Roger Ascham's
Themata Theologica

BLOOMSBURY NEO-LATIN SERIES

Series editors: William M. Barton, Stephen Harrison, Gesine Manuwald and
Bobby Xinyue
Early Modern Texts and Anthologies
Edited by Stephen Harrison and Gesine Manuwald

Volume 7

The 'Early Modern Texts and Anthologies' strand of the *Bloomsbury Neo-Latin Series* presents editions of texts with English translations, introductions and notes. Volumes include complete editions of longer single texts and themed anthologies bringing together texts from particular genres, periods or countries and the like.

These editions are primarily aimed at students and scholars and intended to be suitable for use in university teaching, with introductions that give authoritative but not exhaustive accounts of the relevant texts and authors, and commentaries that provide sufficient help for the modern reader in noting links with classical Latin texts and bringing out the cultural context of writing.

Alongside the series' 'Studies in Early Modern Latin' strand, it is hoped that these editions will help to bring important and interesting Neo-Latin texts of the period from 1350 to 1800 to greater prominence in study and scholarship, and make them available for a wider range of academic disciplines as well as for the rapidly growing study of Neo-Latin itself.

Also available in this series:
Ermolao Barbaro's On Celibacy 1 and 2 by Gareth Williams
Ermolao Barbaro's On Celibacy 3 and 4 and On the Duty of the Ambassador
by Gareth Williams
Japan on the Jesuit Stage by Akihiko Watanabe

An Anthology of Neo-Latin Literature in British Universities
edited by Gesine Manuwald and Lucy R. Nicholas
An Anthology of British Neo-Latin Literature edited by Gesine Manuwald,
L. B. T. Houghton and Lucy R. Nicholas
An Anthology of European Neo-Latin Literature edited by
Gesine Manuwald, Daniel Hadas and Lucy R. Nicholas

Roger Ascham's
Themata Theologica

Lucy R. Nicholas

BLOOMSBURY ACADEMIC
LONDON • NEW YORK • OXFORD • NEW DELHI • SYDNEY

BLOOMSBURY ACADEMIC
Bloomsbury Publishing Plc
50 Bedford Square, London, WC1B 3DP, UK
1385 Broadway, New York, NY 10018, USA
29 Earlsfort Terrace, Dublin 2, Ireland

BLOOMSBURY, BLOOMSBURY ACADEMIC and the Diana logo are trademarks of Bloomsbury Publishing Plc

First published in Great Britain 2023
Paperback edition published 2025

Copyright © Lucy R. Nicholas, 2023

Lucy R. Nicholas has asserted her right under the Copyright, Designs and Patents Act, 1988, to be identified as Author of this work.

For legal purposes the Acknowledgements on p. viii constitute an extension of this copyright page.

Cover image reproduced by permission of the Master and Fellows of St John's College, Cambridge

All rights reserved. No part of this publication may be reproduced or transmitted in any form or by any means, electronic or mechanical, including photocopying, recording, or any information storage or retrieval system, without prior permission in writing from the publishers.

Bloomsbury Publishing Plc does not have any control over, or responsibility for, any third-party websites referred to or in this book. All internet addresses given in this book were correct at the time of going to press. The author and publisher regret any inconvenience caused if addresses have changed or sites have ceased to exist, but can accept no responsibility for any such changes.

A catalogue record for this book is available from the British Library.

A catalog record for this book is available from the Library of Congress.

ISBN: HB: 978-1-350-26794-7
PB: 978-1-3502-6793-0
ePDF: 978-1-3502-6795-4
eBook: 978-1-3502-6796-1

Typeset by RefineCatch Limited, Bungay, Suffolk

To find out more about our authors and books visit www.bloomsbury.com and sign up for our newsletters.

Contents

Preface and Acknowledgements	viii
List of Abbreviations	ix
Introduction	1
Roger Ascham, the *Themata Theologica*, its formation and composition	2
The Bible and patristics	9
Ascham's biblical approach	9
Sola scriptura and patristics	19
Doctrine and confessionalism	22
Humanist classical theology	35
Ascham as theologian	43
Conclusion	47
Text, Translation and Notes	57
Bibliography	227
Index of Biblical and Patristic Citations	235
Index of Classical Citations	239
Index of Subjects and Names	241

Preface and Acknowledgements

This translation of Roger Ascham's *Themata Theologica* represents a token offering within a more extensive mission on the part of many to make a vast body of Neo-Latin writing accessible to the modern reader. The English scholar, Ascham, like many humanists of the period, composed tracts in the vernacular, several of which are very well-known indeed, but his Latin works have, for the most part, remained unread. Despite a growing recognition in modern scholarship of the bilingualism of the age, still, far less attention is given to the Latin works of early modern savants whose output in their native tongue is much more widely read and discussed. This tendency is especially pronounced when it comes to the mid-Tudor Cambridge circle of which Ascham was a prominent member. This was a coterie of highly learned, devout and powerful polymaths, whose Latin pens were tirelessly active at a time when the intellectual life of England was concentrated in, and therefore dominated by, the universities. They were impelled by the conviction that their works could make a difference, and the available evidence certainly points to that result, and yet this is a group whose immediate and longer-term impact is far from having been fully charted. Thus, at every stage of this volume's construction, naggingly present was a sense of how much more there is to be done. This notwithstanding, I hope that this drop in the ocean can provide another useful step towards understanding the endlessly beguiling ebb and flow of English humanism and the precipitous religious and political flux of the sixteenth-century Reformation.

I owe an immense debt of gratitude to many, but to several individuals in particular. Firstly, to Gesine Manuwald and Stephen Harrison, the editors of this series, who gamely agreed to host the enterprise in the first place. I would, moreover, like to thank Alice Wright, Lily Mac Mahon and Zoë Osman of Bloomsbury Publishing, who have all been so consistently efficient and patient throughout the process; and also Merv Honeywood, who was so helpful at the production stage. I am also grateful to Susan Wabuda for her supportive input and encouragement along the way, and to Daniel Hadas, who shared his enviable learning and expertise so generously at several stages. Finally, I must acknowledge the many long and stimulating conversations that I had about the endeavour with Gareth Williams, whose laser insights I constantly profit from, and of which this edition too is the direct beneficiary.

L. R. N. London

Abbreviations

These are utilised in the footnotes of the main introduction and in the annotations to the Latin text and translation.

Arist.	Aristotle (384–322 BCE)
EN	*Ethica Nicomacheia* (*Nicomachean Ethics*)
Rhet.	*Rhetorice* (*Art of Rhetoric*)
Asc.	Ascham (Roger Ascham, c. 1516–1568)
Apol.	*Apologia pro caena Dominica* (*Defence of the Lord's Supper*)
Schol.	*The Scholemaster*
Tox.	*Toxophilus* (*Lover of the Bow*)
Augus.	Augustine (Aurelius Augustinus Hipponensis, 354–430 CE)
De civ. D.	*De civitate Dei* (*City of God*)
De doct. Chr.	*De doctrina Christiana* (*On Christian Doctrine*)
Enchirid.	*Enchiridion de fide, spe et caritate* (A Treatise on Faith, Hope and Love)
Serm.	*Sermones* (Sermons)
Chrysos.	Chrysostom (John Chrysostom, c. 347–407 CE)
Cic.	Cicero (Marcus Tullius Cicero, 106–43 BCE)
Acad.	*Academica* (*On Academic Skepticism*)
Brut.	*Brutus* or *De claris oratoribus* (*Brutus* or *A History of Famous Orators*)
Cat.	*In Catilinam* (*Against Catiline*)
De am.	*De amicitia* (*On Friendship*)
De inv.	*De inventione* (*On Invention*)
De or.	*De oratore* (*On the Orator*)
Fin.	*De finibus* (*On Ends*)
Font.	*Pro Fonteio* (*On behalf of Fonteius*)
Off.	*De officiis* (*On Duties*)
Orat.	*Orator* (*The Orator*)
Parad. St.	*Paradoxa Stoicorum* (*Stoic Paradoxes*)
Phil.	*Orationes Philippicae* (*The Philippics*)
Quinct.	*Pro Publio Quinctio* (*On behalf of Publius Quinctius*)
Top.	*Topica* (*Topics*)
Tusc.	*Tusculanae disputationes* (*Tusculan Disputations*)
Verr.	*In Verrem* (*Against Verres*)

Coloss.	Paul's Epistle to the Colossians
Colum.	Columella (Lucius Junius Moderatus Columella, 4–c. 70 CE)
Rust.	*De re rustica* (*On Agriculture*)
Corinth.	Paul's Epistle to the Corinthians (I or II, as stated)
DMLBS	*Dictionary of Medieval Latin from British Sources*, eds R. K. Ashdowne, D. R. Howlett, and R. E. Latham (2018), 3 vols, Oxford
Deut.	Deuteronomy
E	Erasmus (Desiderius Erasmus, 1466–1536)
Nov. T	*Novum Testamentum* (initially, *Novum Instrumentum*)
EEBO	Early English Books Online
Ephes.	Paul's Epistle to the Ephesians
Ex.	Exodus
Ez.	Book of Ezekiel
Gal.	Paul's Epistle to the Galatians
Gell.	Aulus Gellius (*c.* 125–after 180 CE)
NA	*Noctes Atticae* (*Attic nights*)
Gen.	Genesis
Giles	Giles, J. A., ed. (1865–7), *The Whole Works of Roger Ascham*, 3 vols, London
GNT	Roger Ascham's own copy of a Greek New Testament: *Novi Testamenti omnia* (Basel, 1531)
Hebr.	Paul's Epistle to the Hebrews
Hom.	Homer (seventh to eighth century BCE)
Od.	*Odyssey* (*The Odyssey*)
Hor.	Horace (Quintus Horatius Flaccus (65–8 BCE)
Serm.	*Sermones* (*Satires*)
H/P	The Hebrew / Protestant enumeration of the Psalms
Is.	Book of Isaiah
Jer.	Jerome (Eusebius Sophronius Hieronymus, *c.* 342/347–420 CE)
L	Martin Luther
LCL	*Loeb Classical Library*, Cambridge, MA
Matt.	Matthew's Gospel
NT	New Testament
Numb.	Book of Numbers
ODNB	*Oxford Dictionary of National Biography*
Oec.	Oecumenius
OLD	*Oxford Latin Dictionary*, ed. P. G. W. Glare (1982), Oxford
OT	Old Testament

Ov.	Ovid (Publius Ovidius Naso, 43 BCE–17 CE)
Fast.	*Fasti* (*On the Roman calendar*)
Pag.	Santes Pagninus' *Veteris et Novi Testamenti nova translatio* (1528)
PG	*Patrologiae Cursus Completus, Series Graeca*, ed. J.-P. Migne (1857–1866), Paris
Philipp.	Paul's Epistle to the Philippians
PL	*Patrologiae Cursus Completus, Series Latina*, ed. J.-P. Migne (1844–1855), Paris
Plat.	Plato (*c*. 429–347 BCE)
Ap.	*Apologia* (*Apology*)
Prov.	Book of Proverbs
Ps.	Psalm/s
Quint.	Quintilian (Marcus Fabius Quintilianus, *c*. 35–100 CE)
Inst.	*Institutio oratoria*
Rev.	Revelation of John
Rom.	Paul's Epistle to the Romans
Sam.	Book of Samuel (I or II, as stated)
Soc.	Socrates (*c*. 470–399 BCE)
Thess.	Paul's Epistle to the Thessalonians (I or II, as stated)
Tim.	Paul's Epistle to Timothy (I or II, as stated)
V	Latin Vulgate
V/S	The Vulgate / Greek Septuagint enumeration of the Psalms
Xen.	Xenophon (*c*. 430–*c*. 350 BCE)
Apol.	*Apologia Socratis* (*Apology of Socrates*)
Cyr.	*Cyropaedia* (*The Education of Cyrus*)
Mem.	*Memorabilia* (*Memorials*)

Introduction

The *Themata Theologica* counts as one of many theological tracts of an earlier era to have fallen out of the consciousness of the modern reader. Scripturally-saturated, piously unswerving and compiled in pompous prose, it is hardly a form of writing that sits comfortably with the sensibilities of today. It is the work of a vanished age, a period of religious ferment and calcification, confusion and controversy, when doctrinal nuance and nous could make or break a career and even a life. The *Themata* was composed in the mid-sixteenth century within the tenebrous halls of Cambridge University by the classical scholar, educator and religious reformer, Roger Ascham. It constitutes one of many Latin documents of the period for which no translation into English exists, a fact which may also help explain the scantiness of reference to it in modern historical accounts. No grand claims can be made for the vital place of the *Themata* in the compass of Western literature or for the urgency of its restitution within that tradition. At the same time, to completely ignore it is to jettison a Reformation source that, read with sensitively directed scrutiny, has the capacity to shine a light not just on a single early modern player but also on a critical phase of the reform movement and biblical scholarship in England, and on the concomitant atmosphere that prevailed within a university setting at that time.

Structured as the *Themata* is, as a series of essays (or 'themes') pursuant to specific biblical quotations and theological propositions, the text also offers insights into intellectual praxis and turns of thought that were not peculiar to Ascham alone. This work represents a very immediate and valuable case-study in how *many* classically-trained humanists and signed-up evangelicals might have read and used their bibles. It provides an opportunity to observe how the Holy Writ was proclaimed and often messily negotiated, appended and even reformulated, as it collided and coalesced with Renaissance skills of rhetoric and philology and a love of classical learning, and also with the seismic impact of Lutheran and Reformed ideologies. To peruse the *index locorum* for this text is to encounter the material repertoire of a sixteenth-century humanist, a 'mental library', which internally shaped its author as much as it outwardly constructed a set of expectations about what a contemporary reader ought to recognise.[1]

Against a broader backdrop of modern scholarship which tends to segregate religious history from cultural studies, this edition will, I hope, offer a helpful reminder of the Bible's centripetal pull on all kinds of early modern disciplines and knowledge.[2] The close study it comprises might also help reorient the history of the Reformation, insofar as it focuses far more on methods and approaches than it makes reductive and teleological inferences about confessional identity.[3] No less revealingly, the *Themata* permits an investigation into the very nature of theology at a time when views about the world and its ways were so shifting and when traditional assumptions about how truth was accessed and assessed were being transformed. It is not insignificant that Ascham was both a layman and a member of the Arts (as opposed to the Theological) faculty, and that, in his capacity as a scholar, he claimed an unqualified right to scour and make sense of Scripture. Perhaps not as pressingly, but as interestingly, the text can help broach a difficult barrier between then and now, and bring us closer to the spiritual psychology of an individual who was resolved, above all else, to get to the heart of the kingdom of God with all the tools he had at his disposal.

The scholarship on display in the *Themata* was not simply an academic matter: it was the 'daily bread' of a *respublica litterarum sacrarum*, whose sixteenth-century participants stood close to the centres of power, policy and influence in England, and also belonged to an international milieu of other like-minded textual thinkers and writers. In short, the assortment of approaches on display in this work has the potential to augment our understanding of the interpenetration of humanism and religious conflict, and the nature of Reformation theology and biblical scholarship within Europe more generally.

Roger Ascham, the *Themata Theologica*, its formation and composition

The author of the *Themata*, Roger Ascham (*c.* 1516–1568), is a name that many will know, and yet he is a figure only partially understood. Generally classified as 'a great mid-Tudor humanist', he is perhaps most familiar to us for his roles as tutor to Elizabeth I and as Public Orator of Cambridge University. His most famous works, his *Toxophilus* (of 1545) and *The Scholemaster*, composed in the final stages of his life and published (in 1570) after his death, have been excavated and anthologised in studies on prose style and English humanism. By contrast, his Neo-Latin works and many of his letters that spoke to key Reformation concerns have languished in the penumbra of modern scholarship. He has rarely been taken seriously as a religious thinker. A handful of discrete studies have attempted to redress this imbalance.[4] Of these, perhaps the most valuable for the purposes of this present edition is a large-scale collaborative volume on Ascham, *Roger Ascham and his Sixteenth-Century World*, published in 2021.[5] This volume very helpfully reappraised and expanded the parameters within which we might place Ascham and his activities. In addition to providing a reminder of the pervasively pious atmosphere of the sixteenth century, this book also helped knit together Ascham's many projects, arguing that his written works were far from unrelated but in dialogue with each other. The *Themata*, a relatively early work in Ascham's career, can now be conveniently placed within this bigger frame, and, in turn, enrich our appreciation of his other writings, both those in Latin and in the vernacular.

The *Themata* itself has been granted very little space in secondary literature. Lawrence Ryan, Ascham's leading modern biographer in the Anglophone world, devoted just over two of *c.* 300 pages to it.[6] Furthermore, Ryan's rather dismissive characterisation of the work as a 'school copy book' does not do justice at all to the generative possibilities the tract offers. To begin with, the *Themata* can fill out Ascham's own story, not least because it captures the output of a man in his twenties, an individual on the go and on the rise as he embarked on a bold spring into the outer world of academe, religion and politics. Indeed, the *Themata* was penned during perhaps the most important juncture in Ascham's cursus, and not long before his more high-profile debut publication, *Toxophilus*. The work points both to an individual developing his command of scriptural navigation, and also to one who was confidently, and with startling empowerment, applying his own linguistic and literary theories to the Bible. Additionally, while Ascham was in some ways testing the temperature of theological field in his *Themata*, he was at the same time developing his own path through a labyrinth of, by then, notorious theological issues, including the nature of sin, justification and Free Will.

When Ascham penned his *Themata*, he was a fully habituated member of St John's College, Cambridge. He had matriculated under that roof at the age of just fifteen in 1530, taken his BA and MA there and, after being appointed a fellow in *c.* 1534/5 was, by 1540, employed as a lecturer. He would, in the fullness of time, and by the late 1540s, become a senior member of the University, serving as acting Master of St John's College for a short spell, and he is often referred to as one of a powerful cluster of Cantabrigians who dominated the academic scene of that period.[7] The *Themata* cannot be dated with total precision, and in any case it is a disparate work that grew through accretion over a period of months, if not several years, but the most likely timespan is between 1539 and 1546.[8] This is certainly the view of Ryan, who attributes some of the themes to Ascham's earlier years in Cambridge, and others to the mid-1540s.[9] In many ways, short-range exactitude as regards dating is less important than the fact that the contents of the *Themata* were assembled during a decade that was critical in English Reformation history: the final schizophrenic years of Henry VIII's reign following his break with Rome, a time when the fire and speed of the European reform movement competed with an increasingly impassioned conservatism, a cross-fire in which the members of Cambridge University were squarely caught and could face or flee.

Like many texts produced during this epoch, Ascham's *Themata* was not published at the time it was written. The manuscript itself has not survived, and the only reason we know about the work's existence is because its various sections were printed (along with other material by Ascham) some years later – and posthumously – by one of Ascham's early modern admirers, Edward Grant, Headmaster of Westminster School.[10] Grant informs us in the preface to the printed version that he was responsible for collating these theological exercises. He further refers to them as pieces which Ascham 'shrewdly thought up and beautifully wrote down'.[11] Grant also states that he did so 'all the more gladly because those exercises themselves seem to follow some blossom of oratory and to diffuse the great piety of the writer'.[12] There is every reason to believe, judging by the few examples of Ascham's calligraphic hand that are extant, that the *Themata* would have constituted an aesthetically elegant medley.

The *Themata* in its printed incarnation runs to approximately one hundred pages, and it was bound within a compact octavo volume together with two of his other theological enterprises of roughly the same timeframe.[13] The first was a Latin translation of the Greek commentaries of Oecumenius,[14] a medieval scholiast on the Pauline Epistles to Titus and Philemon, and composed between 1540 and 1544. Although this may sound a rather recondite project, it constituted an avant-garde sally into the realm of patristics when the discipline was still relatively unchartered, and also a groundbreaking engagement with Greek, and it constitutes the first known translation of these Greek scholia.[15] The second was another Latin text entitled *Apologia pro caena Dominica contra missam et eius praestigias* ('A Defence of the Lord's Supper against the Mass and its Magic'). This was a trenchant and confessionally-charged speech, which addressed one of the most controversial religious issues of the age, the Eucharist, and condemned the Catholic Mass outright. Ascham wrote the *Apologia* at the end of 1547, only months after the death of Henry VIII when evangelical optimism for a Protestant revolution under his son, Edward, was at its zenith. The work was composed pursuant to a university disputation that became so heated it had to be halted through official intervention. This notwithstanding, Ascham subsequently forwarded its manifestly Protestant contents to leading figures at court as a means to exert pressure and influence.[16] In this way then, the *Themata* belonged to a textual package of considerable theological ebullience. Grant would dedicate the entire constellation to Robert Dudley, the Earl of Leicester, a well-known supporter and patron of Protestants, and a sounding board to those who harboured frustrations about the incompleteness of reform under Elizabeth's watch.[17] It is additionally not insignificant that the printer of the compilation was Henry Middleton, whose press would specialise in radical reform tracts, often from or inspired by the continental Reformation.[18]

Ascham's *Themata* comprises a compendium of eleven expositions on scriptural verses (from both Old and New Testaments), patristic statements and/or theological concepts, such as the notion of *felix culpa* (literally, 'happy fault'). The separate themes vary greatly in length but also in tenor, and quite clearly the *Themata* does not constitute a unified work.[19] Indeed, the overarching and rather non-specific label '*Themata Theologica*' does not seem to have been Ascham's, but was rather one applied at the editing stage, almost certainly by Grant. We may also deduce that the arrangement of the sections was an editorial decision rather than Ascham's. But is there any other information that can help make sense of the function of these disparate items? Part of the main title of the collection offers a clue. Grant indicates *cui accesserunt themata quaedam theologica, debita disputandi ratione in Collegio D. Ioan. pronunciata* ('To this [viz. the *Apologia*] were added some theological propositions, delivered on account of the duties of disputation in the College of St John').[20] This explicitly points to the disputational backdrop of the *Themata*, and is entirely consistent with a procedure that was an absolute mainspring of university life, namely the practice of debating.

Even this, however, is too homogenising, and careful study of the individual component parts of the *Themata* points to a more variegated constitution. The materials contain a diversity of genres and modes of operation. Certain sections, for example, read far more like biblical commentaries or paraphrases rather than as straightforward disputational orations, others like philosophical investigations, and several even as sermons. Such an admixture was not so exceptional since there was a good level of overlap between various 'habits' of practice: a famous medieval image of the 'religious house' represented biblical commentary as the foundations, disputation as the walls, and preaching as the roof. Grant himself also appears to qualify the earlier statement that the *Themata* were all delivered via disputation, adding later in the preface that these theological exercises were in part publicly delivered in College, and in part written as an exercise 'in the privacy of his bedroom'.[21]

The amalgam notwithstanding, given the clear pertinence of the disputational process for the formation of much of the *Themata*, a few words may be said about this staple of the sixteenth-century academic world. Disputations were formal debates conducted pursuant to the rules-based practice of logic.[22] Though often these days associated with a moribund scholasticism of a medieval past, the disputation continued to be a key procedure within the academic system, which, for all the increasing importance of print, remained a largely oral culture. Traditionally, disputations permitted considerable freedom of speech, and the rationale was that they provided a forum in which paradoxical and provocative ideas could be mooted without fear or foe.[23] Even before Ascham wrote his *Themata*, there were statutes in place at his college of St John's that prescribed regular disputations by the fellows.[24] These were mandated to happen at every level, from undergraduate to senior fellow, with the most senior in college being expected to preside over and coordinate the proceedings.[25] Revisions and additions made to such rubric by Henry VIII only stand as an index of their growing, rather than their diminishing, importance.[26] Concrete evidence points to Ascham's involvement in disputations, and certainly in 1539/40 when records indicate that he served as an examiner of questionists.[27] But we must also imagine a broader career in which these represented a normal form of exchange and debate, and to read Ascham's disputational write-ups is to meet with the dominant flavour of university life, an intellectual culture that was rooted in a constant and very carefully coordinated logomachy.

Although each of Ascham's themes may be viewed as standing for a particular 'case', only four of the themes (1, 3, 4 and 10) appear to be orations delivered pursuant to a formal disputation.[28] In these, references to the disputational context are explicit and plainly invoke aspects of the actual process of disputations: the cut and thrust of intellectual sparring, clarification of terms of the debate, and the adversarial establishment of competing forces and of 'parties' and 'sides'. Themes 1 and 4 actually register a formal *quaestio* that would serve as the stimulus for a disputation: (theme 1) 'Whether more evil is procured from Adam than good produced through Jesus Christ'; and (theme 2) 'Whether an action [when it is] something simple and without specification of attendant circumstances is a sin or not?'.[29] While we only have in these speeches one side of the debate, it is also possible at certain points to infer the opposing arguments. Further evidence of the disputational backdrop of these themes was the inclusion of a form of prayer, a customary part of the disputations of this period.[30] Ceremonial prayers appear in the conclusions of themes 1, 3 and 4, and one would certainly have been incorporated at the end of the tenth had the surviving version of this theme not been incomplete.

While the disputational procedure may have been a sanctioned requirement within the University, it was also, especially within the theological domain, a potentially disruptive activity. The disputation stood at the front line of the Reformation and began to be increasingly used as a lever to facilitate reform.[31] As the religious fissures became more sharply demarcated and disagreements about doctrine assumed greater significance, disputations were considered by contemporaries to constitute one of the most effective ways to sound out a theological position, to reach 'the truth', and eliminate what was false.[32] The disputations of this period belong to a broader cult of persuasion and conversion in which leading thinkers might deploy their full intellectual energy, textual expertise, and scholarly know-how.[33] Given the vital role of the universities in the wider remit of spiritual affairs, it was inevitable that university debates might have considerable sway in shaping thought and steering opinion at a national level. While it is unlikely that a specific political objective lay behind these particular disputations (1, 3, 4 and 10), it is clear that all four broached in a frontal way key Reformation ideas, especially those set in motion by Luther, and that they helped delineate lines of argument and methods of approach.

Other themes within the work are less easy to place under the disputational umbrella. Some are more sensibly classified as commentaries, for example, theme 2, which comprises a focused analysis of the Psalm verse ('I have been young and I am now old, and I have never seen the righteous forsaken nor his offspring seeking bread'). As Alfred Katterfeld, an earlier German biographer of Ascham, observes, this may well have been composed in the late 1530s, at a time when Ascham was keen to collaborate with the Bishop of Chichester, Richard Sampson, on his edition of the Psalms.[34] A reference to 'some small pages' in a 1539 letter to a friend in which Ascham discusses collaborating with the Bishop may well be an allusion to the very contents of theme 2.[35] The content of this theme exhibits more philological computation than we see in the disputational orations, consisting as it does of a word-by-word dissection of the Psalm verse, a technique also on display in themes 8 and 9, which also appear to be commentaries on Galatians 6.14, 'May I be kept from boasting except in the cross of our Lord Jesus Christ') and John 5.34, 'I receive not testimony from man, but that you may be saved') respectively.

The remaining four themes are more philosophical and didactic in their orientation and bear the qualities of pastoral sermons or lectures, each hinging on individual biblical maxims. The two shorter pieces, themes 6 and 7, centre on motifs of anger and human knowledge, stemming from Ephesians 4.26, 'Be angry and sin not', and 1 Corinthians 8.2, 'If anyone thinks that he knows something, he has not yet got to know as he ought to know'. The other two longer themes 5 and 11 pivot on Numbers 22.20, 'Do only this which I bid you', and John 15.16, 'Whatsoever you ask of the Father in my name he will give it to you', the latter providing detailed guidance on the correct forms of prayer. Ascham was certainly lecturing (in Greek, mathematics and dialectic) at the University the late 1530s,[36] but there is no extant evidence to indicate that Ascham delivered any lectures on Scripture, and it is more likely that in these themes he was trying his hand at sermon-writing. Sermons had become the *desideratum* of the age: Henry's reign marked an important stage in the development of official sermons or homilies, which would be used to guide the beliefs of the nation. The officially issued Bishops' Book, for example, was designed to be read as a series of sermons.[37] That Ascham was responsible for drafting sermons would also not be at all out of keeping with his professed enthusiasm for the preaching of the Word, both in the *Themata* itself and elsewhere.[38] Moreover, it fits with the style he adopted in several of his letters, which he himself described as 'sounding like sermons'.[39]

In sum, on display in the *Themata* was a range of religious activities. All of these were compatible with a scholar who was following routine university protocol; yet these themes were also etched with Ascham's own personality and contain a flavour of his own priorities and ambitions. When reading these themes, we should likewise not ignore the strong likelihood that Ascham was toying with a theological career. In modern scholarship, Ascham is almost uniformly associated with the Arts, and, of course, this was the professional path he ultimately opted to follow. However, it was not the only route he countenanced. Indeed, many of his direct contemporaries would proceed to senior clerical office. There are signs that from the late 1530s and into the 1540s Ascham had embarked on a programme of religious self-fashioning, perhaps with a view to working closely with a man of the cloth, and possibly even with the intention of taking holy orders.

We know that Ascham approached Robert Holgate, Bishop of Llandaff and President of the Council of the North, a figure in sympathy with the reform movement, and also Edward Lee, the former adversary of Erasmus and a Catholic traditionalist, who was then serving as Archbishop of York. Ascham would dedicate manuscript copies of his Latin translation of Oecumenius' commentaries as gifts to the evangelical Thomas Goodrich, Bishop of Ely, and again to Edward Lee. While there is no hard and fast evidence that any of the individual parts of the *Themata* circulated more widely or were sent on to others, each one had the potential to be used as a preferment-angling production. Additionally, it is also possible to view the *Themata* as propaedeutic to one of its sibling Latin works, Ascham's *Defence of the Lord's Supper* (*Apologia pro caena Dominica*) of 1547, a tract with a very single-minded reformist purpose, that he produced at the start of Edward VI's new reign. Certain motifs and passages from the *Themata* were reused (often *verbatim*) in the *Apologia*, in particular, those that related to the Decalogue and biblical references that propped up the sanctity of God's Word.[40] Whatever the case, Ascham's theological endeavours were not as few and frail as some portraits of the man would suggest, and the religious range of the *Themata* offers yet another example of a thoroughly faith-based outlook.

The Bible and patristics

Ascham's biblical approach

Despite the rather disconnected format of the *Themata*, the fragments nonetheless combine and conspire to give the work unity. One connecting thread that runs from theme to theme is Scripture. Biblical citations pervade the entire text, with such phrases often amassed in catalogue form, and Ascham magnetically returns to the Word of God at every turn. Ascham composed the *Themata* at a time when the Bible was viewed as a fortress of faith and 'the natural language', so such a biblical reflex during a religious age may seem axiomatic. That the Bible was a constant presence in Ascham's theological compilation seems almost too obvious a fact to state, but it is worth restating, not least because the Bible, for all its acknowledged centrality in the early modern mind, is so often at the periphery of modern studies.[41]

As well as acknowledging the fundamental role the Bible played in all Reformation thought and discourse, we must also keep in mind the remarkable fluidity of the biblical culture of this time. To speak of 'the Bible' in the mid-sixteenth century is meaningless without further anchorage. And so, before moving to a closer inspection of Ascham's use of Scripture, the broader environment merits a moment's consideration. When Ascham composed his *Themata* a myriad of different bibles were in circulation. These included Jerome's Latin Vulgate but also the older *Vetus Latina*, which survived as a collection of texts rather than a single document, albeit, as Hugh Houghton comments, it is a far from straightforward task to distinguish between these two traditions, and neither was monolithic.[42]

Then, with the rise of Greek learning in the West that coincided with the development of philological humanism, the 'Vulgate' was subjected to multiple challenges, most famously at the start of the sixteenth century by Erasmus' *Novum Instrumentum* (which subsequently went by the name of *Novum Testamentum*).[43] In parallel with other attempts to correct the Vulgate in Latin (via Greek and also Hebrew), such as the Complutensian Polyglot Bible in Spain of 1514, Santes Pagninus' *Veteris et Novi Testamenti nova translatio* (of 1527), and Robert Estienne's revised bible editions in France (from the late 1520s), an important clutch of resolutely Protestant Latin bibles also began to appear.[44]

By now, a humanist attention to language had given way to a much harder attitude that equated linguistic solecism with theological error. These Protestant productions included a (partial) bible produced in Wittenberg in 1529 by a team of scholars led by Martin Luther and Philip Melanchthon,[45] Sebastian Münster's Latin translation of the Old Testament, the *Biblia Hebraica* (Basel, 1534/5), the Zurich Latin bibles of 1539 and 1543, and the *Biblia Sacra Latina* of Sebastian Castellio of 1551, the main goal of which was to reproduce Scripture in polished Ciceronian Latin.[46] In addition, and more commonly known about, there was a proliferation of bibles in the vernacular, the most acclaimed versions in English being by William Tyndale (1526) and Myles Coverdale (1535) and also the King's Great Bible of 1539. This was a time when authorised versions had yet to be officially established. Muddying the waters yet further was the fact biblical quotes might have been garnered from the writings of the Fathers, from a heterogeneous mass of biblical commentaries, such as Nicholas Lyra's *Postillae*, or even from memory; the age was still one of widespread oral mediation of God's Word. Sixteenth-century biblical usage is not susceptible of the scientific and clinical analysis that modern research would perhaps like it to be, and it is with good reason that Eyal Poleg refers to a 'turbid realm of uncertainties' when it comes to the Bible of the early modern period.[47] With this in mind, it seems sensible to broach an individual's Bible use in terms of their scriptural 'management' or even 'biblical mentality'. Amid the instability and the interventions by crusaders like Erasmus, Tyndale and Luther, assumptions about (a) the status of the Bible, (b) its language and wording, and (c) the extent to which it might be altered or supplemented had been thrown into disarray. As we move to assess Ascham's biblical approach, these will all be important factors.

There can be no doubt about Ascham's profound commitment to the Word of God. Ascham gave careful prominence to claims of scriptural adherence throughout the *Themata*. This was true of the entire work, but an especially passionate commitment to the Bible is noticeable in the disputational speeches. In theme 3, Ascham claimed that the Bible would be his sole authority:

> But since the Christian religion is the light and truth itself, and through its own nature admits no divergent opinions, except at first sight or through man's fault – for Scripture does not admit more than one true meaning – for that reason, I will not allow my own arguments to waver, but my speech will proceed only through the Word of God, and in such a way that it seems to have been steered by its authority, on particular sails, as it were.[48]

This and other such declarations are telling. They point to a conviction on the part of some that the *auctoritas* of the Good Book did not enjoy the primacy it should in some quarters. They also point to an atmosphere in which claims of biblical allegiance could be used tactically as a means to discredit and vault over the supporting documents of opponents. For many, the Bible constituted the ultimate fountainhead, and in several places Ascham explicitly applied the *ad fontes* metaphor (by now a well-worn humanistic mantra) to the books of Scripture.[49] But when Ascham was composing his *Themata*, an emphasis on Scripture was also strongly associated with reformist agitation, and the relatively junior Ascham was unequivocal about which side of *this* track he walked. More on that in 'Doctrine and confessionalism' (from p. 22); for now, we may consider an arguably more significant facet of Ascham's bible use, a commitment to and proficiency in biblical humanism that earns him a meaningful, if minor, place in the history of theology.

Pursuant to the 1535 Cambridge Injunctions it had been decreed that all theology lectures should be taught from the Old and New Testaments, and not in the manner of scholastic theologians.[50] Scholars have rightly underscored the significance of this provision in the development of theology at the University;[51] the stipulation completely removed from the curriculum all scholastic authorities and replaced them with a pronounced emphasis on Scripture. In effect, what was being proposed was a sea change in exegesis, one that totally departed from the dictates of traditional scholastic theology and all its interpretative aids, and relied instead on the Bible for the answers.[52] Ascham exemplified this new approach in his *Themata*, and in many of his themes we witness his determination to begin and end with the Word of God. Towards the end of theme 10, for instance, Ascham addresses the conundrum of why Christians suffer persecutions. He does so by leading the reader through the Old Testament, in particular, Exodus and Deuteronomy, which, according to Ascham, represent persecution as a form of test. He then takes us to the New Testament, to John, Paul in Romans, to James and Peter, each of whom offer a slightly different reason for persecution, ranging from its ability to excite conversion and hope, to its status as a token of love.[53] As N. Scott-Amos avers in his detailed investigation into Bucer's biblical humanism, even taking into account the spur that the Injunctions provided, this kind of unalloyed biblicism was completely ground-breaking.[54]

Ascham's *Themata* epitomised another essential quality of biblical humanism: an insistence on language. While the overlapping nature of reformations in both language and religion has long been recognised, the impact of linguistics on the Reformation longer-term and certainly beyond Erasmus has been gathering momentum in recent scholarship. In an age when 'literal truth' was paramount, there was an especially vital relationship between language and literary theory on the one hand, and theology and biblical interpretation on the other.[55] Ascham approached Scripture with a fully linguistic or 'grammatical' attitude. His philological habit of mind can be witnessed early on in the collection. Theme 2, where Ascham examines the Psalm verse, 'I have been young and I am now old, and I have never seen the righteous forsaken nor his offspring seeking bread', entails a clinical lemma-by-lemma examination of the verse. As regards the term 'righteous', for example, Ascham adduces a definition through multiple cross-references to other uses of the word in Old and New Testaments. For the precise meaning of 'seeking bread' Ascham turns to Hebrew, writing, 'Among Hebrew speakers and almost all other peoples, [the phrase] "to seek bread" is construed as "to be abandoned" and "to be forsaken"; indeed, this form of expression is used everywhere in the world ...'.[56] Ascham then proceeds to horse-trade in hermeneutical nuance with Hugo of Saint-Cher, a medieval Church Cardinal and a pioneer of 'biblical relativism', who had compiled the so-called *Correctorium*, a compilation of variant readings of the Vulgate Bible. Ascham writes (with a certain grudging respect):

> Cardinal Hugo twists this sentiment (i.e. 'seeking bread') into another sense, in his opinion, by far the most sound [sense], and in mine, certainly not so absurd.... He says [that] the righteous man will not be forsaken by God, nor [will] his offspring, provided that he seeks bread from God, that is, [that] he has devoted every concern of life towards this.[57]

Theme 2 is far from an isolated example in this regard, and it is clear that Ascham was making active and discerning judgements about verbal meanings at every stage.

Ascham was no less mindful of the textual variants that were possible for the Scripture he cited. As discussed, Ascham composed the *Themata* at time of biblical flux, and it seems he was negotiating potential vocabulary options as judiciously as he was weighing up the precise meanings and etymology of words. As we leaf through the pages of Ascham's *Themata*, we quickly run into his very motley (to modern eyes) citation of God's Word. While annotations to the text itself draw attention in detail to the potpourri nature of Ascham's biblical quotations, a quick overview here might also offer some useful navigation.

In certain places, Ascham would reproduce the language of Jerome's Vulgate. A degree of conformity with Jerome makes sense; Jerome's Latin Vulgate, even in Protestant circles, continued to exert powerful authority and retained much of its status as the standard translation of Scripture well into the sixteenth century.[58] In the *Themata*, however, divergence from Jerome was more the norm than compliance, and in many places, Ascham opted to follow, or was at least influenced by, Erasmus' *Novum Testamentum*. Again, a certain dependence on Erasmus was perhaps not so remarkable in the output of a Cantabrigian; Erasmus had himself resided at the University from 1510 to 1515 and left an indelible mark in his capacity of Professor of Divinity there.[59] But it seems that the principal reason for Ascham's interest in the *Novum Testamentum* was Erasmus' close attention to the Greek.

Ascham, as Erasmus had been, was a formidable linguist and would become one of the most accomplished Hellenists of his generation.[60] At the start of theme 7, a piece about human knowledge, he flaunted he own grasp of the language by providing the Greek for each of the references to knowledge in the verse heading itself: εἰδέναι, ἔγνωκεν and γνῶναι (the equivalent of his *putat ... scire, cognovit* and *scire* respectively).[61] Furthermore, parts of the *Themata* point to a preference for Erasmian wording that seemed more faithfully to capture the original Greek than Jerome had. For instance, in theme 8 when quoting John 16.33, 'Be of good courage; I have conquered this world',[62] Ascham's Latin read *Bono animo sis, ego vici mundum*. This was much more in line with Erasmus' *sed bono animo sitis, ego vici mundum* than the Vulgate's *sed confidite, ego vici mundum*, and the reason was almost certainly because Ascham, like Erasmus, considered the idiomatic *bono animo esse* to be a more accurate rendering of the Greek θαρσεῖτε, a verb bound up with 'being confident', as opposed to the Vulgate's *confidere*, the primary valence of which is 'to trust' or 'to rely on'.[63]

In other places, and this is where the situation gets considerably knottier, Ascham casts himself as someone who was willing to snub the authority not just of Jerome but also of 'Saint Erasmus', and we see an Ascham yet more determined than Erasmus was to reflect the Greek in his Latin. In theme 1, when citing Romans 8.37 (which he does repeatedly), 'In all these respects, we conquer through him who loved us', Ascham's Latin reads *In hiis omnibus supervincimus per eum qui dilexit nos*. Erasmus instead of *supervincimus* had opted for *superamus*, a form also used in the Vulgate. The reason for the difference must be that Ascham preferred *supervincimus* because it calques the original Greek ὑπερνικῶμεν. This was despite the fact that (a) the compound verb *supervinco* did not have classical antecedence (indeed, it seems to have entered Latin for precisely this purpose) and (b) Erasmus had eschewed the neologism.[64]

While this emendation might not have had quite the theological punch of Erasmus' adoption of *sermo* for λόγος (in place of *verbum*) or *resipiscite* for μετανοεῖτε (in place of *poenitentiam agite*), Ascham was engaging in a process that had the potential to undermine orthodoxy. He can hardly have been unaware that Greek was increasingly perceived as a threat to theology, tied as it was to a different approach to the Bible.[65] However, for Ascham, as for many reformers, Greek was where the true meaning of the Bible resided. A quote from Ascham's slightly later *Apologia* is revealing on this score: 'I am compelled to intersperse Latin with Greek... and I do this now, not so that I can show off with Greek words, but so that I can show the truth with their light'.[66] As Ascham saw it, there must be a verbal calibration between Latin and Greek, and the latter should always be the ultimate source for the former; indeed, this symbiotic relationship between Greek and Latin was one that exercised Ascham through his life.[67]

We can be sure that for Ascham Greek was a fundamental factor in his engagement with Scripture. Indeed, it has been possible to identify one of the main Greek resources Ascham was using as he drafted his *Themata*: a Greek New Testament of 1531, now held at Hatfield House, and inscribed very neatly with the autograph *Rogerus Aschamus*.[68] The volume is heavily annotated, especially in the four Gospels, and it is clear that this was a resource that Ascham returned to again and again.[69] While some of the notes are in Latin, the vast majority are in Greek. A number consist of cross-references to other parts of Scripture (especially to the Old Testament), but the majority are philological in nature, and tend to gloss or comment on the detail of the Greek New Testament, providing further testimony of Ascham's affinity with the language. Apart from the thrill of contact-across-the-ages that time spent with this elegant volume occasions, it soon becomes apparent that many of the biblical references in Ascham's *Themata* are ones that he has highlighted or remarked on in his own New Testament, and the two are clearly synergetically connected. All such cases have been recorded in my annotations to the text, but a couple of examples can be mentioned here.

In theme 11, where Ascham provides guidance on prayer, he writes *neque βαττολογίαν in precibus accumulate* ('And don't amass idle talk in your prayers').[70] This is a clear allusion to the Greek of Matthew 6.7, which reads προσευχόμενοι δὲ μὴ βαττολογήσητε ('But when you pray, don't be talking idly'). Adjacent to this verse in his Greek New Testament, Ascham has added in his exquisite hand the word βαττολογία, the very noun (as opposed to the verb of the New Testament) he would use in the *Themata*. Another connection can be seen in theme 5, where Ascham, in order to buttress his argument about pursuing a life of Christ, tracks John 14.6, and, in particular, the three elements of *via et veritas et vita* ('the way, the truth and the life') which Jesus declares himself to be.[71] Remarkably, these three elements are highlighted in Greek by Ascham in the margin of John 14.6, where he writes ὁδός, ἀλήθεια, ζωή.

Josef Eskhult has identified two different functions of Protestant Latin bible translations: (i) the scientific exegetical mode which prioritises fidelity to Hebrew and Greek; and (ii) the humanistic rhetorical-educational mode.[72]

Ascham was invested in both, which of course sometimes meant for a tension between them. Notwithstanding Ascham's obvious respect for the philological integrity of the Bible, especially his commitment to the original Greek, his *Themata* highlights another facet of his biblical approach, one that once again often led him to deviate from the Latin of Erasmus' *Novum Testamentum*. This was a concern for the form and style of the Latin itself. A good example comes in theme 6 with a reference to part of Romans 8.28. The Greek has τοῖς ἀγαπῶσι τὸν θεὸν πάντα συνεργεῖ εἰς ἀγαθόν ('for those that love God, everything works together unto good'). Jerome's Vulgate rendered this as *diligentibus Deum omnia cooperantur in bonum* and Erasmus opted for *qui diligunt Deum, omnia simul adiumento sunt in bonum*. Ascham would write *bonis omnia cooperantur in bonum*. While Ascham's version remains faithful to the Greek in essentials, he preferred to use in Latin the same word to translate both ἀγαπῶσι and ἀγαθόν, rather than using different words as the other two versions do. We can only conclude that this was because Ascham favoured the polyptoton effect of *bonis* and *bonum*. Henk Jan de Jonge mounts a compelling case that Erasmus' reproduction of the text of the Greek New Testament was intended only an aid to the preparation (a *castigatio*) of a revised Latin translation.[73] Indeed, as the Reformation progressed, a Latin bible was the jewel in the crown of Protestant scholarship.[74] For all the importance of the vernacular bible translations, a bible clothed in the language of the learned world and the Church, namely Latin, remained the most prestigious.[75]

Richard Muller comments that there was an increased tendency in the early modern age for more philologically capable commentators to offer their own translations of the Bible.[76] In Ascham's *Themata* there are numerous places where he offers his own *sui generis* Latin version of biblical verses, using wording that is not to be found in other translations, and in which felicity of expression and good classical Latin are evidently primary concerns. At the start of theme 10, for example, Ascham, when referring to the beautiful Song of Zechariah in Luke 1.78–79, used the following phrasing:

per viscera misericordiae suae visitare nos, veluti oriens ex alto, dignabatur: ut omnes homines in hunc mundum venientes, qui lucem illam non reiecerunt, vultus sui splendore illuminaret: et omnium hominum pedes, qui in tenebris, et in umbra mortis sederent, in viam pacis dirigeret atque confirmaret.

[Christ] deemed it worthy, through the inmost workings of his mercy, to visit us, just as if rising from on high, in order that he might illuminate with the lustre of his countenance all men coming into this world who did not reject that light; also [in order that] he might direct and secure the feet of all men, who tend to sit in darkness and the shadow of death, unto the way of peace.[77]

This diverged quite markedly from the Vulgate phraseology, which has:

> per viscera misericordiae Dei nostri, in quibus visitavit nos oriens ex alto, inluminare his qui in tenebris et in umbra mortis sedent, ad dirigendos pedes nostros in viam pacis.

It is noteworthy that Ascham avoided the infinitive *inluminare* and prefers a more classically conventional clause of purpose *ut . . . illuminaret* in line with Erasmus, who also amends this to *ut illucesceret*. However, unlike Erasmus (who then followed the Vulgate), Ascham preferred parallel *ut* clauses using [*ut*] *dirigeret atque confirmaret* in preference to *ad* plus the gerundive *dirigendos*. In other places, we find Ascham substituting items of vocabulary with a more classical-sounding lexicon. In theme 8, when citing Psalm 43/44.22, Ascham amended the Vulgate's *propter te mortificati sumus tota die* to *propter te Domine occidimur tota die*,[78] thus replacing the distinctly medieval *mortificati sumus* with a verb of greater classical stamp, *occido*.

We should not forget that, shortly after writing the *Themata*, Ascham would become the Public Orator at the University (serving in that post for eight years from 1546 to 1554). Indeed, in multiple themes we see Ascham applying a sort of religiously-inspired orator's prerogative, a licence to frill, regarding Scripture.[79] At the start of theme 2, Ascham modified Luke 2.32, the Vulgate and Erasmus, each of which read *lumen ad revelationem gentium et gloriam plebis tuae Israel*: Ascham adopted the rather more elaborate *lumen de lumine, ad revelationem gentium et gloriam plebis Israel illuxerit*,[80] wording that embellished (without necessarily undermining) the original Greek, and which rhetorically accentuated the motif of light, with its duplex use of *lumen* and *lumine* and its addition of the verb *illucesco*. There are further aspects of Ascham's rhetorical practice, which are broached in the section 'Humanist classical theology' (from p. 35). For now, we may note that this was no surface gloss; in casting such phrases, Ascham was evidently driven by a deep desire to gild the Word of God for onward consumption.

Ascham's close attention to the effect of language was hardly surprising, for it fits with a much broader concern exemplified in the writings of many humanists, especially the Cambridge set of which Ascham was a prominent member. Ascham absolutely shared the 'Cambridge Connection's' linguistic commitment and philosophy of 'perfection' as identified and powerfully described by John McDiarmid.[81] This entailed a sort of classically-cleansing policy whereby perfect modes of action from the past could be recovered and even outmatched, and the ideal of perfection in language, political order and religion was part of this coordinated enterprise.[82] What is perhaps more startling to observe in the *Themata* is how this desire for 'perfitnesss' extended to the wording of Scripture. Yet if we accept McDiarmid's analysis, this makes total sense, because, for Ascham, if one is to live in Scripture, one must also inhabit its words; the more appealing and animating these were, the greater the chance that the flawlessness of its message might be embraced. As far as Ascham was concerned, to preach the Gospel was to muse and thunder in beautiful language, and true Christian behaviour comprised the ethical equivalent of that language: we *are* what we speak and hear.

In some senses, this *modus operandi* puts Ascham in the company of Sebastian Castellio, the French humanist mentioned above, who would go on to produce a bible in Latin that simulated Ciceronian style. Castellio's rationale was that the language of Scripture was not a fixed one but a spiritual one, and that a translation was most effective when it best served the piety of Christians.[83] It is not insignificant that in 1542 Ascham commented on his reliance on Cicero in his translation of Oecumenius' commentary on Paul's Epistle to Philemon, writing (in a letter):

> I have followed Erasmus in all regards in the version of this epistle, except that for *rogo*, I translate *deprecor*, having as my authority the great Marcus Tullius Cicero, who says that we use *deprecor* not so much when we prevent something from happening, as when we ask forgiveness for an affront.[84]

Castellio's Ciceronian devotion in the biblical sphere would meet with severe criticism and charges of paganism.[85] For many, the notion of bringing human eloquence to a subject as sacred as the Bible was impious.[86] While Ascham's approach to Scripture was not as radical as that of Castellio, and, as we shall see in a moment, Ascham was also relying on other generally more orthodox authorities for his biblical phrasing, glimpses of Castellio's experimentalism are nevertheless apparent in Ascham's *Themata*.

Thus far, I have suggested that Ascham was relying on the Vulgate, Erasmus, his own Greek Bible, and his rhetorical skills when citing the Bible. But the picture is yet still more layered. Ascham was sometimes reproducing particular biblical wording used in the Fathers, especially by Augustine and from Jerome's corpus beyond the Vulgate. On occasion too, it seems he also borrowed wording from the biblical commentaries of contemporary reformers, mainly Luther, especially in theme 8 on the Galatians. Owing to lack of space here, I refer the interested reader to the actual annotations to the text which provide illustrations of such approaches.

In other cases, we can attribute biblical idiosyncrasy to the simple fact that Ascham was sometimes working from memory; this was certainly the view of Maurice Hatch, the translator of Ascham's Latin letters, who repeatedly comments on Ascham's 'faulty' recollection of particular scriptural passages in his correspondence.[87] We can be certain that Ascham knew much of the New Testament by heart, and there are scattered instances where a lapse of recall is in evidence. In theme 10, for example, Ascham formulates the heading, a verse from 2 Timothy 3, verse 12, as follows: *Omnes qui volunt pie vivere in Christo Iesu persequuutiones patientur.*[88] Both the Latin Vulgate and Erasmus' *Novum Testamentum* have *persecutionem* rather than *persequuutiones*. However, slightly later in the theme when Ascham quotes the verse again, he reverts to the standard wording.[89] The plural *persequuutiones* is in fact used in verse 11, and the likelihood is that Ascham was on this occasion composing without consulting his Bible. That Ascham was relying on his powers of retrieval rather than on the Bible in front of him offers an important reminder of the extreme level of internalisation of Scripture during this age. He was certainly not alone in such an approach.

A fallible memory may account for a handful of Ascham's biblical quotations, but the more learned variants are unlikely to be the product of this: in the majority of cases we can be sure that Ascham had in mind a very specific rendering for aural impact or because it better conveyed the Greek. On the odd occasion, it appears that Ascham even demonstrated a willingness to alter biblical phrasing when it suited his argument. In theme 8, for instance, Ascham cited Matthew 5.12 as follows: *gaudete et exultate cum persequuuti vos fuerint homines propter me, quoniam merces et gloria vestra copiosa est in coelis* ('Rejoice and be exceedingly glad when men have persecuted you for my sake, since your reward and glory in heaven is plentiful').[90] The Vulgate reads: *gaudete et exultate quoniam merces vestra copiosa est in caelis sic enim persecuti sunt prophetas qui fuerunt ante vos* ('Rejoice and be exceedingly glad, for your reward is plentiful in heaven. For so they persecuted the prophets that came before you'). The term *gloria*, which Ascham inserts into his arrangement of the verse, is not present in any Latin version (including Erasmus'), not even in the original Greek. Ascham included it because it was relevant to the proceedings at issue, namely Galatians 6.14, which centred on the act of boasting (*gloriari*). He does exactly the same thing (adding the term *gloria*) when citing 2 Corinthians 12.7.[91] These were bold manoeuvres and certainly speak to a certain confidence.

Evident in the *Themata*, then, is what we might perceive to be an extraordinary latitude. Despite Ascham's repeated emphasis on the all-important gravity of God's Word, he showed himself inclined to bend it, edit it and veer from it. Where does this all leave us when we hear Ascham declare to his opponents in theme 4: 'That [point] which you attack we will make evident with examples from sacred Scripture'?[92] Ascham's *Themata* serves as a reminder of the power of private scholarship of this earlier age – a period of startling unpredictability but also unregimented flexibility – when individuals tasted, chewed on, and ingested the words of the Bible, which then became part of themselves.

Sola scriptura and patristics

The omnipresence of Scripture in Ascham's *Themata*, along with its professions of its supremacy, point to a stance that is often termed *sola scriptura* in Reformation studies. This was a theological doctrine that hailed the Bible as the sole unerring source of authority for Christian faith and practice. While it must be emphasised that Scripture served as a touchstone as much for conservatives as Protestants, *sola scriptura* is a credo generally associated with Protestantism.[93] The significance of such an outlook against the backdrop of sixteenth-century schism is explored in more detail below in the section 'Doctrine and confessionalism' (from p. 22). For now, it has pertinence for the patristic context, and the degree to which it permitted meaningful engagement with the writings of the Church Fathers.

As scholars have commented, the *sola scriptura* stance is in some ways more illuminating for its polemical force than the *de facto* reality of its practice. The term was in fact an early modern smoke-screen, an inadequate and misunderstood descriptor, for *sola scriptura* did not mean that Reformation biblical scholars had committed themselves exclusively to interpreting Scripture armed only with their intellects and the guidance of the Holy Spirit, or that other sources of knowledge were excluded.[94] Indeed, Henk van den Belt, while not denying its employment as a slogan, argues that the term *sola scriptura* obscures the continuity between Protestantism and tradition, and also that both Reformed and Lutheran reformers had a deep respect for, and interpreted Scripture in a congenial communion with, the Church of all ages and the theology of the Fathers.[95]

As passionate as Ascham was about Scripture (and he was), Fathers feature in no small degree in the *Themata*. Indeed, recycling language that he had already used about Scripture, Ascham declared in theme 10 his intention that 'the entire discourse and progress of my speech be governed and steered either by the authority of the Word of God or the testimonies of the Fathers' and that he would defer to the 'fountainhead of the Scriptures and the streams of the holy Fathers'.[96] Ascham was someone who understood that the contours of Reformation conflict had come to hang on patristic evidence to a considerable degree. In 1547 he would contribute to a controversy about the Eucharist pursuant to which he composed his *Apologia*, a work in which the Fathers would play a major role. In his *Apologia*, while he voiced disapproval about reliance on the Fathers without the primary sanction of Scripture, Ascham would nonetheless participate fully in the patristic gamesmanship, citing in support of a spiritual Lord's Supper an array of Fathers: Ambrose, Augustine, Cyprian, Jerome, Tertullian; and three Greek Fathers: Chrysostom, Clement and Irenaeus.

In the *Themata*, a less – at least in Reformation terms – evolved tract, Ascham cited Jerome and Augustine multiple times. Augustinian references, in particular, as will be discussed at more length in the section 'Doctrine and confessionalism' (from p. 22), served as far more than garnishing. We can be sure that Ascham was consulting Augustinian texts, and that they were formative in his own theological growth. While Augustine may also have engendered in Ascham a greater receptiveness to a more manifestly Protestant belief system, as we shall see, it was certainly not the case that Protestant doctrine was the influence that finally 'won out'; Augustine remained a commanding force. It is interesting to note, for example, the importance accorded to Augustine in Ascham's description of the scholarly *mores* at the University of Cambridge in a letter to Thomas Cranmer: 'Some for the daily reading of God's word unite the propositions of Augustine, principally, and their knowledge of languages as far as they can as an auxiliary strength'.[97]

Theme 10 features two early Greek Church Fathers, and this assimilation of Greek Fathers ought to be lingered over for a moment. Sheer awareness of them, let alone access to their works, was relatively unusual at this point, certainly in England. Indeed, across Europe, the study of the Greek Fathers was a fledgling field, and an unfamiliar theological tradition was further compounded by a limited linguistic knowledge.[98] In this tenth theme Ascham firstly adduced a Greek Father of the fourth century, Athanasius, and his Latin *Symbolum Athanasianum* (or 'Athanasian Creed'). Ascham had identified a congruence between (a) the argument he was mounting about *recta et sana fides* ('an upright and wholesome faith') and its cultivation of a piety through Christ and (b) the dominant christology of the Athanasian Creed. In fact, Ascham's attribution to Athanasius of the Latin *Symbolum Athanasianum* was a misstep; the Latin creed is almost certainly not the work of the Greek Athanasius, and was probably written a century later. It was, however, only in the 1600s that scholars began to cast doubt on its authorship. When Ascham was producing his *Themata*, it was a tenet of belief considered authoritative in many early Protestant churches,[99] and Ascham's assimilation of it here fits with the increasing determination to prop up a breakaway evangelical movement with as weighty sources as possible.

Ascham also used Chrysostom to bulk out his definition of *recta et sana fides*. We know that Ascham encountered Chrysostom in the original Greek around this time. Ascham requested to borrow a book of Chrysostom from both John Redman and John Cheke in 1543.[100] He would also meet Chrysostom in the commentaries of Oecumenius that he was translating from Greek into Latin. Here in theme 10, Ascham supplements his definition of 'piety in Christ' with what he declares to be the Greek equivalent, 'εὐσέβεια', writing, 'And accordingly, there is a piety in Christ which the Greeks appropriately and clearly call "eusebeia", that St Chrysostom defines [as] "the concern of life with upright faith"'.[101] Ascham then cited the Greek words that he understood Chrysostom to have used in his commentaries on the first Epistle of Timothy: *Graeci apte et plane εὐσέβειαν vocant, ut definit D. I. Chysost. ἡ μετὰ πίστεως ὀρθῆς, ἐπιμέλεια τοῦ βίου*. However, if we probe Ascham's wording in a little more detail, we in fact see that Ascham has almost certainly on this occasion accessed Chrysostom via Oecumenius. Ascham's wording was in greater alignment with Oecumenius' commentary which reads, τοῦτο γὰρ εὐσέβεια, ἡ μετὰ πίστεως ὀρθῆς ἐπιμέλεια τοῦ καθαροῦ βίου, whereas Chrysostom used [Ἅγιοι δέ εἰσι πάντες, ὅσοι] βίον καλὸν μετὰ πίστεως ὀρθῆς [ἔχουσιν ἄν].[102] Ascham, it seems, although he fully intended to cite Chrysostom, was compelled to do so via the material then available.[103] This notwithstanding, Ascham's priority was to draw on Chrysostom and to be overt about it. For many, these earliest patristic sources constituted the most *bona fide* guarantee of religious verity. The words of the first Greek Reader in Cambridge, Richard Croke, set the tone not just for the desirability of such sources but also for their expediency: 'Where, I ask, does religion come from, if not from Greece? What of the New Testament: with the exception of Matthew, was it not all written in Greek? What, likewise, of the Old Testament? Was it not translated into Greek with God's guidance by the Seventy? – not to mention Athanasius, Gregory of Nyssa, Gregory of Nazianzus, Origen, Chrysostom?'[104] In these fitful times, Greek offered an archive of authenticity, and, the older and purer, the better.

The *Themata* belongs to a period of broader revisionism regarding materials that might buttress the Bible. It was a time of canon re-formation as much as other kinds of recalibration, a time when scholars could exercise their own judgement about what was and was not consonant with sacred Scripture. As we shall see in the section 'Humanist classical theology' (from p. 35), Ascham, perhaps even more creatively, treated the classical corpus as a fitting counterpart to the biblical message. Yet alongside such 'entrepreneurship', there was also a growing conservative constituency that feared the loss of traditional authority over reading the Bible, and began to view private opinion as a direct threat to social stability more generally.[105] Many were growing increasingly troubled by the results of unmonitored approaches to the Bible's plurilingual textual tradition. Thus, while Ascham's approach to Scripture in many ways reflected a broader zeitgeist, it was also one that not all agreed with.

Doctrine and confessionalism

Given the *Themata*'s ostensibly theological core, it is a work that has obvious implications for the placement of Ascham on the confessional spectrum. The confessional identity of Ascham has long been a matter of dispute, and over the years, he has been designated as anything from 'an ardent Puritan' to a 'fair-weather friend to religion'.[106] The *Themata* is not a work that has been analysed in any depth, but of the few evaluations that exist, the one that prevails is that of his modern biographer, Ryan. As Ryan saw it, a mild Protestantism of the *Themata* was the single and most consistent doctrinal viewpoint in an otherwise episodic work, and, in fact, Ryan would place full reliance on Ascham's *Themata* in his assessment of Ascham as a 'relatively conservative Protestant'.[107] This assessment has been influential, and was restated in the initial reference-point of every modern student and scholar, the entry on Ascham in the *Oxford Dictionary of National Biography*.[108]

In what follows, I hope to show that Ryan was both right and not so right. While it is certainly possible to argue that the overall arc of the *Themata* presents a consistency of approach, I will be suggesting that it is one that transcends and confounds the narrow label 'relatively conservative Protestant'. The coherence of Ascham's approach is predicated instead on a rather more complex compound of priorities which were often in different stages of development in a collection that grew over several years of increasing religious polarisation. In order to do full justice to Ascham's programme, we need to look through a wider-view lens that takes in more than a single doctrinal stance and extends to the broader contexts of Henrician England and also Cambridge University. We must also consider the fuller trajectory of Ascham's own intellectual maturation across time. Certainly, by the time he wrote his *Apologia*, it seems that Ascham was moving in a more Reformed direction.[109] However, in parallel with confessional considerations, we might also take our cue from a recent swing in early modern scholarship towards a more aggregate analysis that encompasses factors such as pragmatism, ties of friendship and patronage, and networks that could result in a writer inhabiting diverse and even contradictory positions.

Ascham composed the various parts of his *Themata* at a time when the English Reformation was underway in earnest. Henry had broken with the

Pope in Rome, declared himself 'God's Anointed' and *Defensor Fidei* of the Church of England. He had launched an attack on what he perceived to be superstitious forms of religion, dissolved monasteries, and encouraged widespread access to Scripture, commissioning a vernacular translation, the Great Bible of 1539, the title page of which trumpeted its own trilingual pedigree with the claim that it had been 'truly translated after the veryte of the Hebrue and Greke textes'. John Fisher, the founder of Ascham's own Cambridge college, St John's, along with the reactionary Thomas More, had been executed for refusing to recognise Henry's Caesaropapism.

Yet, as Peter Marshall puts it, Henry was no Protestant role model.[110] Historians over the years have struggled to define Henry's religious identity, and although he introduced conditions in which Protestantism might flourish, his own commitment to this movement was far from clear. This was especially so during the last part of his reign, when, despite his earlier enthusiasm, Henry sought to limit Bible reading and control Bible production,[111] and he issued the doctrinally very conservative Six Articles and also in 1543 the King's Book, which contained an unambiguous condemnation of the Lutheran justification by faith. And as the King's health slowly failed, the future direction of the English Church was contested, with bishops and others in authority competing to control its course. It is a reign that, at least with hindsight, appears confusing and doctrinally indeterminate. While some have (very validly, as will be discussed later) understood it as a *via media* model, others have argued that the only real way to make sense of Henry's religion is not on the basis of soteriological issues but rather through the institution of the royal supremacy itself.[112]

The universities were unable to stay aloof from the barrage of propaganda and this broader backdrop of ebb and flow. Henry drew Oxford and Cambridge into his decision-making, placing reliance on their counsel and also the ratification of his edicts.[113] In 1535 regulations were also issued to the universities, including new college statutes following visitations in 1535.[114] Cambridge's embroilment in the royal agenda was all the deeper for the fact that the figure who had encouraged Henry in so many of these policies, the arch-reformist Thomas Cromwell, served as University Chancellor 1535–1540. To quote Alex Ryrie, the universities became the 'flagships' of Henry's Reformation.[115] Yet for all the intellectual heft the academies offered, the position of universities (and their personnel) was never wholly assured; the dissolution of the monasteries stood as a potent emblem of wholesale institutional disposability. In effect, it meant that religious affiliations within Cambridge became not just heightened, but also skewed, as its members realised that its survival and their livelihoods depended to a great extent on the religious disposition of the monarch. Certainly, by the later stages of

Henry's reign, evangelicals and conservatives sought advantage from the very shifting nature of the King's caprice.

The Henrician (and by the same token the 'Cromwellian') backdrop is a constant presence in Ascham's *Themata*. To begin with, the more foundational aspects of the royal manifesto are fully on display. Indeed, a feature that immediately catches the eye is Ascham's papal hostility: in theme 4, he equated the *pestem illam Babylonicam* ('that Babylonian plague'), namely the Roman bishop, with the Anti-Christ, and lampooned 'the Roman curse';[116] in theme 5 he suggests that Church rites that had been infected by 'the discharge and dregs of Roman sewage' ought to be 'corrected or altogether annulled';[117] and he embarks on a yet more muscular rant in theme 10, accusing at length those who are 'more devoted to Papism than Christ' and prefer to 'obey the Pope than the King in Jesus Christ' of immersion in an amoral mire.[118] A very specific (and pungently ribald) reference in this same theme to Reginald Pole, a figure who had decisively broken with Henry and pledged loyalty to Pope Paul III, as well as adding fuel to the anti-Roman furnace, may also give us a *terminus post quem* of 1538/9 for this particular theme.[119] It was at this point in time that King Henry, led by Cromwell's supporting hand, exposed the so-called Exeter Conspiracy, in which the Pole family met with the full retaliative weight of the State.[120]

As the regime had done, so Ascham too would inveigh against Romish abuses and superstition, and he reserved some especially offensive invective for brothers and monks.[121] Ascham was also careful to draw special attention to a monastic-monarchical fault line: 'What a crowd of our brothers and monks ... These men, repudiating the might of monarchs and removing themselves from all respectable state business ...'.[122] He is explicit in his conviction that service to God and service to the Christian state are in fact inseparable; and perhaps the best articulation of his support for the royal supremacy appears in the statement:

> ... because all churches, the heads of which are kings after Christ, advance not their own edicts but those of Christ, for there is no power unless from God, and those churches that exist have been decreed by God. Accordingly, the man who resists [these] powers resists the decree of God.[123]

One thing we can be in no doubt about is Ascham's loyalty to royalty. In every part of his corpus there are expressions of his commitment to the Crown, perhaps most significantly in his *Toxophilus*, published soon after he drafted the *Themata*.[124] This would even be the case later during the reign of Mary I, whose traditional Catholicism Ascham must have baulked at, but whose temporal and spiritual power he bowed before.[125]

Despite the undeniably adversarial impulse of the *Themata*, Ascham was nevertheless keen to brandish the motif of compromise. There is, for instance, an inclusivity on display, and in theme 10 Ascham expressly includes in the 'church militant' both 'heretics and Papists' in addition to true evangelical believers. In several themes Ascham also appeals to a *via media*, a 'middle way' or 'mean', between two extremes. In the tenth theme, for instance, he refers to holding a course between two crags, so that one is neither forced towards the Charybdis of 'gospellers', nor enfeebled and devoured by the Scylla of religious radicals.[126] As discussed below, any *via media* claim is one that requires sensitive construction. For now, it suffices to treat this affecting of the middle way as one bound up with Henry's own self-image.[127] The stance of the 'middle way', a mode of governance that historical narratives standardly treat as a form of balancing act between religious extremes, was one that found its most well-known expression in the reigns both of Henry VIII and also of his daughter, Elizabeth I.

That Ascham's *Themata* was in full alignment – and ostensibly so – with the broad politico-religious impetus of the Henrician Reformation is not insignificant, and scholars have compellingly pointed to Henrician loyalty as form of identity in its own right.[128] We cannot, however, easily say the same for the doctrine of the *Themata*. This is in part because it is impossible to speak of an Henrician theology as such, religion being treated by him more as a bargaining tool than anything, and the latter part of his reign, in particular, being characterised primarily by its contradictory theological swings. For all the strategic positioning that this provoked, religious convictions did become increasingly entrenched, especially in the universities. Ascham's college, St John's, was one of the most dynamic communities in academe, and there he would join a circle that would become known for its sympathy to the evangelical cause, and one that helped shape the religious settlements of Edward VI and Elizabeth I.[129] But alongside this circle, also nestling at St John's was a committed conservative faction,[130] which remained steadfastly faithful to the memory of their founder, John Fisher. And so, even as the *Themata* reflected the broader background of national turbulence and a fraught university sector, it was also deeply implicated in a charged intramural antagonism at college level.

In doctrinal terms, the thrust of the *Themata* presents a generally more Protestant face than Henry ever did, not least through its direct engagement with the core tenets of Lutheranism, ideas that Henry had been careful to try to stem. Seminal Lutheran ideas, including justification by faith alone and sin, are prominent throughout the work, and indeed form the central axis of several of the themes. The work as a whole shows that Ascham was familiar with Lutheran ideology that had, despite the King's best endeavours, taken root in England, and noticeably in Cambridge. Beyond this, it is far less straightforward to pin down Ascham's doctrinal convictions with any firm precision. An obvious complicating factor is that Ascham was himself evidently consulting St Augustine, the primary authority for Luther's own theological breakthroughs. Furthermore, by the time Ascham penned his *Themata*, so many of the doctrinal points that had once been distinctively Lutheran had already became stock-in-trade categories of magisterial Protestantism.[131] Even as Lutheranism remained the authentic voice of English reformism through the later 1530s and early 40s,[132] appropriation of his texts and ideas was an eclectic process and involved certain modifications of Lutheran emphases.[133] In England, while one common direction of travel from this Lutheran starting block was Reformed theology, the sheer untidiness of the theological landscape in this final decade of Henry's reign makes the application of firm confessional designation too prematurely precise.[134] Additionally, while there is good evidence that Ascham would come to be attracted to the reform movement of Strasbourg, especially the programme of Martin Bucer,[135] in the late 1530s someone like Bucer was still predominantly Lutheran.[136] In short, during this period, we need to be much more open to the idea of unevenness, to some obedience to more established authorities, but also much solo supposition and private conscience-following.

Despite all these variables and the fact that we cannot be totally certain that any particular 'suit' in the *Themata* is *wholly* representative of Ascham's own private beliefs, read cumulatively, this work does point to some general tendencies in outlook. The issue of justification was an especially live and present one, particularly in the first three themes.[137] Although it is important to remember that God's justification of sinners was mainstream Catholic theology, we can be certain that the broader Reformation backdrop was the initial stimulus for each of these propositions and for the way they were broached. At the same time, however, these themes serve as a reminder of how Cambridge scholars might also reach their own theological formulations about ideas such as justification through the reading of the Fathers, most prominently Augustine. As Alastair McGrath points out, Augustine was the centre of gravity in the development of Western theology and his writing established the framework via which all future discussion of justification would be conducted.[138] A very prominent influence on both the wording and argumentation of theme 1 was Augustine. In the works of Augustine the issue of justification remains unintelligible if disassociated from the Adamic fall and its implications for humanity,[139] and this too is the drift of Ascham's first theme. This theme centred on the concept of the *felix culpa* ('the fortunate fall or 'fault'), a theological paradox which embraces the idea that there can be fortunate consequences from an unfortunate event, and, more specifically, that the fault of Adam (as recounted in Genesis 3) can be viewed positively since his sin enabled a redemption so great that it gained more via God's subsequent justification of man than was lost by humanity's fall into sin. Ascham followed Augustine in concluding that justification trumps.

The next obvious next question is to what extent Ascham subscribed to the rather more contested doctrine of justification by faith alone. We can be in no doubt that Ascham considered that faith was the one essential prerequisite for salvation, but quite how he envisaged that Christian faith as functioning and what he understood to be the nature of faith's relationship to God's gift of justification requires some disentangling. Let's begin with the faith element of the equation. In many ways faith itself constitutes the *Themata*'s centre of gravity, but Ascham presents it throughout, and explicitly so, as a faith entirely contingent on Scripture. Again, such a view could well be attributable, at least in part, to an Augustinian influence. For Augustine, 'faith' described the act of believing the Gospel on the basis of the authority of the apostolic message. However, we can also explore other spurs. We could, for instance, return to the matter of *sola scriptura*, the mechanics of which were discussed in the section 'The Bible and patristics' (from p. 9), but its positional ramifications may also now be considered. By the time Ascham was composing his *Themata*, *sola scriptura* (or 'Scripture alone') had been rendered a confessional position. Protestants accused the Roman Church of withholding the Gospels from the people and also of obscuring the pure Word of God with superfluous extra-biblical customs. They began to weave an identity for themselves around the authority of Scripture, an authority that increasingly stood in contradistinction to that of the institutional Church.[140] Luther, in particular, espoused a sort of scriptural fundamentalism, and set great store by Scripture's ability to resolve theological issues.[141] Such an outlook is very clear in the *Themata*, and at each stage Ascham invested the greater part of his energies in rendering God's Word as a cornerstone of faith. A key objective throughout was to establish a watertight theological case for the primacy of God's commandments on the basis of the testimony of God himself in Scripture, and we often find in the *Themata* a forest of Scriptural passages that underscore Scripture's own sovereignty.[142] It might be argued that Ascham exhibits the same dogmatic certainty that Luther did when it came to the hegemony of the Bible.[143]

The doctrine of justification by faith alone entailed not just a full submission to God in faith but also a belief that righteousness comes only from Christ and is imputed to us by God's grace. Many of Ascham's themes point to a belief in sufficient grace. Even as Ascham almost certainly arrived at such a position via Augustine, just as Luther had done, there are signs that the way in which he comprehended the nature of its operation was this time inspired by Luther. In the Heidelberg Disputation of 1517, Luther had posited particular theses which would capture the essence of his conception of justification: his 'theology of the cross'. Luther maintained that the suffering of Christ on the cross was the only source of knowledge concerning who God is and how God saves. To put that another way, it was only through a focus on Christ's cross that the 'logic' of God's power and his gift of justification could be grasped.

This was a perspective especially visible in theme 8, where Ascham explores Galatians 6.14 ('May I be kept from boasting (*gloriari*) except in the cross of our Lord Jesus Christ'). Indeed, it is likely that Ascham was consulting a Lutheran text when penning this theme – Luther's commentary on the Galatians – which, as scholars have observed, was the most popular of all Lutheran works in translation in the Tudor period.[144] Beyond several linguistic points of correspondence, there is also what is essentially a recapitulation of Luther's theology of the cross, for example:

> God of everything on behalf of the slaves of death and sin, an innocent on behalf of the accused and the sons of anger, taking on the form of a slave, became a man in the likeness of men, and bore the wood of the cross, the wood of torment and dishonour, with the result that he not only expelled the wood of wickedness with this wood, as if a nail with a[nother] nail, and liberated the human race from the curse of the Law and the prison of death, [restoring it] unto the ancient dignity of freedom, but [also] established and erected as an eternal monument to sin, death and victory over the Devil, a sign of the cross and a trophy in heaven at the right hand of the Father for the perpetual glory of Christ and of all Christians with Christ.[145]

Also in keeping with Luther, Ascham appears to have differentiated sharply between the Law (which demanded obedience to God's will) and the Gospel (which promised remission of sins through Christ), a distinction that became a critical hermeneutic in Lutheran exegesis and the Protestant understanding of justification.[146] In sermons Luther would address the Law to rebellious sinners, the Gospel to troubled, despairing sinners.[147] In this respect, there was an inseparable connection between God's work of justification and Luther's treatment of consolation,[148] an approach which is also observable in Ascham's *Themata*. For Luther, the doctrine of justification of faith alone brought assured consolation to troubled consciences amid genuine terrors, and his sermon on the Galatians culminated in a victorious climax of consolation for life's troubles, including the ultimate predicament, death.[149] In the *Themata* there is likewise an unmistakable tendency to turn adversity to profit via justification by faith, and the consolatory accent certainly ought to be viewed as part of Ascham's theology. In theme 1, for example, Ascham suggests that the postlapsarian ills introduced by Adam are themselves converted into benefits, and that the blights of fear and toil could be productively channelled into a positive expression of faith. Time and time again, Ascham refers to the comfort and succour Christ can offer us amid the despair. A repeated technique that he adopted in three themes, 1, 5 and 8, was to ask a series of imagined questions redolent of helplessness, followed by an answer (in the persona of Christ) that is intended to console. A short example from theme 8 will suffice here:

> Are you deprived of your parents and the help of friends? Heed the comfort of the cross, 'I will not abandon you as orphans; I will come to you'..... Do you fear the violence and persecution of this world? 'Be of good courage; I have conquered this world'.[150]

For Ascham, the state of humankind is so abject that it makes us worthy objects of nothing but consolatory comfort.

This leads us to a related aspect of Lutheran justification by faith alone that Ascham and evidently others at the University were evidently anxious to explore – the issue of human sin. The doctrine of justification by faith alone involved the paradox that although man may be made *iustus* ('righteous'), he remains a *peccator* ('a sinner'). Although Luther did not produce a specific treatise solely on sin, there are few places in his oeuvre where the topic of sin does not appear. Under the umbrella term *peccatum*, Luther identified a range of sins, from *peccatum originis*, which denoted the first sin of Adam and Eve, to *peccatum originale* ('original sin') and also *peccatum hereditare* ('inherited sin'), each of which captured the wholesale submersion of the human race in sin, and all of which he distinguished from *peccatum actuale*, a more specific transgression of the law of God. As Luther's theology matured, the form of sin that came to dominate his thinking was an all-encompassing version, a radical and total sin, or rather sinful state, a critical sin theory, if you like, that went yet further than Augustine.

Several themes in the *Themata* try to puzzle out the relationship between these different types of sin. In theme 3, one of the most doctrinally conservative and probably chronologically earliest of the collection, Ascham marshals an argument in support of a proposition contained in a verse from Ezekiel, 'The son will not carry the sinfulness of the father'. While Ascham does not deny the existence of original sin, he shows himself far more preoccupied with *peccatum actuale* or, as he puts it, *actuale et voluntarium peccatum* ('actual and willed sin'), the sin of individual conduct.[151] In other themes, however, a greater focus on man's innately sinful condition is more conspicuous. In the first theme, even as Ascham was adamant that God's gift of justification ultimately outflanks the damnation of men caused by Adam's fall, he nonetheless devotes more space to the ill-effects introduced by Adam than to the benefits of Christ. He sets out a whole catalogue of sins under separate headings of 'blindness', 'flesh' and 'weakness', and dwells to no small extent on man's powerlessness.[152] In this same theme Ascham also incorporates the Pauline image of donning the armour of God for spiritual warfare, a motif used frequently in Protestant literature and one that captured well the struggle that bedevils a sinful mankind.[153] By the time we get to theme 11, we meet with sentiments that sound quintessentially Lutheran. Here Ascham is quite blunt about the inherent sinfulness of the person at prayer, writing at one point (and paraphrasing John), 'For as long as you are in this world, you have in no way the power to escape the act of sinning. Indeed, if you say that you have no sin, you are liars, and there is no truth in you'.[154] A favourite maxim of Luther was *omnis homo mendax* ('Every man is a liar'), an aphorism that would also, as it happens, appear in Ascham's *Apologia* of 1547.[155]

A rather more noticeable disequilibrium between Luther and Ascham, and a potent reminder that Lutheran theology was as much negotiated as straightforwardly accepted, concerned 'works' and man's morality. Luther in his totemic work, *Bondage of the Will*, had concluded that an inexorably unredeemed humanity that was locked in a permanent state of wretchedness, was incapable of good works except through God's grace, and that the value of any good works for justification was precisely nil. The balance of Lutheran theology was heavily tilted towards the persistence of ineradicable human sin and lack of agency. Ascham, by contrast, although the stress on sin, as we have just seen, was very much present in the *Themata*, placed as much emphasis on individual conduct. In contrast to Luther's ruthless critique of 'works righteousness', Ascham demonstrated a resolve to explore the ways in which faith in Christ might help us to lead a righteous life. But, and this is an important adversative, in the majority of themes, Ascham casts works as the manifestation of *iustitia* ('righteousness') and understands them as part and parcel of the *sola fide* infrastructure. In theme 2, for instance, Ascham discusses individual behaviour and personal responsibility, but within the confines of *iustitia*, offering over two pages an outline of the conduct of a *iustus* (the 'righteous man').[156] In theme 4, pursuant to the Augustinian proposition, 'Fault lies not in the action, but in the way [it is done]', Ascham draws a distinction between *factum* ('deed') and *modus* ('way') and urges the reader to attend to the precise make-up and moral progress of their actions. However, even as the argument suggests that an individual's own conduct contributes to the classification of an action as a sin or as something good, ultimately, as Ascham also makes clear, the quality of conduct is determined in accordance with the strictures of Scripture and the presence or absence of faith.

For Ascham, the constitution of one's conduct was of vital importance, and he did not treat it as a marginal matter or an incidental byproduct of God's grace in the way Luther did. It may be that in this respect we can once more look to an Augustinian influence. One of the key differences in emphasis between Augustine and Luther was that the former elected love as the great distinctive characteristic of justifying faith, whereas Luther selected humility. Not all reformers broke as starkly with the Augustinian paradigm as Luther did; indeed, several scholars have shown the extent to which Luther's successors forged their own versions of justification that put morality back at the centre of their manifestos.[157] For Ascham, the lived experience of religion, the practical realities of a pious Christian life, and the need for moral law and order were as much a priority as the acknowledgement of man's abject condition. Indeed, it was this interest in a quotidian Christianity, in conduct over concept, that seems to have motivated Ascham's overt denunciation of predestination in the *Themata*:

> Thus, these men, who, as they dream up all sort of things about predestination, have no regard either for a pure or profligate life, except only the surest way to their own salvation. Since, with a certain remarkable foolhardiness and in their lazy indifference, they have entangled themselves in a totally inexplicable matter ... [they] confine their own lives within such narrow bounds of predestination, as though [within] certain railings and, in that matter alone, cast their thoughts constantly and exclusively in the direction of 'fascination', except that they reject all wisdom and all concern and regard for conducting a better life.[158]

Ascham's focus on 'exterior actions' played a significant role in Ryan's adjudication of the tract as relatively conservative.[159] Such a verdict is in some ways understandable and certainly in keeping with a standard Reformation narrative, which has tended to classify any position that allowed for man's natural capacities as well as God's grace to bring about 'good works' as more traditionally Catholic. This tendency owes much to the famous quarrel between Luther and Erasmus over the role of the will, which has in turn resulted in an overly crude associative web: Protestant reformers being credited with the development of hard doctrine; Erasmian humanism with a concern for ethics and an optimism about the course of human life.[160]

It would, however, be a mistake to suppose that Protestants of the next generation, when theology had to be put into practice, were uninterested in the actuality of a pious existence and the role of 'works', and it is far too simplistic to evaluate such an agenda in terms of two opposed schemes of salvation. In any case, Ascham was a far cry from the medieval view of a Christian life in which the contrite human will was capable of cooperating with God towards an individual salvation by the performance of good works. As John McDiarmid argues, for Ascham and others in his reformist circle, as well as for many second and third generation Reformed Protestants across Europe, the exercise of the will was not abandoned but repackaged within a framework of divine grace.[161]

Time and time again in the *Themata*, Ascham alerts us to the indispensable deposit of Christ's *gratia* (grace) in all our actions. Theme 5 closes with the words:

> We are born and we live by the grace of God, and from this grace we have learnt from the day we were born, just as though suckled by the milk of a wet-nurse, to conserve ourselves, [our] life and body, and to avoid all those things that seem bound to harm us.[162]

Ascham is clear that virtuous action is *only* possible within the strict confines of God's Word, as reflected in the peroration in theme 4:

> For this reason, since our actions count for nothing unless the way [that is] ordained by me directs them, let us pray to God that he restricts our actions, and [then] not only will we bring about truly good works and our salvation, but we will also run on the correct courses and take our reward.[163]

Again in theme 4, Ascham was categorical that any virtue in us was dependent, not on private human agency, but on the unilateral efficacy of Christ in us: 'Our actions, *not* because they are done by us, but because they are confined within God's commandment, are to be considered good';[164] and 'The ordinance and the will of God, not our own deeds, makes us good'.[165] It might be tempting to conceive of Ascham's *Themata* as a fusion of Erasmus' *philosophia Christi* and Luther's philosophy of grace, but this is too glib; it attributes overmuch importance to Reformation 'models' or 'schools' and not enough to the personal faith Ascham had placed in the salutary power of the Gospels.

The upshot of this is that when we ask what Ascham's view is of, say, good works or the human will, we need to be very mindful of the degree to which *sola scriptura* was the real turbine for his doctrine. For Ascham, it was the Bible, which he viewed as a practical mine of truth, rather than a disembodied set of credal theories, upon which everything else hung. While Luther may have been the impetus for this, it was Ascham who was the arbiter of *how* or *whether* the Bible could prove or disprove a theological point at issue. Sometimes that meant bumping up against the limits of the unknowable, and resulted in an acknowledgement that God's inscrutable verities might lie beyond human logic. And so at the end of theme 3, Ascham, writing about the matter of damnation, announces, 'But we should entrust this entire matter to the unfathomable judgement of God, to the wisdom of one on a higher plane, as it were'.[166]

Elsewhere, we see Ascham registering a certain reticence about broaching certain doctrines, for example, in theme 10, that of Free Will, ' ... I do not consider that the bewildering and involved principle of Free Will must be unravelled here'.[167] Ascham had a strong antipathy for theological subtlety and abstraction, an outlook prominently on display in his above-cited criticism of those 'entangled' in the 'inexplicable' question of predestination. This did not mean, however, that Ascham was averse to any sort of theological inquiry, but he was insistent that such inquiries must be pursued according to the terms set by Scripture. In this same tenth theme, he would scrutinise the nature of *voluntas* ('will') – a term that appears throughout Ascham's *Themata* – doubtless because it is attested to in the Bible, and because it was cognate with the verb *volunt*, which featured in this theme's caption (*omnes qui volunt pie vivere in Christo Iesu persequutiones patientur* from 2 Timothy 3.12). Ascham does in fact offer a definition of the 'will', but one based on his reading of Psalm 34.12 (or 33.13) and Hebrews 6.11 and Romans 10.2.[168] Relying cumulatively on these verses, he asserts that 'to be willing' is 'to have a certain quick and ready inclination of the mind to discharging anything which you have attempted'.[169] As the theme develops, however, this statement becomes heavily qualified by his broader argument that ultimately human will, even if piously-inclined, is completely redundant unless it chimes with God's ordinance. Ryan, it seems, misread Ascham's *Themata*: Ascham's reluctance to become entangled in speculative theological theory, such as that of the Free Will, did not signal, as Ryan averred, a deficiency in divinity.[170] Ascham was very ready to 'do divinity', but with Scripture as his guide, and according to the simple, pure and natural signification of its words.

The *Themata*'s biblicism was entirely congruent with a broader Aschamian outlook. The same biblical fundamentalism permeates all his other works, and in particular another theological Latin tract, the *Apologia*, in which he used the words of the Bible to semantically stress-test the doctrine of the Eucharist. Here too extrascriptural arguments about what happened in the Eucharist were simply not part of Ascham's theological approach and can explain the absence of any mention of 'transubstantiation' in this treatise; Ascham circumvents the term primarily because Scripture does not mention it.

It remains common practice in Reformation studies to view questions of doctrine and confessional orientation as the parent territory of theology; doctrinal affiliation then becomes the primary benchmark for measuring radicalism or conservatism. However, arguably one of the most radical activities during the Reformation was the independent interpretation of Scripture. If we parse Ascham's religious system along these lines, the label 'relatively conservative Protestant' seems far less apt: a professional biblical industry was his driving force, not settlement. The Bible was for Ascham the mistress science without which the entire structure necessarily lacked its final synthesis. That said, the ensuing theological synthesis was necessarily an expression of individualism. Taking into account Ascham's intellectually unafraid and closely-focused scriptural approach, it was, as Ryan comments in passing, 'probably as well for him [Ascham] that the *Themata Theologica* was not published at the time'.[171]

It should be added that Ascham's representation of his own approach in the *Themata* was very carefully sculpted. As regards the management of Scripture, for instance, he is the self-appointed moderate. In the tenth theme, he inveighed against the excesses of extremist 'gospellers':

> And to move from here to another type of men, ... there are some, as those who, according to the principle of opposites, were 'religious' even though very far [removed] from religion. Accordingly, they scramble both to be called and to be considered 'gospellers' from the [term] 'Gospel'. Yet these men, with the appearance of piety because of their reading of the Gospel, nevertheless, by negating its goodness through the immorality of their lives, desecrate the testament of God. For they lay claim to every licence of the flesh and they tear away all good observances which, along with Scripture, have been handed down for our salvation with the result that everything is performed properly in the Church. They are disturbers of correct piety and instigators of a misguided mode of hearing the Word of God.[172]

We must be careful how we approach the pose of moderation in Reformation tracts. As Luc Racaut and Alec Ryrie have observed, there were often tactical motives behind moderation (which were not necessarily moderate) and the voice of moderation was as much about rhetoric as conviction, a stance that could be and was easily weaponised.[173] Even as Ascham fashions himself as an upholder of nonscriptural laws and ceremonies of the Church, some pages earlier, Ascham would belligerently advocate the summary removal of the more problematic aspects of Church liturgy, writing, 'I am not here looking down on approved liturgy of the Church, but I do feel that all rotten and unfruitful branches of misuse must be cut down'.[174] Evangelicals were in general more bitter about radicals than traditionalists were.[175] As ever with polemic and aspersion, it often exposes the narcissism of small differences rather than any real distance.

Humanist classical theology

We have thus far considered ways in which Ascham's *Themata* defies straightforward designation. The work's Henrician but also patristic and Lutheran spirit, its biblical commitment and Ascham's personal stamp merged with various doctrinal precepts, which, in turn, gave rise to a more multifaceted theological mélange. In this final part, I hope to add to this mosaic, and to argue that is possible to enter the work's theological radius from yet another angle – the classical tradition.

Before embarking on this, a few observations on the conventional treatment of the classics relative to the reform movement may be ventured. There is a habit of thought, now fairly hardwired in historiography, that detaches classical learning from the religious convulsions of the Reformation. It means that very often historians treat the classical humanist tradition as running on a different track from religion. One reason for this may be the immense attention that has been given over the years to the Christian humanism of Erasmus; Erasmus' own urbane apologies that he was subordinating the classical to the religious have perhaps coloured all subsequent developments, which are then assessed along the same lines. The result has been a general decoupling of classical learning and religious reform in the historical accounts of the Reformation beyond Erasmus. In place of an openness to harmonisation between the two, it has become commonplace to sequester classical learning from the 'serious' business of reform, and instead associate it with gentler pursuits and irenicism. The *Themata*, a work in which classical thought is deeply woven into its religious mission, is a useful text with which to challenge this master narrative.[176]

Ascham was an individual at the front-line of the campaign to improve biblical language, and, like many humanists, he deemed language the outward expression of an inner condition. The section 'The Bible and patristics' (from p .9) explored Ascham's aspiration for a rhetorically affective Latinity when quoting the Good Book. Yet Ascham's *Themata* as a whole can be viewed as an exhibition of classical oratory. A short paragraph of Latin from the start of the first theme illustrates the point:

> *Primus homo parens noster Adamus, partim veteris serpentis malitia adductus, partim mulieris levitate allectus, propria tamen culpa et consensione, nimis praeceps et lubricus, se, ac omnes qui ex illo in posterum nascerentur, ab excellenti quodam dignitatis gradu, in quo positus fuit, in summam miseriam et confusionem perduxit.*

> The first man, our parent, Adam, was in part led astray by the wickedness of an ancient serpent, and in part seduced by the shallowness of a woman. All the same, it was through his own fault and submission, [that he], all too swift and slippery, brought [both] himself and everyone who was born of him hereafter from a superior position of worth, in which he had [originally] been placed, into the most wretched condition and disorder.[177]

The bugle-horned opening of this oration on the nature of Adam's sin relative to Christ's gifts captures well Ascham's eye for style, with its Ciceronian symmetry – *partim veteris serpentis malitia adductus* on the one hand, and *partim mulieris levitate allectus* on the other – as well as his ear for sound, and one may note the euphonius pairings, *culpa et consensione, praeceps et lubricus*, and *miseriam et confusionem*.

Ascham was very alive to the aural experience of his audience, and he speaks to them with a directness, often, for example, through repetition and rhetorical questions. A favoured pattern, and one Ascham deploys more than once in the *Themata*, is the bullet question-and-answer structure (also discussed above, p. 29). In one of these sequences, in this case, at the end of theme 8, Ascham uses in close succession several second person singular verbs of fearing: *times, extimescis, abhominaris, vereris* and *exhorrescis* to ask questions such as, 'Do you fear the violence and persecution of this world?' Although the answers to each of these comprise biblical citations, these are transmitted through the lattice of classical rhetoric, including the *variatio* of the accumulation of verbs of fearing that make up the questions. The biblical maxims gather fire and speed because of the overarching rhetorical configuration. On display here is a pneumatic drill effect, which not only conveys the intensity of the Gospel voice, but also provides a sort of mnemonic immersion. Ascham adopts this scheme three times in total,[178] and it certainly points to the performative dimension of the tract, and also to the broader oral culture within which we must read Ascham's *Themata*, and indeed so many early modern productions.[179]

Ciceronian formulations are also much in evidence, and, as recorded in the annotations to the text, the vast majority of the more arresting phrases have been taken by Ascham from Cicero. Ciceronian harmonics often help round out a clause or sentence in which Ascham has mounted an especially crucial theological argument, and Ascham regularly has a particular passage culminate in a rhetorical clausula, the Ciceronian *esse videatur* being deployed five times.[180] The prescription for prayer found in theme 11 and discussed below in 'Ascham as theologian' (pp. 44–45) likewise depends on classical rhetoric for much of its potency. When Ascham makes his recommendations and explains how prayer works, he speaks as Christ, utilising the rhetorical device of prosopopoeia, just as Cicero would do in his *De oratore*, when he adopted the persona of Crassus, or in his *In Catilinam*, when he appeared as Rome itself.[181]

The Ciceronian rhetorical complexion certainly fits with a more widespread preference for the imitation of Cicero that many of Ascham's circle espoused. Yet the assimilation of a classical rhetorical style into an overtly religious remit was not just about stereo; it slots into a much larger context of vigorously-debated Renaissance squabbles that helped ensure rhetoric's relevance to religion. These included a long-running series of Ciceronian controversies which centred on the imitation of Cicero,[182] and that also, by the mid-sixteenth century, came to dominate translation theory as well.[183] These also related to wider discussions about the relationship between rhetoric and philosophy (in particular dialectic), oratory and epistemology.[184] Since the rediscovery in the fifteenth century of Cicero's *De oratore* and a renewed interest in Aristotle's *Rhetoric*, humanists had rejected scholastic forms of philosophy, which they claimed distorted Aristotelianism. A central complaint was that scholastics had neglected knowledge through their failure to attend to the 'discovery' of arguments (*inventio*) and forms of organisation called 'topics' or *loci* as espoused in the ancient manuals. Humanists, inspired by the synthesis of rhetoric and philosophy that they identified in the classical corpus, attempted to correct this, to recalibrate the role of rhetoric, and to forge a new relationship between it and dialectic. This, it was hoped, would create a more fructifying dynamic between *res* (the substance of the thing) and the *verba* (the linguistic medium that animated it). These ideas may sound rather esoteric nowadays, but they were of the utmost importance right through the fifteenth and sixteenth centuries, accentuated no doubt by a greater accessibility to the Word of God and its communication. They were ideas that would grip Ascham too, and a substantial portion of his oeuvre more generally would revolve around this dyad of *res* and *verba*.[185]

The *Themata* is in many ways an exemplary textual expression of the combination of dialectic and rhetoric. A tendency for taxonomy is discernible in several themes. In theme 1, for instance, we see Ascham organising the sins and sufferings of Adam under several heads, 'Accordingly, all [these] sins which have originated from Adam, while they are infinite in number, we suggest they belong to blindness, flesh and weakness, just as if to certain categories (*tanquam ad certa capita*)'.[186] As for the sufferings introduced by Adam, although again these are said to be infinite, Ascham suggests that they can be divided into certain types (*certis tamen generibus describi possunt*), which he then sets out.[187] In theme 6, Ascham's response to the injunction from Ephesians 4.26, 'Be angry and sin not', is to identify types of anger. These are then the chief points via which he can arrange his argument. So, following a twofold division of anger into 'anger of flesh' and 'anger of faith', Ascham proceeds to codify the latter into further (positive) categories: the anger of 'correction', of 'advice', of 'sin (or repentance)', and of 'the mind'. However, such designation is always combined with a rhetorical sound-and-light show, through, for instance, the use of tricola (blindness, flesh and weakness) and the symphonic-sounding verbs in theme 6, which provide the fundamental cement for the types of anger he itemises: *dicimus:...[quorum beneficio] vivimus... [quorum praesidio bene] vivimus... dicitur... irascitur... consequitur.*[188] Inherent in the *Themata* is sort of living language system in which classical rhetoric re-parcels the Christian *res* in such a way as to draw the reader into a true participation in God's Word. The Reformation has, and not without good reason, been referred to by historians as a 'language event', and in Ascham we see the degree to which ancient rhetoric could assist in a reform campaign that centred on teaching a fluency in God and a life in the Logos. Elegant, eloquent and well-chosen language had the ability to transport a worshipper to a different plane of value. Thus, for civic-minded reformers and humanists steeped in notions of the *vita activa* of writers like Cicero, rhetorical training was being drafted into the most important *res* of all: Christian worship.

Rhetoric also fed the confessionalising thrust of the *Themata*, and, as such, contributed to rant as much as to rhapsody. A prime example comes in Ascham's assault on Cardinal Pole in theme 10 (mentioned on p. 24). By the time Ascham was working on the *Themata*, Pole was not only associated with popery but also with treachery, and Ascham applied his full rhetorical weight against him:

> Sed Deus optimus est orandus, ut nec hiis nec consimilibus peccata sua imputare velit. An-non nominatim perstringam Reginaldum illum Polum, quo, inter utrumque polum, sceleratior et abhominabilior numquam extitit, qui pietate, si diis placet, extra Christum? non, sed impietate

inaudita in Diabolo, non solum a Patria ingrate, a Rege perfidiose, a Christo impie veluti ignavissimus quidam Demas ad Papam et Diabolum deficit: sed ingentem quandam perditorum hominum faecem et coluviem in easdem sordes involvit.

But we must pray to God pre-eminent to will it that his (i.e. the Pope's) sins are not imputed to these men nor to similar men. Or should I not mention that fellow Reginald Pole by name? Than *Pole* there has never lived [anyone] between each *pole* more wicked and more execrable, who, if it pleases the gods, [lives] with 'piety' beyond Christ. And not [just that], but with an impiety unheard of in the Devil, not only has he gone over ungratefully from his fatherland, treacherously from his King, and impiously from Christ, to the Pope and the Devil, just like some very cowardly Demas, but he has [also], swept up into the same state of uncleanliness a certain immense detritus and swill of the most degenerate men.[189]

In a passage that can only be properly appreciated in the Latin, Ascham relies on wordplay (on Pole's name), amplification through a tricolon of adverbs (*ingrate, perfidiose* and *impie*), binary opposition via the polyptoton of *pietate* and *impietate*, the use of coupling *a Patria ... a Rege* and *ad Papam et Diabolum*, and the Ciceronian invective *perditorum hominum*.[190] Eruptive classical rhetoric is here applied in such a way as to demarcate division at a time when the confessional delineations of the Reformation were still forming. The modern narrative often has us believe that humanism was an irenic force in contrast to the polemic of theology; but, as Peter Matheson rightly points out, the picture is infinitely more complicated.[191] The ancient rhetorical inheritance was at this point actively contributing to religious schism and determining lines of combat. We should perhaps conceive of the Reformation not so much in terms of the 'confessionalization of humanism', as Erika Rummel puts it,[192] but humanism as an agent of confessionalisation.[193]

As crucial as classical stylistics were to Ascham's communication of the Word of God, pagan principles also gave shape to the tract's dialectical structures and, in turn, its theological direction. At the start of the fourth theme, where Ascham explores the Augustinian proposition, 'Fault lies not in the action but in the way [it is done]', he analyses the term 'action' under two heads: (i) a general, simple and unlimited action, which the Greeks call 'a thesis'; and (ii) an action that is contingent and limited, which the Greeks term a 'hypothesis'.[194] This exact distinction found in Cicero *Topics*, a work in which Cicero harnesses the Aristotelian system of invention and sets out his loci-theory of rhetoric.[195] Ascham continued to rely on the *Topica* in his suggestion that a 'limited action' is defined by its the attendant circumstances: the person, the place, the time and details of this kind (*res circumstantes: personam, locum, tempus, et quae sunt huiusmodi*). Cicero too had postulated that 'a cause' (i.e. a hypothesis) 'is determined by certain persons, places, times, actions, and things, either all or most of them' (*causa certis personis, locis, temporibus, actionibus, negotiis cernitur aut in omnibus aut in plerisque eorum*).[196] Moreover, in the subsequent part of Ascham's argument about the importance of the *modus* for determining the nature of an action, he appeared to lean on another Ciceronian handbook to oratory, the *De inventione*. However, whereas for Cicero *modus* was a state of mind in which there is judgement and lack of judgement (*eius partes sunt prudentia et imprudentia*), for Ascham it pointed to the presence of absence of faith.[197] Ciceronian principles were being directly coopted by Ascham, but moved into another point of orientation. Whereas some of his contemporaries might have sensed here an uncomfortable blurring of the boundary line between heathenism and faith, Ascham had no such scruples.

Humanist grammar also contributed to Ascham's religious analysis. In theme 4, Ascham delved into the constitution of particular actions relative to the Word of God, with an especial focus on episodes in the Old Testament. As part of this, he suggested that a 'way' (*modus*) might be characterised either as 'permitted' (*permissivus*) or 'compulsory' (*imperativus*). For example, he argued that it is 'permitted' when Abraham, because of Sarah's barrenness, slept with his maidservant, or when Jacob deceived his father and defrauded his brother of his blessing and inheritance. It is 'compulsory' when God ordered the sons of Israel to plunder Egypt, or when God bade Hosea the Prophet to lie with a prostitute and beget sons of fornication. *Permissivus* and *imperativus* were technical terms used by grammarians; they feature, for example, in William Lily's *Grammar of Latin in English* (*c*. 1540), a resource, or the principles of which, Ascham would have been familiar with. In Lily, these terms were discussed under the heading *modi verborum*, the 'moods of verbs', and instances of use were provided from Virgil and Propertius, Cicero and Martial. What is extraordinary is the way that this grammatical theory then bleeds into exegesis in the *Themata*. The role of these verbal moods influenced Ascham's computation of the different modes of action in the Bible, and he evidently found the contrast between (a) an unequivocal command or injunction, which might be represented by, say, an imperative, and (b) the exceptional licence, that might be conveyed by a hortatory or jussive subjunctive, a serviceable one when it came to expounding Scripture.

But the humanist classical influence can be felt beyond the scaffolding of Ascham's *Themata*. Classical ideas also inform the pith and substance of his enterprise. In theme 2, where Ascham attempts to define 'the righteous man', he cites examples from Psalm 37 and also Ezekiel 18,[198] but in parallel he presses Cicero into service once again. Quoting *De inventione*, Ascham writes, '[Cicero says] he is righteous who worships God with faith and reverence, and who vigilantly discharges his duty to fatherland, parents and every single man'.[199] Ascham effectively creates here an equivalence between classical and Christian. A similar approach is evident later in this same theme, when Ascham enlarges on an argument against the notion of inheritance within the remits of sin and righteousness with an allusion to Columella's work on agriculture, *De re rustica*, and Columella's description of the deterioration of quality wheat into worthless '*siligo*'.[200] Such examples are not exceptional. Ascham opened theme 7, the heading of which was the Pauline verse, 'If any man thinks that he knows anything, he has not yet got to know as he ought to know', with a discussion of the ancient Greek philosopher Socrates in Plato's *Apology*.[201] In theme 10, which is organised around a verse from 2 Timothy 3, 'Everyone who is willing to live piously in Jesus Christ will endure persecutions', Ascham cites the Roman poet Ovid among a catena of other biblical references in order to highlight the reward in heaven that follows the oppression experienced by Christians in this life.[202] In the last part of the fourth theme where Ascham emphasises the importance of constant and careful adherence to God's bidding, he defers to an ancient model of behaviour, which entails finding a balance between too much and too little virtue, at which point Ascham proceeds over two pages to namecheck Aristotle, Horace and Xenophon.[203]

The reference in this fourth theme to Xenophon and his portrayal of Socrates in *Memorabilia* is especially important,[204] for it points to a fundamental dynamic in Ascham's relationship with the ancient authors. The counsel Xenophon offers (as articulated by Socrates), that the best way to honour God is to follow his bidding, is then recontextualised by Ascham in such a way that it is almost seamlessly transformed into a requirement for an unwavering adherence to the Word of God. In effect, the Socratic example acts as a vector for correct Christian insight. It is telling that this same passage from Xenophon is set out in full in Ascham's handwriting on the very first page of his Greek New Testament. Just as in the copy of his Greek New Testament, where Ascham's Xenophon handwritten insertion literally and visually serves as a the textual launchpad into first chapter of Matthew (see Figure 1 at p. 56), so too we witness here in the *Themata* a clear belief in the springboard power of the pagan canon and its ability to impart sacred knowledge.[205] Ascham, it seems, did not just perceive a 'Christian spirit' residing within many of the ancient authors, he also saw how the ancients could help awaken the Christian spirit residing in religious texts.

On display in the *Themata* is an incredibly fertile form of classical intertextuality, the dexterous weaving of related works of literature – in both concept and word – into a new text. The practice of intertextuality is often associated in modern scholarship with a demonstration of learning, a sort of literary 'game' and outward show. However, in Ascham, classical citations do not play a superficial role but a fundamental one. Classical examples, which drew on the best that has been thought and said, appear side by side with the religious, and are reconciled with the biblical citations with which they are yoked. Classical and Christian operate in synthesis: Ascham actively 'converts' the classical texts that he builds into his *Themata*; at the same time, his classical examples help underscore the sacrosanctity of the Christian texts they are read alongside. Most crucially, Ascham appears to treat classical authors as authorities, as a means to establish the truth. Concerning his reliance on Cicero for the definition of 'the righteous man' in theme 2, Ascham wrote 'I won't set out what he says [so much] for that reason, but because truth demands it be so (*quia veritas sic postulat*); for this reason, I shall bring it forth into the mix'.[206] In theme 4, albeit in conjunction with a certain self-reflexive critique whereby he suggests that the ancients had 'no concrete and manifest image of the true law and of genuine justification,' Ascham nevertheless suggests that they '[arrived] more effectively at a comprehension of the truth (*veritatis cognitionem*) than we'.[207]

It is difficult to read Ascham's *Themata* without reaching the conclusion that the classical tradition informed his own Christian faith to a profound degree. Indeed, there were in Ascham's classically-rooted work wider implications for the Reformation, and we may consider two instances here. The first centres on a principle that would play a crucial role in the plate tectonics of the broader European reform movement. This was the notion of adiaphoron or 'something indifferent'. Ascham marshalled this classical notion in his fourth theme while explaining the 'simple and unlimited' type of action. This, he suggested, was an action 'without any attendant circumstances prescribed by us', and 'is neither good nor bad (*neque bonum neque malum*), but something indifferent (*indifferens*) and an "adiaphoron" (ἀδιάφορον)'.[208] The idea was a bastion of Stoicism,[209] but Ascham's actual wording is unmistakably Ciceronian, and appears to have been borrowed almost word for word from the third book of *De finibus*, where Cicero reconstructs the main tenets of Greek (and, more precisely, Stoic) philosophy into Latin.[210] Ascham evidently viewed the concept as a theologically productive framing device, as too would a number of reformers across Europe. This included key architects of the Leipzig Interim of 1548, a religious settlement between the Catholic Emperor, Charles V, and the German Protestants.[211] That a compromise between these two sides was (in the end) secured was entirely owing to the concept of adiaphoron – Melanchthon managed to persuade certain Lutherans that beyond the essential article of faith, justification, other points of doctrine were 'inessential' or adiaphora.[212]

The idea had traction in England too: Bernard Verkamp has claimed that adiaphorism, following its full absorption into the national mindset, was the keystone of the entire English religious settlement.[213] I am not for one moment suggesting that Ascham was himself directly influential in any of these pan-European developments. What I would propose, however, is that he was part of larger intellectual movement in which Graeco-Roman lines of thought, of which so many at the time had an intimate knowledge, had a pivotal agency in the evolution of new forms of religious ideology and in theological 'due process'.[214]

A second (related) example can help illustrate the same point. Ascham places heavy stress in his *Themata* on 'the middle way', τὸ μέσον or *modus* ('the mean'), in matters of morality. We considered this idea above in relation to the Henrician reign, be it a deliberate policy of balance between religious extremes or some kind of fudge. Yet the golden mean was also a product of classical philosophy, as Ascham would himself announce when he evokes the concept in theme 4, deferring to the 'ancient philosophers' and Horace.[215] It has been argued that Ascham played a significant role in the formation of Elizabeth I's 'religion'.[216] If this is correct, then we might also be open to the idea that the pagan literary tradition, transmitted by reform-minded humanists like Ascham, contributed in some way to the bedrock of the various religious settlements rooted in the *via media* that took shape in England and possibly even elsewhere during the course of the Reformation.[217]

That Ascham's classical proclivities had a direct bearing on his religious engagement certainly fits with a small but growing body of studies which surmise the same. Scholars who are prepared to delve into the rather more neglected Neo-Latin material, and whose investigations work upwards from the primary material, are similarly pointing to the considerable bearing that classical sources might have had on controversial theological questions and the very process of confessionalisation.[218]

Ascham as theologian

On the basis of the previous sections, is it at all legitimate to refer to Ascham as a 'theologian'? His *Themata* captures well a dovetailing of priorities of biblical scholarship, philology, patristic input, an engagement with established doctrine, and the application of classical learning and rhetoric. But do these cumulatively count as 'theological'? When Ascham penned the sections of his

Themata, while he may well have been toying with the possibility of an ecclesiastical pathway, he was not a Bachelor of Divinity. Indeed, he had no formal theological qualification at all, and he was emphatically a member *not* of the Theological Faculty but the Arts, a faculty in which he would remain. And even though Ascham attended St John's, Cambridge's theological college, strictly speaking and according to the conventions of the sixteenth-century academy, he was not a theologian. And yet the *Themata* was produced at a time when the nature of theology – its remit, practice, purpose and personnel – was increasingly subject to challenge and change.[219]

This contest over theological territory was rooted in the rivalry between humanism and scholasticism that had started in the fifteenth century with thinkers like Leonardo Bruni, Pico della Mirandola, and Ermolao Barbaro. As Erica Rummel's valuable review of these cultural collisions highlights, issues such as the value of dialectic in theology, the relative merit of patristic and scholastic authorities, and the utility of classical learning would persist and eventually result in questions being asked about the very authority of theologians to dispense theology.[220] The situation was further compounded when, against a backdrop of university curricula reforms and a growing sense of the validity of humanism as an intellectual method, Erasmus argued that every Christian should be a theologian and Luther suggested that every Christian was a priest.[221] Perhaps the most acrimonious aspect of this dispute was the argument over who was competent to interpret Scripture, which ultimately led to the broader question of what constituted the proper theological method.[222] Even the notion of what theology should constitute was now a debatable one: should it in essence be a practical rather than a speculative enterprise? Bucer, a figure who would become an important mentor for Ascham, remarked in a commentary on the Gospels of 1530 (in a passage on John 14), 'True theology is not theoretical or speculative, but active and practical. Indeed, the end of it is to act, that is to live a godly life'.[223]

If this was now the definition (at least for some) of valid theology, we can certainly consider Ascham's methodology in this light. One manifestation of this more pragmatic theological approach comes in the final theme of Ascham's *Themata* which relates to the realm of prayer. Theme 11 comprises a general exhortation to prayer, and the bulk of its contents comprises template wording for the ordinary worshipper. The inspiration for the theme, as the heading indicates, was John's Gospel, and in particular Jesus' prayer to God in chapter 17; only here, Ascham has Christ speak not to God but directly to the reader. Many of the prescriptions spring straight from Scripture, including other parts of John and the Sermon on the Mount in

Matthew and the Lord's Prayer, but Ascham has for the most part dressed the sentiments in his own words. The guidance covers the types of requests that should be avoided in prayer (essentially worldly matters, such as popular acclaim). It also addresses the appropriate modes of prayer – excessive talkativeness should, for example, be eschewed – and Ascham urges individuals to attend carefully to the form of words they use. Ascham via Christ then proceeds to outline what ought to be prayed for: only what is spiritual, germane to the kingdom of God, and in conformity with the will of God. Provided the imprecatory focus is God, the daily necessities, such as bread, daily sustenance, soundness of body, quietude, and peace of mind, will, according to Ascham, duly follow. Over two pages (95–96), Ascham also conveyed, as does John's Gospel, a full sense of the centrality of Christ in a life of prayer.

The tutelage Ascham offers here can be viewed within a larger evangelical programme to reformulate the traditional practice of prayer. Prayer was intensely valued by Protestants of every shade. It was defined simply as an urgent and heartfelt communication with God, a 'pouring out' of the self, and normally conceived of in verbal terms.[224] Reformers from Erasmus to Luther and Melanchthon not only reflected on prayer, but also wrote squarely on and at length about it.[225] The role of saints was minimised and mechanical forms of prayer were replaced by a more unmediated discourse with God. Prayers should be sincere, humble and scriptural, and employ an exalted language. Biblical prayers were particular favourites.[226] Ascham's theme, which adheres to this paradigm, then slots into a much larger theory of prayer. While it might in some senses be pigeonholed as an exercise in Reformation piety, it was also a production that was pushing the frontiers of theology. It stands as yet another example of how those who were excited by the Reformation had started to make their own reconstruction of Christianity based on a subjective understanding of theology.

Although Ascham nowhere indicates that he was practising theology *per se* in his *Themata*, it is tempting to view its various parts as just that. He came to the Bible with a thoroughly humanist mindset; one might call it a philological faith, the corollary of which was the perception of orthodoxy – or otherwise – on the basis of the words someone uses. The fruits of rhetoric must be counted as a chief energising principle in his campaign to repair and restore Christian worship. Ascham was also certainly on home academic territory as far as the Greek of the Bible was concerned, and it is evident that for Ascham Greek offered a resource that could not just help provide the underpinning of a theological case, but also symbolically drive the very process of a theological recovery of an apostolic past. Armed with these skills,

Ascham also offers counsel at each stage of the *Themata* on a life in Christ and on how to negotiate a pious existence through the inevitability of sin. He supplies guidance on righteousness, on the necessity of biblical attentiveness and devotion, on valid and invalid forms of anger, on the emotional management of oppression, and on successful models of prayer. This learned layman sounds to all intents and purposes like a priest.

It seems reasonable to ask whether university men like Ascham, with all their classical prowess, viewed themselves as the 'theologians' or even 'secular clerics' of a new religious revival. Many from Ascham's Cambridge cadre who had specialised in the Arts would also go on to perform important roles in Church and State, figures like John Cheke, Walter Haddon and Thomas Smith. That Ascham also considered his contemporaries as theologically instrumental is hinted at in theme 10. In a particualrly scriptural part of this theme Ascham quotes his Cambridge colleague John Redman:

> I will supplement these holy passages of Scripture, as if by way of a *coronis*, with a certain distich [written] by a man supremely learned and honourable in equal measure, John Redman: 'A vexation that is not indecent disturbs the flesh that is indecent / so that the spirit can be kept in safe water'.[227]

Redman was not an out and out Protestant, but a committed royal champion and an important spiritual leader during the Henrician and Edwardian Reformations.[228] He was revered by his peers at Cambridge as a heavyweight classicist but also for his steadfastly godly lifestyle along biblical lines. His elegiac couplet, with all its classical concision and alertness to sound effects and Ovidian paradox, captures beautifully the amalgamation of classical virtuosity and religious animation that Ascham so admired. The fact that Ascham placed this distich on a par with biblical authority tells us so much about Ascham's outlook at a time of such expectation and ambition about the scope of the spiritual renewal that Henry's break from Rome had enabled. Individuals like Redman, and indeed like Ascham himself, were applying all their humanist expertise to a Christian project which impinged not just on this life but on the next as well, and networks of classically-steeped kindred spirits were forging new ways to 'do' theology. The actual position of Redman on the confessional scale relative to Ascham and others was of less importance than a resolve to combine the *ad fontes* discipline of Renaissance humanism with the restoration of a morally repristinated Christendom. While we cannot classify Ascham as a premier league theologian, he did belong to a group who were not only encroaching, by virtue of their skills, into the jurisdiction of theology, but were also developing a viable vision for how to overhaul it.

Conclusion

In this introduction, I hope to have persuaded at least some readers that in Ascham's *Themata*, a book of less than a hundred pages, a tract that is available in Latin and perfectly legible, but one that has been practically ignored by modern scholarship, can present the largest point of views. At the same time, through a process of thick description, these types of text can offer some wonderfully nuanced vantage points, revealing as they do a jockeying of different priorities and properties that cut across the more established historical lines for evaluating the past. Investigative research into the Latin texts can illuminate the 'lesser' figures, yes, but they can also help to resituate what have unfortunately become intellectual hinterlands into the mainstream.

Notes

1 Asc's library does not survive intact, but see Lazarus 2021 for a handlist of books he owned and annotated.
2 To borrow the words of Debora Shuger in Shuger 1994: 3.
3 A powerful point made by Hannah Crawforth and Russ Leo in their tribute to Shuger's field-changing study on the Renaissance Bible (Crawforth / Leo 2021: 3).
4 Hatch 1946; Vos 1989; and Nicholas 2015a, 2015b, 2016, 2017 and 2022.
5 Nicholas / Law 2021.
6 Ryan, 1963: 99–101. The *Themata* was discussed in a similarly cursory way in a nineteenth-century German biography, Katterfeld 1879: 23–24 and 40–41.
7 For more on Asc's early career at St John's, see Ryan 1963 and Nicholas / Law 2021. For the importance of his Cambridge circle in particular, see McDiarmid / Wabuda 2022.
8 It is unlikely, but not impossible, that Asc. also worked on the *Themata* during an absence from Cambridge 1541/2, as he recovered from a debilitating illness at his home in Yorkshire.
9 Ryan 1963: 99.
10 For more on Edward Grant, see S. Wright, 'Edward Grant (c. 1546–1601)', *ODNB*.
11 For a full translation of Grant's preface and dedication (to Robert Dudley, the Earl of Leicester), see Nicholas 2017: 212–21, at 216–17.
12 ibid.: 220–21.
13 *Apologia doctissimi viri Rogeri Aschami, Angli, pro caena Dominica contra missam et eius praestigias: in Academia olim Cantabrigiensi exercitationis gratia inchoata. Cui accesserunt themata quaedam theologica, debita disputandi ratione in Collegio D. Ioan. pronunciata. Expositiones item antiquae, in epistolas Divi Pauli ad Titum et Philemonem, ex diversis*

sanctorum Patrum Graece scriptis commentariis ab Oecumenio collectae, et a R. A. Latine versae, ed. E. Grant (London, 1577).
14 Ascham's identification of 'Oecumenius' as the author of the commentaries was an over-simplification; the material he translated included authorities like Chrysos., Theodoret and Cyril.
15 Kennerley 2021: 61–81.
16 On January 5, 1548, Asc. wrote to William Cecil, the then Master of Requests, indicating that, subject to the agreement of Cecil and John Cheke, he intended to forward his *Apol.* to the Lord Protector, the Duke of Somerset, Edward's uncle and *de facto* leader (Letter 83, Giles, vol. I.I, 157).
17 Adams 2002: 228. See also Nicholas 2017: 212–17.
18 For more on Henry Middleton, see McKerrow 1949 and 1968; the publisher was Francis Coldocke. *Fifty Godly Sermons* by Heinrich Bullinger was printed by Middleton in 1577, in the same year as *Apol.* Asc's *Apol.* was not printed *cum privilegio*.
19 Ryan 1963: 99.
20 Nicholas 2017: 212–13.
21 ibid.: 220–21.
22 For more on this discipline generally, see Novikoff 2013; Rodda 2014; and Friedenthal / Marti / Seidel 2020.
23 Rex 2019: 15.
24 Mayor 1859: 110–15.
25 ibid.: 112–15.
26 ibid.: 110–15.
27 *Grace Book Delta* 1910: 571. In Letter 4 in Giles, vol. I.I, 6 (1539) Asc. asks Thomas Watson to read through 'a disputation of last week'.
28 Although theme 6 contains at the end the wording *hanc quaestionem conclusimus* ('We have concluded this investigation'), it does not read like a piece written pursuant to a formal debate.
29 *Themata*, 1 and 29.
30 Nicholas 2020: 114–15; and Leeuwen / Stanglin / Tolsma 2009: 265.
31 Rodda 2014: 1; and Craig 1950: 22.
32 Rodda 2014: 2–3 and 82.
33 Kirby 2013: 1 and *passim*.
34 Katterfeld 1879: 23 and 41; and Hatch 1946: 14. As Katterfeld suggests, this project had begun on the initiative of Edward Foxe, the Bishop of Hereford, but upon his death in 1538, it was taken in hand by Richard Sampson. The work in question was almost certain *In priores quinquaginta psalmos Daviticos familiaris explanatio* (London, 1539). There are no obvious overlaps in content between this work and Asc's commentary in theme 2.
35 The *pagellas eas* are referred to in Letter 17, Giles, vol. I.I, 34 (1543, though Hatch persuasively dates the letter to 1539 (Hatch 1946: 14)).
36 Ryan 1963: 25–26.
37 MacCulloch 1996: 206.
38 *Themata*, 73, 90 and 93; and *Apol.* in Nicholas 2017: 97, 137, 169 and 187.

39 For example, Letters 9 and 12, Giles, vol. II, 22 and 28 (both of 1559).
40 See esp. notes to themes 4 and 5.
41 Killeen / Smith 2015: 2; and Shuger 1994.
42 Houghton 2016: viii
43 This was a work (issued in several editions) that set out the original Greek of the NT alongside a revised Latin translation.
44 For general overviews of this complex history, see Poleg 2020; Cameron 2016; Hamel 2001; and Killeen, Smith / Willie 2015.
45 This was then revised by Andreas Osiander and Johannes Brenz (Gordon 2010: 9–10).
46 Gordon 2010; and Backus 2012.
47 Poleg 2020: xxi.
48 *Themata*, 26.
49 ibid., 49, 77 and 84.
50 Mullinger 1873: 630.
51 Scott-Amos 2015: 44.
52 See, for example, Muller 1996.
53 *Themata*, 84–85.
54 Scott-Amos 2015.
55 Cummings 2002: 15–53.
56 *Themata*, 19. There is little evidence that Asc. knew or worked with specifically Hebrew materials.
57 *Themata*, 19.
58 Muller 1996: 13.
59 E worked on his *Nov. T* during his Cambridge sojourn (McConica 1991: 40).
60 Nicholas / Law 2021.
61 *Themata*, 55.
62 This was also quoted by Asc. in themes 1 and 5.
63 Asc.'s singular *sis*, rather than E's plural *sitis* is also interesting, and may have been selected with the individual reader or auditor in mind.
64 It may be noted that *supervincimus* had attestation in Cyprian.
65 Leader 1988: 297–99.
66 *Apol.* in Nicholas 2017: 216–17.
67 For more on this and the power of Greek, see Nicholas' paper for the 'Latin-Greek Code-switching in Early Modernity' workshop held in Leuven, October 2022.
68 Τῆς καινῆς διαθήκης ἅπαντα. *Novi Testamenti omnia* (Basel, 1531), Hatfield House 7522. The preface was written by Johannes Oecolampadius, one of the chief assistants in Erasmus' *Nov. T* project.
69 In addition to Asc.'s own larger autograph, there is a secondary (fainter) reference on the first page to 'Roger Ascham and friends', but the hand of the annotations through the Bible is clearly Asc.'s.
70 *Themata*, 92.
71 ibid., 45–46.
72 Eskhult 2012: 171.

73 Jonge 1988: 97–110; and Hamilton 1996: 110
74 Gordon 2010: 22.
75 Eskhult 2012: 168–70.
76 Muller 1996: 14.
77 *Themata*, 73.
78 ibid., 63.
79 Eskhult makes a good case for the extent to which classical rhetorical theory was fundamental to the translation principles used in the early modern period (2012: 171–74).
80 *Themata*, 11.
81 McDiarmid 2022: 21–50.
82 ibid.: 25 and 42–43.
83 Gordon 2010: 21.
84 Letter 11, Giles, vol. I.I, 24 (1542).
85 Gordon 2010: 20–21.
86 Eskhult 2012: 175.
87 Hatch 1946: *passim*.
88 *Themata*, 73.
89 ibid., 75.
90 ibid., 64.
91 ibid., 61.
92 ibid., 29–30.
93 This was in part, of course, because Protestants actively adopted the slogan for themselves against Catholics.
94 Muller 1996: 20; and Belt 2016.
95 ibid.: 210 and 204–26. Belt advocates the use of the phrase '*scriptura prima*' instead (225).
96 *Themata*, 77.
97 Letter 27, Giles, vol. I.I, 68 (1545).
98 Kennerley 2021: 61.
99 Doctrinal Protestant statements, including the Augsburg Confession, the Formula of Concord, the Second Helvetic Confession, the Belgic Confession, the Bohemian Confession and the Thirty-nine Articles, commended the Athanasian Creed to their followers.
100 Letters 20 and 21, Giles, vol. I.I, 43 and 47 (both of 1543).
101 *Themata*, 77.
102 For a full citation, see n. 514 in the annotations.
103 It is likely that Asc. was using the 1532 edition of scholia that had been attributed to Oec. by Bernadino Donato (and was printed in Verona).
104 Richard Croke, *Orationes duae: altera a cura qua utilitatem laudemque graecae linguae tractat, altera a tempore qua hortatus est Cantabrigienses, ne desertores essent eiusdem* (Paris 1520), sig. c. viiir. For the Latin text and trans., see Kachuck and McDougall 2022: 76–77.
105 Hamlin 2015: 2 and also 1–21 for further discussion of individualistic approaches to Bible reading with a focus on the vernacular.

106 Ryan 1963: 100; and Rex 1999: 29–30.
107 Ryan 1963: 99. This assertion was made by way of rejoinder against a cluster of voices casting Asc. as a religious radical.
108 O' Day, 'Roger Ascham, c. 1515–1568', *ODNB*.
109 See Nicholas 2017.
110 Marshall 2006: 2.
111 MacCulloch 1996: 241 and 310. There was a very real possibility of an outright ban on English bibles in the final years of Henry's reign, and between 1541 and 1548 no English bible reached print (Shuger 2022: 62)
112 Marshall 2006: 13. The references to an Henrician *via media* are ubiquitous in modern historical assessments.
113 For example, concerning the legality of his marriage and then the legitimacy of papal dispensation (Law 2021: 26).
114 Logan 1991.
115 Ryrie, 2013: 261, 471 and 474.
116 *Themata*, 40. In the decorative frontispiece of *Tox*. a reference to the banishment of *Babylonica pestis* appears on the outer banderol (Giles, vol. II), and see also n. 124 below.
117 *Themata*, 50.
118 ibid., 80–81
119 ibid., 81.
120 MacCulloch 1996: 215–16. Exposure of this attempted coup was one of Cromwell's most spectacular triumphs (216).
121 *Themata*, 80.
122 ibid.
123 ibid., 49.
124 The abovementioned frontispiece of *Tox*. also displays the royal coat of arms, and overtly celebrates the Henrician promotion of the Bible, the rejection of the Church of Rome, as well as the fall of the Pope. This is followed by a dedicatory letter to Henry and, as Cathy Shrank puts it, 'from the first page onwards Ascham's work is designed to display its author's usefulness to the Henrician regime and its imperial and anti-papal projects' (Shrank 2021: 209–10).
125 Asc. would conform under Mary and serve as her Latin Secretary. During this reign he might be best understood as a 'Nicodemite': one who was privately committed to Protestantism, but who was willing to make public accommodations with the Marian regime and a restored Catholic Church in England, once God had shown his will in making Mary queen.
126 *Themata*, 82. A similar nod to the *via media* paradigm as regards Bible use can be found in the opening sentence of Cranmer's preface to the Great Bible of 1539 (Shuger 2022: 61).
127 MacCulloch 1996: 137.
128 Ryrie 2009.
129 Rex 2011: 44–93; and Hudson 1980.
130 Rex 2011 and 2021.

131 Trueman / Euler 2010: 63.
132 Ryrie 2002: 92.
133 Trueman / Euler 2010: 67–68.
134 MacCulloch 1996: 174; and Ryrie 2009.
135 Nicholas / Law 2020. There is also a handwritten reference to 'M. Bucer' in GNT at the start of Ephes.
136 MaCulloch 1996: 174 and 176.
137 It is likely that Ascham transcribed Redman's treatise on justification (*Opus De Justificatione*) for presentation to the King in 1542 (Letter 20, Giles, vol. I.I, 46, and also see Hatch 1946: 86).
138 McGrath 1986: 24.
139 Pereira 2013: 22.
140 Marshall 2006: 7.
141 Rex 2019: 166.
142 *Themata*, theme 5 generally, esp. 47–48.
143 For Luther's 'certitude', see Rex 2019: introduction.
144 Trueman / Euler 2010: 69.
145 *Themata*, 58–59.
146 Kolb 2014.
147 ibid.: 170.
147 Cubillos 2009.
149 ibid.: 52.
150 *Themata*, 69.
151 For example, *Themata*, 24.
152 *Themata*, 2–5.
153 *Themata*, 10: Asc. draws on Ephes. 6.13–17.
154 *Themata*, 94.
155 Rex 1991: 95. It is a phrase derived from Ps. 116 and found in 1 John 8 and 10 (and is echoed by Paul in Rom. 3.4). Asc. stated clearly 'every man is given to lying' and using precisely the same Latin words as L had – *omnis (enim) homo mendax* (*Apol.* in Nicholas 2017: 30–31).
156 *Themata*, esp. 12–13.
157 Yost 1975; McGrath 1982; and Green 2009: 110–14. See also Lugioyo 2010.
158 *Themata*, 74. In the fullness of time, and judging by Asc.'s annotations on a treatise by St Ambrose on election and justification, it appears that he did come to embrace the doctrine of predestination, but still with the proviso that this did not negate the importance of living a godly life. The tract was *Divi Ambrosii ... de vocatione omnium gentium libri duo* (Geneva, 1541), a printed work held at the Bodleian Library (8° Rawlinson, 169 (2)). On the title page is written *manus haec est Rogeri Aschami* 1555; it is likely that his annotations belong to that date.
159 Ryan 1963: 99.
160 In particular, E's *philosophia Christi*, with its emphasis on a life in Christ and on the duty of *pietas*.
161 McDiarmid 2022: 44.

162 *Themata*, 51.
163 ibid., 41–42.
164 ibid., 35.
165 ibid., 37.
166 ibid., 24.
167 ibid., 75.
168 ibid., esp. 75–76.
169 ibid., 76.
170 Ryan 1963: 95 and 97.
171 ibid.: 101.
172 *Themata*, 81–82.
173 Racaut / Ryrie, 2005: 5. On the degree to which 'moderation' dominated early modern discourse and was bound up with power politics, see also Shagan 2011.
174 *Themata*, 65.
175 MacCulloch 1996: 145.
176 In recent years, several studies have started to challenge this narrative, some of which are cited below.
177 *Themata*, 1.
178 ibid., 10, 45–46 and 69.
179 Richards 2019.
180 *Themata*, 12, 26 (twice), 35 and 37.
181 ibid., theme 11.
182 This has been discussed extensively in secondary literature, but see esp. McLaughlin 1995.
183 Brammall 2018: 58. This also involved the vexed distinction between *interpres* ('a translator') and *orator* ('an orator'). Asc.'s *Schol.* reflects a direct engagement with these developments.
184 See Gray 1963; Mack 1996; and Spranzi 2011.
185 See Nicholas 2021: 150-1; and Shrank 2021.
186 *Themata*, 5. Interestingly, Asc. uses this wording in *Schol.*, Giles, vol. III, 201.
187 *Themata*, 5–6.
188 ibid., 53.
189 ibid., 81
190 ibid., 88.
191 Matheson 2004: 159.
192 Rummel 2000.
193 And as Aseph Ben-Tov puts it, 'There is much to be learned about confessional humanism as opposed to humanism under confessionalism' (Ben-Tov 2009:16).
194 *Themata*, 27.
195 ibid. Cic. *Top.* 21.79–80, and for more on this influential work of Cic., see Reinhardt 2003: introduction.
196 *Themata*, 27; and Cic. *Top.* 21.79–80.

197 *Themata*, 26–27; and Cic. *De inv.*, esp. 1.27.41.
198 *Themata*, 12–13.
199 ibid., 13. In 2.53 and 54 of *De inv.* Cic. develops the concept of *iustitia*.
200 *Themata*, 18.
201 ibid., 55–56.
202 ibid., 86.
203 ibid., 35–36.
204 ibid., 36.
205 A point made by Ben-Tov 2009: 9.
206 *Themata*, 13.
207 ibid., 36
208 ibid., 26.
209 Long / Sedley 1987: 354–59.
210 See n. 179 in theme 4.
211 The issue of what constituted *adiaphora* became a major dispute during the Protestant Reformation (sometimes referred to as the 'Adiaphorist Controversy', 1548–1552). Following the death of L, Melanchthon tried to reach some accommodation with Catholics, in particular with the Holy Roman Emperor, Charles V, and Melanchthon was eventually persuaded to sign up to the Leipzig Interim of 1548, his rationale being that doctrinal differences unrelated to justification by faith were *adiaphora* or matters not essential for salvation. However, this compromise was vehemently opposed by some, especially by the Gnesio-Lutherans, a sect who saw themselves as the 'authentic' followers of L.
212 Thereafter, the issue would cause constant tensions between hardline Lutherans and more moderate Philippists.
213 Verkamp 1977.
214 For more on this tendency, see Lazarus / Nicholas forthcoming.
215 *Themata*, 36.
216 Clegg 2021. And for more on the influence of Ascham and his circle on the Elizabethan Settlement, see Hudson 1980.
217 See also Yost 1975.
218 For example, Shuger 2022; Hardy 2017; Ben-Tov 2009, and Lazarus / Nicholas forthcoming.
219 For more on the sixteenth-century challenges to the jurisdiction of theology, see Rummel 1995 and Scott-Amos 2015: 1–4.
220 Rummel 1995.
221 Ryrie 2013: 1. The universal claim to priesthood was espoused in a number of L's works, including his address *To the Christian Nobility of the German Nation* and his *Babylonian Captivity of the Church* (both of 1520).
222 Scott-Amos 2015: 31.
223 ibid.: 7. At the start of the seventeenth century, further insight into the meaning and value of theology as an intellectual discipline was provided by Matthew Sutcliffe, the chaplain of Elizabeth, in his *De recta studii theologici*

ratione (1602), which suggested that teachers and students of theology needed languages, a good memory, dialectic and poetry (Binns 1990: 310).
224 Ryrie 2013: 99.
225 Cratty (forthcoming). 1522 saw the publication of L's *Personal Prayer Book*. Tracts by E on or pertaining to prayer included his *Lord's Prayer Divided into Seven Parts* (1523), *Method of Praying to God* (1524), and *Precationes aliquot novae* (1535) (and see also Pabel 1997). Melanchthon wrote a treatise *De precatione* (1552), and his *Loci communes* from 1543 onwards contained a chapter entitled *De invocatione Dei seu de precatione* (and see also Weaver 2022). Calvin's *Institutes* also discussed forms of prayer.
226 Ryrie 2013: 226.
227 *Themata*, 85.
228 A. Null, 'John Redman (1499–1551), Theologian and College Head', *ODNB*. See also Ryrie 2009: 12–17. Not all humanist allies were theological soulmates.

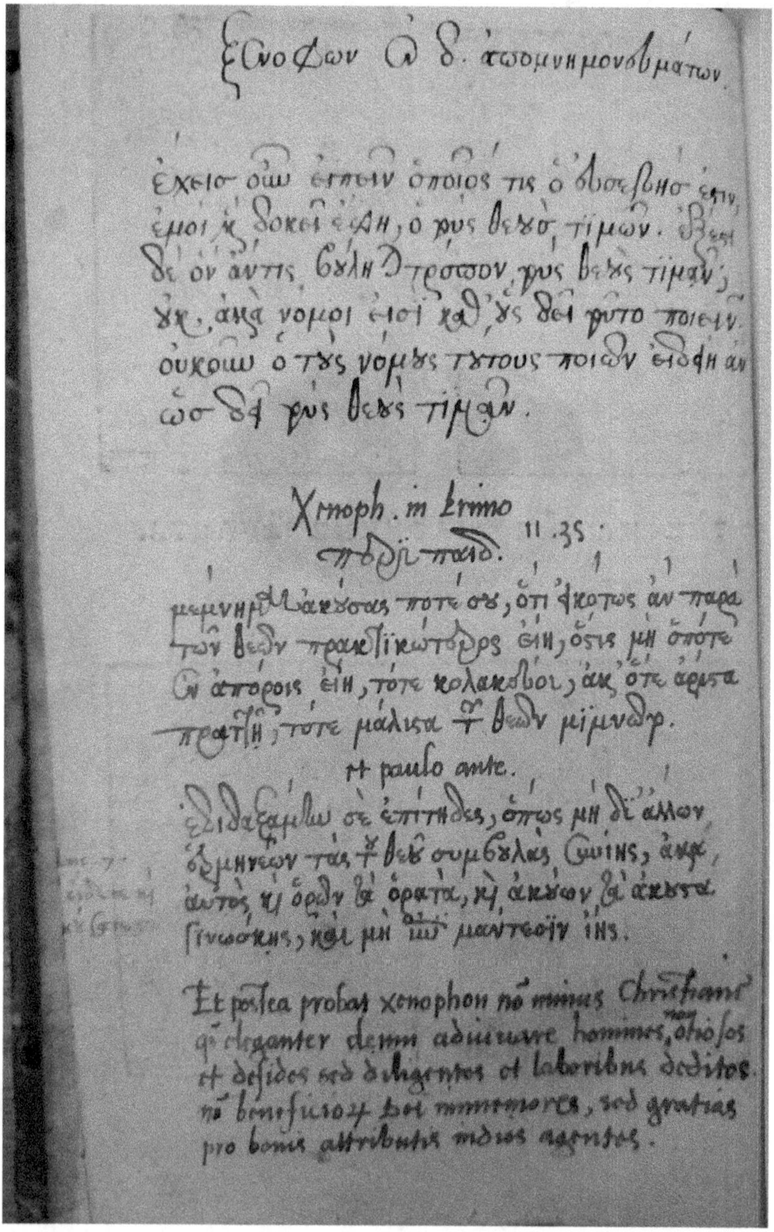

Ξενοφῶν (ω δ. τῶ ὑπομνημονεύματων

Ἔχεις οὖν εἰπεῖν ὁποῖός τις ὁ δυσσεβής ἐστιν
ἐμοὶ κ̄ δοκεῖ ἐιᾶη, ὁ τοὺς θεοὺς̄ τιμῶν. βελ-
δε οὖν ἀντις ἔχλη διτρόπων τοὺς θεοὺς τιμᾶν·
ἂν. ἀλλὰ νόμοι εἰσὶ κᾱθ᾽ ἂς δεῖ τοῦτο ποιεῖν.
οὐκοῦν ὁ τοὺς νόμους τούτους ποιῶν εἰδείη ἂν
ὡς δεῖ τοὺς θεοὺς τιμᾶν.

Xenoph. in primo
11.35
περὶ παίδ.
μεμνήμ̄ μακόας τότε οὖ, ὅτι ἀκρῶς ἂν παρὰ
τῶν θεῶν πρακτικώτερος εἴη, ὅστις μὴ ὁπότε
ἐν ἀπόροις εἴη, τότε κολακεύοι, ἀκ ὅτε ἄριστα
πράττη, τότε μάλιστα τ̄ θεῶν μιμνῇρ.

Et paulo ante.
Ἐδίδαξεν̄ δὲ ἐπιτηδες, ὅπως μὴ δι᾽ ἄλλον
ὁμηνύων τὰς τ̄ θεῶν συμβολὰς ζωίης, ἄχε,
ἀυτὸς ἧ ὁρᾶν ἃ ὁρᾶτα, ἧ ἀκούων ἃ ἀκουστὰ
γινώσκης, καὶ μὴ τῷ μαντεύῃν ἴης.

Et postea probat xenophon no minus Christiani
q'elegantèr deum adiuvare homines, otiosos
et desides sed diligentes et laboribus deditos
no beneficiou dei immemores, sed gratias
pro bonis attributis modis agentes.

Figure 1 An image of Ascham's handwritten notes on Xenophon just before the start of Matthew's Gospel in his Greek New Testament. Reproduced with permission of the Marquess of Salisbury, Hatfield House.

Text, Translation and Notes

Latin text and English translation

The text below has been taken from a printed book of 1577, *Apologia doctissimi viri Rogeri Aschami, Angli, pro caena Dominica contra missam et eius praestigias: in Academia olim Cantabrigiensi exercitationis gratia inchoata. Cui accesserunt themata quaedam theologica, debita disputandi ratione in Collegio D. Ioan. pronunciata. Expositiones item antiquae, in epistolas Divi Pauli ad Titum et Philemonem, ex diversis sanctorum Patrum Graece scriptis commentariis ab Oecumenio collectae, et a R. A. Latine versae*, ed. E. Grant (London). 'A Defence of the Lord's Supper against the Mass and its magic, by the most learned Englishman, Roger Ascham, and embarked upon some time ago as an exercise in the University of Cambridge. To this were added certain theological propositions delivered on account of the duties of disputation in the College of St John. Also [included] is an early interpretation of the letters of St Paul to Titus and Philomen collated by Oecumenius from various written commentaries of the sacred Fathers in Greek, and translated into Latin by Roger Ascham'.[1] As the long title suggests, the *Themata* is one of three pieces bound within this 1577 volume, and runs from pages 149–246. For ease of reference, a stand-alone page numbering scheme, starting with the number 1, has been employed in the present edition, and references in the annotations, in the main introduction, and in the short preludes to each proposition (or 'theme') adhere to the same organisational principle. However, should readers wish to consult the printed version, the original page and signature numbers have additionally been included in the Latin text and translation below.

---

[1] In addition to the physical copies of this volume housed in certain libraries, an online version is available in *EEBO*.

I have reproduced the orthography used in the printed version, but any Latin accentuation has been removed. Variant spellings (usually the more familiar classical forms) are indicated in the notes where the word is initially used, and readers are encouraged to note not only the diversity possible in early modern orthography but also the variety of spelling within a single text. Early modern abbreviations and contractions have been resolved (except names, the abbreviated forms of which might be of interest, and that are in any case obvious), and I have changed the ampersand to *et*. Although early modern punctuation habits can seem odd, I have retained the punctuation, not least because this was almost certainly used as a means to direct the original oral delivery (a factor that is important always to keep in mind). In certain themes Ascham also included Greek, which I reproduce, but in accordance with modern conventions regarding the layout and accentuation of Greek.

Hanging notes were used in the margins of the printed edition, and these have been incorporated into the main text below, using square brackets and italics. It is likely that these are the printer's notes rather than Ascham's. Although these may, at first glance, seem to clutter up the main text, they were retained in this edition on the grounds that readers who have an interest in early modern print culture may find them useful.

The overriding aim of the English translation is to offer a version that the reader can easily map onto the Latin and read simulataneously with it. To this end, readers will note the use of square brackets in the translation to indicate places where words in English have been used that go beyond what is contained in the Latin (although these have not been used when a word in a sentence is resupplied, the simple verb 'to be' is assumed, or in cases where I have used the conjunctions 'and' or 'but'). Clarity was a *desideratum*, especially given that this is a tract which contains so much – at least to our twenty-first-century eyes – esoteric theological analysis. Theological Latin can be an alienating and rather off-putting form, but this volume is designed to offer a translation 'practice ground', an opportunity to encounter the myriad of awkward word choices that have to be made when translating a work that belongs to such a biblically-freighted and tangled confessional context. Indeed, if we are to grapple meaningfully with the religious thought of the past, the ability to read Latin is a prerequisite. Latin had been the language of Western Christian theology since Late Antiquity, and it has been estimated that well over half of the books published during the European Reformation were in Latin. The hope is that this edition, as well as providing a further resource, will also act as a spur to further translation work in this field.

In assembling the translation, another important consideration was the tract's rhetorical style, and, as far as the above-mentioned fidelity to the Latin allows, my version has attempted to convey the power of Ascham's pen, with all its sound effects, orotundies and rounding periods. James Binns included

Ascham in a cluster of Tudor authors whom he credited with writing 'the best Latin prose', a form that was lively, flowing, flexible, clear, elegant and pleasing.[2] It is important, moreover, to keep in mind that, for Ascham and his contemporaries, linguistic flair was no superficial matter, but inextricably tied up with the theological message (and for more on this, see the section 'Humanist classical theology' from p. 35 of the main introduction).

Short preludes to each of the eleven themes will, I hope, set the scene for the reader in a more targeted way, as well as allowing individual themes to be more quickly selected and read in isolation according to the aims and interest of the end-user.

Biblical references and translations

As was true of many early modern texts, Ascham's approach to the Bible is far from straightforward. 'Ascham's biblical approach' (from p. 9 in the main introduction) outlines some of the difficulties in general terms: it describes how Ascham was not using a single version of the Bible, and tries to convey something of the complicated back-story that lies behind his scriptural quotations. The story is substantiated in a more detailed way by the notes to the text, where the precise wording of Ascham's biblical quotations is considered in relation to: (a) the Latin Vulgate; (b) Erasmus' *Novum Testamentum*; and (c) where it seems relevant, the Greek New Testament. While these sources, given their authority at the time, constitute obvious yardsticks by which to evaluate Ascham's biblical practice, other versions of the Bible (for example, Pagninus' Hebrew-based version of 1527),[3] are mentioned along the way and, in some cases, patristic tracts and other contemporary writers. Given the proliferation of bibles and biblical resources that circulated in the early-mid sixteenth century, an exhaustive comparative survey has not been possible. However, silence about a particular text does not necessarily point to lack of consideration; during the course of my investigation, many versions were checked that offered little in the way of broader correspondence. In any case, a scholarly independence is probably the key factor in understanding Ascham's *modus operandi*.

Further qualification must be made regarding the textual *comparanda* referred to above. Despite the relative stability of the fifth-century Latin Vulgate by Jerome, different incarnations of it did emerge. Aside from the copyist errors that crept into versions from Late Antiquity onwards, a number

---

[2] Binns 1990: 301.
[3] Also used by Jean Calvin (Gordon 2010: 11). An online version can be found at: https://archive.org/details/bub_gb_vgsr-LkRoyEC/page/n773/mode/2up?view=theater

of official Counter-Reformation revisions were also made, the most famous version of which was the Clementine Vulgate, first published in 1592. In the twentieth century a restoration project resulted in the 'Stuttgart Vulgate', often known as the 'Weber-Gryson Vulgate' as it was initiated by Robert Weber and completed by Roger Gryson in 2007.[4] Their objective was to reconstruct the text of *c.* 500 CE, and, for academic purposes, this tends to be the most widely accepted critical version, and the one to which my notes refer.[5] There were also several editions of Erasmus' *Novum Testamentum* (five in total, in 1516, 1519, 1522, 1527, and 1536). Although Erasmus' fourth edition of 1527 is helpful because of the addition of a third column which sets out the Vulgate alongside Erasmus' Greek and his own Latin version, the one primarily referred to in this volume is the third edition of 1522. In the history of the New Testament, this third edition was the most significant; it incorporated all the main textual adjustments, and was relied upon by, for instance, William Tyndale for the first *English New Testament* (1526), Robert Estienne as a base for his editions of the Greek New Testament printed in 1546 and 1549, and by the translators of Geneva Bible and King James Version.[6] I have not tended to supply translations for alternative biblical wording referred to in the annotations unless this is radically different to Ascham's formulations, or in cases where Ascham has simply paraphrased a particular passage; any such translations are my own.

A biblical resource of critical value to Ascham was the Greek New Testament, and it is evident that this influenced his choice of Latin wording in several places. Occasionally too Ascham makes express reference to Greek. We can be sure that one Greek New Testament Ascham was definitely consulting was Τῆς καινῆς διαθήκης ἅπαντα. *Novi Testamenti omnia* (Basel, 1531), now held at Hatfield House (7522), for it is inscribed with Ascham's autograph and covered with his own handwritten annotations. All cases of obvious consonance between the *Themata* and the marginalia in his Greek New Testament are identified in the notes below.

The final difficulty to mention is that of Psalm numbering. Different systems were developed, settling into what are now commonly known as

---

[4] An online version can be found on the Latin Library at: http://www.thelatinlibrary.com/bible.html
[5] Houghton 2016: viii.
[6] The third edition can be found at: https://www.e-rara.ch/bau_1/content/zoom/1240896

(a) the Vulgate / Septuagint and (b) the Hebrew / Protestant traditions. The Psalm numbers used in the headings and hanging notes of the *Themata* belong to the Hebrew / Protestant system. It is, however, far from clear that Ascham was responsible for this numbering scheme, which may be attributable either to the editor, Edward Grant, or the printer. We thus ought not place too much stress on the use of the Hebrew / Protestant numbering in these instances, not least because annotations in Ascham's Greek New Testament suggest in fact that he was following the Vulgate / Septuagint enumeration; the hanging notes in the *Apologia pro caena Dominica*, a slightly later Latin tract bound within the same volume, indicate likewise. Indeed, many signed-up evangelicals at the time similarly observed the more traditional Vulgate / Septuagint scheme. In any case, for the avoidance of confusion, clear references to both sets of numbering are made in the annotations that follow.

Patristic and classical references and translations

Patristic citations are from J.-P. Migne's *Patrologiae ... Latina* and *Graeca*, unless specified otherwise, and the source of translations are indicated in each case, and if not, are my own.

Classical texts and translations are taken from the Loeb Classical Library series.

Theme 1
(1–10)

This first theme is discussed over ten pages, and comprises what appears to be the write-up of a disputational oration. The *quaestio*-like wording ('Whether more evil is procured from Adam than good produced through Jesus Christ')[7]

---

[7] This is then restated in a slightly fuller way on the following page, 'But whether that first earthbound man from the earth introduced more evil through his transgression and fault for [our] damnation and death, than that second man [and] Lord from heaven, produced good through his obedience and grace, for [our] justification and life, is of course the question, albeit an extremely complex and involved one' (2). It is difficult to know whether it was in fact this or the heading of the theme that served as the official *quaestio* in the original disputation.

which heads the piece appertains to the concept of the *felix culpa* ('the fortunate fall' or 'fault').[8] The notion had its roots in Romans 5.14–21, a series of verses which directly compare and contrast the sinful transgression of Adam with the grace of God and the justification offered by Christ. From the fourth century on, it became a category of theodicy (i.e. one that attempted to resolve the presence of evil in the world), and was broached by Ambrose, Augustine and, later, Aquinas, all of whom gave a similarly positive account of the fall. The exact phrasing of the heading of this theme almost certainly drew inspiration from Augustine's *De civitate Dei* 22.24, where Augustine writes [*sed utrumque simul currit isto quasi fluvio atque torrente generis humani,*] *malum quod a parente trahitur, et bonum quod a creante tribuitur* ('['But in this rushing stream of human life two currents, as it were, flow together], the evil derived from our parent and the good bestowed by the Creator').[9]

Ascham, in fact, nowhere uses the formulation '*felix culpa*', but his central argument, in keeping with the traditional position, cleaves to the view that the *lapsus Adami* was turned to man's advantage because of Christ, a victory Ascham expresses through his constant repetition of St Paul's Romans 8.37, 'In all these things we conquer through him who loved us'. In addition to the articulation of the theme's heading, there are other indications that Augustine's *De civitate Dei* 22.24 formed a base text for Ascham's theme more generally. Ascham not only borrowed phrasing from Augustine (as detailed in the notes below), but he also held fast to the Augustinian position that God chose not to withdraw the blessing after the sin which he granted before the sin. Irrespective of this, Ascham dwells far more than Augustine does (in this part of his *De civitate Dei* at any rate) on the sin and suffering of mankind on account of Adam; over half of Ascham's theme is devoted to the sin and suffering (*peccatum et supplicium*) actualised by the fall of Adam. The first half of the theme sets out a full taxonomy of both sin and suffering; Ascham then divides the fomer into blindness, flesh or weakness, each of which he also proceeds to anatomise. This culminates in Ascham's declaration that 'if we give careful thought to this most disordered [state of] man's wretchedness, we can be certain of finding in ourselves nothing to celebrate' (6–7).

It is possible that Ascham's (and possibly the disputation's) focus on sin was, in part, driven by Augustine's anti-Pelagian publications. It may also

---

[8] See entry on *felix culpa* in Olsen / Petersen / Rosengarten 2014, vol. 8.
[9] Augus. *De civ. D.* 22.24 (*PL* 41, col. 788) and translations of this are from *LCL*, trans. W. M. Green (1989). The *felix culpa* is also discussed elsewhere in his corpus, for example, Augus. *Enchirid.* 8 on 'The Plight of Man after the Fall'.

point to a high degree of infiltration of Lutheran ideology at the University. It is certainly the case that Ascham accords man no real part or agency amid these competing forces. Also visible in this theme are the first glimpses – ones which become more apparent through the work – of a clear distinction between Law and Gospel, a major topic in Lutheran theology. There is also a Lutheran dogmatism on display in the last part where Ascham speaks about the certitude of Christ's blessings. At the same time, however, we cannot discount the fact that Ascham's argument was determined by his own reading of the Bible, in particular, Romans, 7 and 8, the contents of which move from an account of man's captivity to a celebration of his subsequent freedom from sin through Christ's intervention and the many benefits of a life in Christ. As evidence of the power of Christ's benefactions through justification, Ascham includes at the close of the theme a question and answer sequence (which may in part mimic the questions at the end of Romans 8) that incorporates a volley of New Testament quotes and was evidently designed to reassure any doubters.

Themata Quaedam Theologica disertissimi viri Rogeri Aschami

[1] [149] [K.iii.] An plus mali ab Adamo trahitur, quam boni per Iesum Christum tribuitur.

Primus homo *[primus homo]* parens noster Adamus, partim veteris serpentis malitia[10] adductus, partim mulieris levitate allectus,[11] propria tamen culpa et consensione, nimis praeceps et lubricus,[12] se, ac omnes qui ex illo in posterum nascerentur, ab excellenti quodam dignitatis gradu, in quo positus fuit, in summam miseriam et confusionem perduxit. Secundus

[2] [150] homo, Dominus noster Iesus Christus, *[Secundus homo]* Dei Patris Spiritusque sancti voluntate et consilio, sua tamen erga homines benignitate et amore praecipuo, universos qui participes illius beneficii esse volunt, in immensum decus, et amplissimum splendoris locum evexit. Verum, an primus ille homo de terra terrenus, plus mali, per delictum suum et culpam, ad condemnationem et mortem invexit, quam secundus ille homo de coelo Dominus, boni, per oboedientiam suam et gratiam, ad iustificationem et vitam tribuit, quaestio sane est,[13] licet difficilis admodum et perobscura, ad cognitionem tamen pulcherrima, et ad omnem usum ac religionem nostram continendam maxime necessaria. Nihil enim pulchrius est, quam humani generis interitum per Adamum, et eiusdem redemptionis mysterium, per IESUM CHRISTUM perpetua recordatione recolere: nec quicquam contra magis necessarium est, quam quanta in homine propter Adamum imbecillitas sit et desperatio, (ut timor Dei nobis incutiatur)[14] et quanta iterum in homine per Christum Iesum

---

[10] *malitia*: possibly a play on the word for apple, *malum*.
[11] *allectus*: from the verb *allicio* rather than *allego*. This is also the first example of verbal symmetry in the tract.
[12] *praeceps et lubricus*: with these adjectives, Adam is made to sound like the snake by which he has been deceived. The combination of epithets is one also found in the classical

Certain Theological Propositions of the most learned man, Roger Ascham

'Whether more evil is procured from Adam than good produced through Jesus Christ'.

[1] [149] [K.iii.] The first man *[first man]*, our parent, Adam, was in part led astray by the wickedness[10] of an ancient serpent, and in part seduced[11] by the shallowness of a woman. All the same, it was through his own fault and submission [that he], all too swift and slippery,[12] brought [both] himself and everyone who was born of him hereafter from a superior position of worth in which he had [originally] been placed into the most wretched condition and disorder. The second

[2] [150] man *[the second man]*, our Lord Jesus Christ, through the will and design of God the Father and the Holy Spirit, nevertheless, [also] through his own kindness and special love towards mankind, has elevated all those who are willing to be partakers of that favour into great honour and the most bountiful state of magnificence. But whether that first earthbound man from the earth introduced more evil through his transgression and fault for [our] damnation and death than that second man and Lord from heaven produced good through his obedience and grace for [our] justification and life is of course the question,[13] albeit an extremely complex and involved one. Still, [it is a question that is also] most glorious to consider and so very vital as regards a full comprehension of all practice and our religion. Indeed, nothing is more more glorious than to contemplate in perpetual remembrance the destruction of the human race though Adam and the mystery of its redemption through Jesus Christ. And nor, in turn, is anything more crucial than to store in [one's] daily memory [the fact] that, however great the powerlessness and despair that exists in man because of Adam (with the result that fear of God is struck in us),[14] as great again

---

canon, including in Cicero, e.g.: *cupiditatem dominandi praecipitem et lubricam* ('a hazardous, treacherous desire for domination'), Phil. 5.18.50.

[13] *Verum ... est*: this restates the main proposition in a fuller way. *coelo* is an alternative form for *caelo*.

[14] *timor incutitur*: a phrase found in Cic. *De or.* 2.51.209.

[3] [151] [K.iiii.] possibilitas sit et expectatio, (ut amor Dei in nobis incendatur) quotidiana memoria complecti. Utriusque igitur, et Adami parentis incommoda, et Domini nostri Iesu Christi beneficia, ita persequar, ut nec universa mihi assumam, ut fuse explicentur, ad rei ipsius dignitatem: sed nonnulla potius leviter attingam,[15] ut brevi significentur, ad loci huius et temporis rationem. Adami lapsu perdidimus omnia dona supernaturalia *[Dona supernaturalia Adami lapsu amissa]*, quae potius debent ab omnibus defleri, propter certam illorum amissionem: quam a me hoc tempore possunt recenseri, propter ullam illorum cognitionem. Sunt tamen (ut docti ferunt) ista. Scientia Dei, Puritas et Innocentia vitae, Iustitia, Constantia, Potestas non moriendi.[16] Adami lapsu irrepserunt in eorum loca, duo gravissima humanae vitae flagella, et extrema damna, Peccatum atque Supplicium:[17] *[Duo gravissima vitae humanae flagella peccatum et supplicium per Adamum invecta]* nam propter peccatum calamitosi, propter supplicium miseri semper homines existunt. Omnis[18] peccati faex et eluvies, in quam nos Adami lapsus involvit, e tribus potissimum puteis hauritur: qui etiam putei, licet stagnent in

[4] [152] homine, derivantur ab eodem lapsu Adami: nam, aut ex caecitate, aut carne, aut infirmitate,[19] peccatum omne proficiscitur *[Peccatum]*. Caecitas, ne quid rectum cognoscamus, iudicium obscurat: caro, ut a recto deflectamus, voluntatem sollicitat: infirmitas, in recto persequendo, constantiam omnem labefactat. Caecitas viam aut non aperit veram, aut patefacit falsam; caro aut cognitam viam contemnit, aut in devia seducit; infirmitas iam inceptam viam, aut tedio[20] relinquit, aut immensis difficultatibus prope confectam, viam obstruit: mirum ergo non est, si homo ad arcem felicitatis pervenire non poterit. *[Caecitas]* Caecitati subiiciuntur, ignorantia, errores, superstitio,

---

[15] *attingam*: Although I have rendered this a future simple, it is technically a present subjunctive (in parallel with *assumam*) following *persequar, ut* . . . .
[16] *Scientia . . . moriendi*: This is the first of many examples where Asc. applies a taxonomic approach and a series of categories.
[17] *Peccatum atque Supplicium*: these are the two parts of evil ultimately derived from Adam's fall; cf. Augus. *De civ. D.* 22.24, (*PL* 41, col. 788). *Supplicium* also has connotations of 'punishment'.

[3] [151] [K.iiii.] is the creative potential and prospect in man through Jesus Christ (with the result that love of God is kindled in us). Accordingly, I will review [the properties] of each – both the ill-effects of our parent Adam and the benefits of our Lord Jesus Christ. [I will do so] in such a way that I do not try to include everything for the purpose of explaining it at some length, which the business [in fact] merits. Rather, I will touch[15] on some things lightly for the purpose of conveying [my case] in brief, which the constraints of the space and time require. With the fall of Adam, we lost all divine gifts *[All divine gifts were lost through the fall of Adam]*. This ought to be lamented by everyone because of the inescapable loss of those gifts, rather [more] than they can be enumerated by me at this time for the reason of any examination of them. But [if I were to enumerate them], these gifts, as learned men report, comprise: knowledge of God, purity and innocence of life, righteousness, steadfastness, and power over death.[16] With the fall of Adam, there crept into their place two very serious scourges of human life and the worst kinds of defects: sin and suffering[17] *[Two very serious scourges of human life – sin and suffering – were introduced through Adam]*. Indeed, it is because of sin that men are always ruinous, and because of suffering that they are always wretched. The dross and discharge of every[18] [sort of] sin in which Adam's fall has mired us is drawn from three cesspits in particular. And to press the point, these cesspits, although they fester in

[4] [152] mankind, descend from that same fall of Adam. Certainly, all sin *[Sin]* originates from blindness, or flesh, or weakness.[19] Blindness, that we might not recognise what is right, obscures judgement. Flesh, that we might veer from what is right, disturbs the will. Weakness, when it comes to pursuing what is right, causes all steadfastness to totter. Blindness either fails to reveal the true path or throws open a false one. Flesh either condemns the known path or entices [people] into the wrong paths. Weakness either abandons in weariness[20] a path already started or, with insurmountable obstacles, blocks a path almost completed. And so, it is no wonder if a man is unable to reach the summit of [good] fortune. Annexed to blindness *[Blindness]* are: ignorance, errors, superstition,

---

[18] *Omnis*: I have taken *omnis* as a genitive with *peccati* rather than as a nominative with each of *faex* and *eluvies*. *in quam* refers to both *faex* and *eluvies*.

[19] *caecitate, aut carne, aut infirmitate*: blindness, flesh and weakness were regarded more generally as the three residual aspects of original sin. The unit of three serves as a structuring device for what follows.

[20] *tedio*: an alternative form for *taedio*.

haeresis, vanae opiniones, praepostera iudicia, temeritas, assertio incognitorum pro cognitis, invectio inutilium pro necessariis, amor sui, contemptus aliorum, pro bonis mala, pro malis bona, stultitia, vanitas, arrogantia, et eius generis alia infinita. *[Caro]* E carne proficiscuntur multa ad fraudem excogitata, plura ad vim et acerbitatem excitata, plurima ad voluptatum illecebras comparata.[21]

[5] [153] [K.v.] Fraudis sunt blasphemiae, periuria, calumniae, perfidia, falsa testimonia, circumventiones, insidiae, adulatio, et sexcenta his finitima. Ad vim et acerbitatem pertinent, discordia, lis, inimicitiae, aemulationes, homicidia, crudelitas, rapina, furta, caedes, saevitia, tyrannis, ambitio, et cetera his confinia. Voluptatis comites sunt, nequitiae, libidines, impudicitia, fornicationes, adulteria, incesta, immundiciae,[22] lascivia, ebrietas, commessationes,[23] et omnia luxuriei genera. Infirmitatis vitia sunt, *[Infirmitas]* levitas, inconstantia, mobilitas, fastidium, desidia, segnities, incuria, et quaecunque sunt ad negligentiam referenda. Peccata ergo omnia, quae ab Adamo profecta sunt, cum numero sunt infinita, ad caecitatem, carnem, et infirmitatem, tanquam ad certa capita, pertinere dicimus. Et haec de peccato.

Alterum malum quod ab Adamo proficiscitur, supplicium ponimus *[Supplicium]*, quod non ad improbitatem iniquorum, sed potius ad conditionem et sortem miserorum referri debet. Supplicia, cum re ipsa peccata non sunt, antecedunt tamen aut consequuntur

[6] [154] vel cum ipsis peccatis coniuncta sunt: haec numero infinita, certis tamen generibus describi possunt. Domestica supplicia sunt, labor, dolor, metus, luctus, penuria, fames, morbi, naturalis mors, et quae in propriae nostrae vitae medullis inhaerent. Foris assumuntur, orbitas, sollicitudo, bellum, captivitas, vincula, plagae,[24] carceres, exilia, violenta mors, et id genus alia. Longissime[25]

---

[21] *multa ... plura ... plurima*: produces a powerful amplificatory effect through the movement from positive adjective to comparative to superlative, underscored by the assonance of 'a'.
[22] *immundiciae*: an alternative form for *immunditiae*.
[23] *commessationes*: more likely an alternative form for *comissatio* rather than *commensatio*, a late medieval Latin word (cognate with *comedo*, 'to eat with', as attested to in *DMLBS*).

heresy, empty beliefs, wayward judgements, rashness, an avowal of the unknown in place of the known, an insistence on the pointless in place of the necessary, love of self, contempt for others, evil in place of good, good in place of evil, stupidity, vanity, haughtiness and other numerous traits of this type. From flesh *[Flesh]* much originates that has been contrived for deception; more that has been incited for violence and affliction; and very much that has been prepared for the inducement of passions.[21]

[5] [153] [K.v.] These are: the profanity of deception, falsehoods, subterfuges, treachery, false statements, double-dealing, ambushes, flattery and a huge number [of horrors] like these. Associated with violence and anger are: conflict, contention, enmity, rivalry, murder, cruelty, rape, theft, slaughter, savagery, oppression, bribery and other [atrocities] akin to these. The partners of passion are: profligacy, lust, lewdness, fornication, adultery, incest, filthiness,[22] obscenity, intoxication, revelry[23] and all other types of outrageousness. The failings of weakness *[Weakness]* are: shallowness, lack of steadfastness, fickleness, arrogance, apathy, sluggishness, want of care, and all that can be attributed to neglect. Accordingly, all [these] sins which have originated from Adam, while they are infinite in number, we suggest belong to blindness, flesh and weakness, just as if to certain categories. And this [much] about sin.

The other evil that originates from Adam we refer to as suffering *[Suffering]*. This ought not to be understood as [something] bound up with the depravity of the unjust, but rather the state and lot of the wretched. [Forms of] suffering, while not in essence sins, are nevertheless a prelude to, consequent upon,

[6] [154] or in concert with the sins themselves. These are infinite in number, but they can be divided into certain types. There is suffering of a [more] private kind: toil, pain, fear, grief, poverty, hunger, disease, natural death and that which is appurtenant to the core of our own life. Beyond the home, [the following] are faced: bereavement, worry, war, captivity, chains, beatings,[24] incarceration, exile, violent death and other [scourges] of that type. From further away,[25]

---

[24] *plagae*: the noun *plaga* a broad semantic range and, in addition to 'beating / blow', can denote 'plague' and, more generically, 'misfortune'.
[25] *longissime*: It is more felicitous to render this superlative adverb as a comparative, as the text moves spatially from *domestica* to *foris* and finally to the punishments inflicted by forces beyond man's control.

prospectant nos ea supplicia quae casu accidunt, ut ab aestibus, frigoribus, tonitru, grandine, fulmine, hiatibus terrarum, oppressionibus ruinarum,[26] quas res inopinata mors consequitur. Quid referam mille venenorum genera,[27] e metallis,[28] herbis, fruticibus, auris,[29] et pestiferis belluis[30] provenientia,[31] ad interitum humani generis, per Adami culpam invecta?[32] Daemonum incursiones innumerabiles, quibus humana vita exagitatur, non praeterirem, nisi, ne in immensum oratio mea cresceret, vehementer pertimescerem. Sed satis iam opinor[33] ex his, quae diximus, manifestum esse potest, universum humanum genus vel peccatis calamitosissimum, vel suppliciis miserrimum existere. Et hanc sane hominis confusissimam

[7] [155] miseriam si diligenti cogitatione versabimus, nihil profecto quod in nobis ipsis gloriaremur inveniemus. Et hactenus[34] de Adami lapsu, eiusque incommodis, quae vel peccata ad malitiam, vel supplicia ad miseriam attulerunt,[35] a nobis dictum sit. Et iam a Iesu Christo *[Jesus Christus]* exordiamur cum apostolo Paulo, ubi dicit: In hiis omnibus[36] supervincimus per eum qui dilexit nos,[37] per cuius gratiam solius, ab his omnibus malis gloriosissimam victoriam reportabimus. Christi benignitas in nos nulla oratione comprehendi potest, paucissimis tantum manifestum erit, non tantum[38] Adami mala posse ad[39] mortem et condemnationem, quantum Christi beneficia ad vitam et iustificationem. Nam primum, Deus non totum damnando hominibus abstulit, quod antea benedicendo hominibus tradidit.[40]

---

[26] *oppressionibus ruinarum*: I have translated this in a more specific rather general way, in keeping with the other natural disasters itemised in the list.
[27] *mille venenorum genera*: For more detailed information on poisons in the early modern period, see Gibbs 2018.
[28] *e metallis*: Asc. possibly has in mind the poisoning caused by lead. There was a strong interest in metals through the early modern period. Metals, such as lead, were often used in medicines and alchemy, even though there was a growing awareness during the period that, in the wrong doses, these metals might also have detrimental effects. Georgius Agricola, for example, would survey the health problems of German miners in his *De re metallica* of 1556.
[29] *auris*: I have taken this is an ablative plural from of *aura* rather than *aurum* ('gold [mineral]').
[30] *belluis*: an alternative form for *beluis*.
[31] *quid . . . provenientia*: This is not the only way this list can be rendered; if one were to render *venenorum* more generally as 'mischief', say, the items that follow might be translated as 'mining, crops, shrubbery, air and plague-ridden cattle'.
[32] *per Adami culpam invecta*: This appears to be describing a sort of *culpa* in nature that can also be attributable to Adam's transgressions.
[33] *opinor*: is used parenthetically as if *ut opinor* were intended; the indirect statement follows *manifestum esse potest* . . . .
[34] *hactenus*: literally, 'thus far' or 'till now'.

Licet enim vitam nostram ad poenam Diabolo subdidit,[41] omnem tamen naturam nostram salvam et incolumem texit: et propterea viget in nobis intelligentia,[42] viget mens, cuius beneficio magna honestatis vis ad veri perspicientiam, ad hominum societatem tuendam, ad res fortiter ferendas, ad modum et ordinem in re quavis conservandum, in homine remanet: et hoc

[8] [156] tantum propter Dominum nostrum Iesum Christum. Praeterea, quae sunt ab Adamo ad miseriam nostram invecta, ea sunt per dei bonitatem ad nostram summam utilitatem conversa. In plana re, pauca exempla sufficient. Metus, *[Metus]* cum sit peccati poena per Adamum, magnae commoditatis causa facta est per Iesum Christum: nam metu praeceptores habent tractabiles discipulos,[43] et metu Magistratus habent obedientes subiectos.[44] Et sic de labore *[Labor]*, qui etiam poena peccati est, dici potest. Cum labore discimus, sine labore nescimus: cum labore, boni: sine labore, mali semper, sumus: ad quem modum reliqua omnia persequi potuerim:[45] supervincimus ergo per eum qui nos dilexit.[46] Et haec quae diximus sunt miserorum solatia,[47] non beatorum praemia:[48] quae sane bona, cum data sunt etiam his omnibus, quos praedestinavit ad mortem: quanta sunt ergo illa bona, quae daturus est hiis, quos praedestinavit ad vitam?[49] Totus Adami lapsus in summam bonorum utilitatem est conversus, et plurima capit homo bona, ex eo lapsu, qui[50] insitus est in Iesu Christo, quae nunquam sane

---

[41] *Licet ... subdidit*: it is common to have *licet* (meaning 'although') with the indicative rather than the subjunctive in post-classical Latin.

[42] *intelligentia*: an alternative form for *intellegentia*.

[43] *metu ... discipulos*: Ryan refers to this as a 'curious' argument (1963: 100), but Asc. was a teacher and in the preface of his later *Schol.* (Giles 1865–1867: vol III, 78–87) recounted a debate he took part in about the benefits (or not) of administering corporal punishment to students (see also Ryan 1963: 251–53), and it was evidently a live pedagogical issue at the time. In this discussion between several senior members of the establishment at Windsor Castle in 1563, William Cecil, the then Secretary of State, commented that masters should use more discretion in whipping students for fear that scholars develop a hatred of learning. In opposition, William Petre expressed his approval of beating pupils as a means of keeping 'the school in obedience and the scholar in good order' (Giles, 79). Asc., with Cecil's prompting, then proceeded to explain at some length why he believed that 'young children were sooner allured by love than driven by beating to attain good learning' (Giles, 81). Asc. had, by the time he wrote his *Schol.*, modified the stance expressed here in the *Themata* about the advantages of fear.

awaiting us are those forms of suffering which occur by chance, [such] as [thos
occurring from] from extreme heat, cold, thunder, hail, lightning, sinkholes in th
land, the catastrophe of subsidence,[26] the [sort of] events that lead to sudden deat!
Why should I report a thousand types of poison[27] emanating from metals,[28] plan[
bushes, vapours[29] and [certain] plague-ridden animals,[30] which were introduc(
through the fault of Adam[32] for the destruction of the human race?[31] I would [als
not omit countless assaults [at the hands] of evil spirits by which human life
troubled were I not very worried that my speech would grow [too] unwiel
Rather, as far as I see it,[33] from all I have already said, it can be sufficiently establish
that the entire human race lives either very ruinously with sin or very wretche
with suffering. Indeed, if we give careful thought to this most disordered

[7] [155] [state of] man's wretchedness, we can be certain of findin$
ourselves nothing to celebrate. Let us have spoken enough[34] about the fa[
Adam and its ill-effects, that have added either sins to wickedness or suffe
to [that] wretched condition.[35] We should begin [again] now from J
Christ *[Jesus Christ]*, and with the apostle Paul, when he says 'In all[36] t
respects, we conquer through him who loved us';[37] through his grace a
we will secure the most celebrated victory from all these evils. The kin(
of Christ towards us can be captured in no speech, but it will be(
obvious in just very few [words] that the evils of Adam do not have as m
influence over[39] death and damnation as the benefactions of Christ hav(
life and justification. For, to start with, God did not snatch from ma:
to their utter damnation that which he had gifted to men for their bei

---

[35] *de ... attulerunt*: The idea is that Adam's initial wickedness is compounded by fur and his initial wretchedness by further suffering.
[36] *omnibus*: The printed version has *hominibus*, but this must be a typographical er[should read *omnibus*, as per Rom. (below), and makes better sense as *omni* confusion may have arisen through the use of *hominibus* a couple of sentences]
[37] *In ... nos*: Rom. 8.37; V: *sed in his omnibus superamus propter eum qui dilexit* prefers *supervincimus*, a verb used also by, for example, Cyprian, Augus. and Pa(V or E, who retained *superamus* in each edition of *Nov. T.* The verse appears f through this theme. *supervincimus* calques the original Greek ὑπερνικῶμεν; tl underlined and has a manicule pointing to it in GNT.
[38] *tantum*: The *errata* of the printed version inserts *tantum* in place of *tam* in th version.
[39] *posse ad*: *posse* + *ad* + accusative has a specific meaning of having a power or eff something (*OLD* 8(b)).
[40] *Deus ... tradidit*: This follows Augus. *De civ. D.* 22.24, which, for example, sta *enim damnando aut totum abstulit quod dederat, alioquin nec esset omninc removit a sua potestate, etiam cum diabolo poenaliter subdidit ...* ('For in cond(did not take away from that nature everything which he had given, otherwis not exist at all. Nor did he release it from his power, even when he subjected it 1 as a punishment ...') *PL* 41, col. 788.

For although he yielded[41] up our lives to the Devil by way of penalty, he nonetheless kept our whole nature intact and unimpaired. And so, understanding[42] flourishes in us and our mind flourishes, thanks to which a great force of virtue remains in mankind for a full knowledge of the truth, for protecting the fellowship of man, for bearing things stoutly, and for conserving the measure and the order in any matter whatsoever.

[8] [156] And [all] this [comes about] only because of our Lord Jesus Christ. Besides, whatever has been introduced by Adam for our wretchedness, this has been transformed through the goodness of God for our supreme advantage. [To explain] the matter clearly, a few examples will suffice. Fear *[Fear]*, although through Adam [it was] a penalty of sin, through Jesus Christ, it became an opportunity for great advantage. For it is through fear that teachers have manageable pupils,[43] and through fear that those in power have obedient subjects.[44] And the same can be said of toil, which is also a penalty of sin. We learn with toil; without toil we know nothing. With toil we are good; without toil, we are always evil; [and it is] in this way that I could have[45] explained everything else. 'We thus conquer through him who loved us'.[46] And that which I discuss [here] constitutes a comfort[47] for the wretched not a reward for the blessed.[48] [While] such [gifts] are of course good when they have been granted to all these men whom he (i.e. God) has predestined to death, how great, then, are those [gifts] which he is going to give to these whom he has predestined to life?[49] The whole fall of Adam has been redirected to the supreme advantage of good men, and the man who[50] takes the greatest good from that fall is the one who is grafted in Jesus Christ; such good he (i.e. man) would, of course, never have

---

[44] *metu ... subiectos*: Ryan connects this line of argument with a broader position held by Asc. about the inseparability of service to the state and service to God (1963: 100). *obedientes* is an alternative form for *oboedientes*.

[45] *potuerim*: is a potential perfect subjunctive. Asc. means here that he could explain other aspects of life along these lines.

[46] *supervincimus ... dilexit*: Rom. 8.37 again.

[47] *solatia*: an alternative form for *solacia*.

[48] *Et ... praemia*: words borrowed and adapted from Augus. *De civ. D.* 22.24: *Et haec omnia miserorum sunt damnatorumque solacia, non praemia beatorum* ('And all these are the comforts of men unhappy and condemned, not the rewards of the blessed'), *PL* 41, col. 792.

[49] *quae ... vitam*: Again, words used in Augus. *De civ. D.*: *Quid dabit eis quos praedestinavit ad vitam, qui haec dedit etiam eis quod praedestinavit ad mortem?* ('What will [God] give to those whom he has predestined to life, when he has given these things even to those predestined to death?'), *PL* 41, col. 792.

[50] *qui*: It makes much more sense for *homo* to be the antecedent of *qui* than *lapsu*.

[9] [157] percepisset in ipso innocenti Adamo. Verum si Adamum et eius incommoda, cum Iesu Christo et eius beneficiis cominus conferamus, facilime,[51] quantum per eum, qui nos dilexit, supervincimus,[52] considerabimus.[53] *[Adamus et eius incommoda, cum Iesu Christo et eius beneficiis comparantur]* Adamus culpam invexit; Christus paenitentiam adduxit. Adamus, culpa sua, solum peccatum originale attulit; Christus, gratia sua, et originale, et omnia etiam actualia abstulit. Adamus afflictionem, laborem, et certamen proponit; Christus patientiam, praemium, et coronam tribuit.[54] Adamus inobedientia[55] sua, tantum mortem nobis impartit:[56] Christus, gratia sua, et mortem morte destruxit, et vitam vita restituit: supervincimus ergo per eum qui nos dilexit.[57] Sed Adamus reddidit nos filios irae,[58] filios indignationis, obiecit nos faucibus crudelissimorum hostium, Carnis, Mundi,[59] Diaboli, Peccati, Mortis, Inferni. Christus omnem captivam duxit Captivitatem,[60] Infernum divicit,[61] Morti aculeum[62] abstulit, Diaboli vires fregit. Diabolus iam voluntatem nocendi, non potestatem ullam habet, nisi quatenus nos ei concedamus. Ergo si tu

[10] [158] vis, Diabolus non potest: si tantum resistis, fugiet a te,[63] quemadmodum ait Apostolus. Et contra tam fractos hostes, munitissima tamen arma donat Christus, ut omnibus modis per eum supervincamus. Nam pro baltheo,[64] veritatem; pro thorace, iusticiam;[65] pro scuto, fidem per spiritum suum nobis infudit.[66] Verum, ut intelligamus totum peccati imperium, per Christi beneficium esse sublatum, audi tu, quisquis es, qui dubitas. Errore duceris?[67] Christus via et ianua est.[68] In ignoratione et tenebris

---

[51] *facilime*: an alternative form for *facillime*.
[52] *per ... supervincimus*: Rom. 8.37 again.
[53] *si ... conferamus ... considerabimus*: a subjunctive (*conferamus*) is used in the protasis of the conditional and an indicative (*considerabimus*) in the apodosis: the act of contemplating Christ *will* follow.
[54] *Adamus ... abstulit ... tribuit*: The *comparanda* are made all the more direct through the use of symmetry and similar sounding verb forms.
[55] *inobedientia*: an alternative form for *inoboedientia*, a Latin word first used in the Church Fathers.
[56] *impartit*: an alternative form for *impertit*.
[57] *supervincimus ... dilexit*: Rom. 8.37 again.
[58] *filii irae*: the phrase comes from Ephes. 2.3.
[59] *Mundi*: In Christian writing, *mundus* denotes 'this world', namely the realm of sin and death, as opposed to Christ's kingdom of holiness and life.
[60] *Christus ... Captivitatem*: wording inspired by Ephes. 4.8: *captivam duxit captivitatem* ('He led captivity captive').
[61] *divicit*: an alternative form for *devicit* (from *devinco*).

[9] [157] taken possession of in the time of Adam's innocence. Truly, if we were to directly compare Adam and his ill-effects with Jesus Christ and his benefits, without any difficulty at all,[51] [it can only be the case that] we will reflect on[53] how much we conquer through him who has loved us[52] *[Adam and his ill-effects are compared with Jesus and his benefits]*. Adam introduced fault; Christ brought repentance. Adam, through his fault, set in motion only original sin; Christ, through his grace, removed original sin and also all individual acts of sin. Adam offers punishment, toil and strife; Christ imparts forbearance, profit and the crown [of martyrdom].[54] Adam, through his disobedience,[55] assigns[56] us only death; Christ, through his grace, weakened death with death and restored life with life. Thus, we conquer through him who loved us.[57] Adam, for a fact, rendered us the sons of anger[58] and the sons of discontent; he exposed us to the jaws of the most ruthless enemies: Flesh, this World,[59] the Devil, Sin, Death and Hell. Christ led the whole of Captivity captive,[60] subdued[61] Hell, deprived Death of her sting,[62] and broke the strength of the Devil. Now the Devil possesses [only] the will to harm, but no power, except to the extent that we grant it to him. Well then, [even] if you

[10] [158] want it, the Devil has no capacity. If you [can] only resist, he will flee from you,[63] just as the Apostle suggests. And against so weakened an enemy, Christ nevertheless provides the strongest weapons so we might conquer through him in every way. Indeed, he has provided us with truth for a sword belt,[64] righteousness[65] for a breastplate, and faith through his spirit for a shield.[66] Yet to [fully] grasp [the notion] that the entire dominion of sin has been removed through Christ's favour, pay heed, you, whoever you are who doubts [this]. Are you guided by error?[67] Christ is the path and the entrance.[68] Do you lie in ignorance

---

[62] *Morti aculeum*: Paul refers to the 'sting of death' as 'sin' (*peccatum*) in 1 Corinth. 15.56.
[63] *si . . . te*: A paraphrase of James 4.7: *resistite autem diabolo, et fugiet a vobis* ('But resist the Devil, and he will flee from you').
[64] *baltheo*: an alternative form for *balteo*.
[65] *iusticia*: an alternative form for *iustitia*. However, this often appears as *iustitia* in the *Themata*. This may reflect the fact that in early modern script 'c' and 't' looked very similar and the original manuscript may not have been clear; there are similar instances of this phenomenon through the tract.
[66] *Nam . . . infudit*: images found in Ephes. 6.13–17, where Paul outlines the 'armour of God': how the loins may be girt about with truth; having the breastplate of righteousness; having feet shod in preparation of the Gospel; taking the shield of faith; the helmet of salvation; and the sword of the spirit. Asc. would draw on this again in a more expanded way in *Apol.* (Nicholas 2017: 14–15).
[67] The question-answer approach is one used in themes 1, 5 and 8 and the content overlaps in each case.
[68] *Christus via et ianua est*: a possible adaptation of John 14.6, where Christ says of himself *sum via et veritas et vita*. This is the first of a volley of biblical quotes that forms the climax of this theme.

iaces? Ipse veritas et lux est, illuminans omnem hominem venientem in hunc mundum.[69] *[Eadem propemodum verba recensentur themate inscripto, Absit mihi gloriari. etc. Gala. 6.]*[70] Peccati magnitudinem metuis?[71] Ecce agnus Dei qui tollit peccata mundi.[72] Maledictum legis[73] extimescis? Perfectio legis ipse est, ad iusticiam omni credenti.[74] Mundi tyrannidem times? Bono animo sis; ille vicit mundum.[75] Diaboli fraudem vereris? Venit princeps huius mundi,[76] in illo non habet quicquam.[77] Inferni voraginem exhorrescis? Hic nihil praevalent portae inferni.[78] Mortis ultimi hostis aculeum formidas? Absorpta est mors in victoriam:[79] et qui credit in illo, etiamsi mortuus fuerit, vivet.[80] [159] Quid ergo restat ut dicamus, nisi quod omnibus modis supervincimus per eum qui nos dilexit, cui honor et gloria in omne aevum. Amen.

---

[69] *lux ... mundum*: John 1.9. V: *erat lux vera quae inluminat omnem hominem venientem in mundum*; Nov. T: *erat lux illa, lux vera: quae illuminat omnem hominem venientem in mundum*. E's version comes closest to the Greek: ἦν τὸ φῶς τὸ ἀληθινὸν ὃ φωτίζει πάντα ἄνθρωπον ἐρχόμενον εἰς τὸν κόσμον, but the version here is perhaps more powerful because of its use of the doublet, *veritas et lux*. On the use of *veritas*, see n. 282.

[70] *Eadem ... Gala. 6*: This hanging note suggests that the biblical quotes are repeated almost word for word in theme 8, but in fact they come in theme 5, under the heading 'Numb. 22'.

[71] *metuis ... formidas*: Here and in what follows, there are six Latin synonyms of the verb 'to fear', *metuis, extimescis, times, vereris, exhorrescis* and *formidas*. Each appears in the second person singular and their deployment in a series of rhetorical questions is very arresting.

[72] *Ecce ... mundi*: John 1.29. The citation matches both V and Nov. T. This is what John says when he sees Jesus coming towards him.

[73] *Maledictum legis*: see n. 382 for more on the significance of this notion of the 'curse of the Law'.

[74] *Perfectio ... credenti*: Rom. 10.4. Asc. diverges slightly from both V: *finis enim legis Christus ad iustitiam omni credenti*, and from Nov. T: *nam perfectio legis Christus, ad iustificationem omni credenti*. This and the previous sentence taken together reflect an

and darkness? He himself is the truth and the light, illuminating every man coming into this world.[69] *[Practically the same words are rehearsed in the theme with the title, 'May I be kept from boasting' etc. Galatians, chapter 6].*[70] Are you afraid[71] of the enormity of sin? Behold, the lamb of God who removes the sins of the world.[72] Do you dread the curse of the Law?[73] He himself is the fulfilment of the Law unto righteousness for every man who believes.[74] Do you fear the oppression of this world? Be of good courage; he has conquered this world.[75] Are you fearful of the Devil's deceit? The prince of this world[76] is coming, but has no claim over him.[77] Do you tremble at the abyss of Hell? Here the gates of Hell have no power.[78] Do you shudder at the sting of death from your most formidable opponent? Death has been swallowed up in victory,[79] and whoever believes in him, even though dead, will live.[80] [159] In conclusion, what is left to say except that we conquer in every way through him who loved us, and for whom there [will be] honour and glory in every age. Amen.

---

awareness of and articulate well a key difference between Law and Gospel (sometimes termed 'Sin and Grace'). The former might provide a useful curb though fear of punishment (a point highlighted in the later authoritative Lutheran statement of faith, the Formula of Concord of 1577), whereas the latter offered forgiveness of sins.

[75] *Bono ... mundum*: A reworded version John 16.33. V: *sed confidite, ego vici mundum*. Asc.'s idiom *bono animo sis*, which is also used by E in *Nov. T*, *sed bono animo sitis, ego vici mundum*, is much closer to the Greek, ἀλλὰ θαρσεῖτε, ἐγὼ νενίκηκα τὸν κόσμον.

[76] *princeps huius mundi*: The 'prince of this world' is the Devil.

[77] *Venit ... quicquam*: John 14.30. V has *in me* rather than *in illo* as Jesus speaks these words; *in illo*, is of course a reference to Christ, and John means that the Devil will have no power over Christ, who has no sin in him. The verse is flagged up in GNT.

[78] *Hic ... inferni*: Matt. 16.18. V: *portae inferi non praevalebunt*; *Nov. T: portae inferorum non valebunt*. Asc.'s *portae inferni* here is closer to wording used in Pag: *et portae inferni non valebunt*.

[79] *Absorpta ... victoriam*, 1 Corinth. 15.54, wording identical to V and *Nov. T*.

[80] *qui ... vivet*: John 11.25. Asc. follows V and *Nov. T* (albeit they have *in me* rather than *in illo*). He also underlines the entire verse in GNT and summarises the words in Greek in the margin.

Theme 2
(11–19)

This theme has the flavour of a biblical commentary, and also, in parts, of a (medieval thematic) sermon. It may be one of the earliest themes of the collection and, read separately from the others, seems relatively conservative in its doctrinal tenor, even as the use of Hebrew / Protestant Psalm numbering possibly points to a more evangelical biblical outlook (albeit with the caveat lodged above).[81] It centres on a particular verse from Psalm 37 (or 36), 'I have been young and I have also become old, and I have never seen the righteous forsaken nor his offspring seeking bread', a statement made by David in the Old Testament. Over the course of his account, Ascham carefully defines and fleshes out each element of the verse, which often entails an investigation of the semantic range or origin of a particular term. This theme offers an early glimpse of Ascham's philological exegesis, one that would emerge with fuller force in his *Apologia pro caena Dominca* of 1547. It also demonstrates a lively interest in the Fathers and other religious thinkers but, more conspicuously, it points to a concern that would emerge in theme after theme, namely the literal meaning of God's Word in the Bible.

Theologically, one element of the heading's verse quotation takes centre stage in the theme – that of *iustitia* ('righteousness'). In fact, the theme becomes most sermon-like when Ascham explains how it operates and exhorts whoever reads or listens to this piece to reflect actively on how to be righteous. The concept of righteousness was one of the most important issues to come under the soteriological spotlight in the Reformation, with Luther arrogating all responsibility for it to God alone, and viewing righteousness as a quality that could only be divinely imparted, rather than something humans could produce of their own accord or through their own good behaviour. In contrast to the Lutheran stress on systemic sin and on the impossibility of 'good works' which are always sinful, in this theme, Ascham focuses far more on man's conduct. He grants to each individual a certain agency and suggests that the degree to which a man falls from righteousness will vary from generation to generation. Such an outlook is hardly surprising (especially if it does belong to an earlier timeframe): Luther's unyielding insistence on wholesale sin was staunchly resisted by Henry VIII, and, in any case, many

---

[81] See p. 61.

Protestant reformers also resisted the antinomian implications of Luther's message, and placed far greater weight on each individual's morality. Ascham may also have had a patristic model in mind, whereby, once baptism took away sins, the divine and the human cooperated in salvation. More impotantly, though, Ascham is adamant that actions are only righteous *provided* that they conform to God's Law and *provided* that they are done in faith, a conviction that will emerge more conspicuously in other pieces. Such a proviso is perhaps suggestive of a belief-system that might mature into a view that good works do not *per se* effect justification but, rather, are an expression of it.

Another interesting feature of the argumentation in this theme is Ascham's incorporation of classical sources. Despite Ascham's claim that all his points are 'evident and sufficiently established from sacred Scripture and from the Doctors of the Church', when summarising the 'righteous man', he relies (in addition to the Psalm itself and Ezekiel) on Cicero's *De inventione*. A second classical author, Columella, is then cited as evidence that the righteous man does not necessarily remain so. The classical influence is further felt in Ascham's deployment of *exempla*, which were a fundamental facet of ancient rhetorical practice (germane to *inventio*). Furthermore, his frequent use of examples to support his argument points to a keen awareness of the interconnectness of rhetoric and dialectic.

[11] [159] Iuvenis fui et etiam senui et nunquam vidi iustum derelictum, nec semen eius quaerens panem. Psal. 37.[82]

Cum[83] Eccelsia Dei, in qua nos militiam quandam adversus Dei hostes et tenebrarum[84] perpetuo sustinemus, ortum habere et gigni, et aliquando diem suum obitura[85] (iuxta patrum sententias)[86] videatur, propterea David spiritus sancti plenus, hoc loco in nomine totius ecclesiae, in eorum consolationem qui iustam vitam traducere, et capiti suo[87] adhaerescere velint, in hanc sententiam[88] irrumpit. Cum me cogitatione refero in memoriam infantiae meae sub Abel: et ante legem, adolescentiae meae, in tempore Patriarcharum, Iudicum, et Regum,[89] et cum intueor in florentem meam aetatem, cum lumen de lumine,[90] ad revelationem gentium et gloriam plebis Israel illuxerit,[91] cumque senectutis meae decursam et exactam aetatem[92] prospicio, in qua omnis

[12] [160] fere charitatis[93] sanguis refrigescet, et pene[94] exhaustus fuerit: cum (inquam) universae aetatis meae memoriam, una cogitatione complector et perlustro, ita in ea semper erga iustos Dei bonitatem fusam esse, et prolatatam video, ut nunquam quenquam iustum viderim, sic iacentem et inclinatum, aut in eas miseriae et indigentiae[95] angustias compingi, quin praesens et

---

[82] *Iuvenis ... panem*: Ps. 37.25. The explicit Psalm numbering is significant, as number 37 follows H/P; it is 36 according to V/S. The wording diverges from V: *iunior fui et senui et non vidi iustum derelictum nec semen eius quaerens panes*. Cf. Augus. *Ennaratio in Psalmum XXXVI*, pt. 3: *Iuvenis fui, et ecce senui, et non vidi iustum derelictum, nec semen eius quaerens panem*, PL 36, col. 384. Asc.'s wording also matches exactly Jer. *commentariorum in Amos libri*, 3.viii.: *iuvenis fui et senui et non vidi iustum derelictum nec semen eius quaerens panem*, when Jer. quotes Ps. 36, PL 25, col. 1085.
[83] *Cum ... irrumpit*: I have not translated *cum* as I have broken up the long sentence that follows it.
[84] *tenebrarum*: The genitive plural is odd, and it is much more likely that Asc. meant to (or did) use an accusative.
[85] [*suum*] *diem obire*: an idiom that means 'to die'.
[86] *iuxta patrum sententias*: a reference to the eschatological predictions of the early Church Fathers.
[87] *suo*: I have understood this reflexive adjective as relating back to David rather than to *qui* ('those who...').
[88] *in hanc sententiam*: In the *sententia* that follows, Asc. puts into the mouth of David (in the first person) a long pronouncement, in his own wording, that has been inspired by parts

[11] [159] 'I have been young and I have also become old, and I have never seen the righteous forsaken nor his offspring seeking bread'. Psalm 37.[82]

The Church of God,[83] in which we continously maintain a certain 'military service' against the enemies of God and the darkness,[84] is regarded as having a beginning, as proceeding forth, and, at some point, destined to come to an end,[85] in accordance with the pronouncements of the [Church] Fathers.[86] Bearing this in mind, David, full of the Holy Spirit, in the name of the whole Church, for the comfort of those who are willing to lead a righteous life and to cleave to his[87] principle, bursts forth in the following passage with this pronouncement,[88] 'When I turn in reflection to the remembrance of my early childhood after [the time of] Abel; and before the Law, of my adolescence in the time of the Patriarchs, Judges and Kings;[89] and when I give thought to the springtime of my life, when the light from light[90] shone for the revelation of the Gentiles and the glory of the people of Israel;[91] and when I survey the passage of my old age, advanced and spent,[92] when nigh on all

[12] [160] strength of charity[93] flags and is almost[94] exhausted; when, I say, I contemplate and scan the memory of my entire lifetime in a single reflection, I see in that [reflection] that the goodness of God has always been offered and extended to the righteous in such a way that I have never seen anyone righteous [left] lying [in neglect] and fallen so to speak, or impounded in those narrows of wretchedness and want,[95] but that straightway a present and

---

of Ps. 70 (V/S) / 71 (H/P). In this Psalm, penned in old age, David surveys the arc of his life, referring specifically to his birth in verse 6, youth in verses 5 and 17, and old age in 9 and 18. It was clearly a piece intended for the general use of God's people in their afflictions.

[89] *Patriarcharum, Iudicum, et Regum*: This is the sequence of ruling figures in Israel; prophets were synonymous with judges.

[90] *lumen de lumine*: a flourish on the part of Asc., taken from a form of words applied to Christ in the Nicene Creed.

[91] *lumen . . . illuxerit*: Luke 2.32. Asc. diverges from V and E with his *lumen de lumine* – they just have *lumen* – and with his addition of *illuxerit*.

[92] *senectutis . . . aetatem*: Throughout Ps. 70 (V/S) / 71 (H/P), David asks for help from God to assist him in his old age, and in verse 9 explictly states that his strength is failing: *in tempore senectutis cum defecerit fortitudo mea [ne derelinquas me]* ('in the time of old age when my strength shall fail, [do not forsake me]').

[93] *charitatis*: an alternative form for *caritatis*.

[94] *pene*: an alternative form for *paene*.

[95] *indigentiae*: a rare word used mainly by Cic. It can mean 'want', 'need' or 'desire'.

maturum opis adminiculum, Dei benignitate, quam celerrime sit ei asportatum. Merito ergo Propheta in nomine Ecclesiae, Iuvenis fui et etiam senui etc. Quis sit iustus singula quaeque fere scripturae pagina ostendit, nullibi tamen expressius et pictius ob oculos ponitur, quam in Psalmis: nam sic post in praesenti Psalmo David: *[Psal. 37.]* Iustus est cuius os meditatur sapientiam, et lingua eius loquitur iudicium, et lex Dei eius in corde ipsius.[96] Hunc Dominus non derelinquet, sed haereditabit[97] terram, et inhabitabit in seculum[98] seculi super eam.[99] Talem iusti benedictionem confirmat ipse Dominus noster Iesus Christus, cum dicit: Primum quaerite etc.[100] Si quis vero requirit explicatiorem iusti descriptionem,

[13] [161] [L.] Ezechielem decimo octavo audiat: *[Ezech. 18]* Vir, si fuerit iustus et fecerit iudicium et iusticiam, in montibus non comederit, et oculos suos non levaverit ad idola domus Israel, et uxorem proximi sui non violaverit, nec ullum iniuria oppresserit, pignus debitori reddiderit, per vim nihil rapuerit, panem suum esurienti dederit, et nudum operuerit vestimento, ab iniquitate averterit manum suam et iudicium verum fecerit[101] inter virum et virum, in praeceptis meis ambulaverit, et iudicia mea custodierit ut faciat veritatem, hic iustus est, et vita vivet ait Dominus Deus.[102] Si me feretis describere vobis iustum, eandem inibo rationem, quam M. Cicero in 2. De inventione[103] sequutus esse videatur,[104] quod non impie dictum, sed cum

---

[96] *Iustus ... ipsius*: Ps. 36.30–31 (V/S) / 37.30–31 (H/P). V has slightly different wording: *os iusti meditabitur sapientiam et lingua eius loquetur iudicium. Lex Dei in corde ipsius ....* The fact that Asc. highlights this as an authoritative definition of the 'righteous man' is very revealing, for it serves to connect in the most direct way, through its references to 'mouth' and 'tongue', the spoken word (or rhetoric) with Christian morality, a theme that would dominate all Asc.'s later writings.

[97] *haereditabit*: an alternative form for *hereditabit*.

[98] *seculum*: an alternative form for *saeculum*.

[99] *Hunc ... eam*: Ps. 36.28–29 / 37.28–29 (H/P). Asc. paraphrases here. V: *quia Dominus amat iudicium et non derelinquet sanctos suos ... iusti autem hereditabunt terram et inhabitabunt in saeculum saeculi super eam* ('For the Lord loves judgement and will not forsake his saints ... But the righteous shall inherit the earth and shall dwell therein for evermore').

[100] *Primum quaerite etc.*: Matt. 6.33. The full verse reads: *quaerite autem primum regnum Dei et iustitiam eius et omnia haec adicientur vobis* ('First, therefore, seek the kingdom of God and his righteousness, and all these things shall be added for you'). The verse is underlined in GNT.

[101] *iudicium ... fecerit*: 'to pass judgement' as per *OLD* 6(b).

[102] *Vir ... Deus*: Ez. 18.5–9. This broadly follows V; however, Asc. omits from verse 6 *ad mulierem menstruatam non accesserit* ('and nor has he come near to a menstruating

timely offer of sustenance is brought to him through the kindness of God'. Thus, with [good] reason, the Prophet, in the name of the Church, [said], 'I have been young and I have also become old' etc. [The question of] who is righteous nearly every single page of Scripture adumbrates, but nowhere is it set out more clearly and more vividly before [our] eyes than in the Psalms. Indeed, in this same Psalm *[Psalm 37]*, David afterwards [speaks] thus, 'He is righteous whose mouth observes wisdom and whose tongue enunciates judgement, and the Law of his God is in his heart'.[96] The Lord will not forsake this man; rather he will inherit[97] the earth and will for evermore[98] dwell therein.[99] Our Lord Jesus Christ himself affirms such a blessing of the righteous when he says 'First seek etc'.[100] Indeed, if anyone looks for a clearer account of the righteous man,

[13] [161] [L.] let him listen to Ezekiel in the eighteenth [chapter] *[Ezekiel, chapter 18]*, [when he says], 'If a man is righteous and exercises judgement and righteousness, has not eaten upon the mountains, nor lifted his eyes to the idols of the house of Israel, has not defiled his neighbour's wife, nor has borne down on any[one] unjustly, but has returned a pledge to a debtor, has seized nothing by violence, has given his bread to the hungry and covered the naked with a garment, has turned his hand away from unfairness, has passed true judgement[101] between man and man, has walked in my statutes, and has observed my judgements to act truthfully – this man is righteous and will live with life, says the Lord God'.[102] If you allow me to summarise for you the righteous man, I will offer the same definition that Marcus Cicero appears to have followed[104] in the second book of 'On Invention',[103] [a viewpoint] articulated not irreligiously, but [one that] will

---

woman'), alters *et hominem non contristaverit* to a more classically-sounding *nec ullum iniuria oppresserit* in verse 7, and omits *ad usuram non commodaverit et amplius non acceperit* ('he that has not lent for usury, nor has received any increase') from verse 8.

[103] *De inventione*: This is one of Cic.'s early works on rhetoric, a sort of prelude to his more developed treatise on the subject, *De or*. In 2.53–54 *De inv.*, Cic. develops the concept of *iustitia* as one limb of a broader definition of *honestum* ('what is honorable'). He defines it from the outset as a 'habit of mind which gives every man his just desert, while preserving the common advantage'. Cic.'s definition is more multifaceted than than that offered by Asc., but Cic. certainly points to religion and patriotic duty, writing, 'Religion is that which brings men to serve and worship a higher order of nature which they call divine' and 'duty is the feeling which renders kind offices and loving service to one's kin and country'. Pursuant to customary law, Cic. suggests, equity is fostered, namely 'what is just and fair to all' (*LCL*, trans. H. M. Hubbell, 1949).

[104] *esse videatur*: In Roman rhetoric, a *clausula* was a rhythmic figure used to add finesse and finality to the end of a sentence or phrase. There was a large range of popular clausulae, but most well known is this Ciceronian *esse videatur* type. Other examples of the *esse videatur* unit in this tract can be found at 26 (twice), 35 and 37.

Christi doctrina coniunctissimum erit: neque quod ille ait, ideo proferam: sed, quia veritas sic postulat, ideo in medium producam. Iustus est *[Iustus]*, qui religione et sanctitate Deum colit, et qui pietate, patriae, parentibus, et singulis hominibus diligens officium tribuit: nam qui Deum colit, hoc est, ante omnia toto corde et animo amat, quod est religionis: quique omnem hominem non aliter ac seipsum

[14] [162] diligit, quod est pietatis: hic, iuxta Christum et Paulum, universam Dei legem et iusticiam explet. Quod vir iustus numquam a Deo derelinquetur, plura sunt in sacris scripturis testimonia quam possum recensere, et plura etiam exempla, quam opus fuerit proferre. Nec singularum rerum adversarum exempla persequar,[105] nec quemadmodum Ionas a pisce *[Ionas]*,[106] et pueri a camino ignis liberati fuerant *[Tres pueri in Camino ignis]*:[107] sed tamen unum aut alterum testatius et illustrius exemplum, ubi Deus incredibilem quandam opem iustorum indigentiis attulerit. Quid? Num iustus Elias *[Elias]* cum in torrente Carith magna fame delitesceret a Deo derelictus,[108] cum corvi deferebant ei panem et carnes mane, et similiter panem ac carnes vesperi?[109] Num vidua illa in Sarephtha Sydoneorum *[Vidua in Sarephtha]* in gravissima fame a Deo derelicta est, cuius hydria farinae nunquam defecit, et lecythus olei nunquam imminutus est?[110] An populus Israeliticus *[Populus Israeliticus]*, in nobilissima illa Samaritana fame a Deo derelictus est, cum venundaretur[111] caput asini octoginta argenteis: et quarta pars cabi stercoris columbarum quinque argenteis, cum mulieres

---

[105] *Nec ... persequar*: an example of *praeteritio*, a rhetorical device, whereby a topic can be mentioned in the very denial of its mention.

[106] *Ionas a pisce*: Jonah disobeys God's commandment to go to Ninevah, and is subsequently swallowed by a whale, in the belly of which he remains for three days and nights, only to be freed again once he repents (Jonah, chs 1–2).

[107] *pueri ... fuerant*: Daniel 3.12–30. Three Jewish men (Shadrach, Meshach and Abed-nego) from Babylon, when they failed to observe the form of worship Nebuchadnezzar had

[prove to] be very compatible with Christ's teaching. I won't set out what he says [so much] for that reason, but because truth demands it be so; for this reason, I shall bring it forth into the mix. [Cicero says] he is righteous *[the righteous man]* who worships God with faith and reverence, and who vigilantly and with piety discharges his duty to fatherland, parents and every single man. For the man who worships God, that is, loves him with his whole heart and mind before everything – this is the mark of faith. And the man who loves every man not otherwise than himself –

[14] [162] this is the mark of piety. This man, according to Christ and Paul, accomplishes the universal Law of God and righteousness. As for the fact that the righteous man shall never be forsaken by God, there are more testimonies in the sacred Scriptures than I can number, and still more examples than there is need to set forth. I will not review[105] examples of individual misfortunes, how Jonah was freed from the whale *[Jonah]*,[106] or the boys from the furnace of fire *[three boys in the furnace of fire]*.[107] But [I will] nevertheless [mention] one or two more well-known and remarkable examples when God has offered forth a form of miraculous support to the righteous in need. What [do I mean]? Was Elias, a righteous man *[Elias]*, forsaken by God in great hunger when he took shelter in the Carith stream,[108] insofar as ravens brought him bread and meat in the morning and similarly bread and meat in the evening?[109] And was that widow in Zarephath of the Sidonians *[widow in Zarephath]* forsaken by God in the direst hunger [insofar] as her pot was never short of flour and her flask never without oil?[110] Were the people of Israel *[People of Israel]* forsaken by God in that very well-known famine in Samaria, [at a time] when the head of an ass was sold[111] for 80 pieces of silver, and a quarter part of a corn measure of dove-dung for for five pieces of silver, and when women

---

imposed, were condemned to die and thrown into a fiery furnace. However, they did not die and were left unscathed by the flames.
[108] *iustus ... derelictus*: 1 Kings 17.1–16.
[109] *corvi ... vesperi*: 1 Kings 17.1–6.
[110] *Vidua ... est*: 1 Kings 17.8–16.
[111] *venundaretur*: Sometimes this word appears as two, *venum do, dare*.

[15] [163] [L.ii.] comederent liberos suos:[112] proxima tamen luce, Dei bonitate, tanta omnium copia et frumenti abundantia suppeditaverat, ut modius similae uno siclo, et duo modii hordei uno siclo cuivis volenti venundarentur?[113] Si vero Deus aliquando gravius nos vexaverit, et longiore rerum miseria detinuerit, hoc non ad interitum, ut perdat; sed ad explorationem, ut probet, facit. Ita enim manifestissime loquitur spiritus Domini, Esaiae 54. cum ait *[Esai. 54]*: Ad punctum in modico dereliqui te, at in miserationibus magnis congregabo te. In momento indignationis abscondi faciem meam parumper a te, at in misericordia sempiterna misertus sum tui. Montes enim commovebuntur et colles contremiscent, misericordia autem mea non recedet a te, et foedus pacis meae non movebitur, dixit miserator tuus, et redemptor tuus dominus Deus.[114] Verum, multi pii sanctique viri, non solum rebus ad victum pertinentibus caruerunt, sed dira fame, gravissimo supplicio saepenumero interierunt. Ita est ut dicitur, sed hii minime derelicti videntur esse, qui pro diurno pane aeternum adipiscuntur: pro parva et exigua fame, perennes epulas consequuntur.

[16] [164] Nam qui aurum invenerit, plumbum, quod olim habuit, non amplius quaerendum existimat: cui dies semel illuxerit, candelam ad accendendum non desiderat. Bene hic quidem sitit, qui ita sitit, ut non sitiat in aeternum:[115] bene hic quidem in fame deseritur, ut numquam vel unum pedem a latere Christi discedat[116] in posterum. Si ergo videaris ad tempus in fame, vel ulla alia miseria a Deo relinqui, ne cadas animo, sed audacter confide quod hoc etiam tibi in perpetuum lucrum sit cessurum:[117] dicasque plena spe, et grata animi tui voluntate cum Paulo ad Romanos. 8. *[Rom. 8]* Existimo quod non sunt condignae aut ullo modo aestimandae passiones huius temporis, ad futuram gloriam quae revelabitur in nobis.[118] Iustus nunquam

---

[112] *populus ... suos*: 2 Kings 6.25–33.
[113] *proxima ... venundarentur?*: 2 Kings 7.1.
[114] *Ad ... Deus*: Is. 54.7–8 and 10. This follows V almost word for word.
[115] *sitit, qui ... aeternum*: A nod to John 4.13/14, where Jesus states (as per V) *qui autem biberit ex aqua quam ego dabo ei non sitiet in aeternum* ('Moreover, whoever shall drink of the water which I give him shall not thirst unto eternity'). The last part of John 4.14 is underlined in GNT.
[116] *unum pedem discedere*: I have translated this more colloquially.
[117] *quod ... cessurum*: The use of *quod* plus the subjunctive where we might expect an accusative and infinitive is more common in early modern Latin than in classical, but

[15] [163] [L.ii.] began to eat their own children?[112] Yet on the next day, by the goodness of God, a cornucopia of produce and an abundance of corn were in such full supply that a measure of the finest wheat sold for one shekel, and two measures of barley for one shekel to whoever was willing.[113] What's more, if God has sometimes troubled us more grievously and impeded us with a more prolonged wretchedness in our affairs, he does this not for our destruction that he may ruin us, but for our examination that he may test us. Accordingly, the spirit of the Lord speaks very clearly when in Isaiah 54 *[Isaiah 54]* he speaks thus, 'For a brief moment, I forsook you, but I will join you in great mercies. In a moment of wrath, I put my face out of sight from you for a little while, but with everlasting pity I had mercy on you. For mountains will be moved and hills will shake, but my pity shall not recede from you, and the covenant of my peace will not be moved, said the one who has mercy on you and your redeemer, the Lord God'.[114] In truth, many pious and holy men not only have lacked the necessities for life, but have [also] perished, often in terrible hunger and in the most severe [state of] suffering. Accordingly, as it is said, these men, who obtain eternity in the place of daily bread, seem to be the least forsaken. In return for brief and shortlived famine they attain an eternal banquet.

[16] [164] This is because the man who has found gold no longer considers the lead which he once possessed worth seeking. The man for whom the day has once dawned does not need a candle to light [the way]. This man certainly thirsts well who thirsts in such a way that he does not thirst unto eternity.[115] And this man is certainly well abandoned in hunger that he never leaves Christ's side by so much as an inch[116] for the rest of time. If therefore you seem to be left for some time in hunger or in any other wretched state by God, don't lose spirit, but courageously trust that even this will result in your continual profit.[117] With full hope and the thankful will of your mind, you should say together with Paul [in his epistle] to the Romans 8 *[Romans 8]*, 'I consider that the tribulations of this time are not worthy of or comparable in any way with the future glory that shall be revealed in us'.[118] The righteous

---

even in classical Latin it is possible to find such a formulation following 'verbs of perceiving' such as *credo* etc.

[118] *Existimo ... nobis*: Rom. 8.18. V: *existimo enim quod non sunt condignae passiones huius temporis ad futuram gloriam quae relevabitur in nobis*; *Nov. T*: *nam reputo, non esse pares afflictiones praesentis temporis ad gloriam, quae revelabit erga nos*. E, unlike Asc. and V, removes the *quod* clause and instead deploys an accusative and infinitive. However (here), Asc. may have opted to retain the less classically acceptable *quod* clause as it apes the Greek's λογίζομαι γὰρ ὅτι.... Asc. interestingly also expands the sentiment contained in Rom., adding the rather stylish gerundive *aestimandae*. This was another verse he summarised in the margins of GNT.

derelinquetur a Deo, nec semen eius quaerens panem.[119] Sancti patres, Christianae religionis doctores,[120] de semine varie sed omnes pie sentiunt. Quidam enim pro operibus, quae quis in hac vita committit, intelligunt: quidam pro filiis et posteritate capiunt, nec pro omnibus filiis: nam boni filii sunt ex malis patribus profecti, et mali filii ex bonis parentibus nati: sed pro his tamen qui in vestigiis

[17] [165] [L.iii.] iusti cuiusvis viri (nam is pater est) sedulo et constanter institerint: nam hii sunt (inquit scriptura) veri filii Abrahae, qui fide sunt filii Abrahae:[121] ergo qui moribus iusti imbutus iustam eius vitam fuerit sequutus, hic semen iusti merito dicendus est, etiam si iustus ille, quem imitatus est,[122] nunquam ei fuerat cognitus. Sentit ergo propheta cum dicit, Iustus a Deo nunquam derelinquetur, nec semen eius quaeret panem,[123] quod benedictio bonitasque Dei, in omnem saeculorum memoriam, in generationem et generationem erga iustos, quocumque tempore extiterint, perpetuo transfundetur. Si vero habueris patrem iustum, nec tamen in viis eius ambulaveris, sed ab his longissime deflexeris, non tu iusticiae eius haeres,[124] non immortalis praemii consors atque particeps: nec magis eius filius, quam hii sunt filii Abraham, qui fide non sunt filii Abraham; nec semen benedictionis ad vitam aeternam demetendam, sed herba damnationis apta materies ad succidendam et in ignem proiiciendam eris.[125] Nam si a patris virtute et probitate degeneraveris, non tu ab illo profectus, sed a teipso, quasi iam prognatus esse videris. Teipsum

[18] [166] exhaeredasti:[126] iusti patris nomen, quod ille tibi reliquerat, insolentia obtritum obliterasti: et teipsum ac omnem vitae necisque potestatem in adoptionem Diabolo emancipasti:[127] et sic pro haerede DEI, mancipium Diaboli: pro filio lucis, tenebrarum nepos, gravissimo nexu[128] factus es.

---

[119] *Iustus ... panem*: a restatement of Ps. 36.25 (V/S) / 37.25 (H/P) and the heading of the theme.
[120] *doctores*: Asc. often refers to 'Doctors' as distinct from 'Fathers' though, as was also the case in his *Apol.*, for him there was clearly some overlap between the two.
[121] *hii ... Abrahae*: Gal. 3.7. V: *cognoscite ergo quia qui ex fide sunt, ii sunt filii Abrahae*; Nov. T: *scitis igitur, quod qui ex fide sunt ii sint filii Abraham*.
[122] *imitatus est*: an interesting verb, since *imitatio* ('the process of imitation') was an important concept for Asc. He discusses the practice at length in *Schol.*, and it is clear that for Asc. and others of his circle imitation extended from imitating words to imitating behaviour. Here the notion of *imitatio* is directly stitched into the Christian inheritance.
[123] *Iustus ... panem*: a restatement of Ps. 36.25 (V/S) / 37.25 (H/P).
[124] *haeres*: an alternative form for *heres*.

man will never be forsaken by God, nor his offspring seeking bread.[119] The holy Fathers and Doctors[120] of the Christian religion think differently about 'offspring', but all [of them] piously. Some interpret it as the deeds which someone does in this life. Some construe it as sons and those after them – and not all sons – for good sons have sprung from bad fathers, and bad sons have been born from good parents; rather, as those who

[17] [165] [L.iii.] have followed assiduously and constantly in the footsteps of any righteous man, for that man is their father. Indeed, as Scripture says, 'These men are the true sons of Abraham, who[ever] are the sons of Abraham in faith'.[121] Consequently, the man who is practised in the habits of the righteous man and has followed his righteous life, [it is] he [who] must properly be referred to as 'the offspring of the righteous man', even if that righteous man whom he imitated[122] was never known to him. The prophet evidently thinks this way when he says 'The righteous man will never be forsaken by God nor will his offspring seek bread';[123] [that's] because the blessing and goodness of God will be continually transferred unto every remembrance of the ages, [and] unto generation and generation to the righteous in whatever age they exist. To be sure, if you have a righteous father, yet do not walk in his ways, but veer very far from them, you shall not not be an heir[124] of his righteousness or a partner or participant in his immortal reward. You shall no more be his son than these men are the sons of Abraham, who are not the sons of Abraham in faith. Nor will you be the offspring of a blessing whereby an everlasting life might be reaped, but [rather] a blade of perdition, a material fit for being mown down and thrown into the fire.[125] Indeed, if you depart from the morality and rectitude of your father, you seem not to have sprung from him but as if really descended from yourself.

[18] [166] You have inherited[126] yourself. You have consigned to oblivion the name of your righteous father which he left to you, [now] degraded through disrespect. And you have allowed yourself and all power of life and death to be adopted by the Devil.[127] Thus, instead of being an heir of God, you have become the adoptee of the Devil; and instead of being the son of light, you have become the grandson of darkness with the most burdensome [bonds of] obligation.[128]

---

[125] *herba ... eris*: Asc. may have in mind here verse 2 of Ps. 36 or 37, although he expresses the point very differently to V: *quoniam tamquam faenum velociter arescent et quemadmodum holera herbarum cito decident* ('Since they will quickly wither away like grass and just as the green herbs shall swiftly fall').
[126] *exhaeredasti*: an alternative form for *exhereda(vi)sti*.
[127] *emancipare ... adoptionem*: is a formula used in Cic. *Fin.* 1.7. It denotes a formal adoption whereby one is still under paternal authority (cf. *arrogatio*, which referred to the process for someone already independent). Asc.'s point is that man has in effect been adopted by God the Father.
[128] *nexu*: nexus is coloured in its meaning by *emanicipare* and *mancipium*, and denotes (here) a new form of personal obligation.

Et quod omnia sanguinis gentisque iura, quae cum iusto patre et Christo ante habueras, exuisti, quanquam in alterius nomen totus transiisti docet Paulus, cum dicit: Nulla cognatio DEO cum Diabolo, nulla necessitudo luci cum tenebris.[129]

Docet hoc etiam ipse Naturae ordo, quod iusti seminis nomen perdideris:[130] nam triticum in genere frumentario longe praestantissimum, quemadmodum in libris rerum rusticarum ostendit *[Columella]* Columella,[131] si solo, in quo seminatur, non diligens cultura paterno[132] quodam modo quotannis adhibeatur, triennii spatio, omne tritici nomen deponit, et in siliginis[133] naturam transit atque commutatur.[134] Sin vero a iusticia patris non discesseris, sed in viis

[19] [167] [L.iiii.] eius ambulaveris: si pauperis miserearis, et inopi commodaveris: tum tu semen illius in perpetua Domini benedictione fueris, et sicut pater tuus ut DEUS promittit, terram haereditate[135] capies, et in seculum seculi super eam inhabitabis.[136] Panem quaerere apud Hebraeos et caeteras fere omnes gentes, (ubivis gentium enim hic loquendi modus usurpatus est), pro deseri et derelinqui capitur.[137] Sensus ergo est, quivis in viis iusticiae ambulans, filius pariter atque pater, iuvenis aeque ac senex, privatus perinde ac magistratus, a Deo non derelinquetur: sed quacumque in aetate, quacumque seculorum memoria, iusticia hominum apparuerit, in eadem effusissima DEI bonitas erga nos illuxerit. Hugo Cardinalis[138] hanc

---

[129] *Nulla ... tenebris*: Asc. almost certainly has in mind here part of 2 Corinth. 6.14 that reads (in V): ... *quae enim participatio iustitiae cum iniquitate? aut quae societas luci ad tenebras?* (' ... For what participation has righteousness with injustice? Or what fellowship has light with darkness?').

[130] *Docet...quod ... perdideris*: another *quod* clause where we might expect an accusative and infinitive in classical Latin. There are a number of examples through the rest of the text (sometimes with the subjunctive and sometimes with the indicative).

[131] *in ... Columella*: The Roman author Columella, whose work *De re rustica* in twelve volumes has been completely preserved, and forms our most important source on Roman agriculture.

[132] *paterno quodam modo*: The theme of paternalism is an emphasis Asc. wants to draw out at this point in the theme; there is no such reference in Colum.

[133] *siliginis*: *siligo* is the term Colum. uses for a degenerate form of wheat (see n. 134 below).

[134] *si...commutatur*: Colum. *Rust.* 2.9.13. The relevant passage is: *Nec nos tamquam optabilis agricolis fallat siligo, nam hoc tritici vitium est et, quamvis candore praestet, pondere tamen vincitur. Verum in umido statu caeli recte provenit et ideo locis manantibus magis apta est. Nec tamen ea longe nobis aut magna difficultate requirenda est, nam omne triticum solo*

That you divested yourself of all the rights of blood and family which you had before with a righteous father and with Christ (even though you passed over entirely to the name of another), Paul teaches when he says 'There is no kinship between the God and the Devil; no relationship between light and darkness'.[129]

Even the very order of Nature teaches this, [namely] that you have squandered the name of 'righteous offspring'.[130] For instance, as Columella illustrates in the books of his 'On Rural Affairs' *[Columella]*,[131] by far the most outstanding wheat in the grain family, if careful cultivation of a paternal[132] kind is not applied each year to the soil in which it is sown, sets aside in the space of three years, the very name of 'wheat' and passes over into the nature of 'siligo'[133] and is wholly transformed.[134] But if it's the case that you have not parted from the righteousness of the Father, but

[19] [167] [L.iiii.] you walked in his ways; if you feel compassion for the poor and have given to the needy, then you will be his offspring in the continuous blessing of the Lord, and just as God – your father, as it were – promises, you will inherit[135] the earth, and you will dwell therein for evermore.[136] Among Hebrew speakers and almost all other peoples, [the phrase] 'to seek bread' is construed as 'to be abandoned' and 'to be forsaken';[137] indeed, this form of expression is used everywhere in the world. And so, the sense is [that] whoever walks in the ways of righteousness, son as well as father, young man and old man alike, private citizen and magistrate equally, he will not be forsaken by God. But [rather] in whatever epoch and as we call to mind any age whatsoever, the righteousness of men has been visible, and in it the most liberal goodness of God has shone towards us. Cardinal Hugo[138] twists

---

uliginoso post tertiam sationem convertitur in siliginem. ('And let us not be misled into thinking that siligo is desirable for farmers; for this is a degenerate kind of wheat, and though superior in whiteness, it is inferior in weight. It does well, however, in a humid climate, and for that reason is better suited to springy places. Still, we need not go a great distance or to great pains to find it; for in wet ground every kind of wheat turns into siligo after the third sowing.' (*LCL*, trans. H. B. Ash, 1941). Ascham uses the same allusion in *Tox.*, Giles, vol. II, 85.

[135] *hareditate*: an alternative form for *hereditate*.

[136] *terram . . . inhabitabis*: drawing on Ps. 36 (V/S) / 37 (H/P) again, here verse 29. V (36.29): *iusti autem hereditabunt terram et inhabitabunt in saeculum saeculi super eam.*

[137] *Panem . . . capitur*: The Hebrew for 'seeking bread' is מְבַקֶּשׁ־לָחֶם, although Asc. does not cite the original Hebrew. This section offers a flavour of Asc.'s broader interest in the history of particular terminology.

[138] *Hugo Cardinalis*: Hugo (or Hugh) of Saint-Cher, often referred to in Latin as 'Hugo Cardinalis' or 'Hugo de Sancto Charo', was a French biblical commentator and papal cardinal of the thirteenth century.

sententiam in alium sensum, et suo iudicio longe tutissimum, nec meo profecto absurdissimum, omnibus tamen Ecclesiae Doctoribus, quos ego vidi, repugnans, et fere inauditum contorquet. Iustus (inquit) a Deo non derelinquetur, nec semen eius, modo quaerat a Deo panem,[139] hoc est, omnem vivendi curam in illum iactaverit: saturat enim catulos [168] leonum, multo magis nos, qui escam a Deo quaerunt. Ergo, quid iustus, quid derelinqui, quid semen, ex sacra scriptura Ecclesiaeque Doctoribus satis liquere et manifestum esse puto.

---

[139] *Iustus ... panem*: Hugo's commentary on Ps. 36 included in *In Psalterium universum Davidis Regis et Prophetae* (Venice, 1703). Asc. must be referring to Hugo's qualification: sic: *nec semen eius quarens panem, id est, principaliter intendens corporalibus, quia si hoc facit aliquis, non est iustus* ('Thus: not meaning his offspring seeking bread, that is chiefly concerned with matters of the flesh, because if someone does this, he is not righteous') (96).

this sentiment into another sense, in his opinion, by far the most sound [sense], and in mine, certainly not so absurd, nevertheless, [one] that is resisted by all the Doctors of the Church that I have seen, and is practically unheard of. He says [that] the righteous man will not be forsaken by God, nor [will] his offspring, provided that he seeks bread from God,[139] that is, [that] he has devoted every concern of life towards this; this is because, [even as] he (i.e. God) sates the whelps [168] of lions, by [how] much more us who seek food from God. To conclude, I think what 'the righteous man' is, what 'to be forsaken' is, what 'the offspring' is, are [all] evident and sufficiently established from sacred Scripture and from the Doctors of the Church.

Theme 3
(20-25)

This piece bears the hallmarks of a dispuational speech, although it is not entirely clear what the original *quaestio* was. The heading of the theme (an Old Testament verse from Ezekiel) seems to constitute the cornerstone of Ascham's argument rather than serving as a debating motion. The guiding principles of this theme are in close alignment with theme 2 and it may belong to a similar (late 1530s) timeframe. Just as in theme 2, where Ascham seemed to grant each individual a degree of agency in determining the extent to which s/he is or is not righteous, suggesting this would vary from generation to generation, so in this theme Ascham contends that each person is individually responsible for their own sin, insisting that sin cannot be passed through a patrilineal line.

It is again noteworthy that this piece pivots on a theological issue – sin – which Luther's campaign had rendered a priority. It is possible to infer that Ascham's opponent/s in the disputation were mounting a case for the ineradicable persistence of sin via Adam: Ascham wrote below, 'But if anyone presses [the point] and insists that we all bear the sinfulness of our father Adam ...' (23). As regards original sin, Ascham does not deny it exists – he refers to a founding sin, which, via Adam's own sin, 'entered into the world, and was passed down to all men' (23). However, Ascham, citing Paul in support, insists that the damnation caused by this sin is cancelled out by the justification offered by Christ. In this way, Ascham alludes again to the tension between *condemnatio* and *iustitia* that forms the fulcrum of the first theme.

In doctrinal terms, at least, Ascham appears to be marshalling a more 'conservative' argument in this theme than his opponent/s. Further indication of this is that he draws on Jerome rather than Augustine to support his suit. Ascham adduces Jerome's commentary on Ezekiel to the effect that sons are not punished in the third and fourth generations because their fathers transgressed; Ascham even alludes to a suggestion in Jerome that God looks positively on sinners (21). This has quite a different feel to the anti-Pelagian stance espoused by Augustine, which dwells on concupiscence of the flesh of every person descended from Adam and Eve.

On the other hand, Ascham's argument can be viewed as rather radical in its biblicism. Ascham stringently probes the wording of Ezekiel and other parts of the Old Testament for insights into the issue of inter-generational transmission of sin. To the extent that Ascham is following Ezekiel 18, his argumentation is entirely logical. Ezekiel 18 expressly states that 'the son will not carry the sinfulness of the father', and it might not have especially concerned Ascham that the contents of the chapter pertained to a general practice in Israel (and elsewhere) of punishing children for *specific things* their parents did rather than any concept of original sin. Furthermore, the instruction provided in this chapter of Ezekiel concerning individual responsibility is, in one form or another, often repeated throughout this Old Testament book. Biblical citations undergird Ascham's case throughout.

[20] [168] Filius non portabit iniquitatem patris. Ezech. 18.[140]

Dominus Deus miseriator et misericors, patiens, et multae misericordiae Deus, nihil unquam fere vel iustis et piis, ad summam laetitiam exoptatius: vel iniustis et perditis, ad omnem doloris acerbitatem gravius: *[Ezechi. 18]* per os Prophetarum eloquutus est, quam cum dicit, Anima quae fecerit iusticiam, in iusticia sua, vita vivet: et anima quae peccavit, ipsa morietur.[141] Neque enim inquit Dominus, pater portabit inquitatem filii, nec filius iniquitatem patris. Praeterea, proverbium illud in terra Israel multum iactatum, (nempe, Patres comederunt uvam acerbam, et dentes filiorum obstupuerunt),[142] quasi falsum, et e vulgi opinione profectum, per os Ezechielis Prophetae ipse refutat Deus. Vivo ego, dicit Dominus,

[21] [169] [L.v.] si erit vobis ultra parabola haec in proverbium in Israel. Ecce omnes animae, meae sunt: ut anima patris, ita et anima filii, mea est: anima quae peccaverit, ipsa morietur.[143] Neque obiiciamus Mosen Prophetae, vel Deum potius Deo, qui ita in Exodi capite vicessimo loquitur: *[Exod. 20]* Ego sum Dominus Deus tuus, Deus aemulator, qui reddo peccata patrum super filios, usque ad tertiam et quartam generationem.[144] Verba quae sequuntur, et hanc gravem comminationem levant, et sententiae, si quae sit, dubitationem explicant: addit enim Dominus, His (inquam) qui me oderunt.[145] Nam, quemadmodum ait Hieronymus, non ideo puniuntur filii in tertia et quarta generatione, quia patres eorum deliquerunt, cum patres, qui peccatores erant, puniri debuerint: sed quia patrum aemulatores extiterunt, et haereditaria[146] quadam pravitate Deum, sicut patres, oderunt.[147] Alium sensum magis latentem et abditum, in quo tamen mirifice patientia et longanimitas Dei erga peccatores elucescit, ostendit Hieronymus. Ait enim primam *[Hieronymus.]* peccandi cogitationem, qua peccatum

---

[140] *Filius ... patris*: The heading of the theme comprises part of Ez. 18.20. The wording follows V.
[141] *Anima ... morietur*: The wording matches V, and comprises a refrain that runs through Ez. 18 (from verse 4), one repeated throughout this theme too.
[142] *Patres ... obstupuerunt*: Ez. 18.2. (The phrase also appears in Jeremiah 31.29). *obstupuerunt* is an alternative form for *obstipuerunt* (from *obstipesco*), though V has the present tense *obstupescunt*.
[143] *Vivo ... morietur*: Ez. 18.3–4, where the maxim directly above is denied. V also utilises this wording, though it has *Deus* after *Dominus*. (As an aside, *si* is too awkward to reflect in the English). Asc. relies on Ez. as means to show that people cannot shirk responsibility for their own guilt. The maxim is similarly undermined in Jeremiah and verse 31.30 reads 'everyone shall die for his own iniquity'.
[144] *Ego ... generationem*: Ex. 20.5. Asc. diverges slightly from V: *Ego sum Dominus Deus tuus fortis, zelotes, visitans iniquitatem patrum in filios in tertiam et quartam generationem ....* Asc.'s wording in fact reads more like a very similar verse in Deut. 5.9: *enim sum Dominus*

[20] [168] The son will not carry the sinfulness of the father. Ezekiel 18.[140]

The Lord God has pity and is merciful; he forbears, and is the God of great mercy. Scarcely ever has he (i.e. God) spoken forth anything more welcome for the ultimate happiness of righteous and pious men, or more serious for every affliction of pain for unrighteous and corrupt men than when, through the mouth of the Prophets, he says *[Ezekiel 18]* 'The soul which has acted righteously shall live with life in its own righteousness; but the soul which has sinned shall itself die'.[141] To be sure, the Lord does not say [that] the father will bear the sinfulness of the son, or [that] the son will bear the sinfulness of the father. Besides, that maxim, 'Forsooth, the fathers have eaten sour grapes and the sons' teeth have been set on edge',[142] that circulated widely in the land of Israel, God himself refutes through the mouth of the Prophet Ezekiel as though it were false and originating from popular prejudice: 'As I live', says the Lord,

[21] [169] [L.v.] 'this saying shall be no more for you a proverb in Israel. Behold, all souls are mine; as the soul of the father, so too is the soul of the son mine. The soul which has sinned shall itself die'.[143] And we should not set Moses against the Prophet or rather God against God, who speaks as follows in the twentieth chapter of Exodus *[Exodus 20]*, 'I am the Lord, your God, a jealous God, returning the sins of fathers upon their sons into the third and fourth generations'.[144] The words that follow both leaven this heavy threat and explain any uncertainty implicit in the pronouncement, as the Lord adds, 'for these, I say, who hate me'.[145] Indeed, just as Jerome says, sons are not punished in the third and fourth generations because their fathers transgressed – it is the case that the fathers who were sinners should have been punished – but because they they followed the example of their fathers and, just like their fathers, hate God with some inherited[146] ungodliness.[147] Jerome points to another more recondite and obscure meaning, whereby the forbearance and patience of God nevertheless shines forth in wondrous ways towards sinners. For he *[Jerome]* says that the initial inclination to sin, via which

---

Deus tuus Deus aemulator reddens iniquitatem patrum super filios in tertiam et quartam generationem. . . . It is noticeable that Asc. has employed *peccatum* in place of *iniquitas*, a term more in keeping with the point at issue.

[145] *His . . . oderunt*: These are the final words of Ex. 20.5. V: . . . *eorum qui oderunt me*. This version again seems to follow Deut. 5.9: . . . *his qui oderunt me*.

[146] *haereditaria*: an alternative form for *hereditaria*.

[147] *Hieronymus . . . oderunt*: Jer. *Commentariorum in Ezechielem libri*, 6.xviii: *non enim ideo puniuntur in tertia et quarta generatione, quia deliquerunt patres eorum, cum patres potius qui fuerunt peccatores puniri debuerint; sed quia patrum exstiterunt aemulatores, et oderunt Deum, haereditario malo et impietate in ramos quoque de radice crescente* (PL 25, col. 168). ('Accordingly, indeed, they (i.e. sons) are not punished into the third and fourth generation because their fathers transgressed – since their fathers who were in fact sinners deserved to be punished – but because they were imitators of their fathers and hated God via an inherited evil and wickedness that also grew into branches from the root').

[22] [170] cepimus, quasi patrem esse: at si quod concepimus,[148] opere perfici, et quasi crescere permittamus, filium vocat: et hos primos ac secundos peccandi stimulos, dicit Graecos προπαθείας vocare, sine quibus, ut nullus homo esse possit, ita eas[149] raro Deus aut numquam punit. Sin peccatum adoleverit, nepotem: si vero insoluerit,[150] et in malitia gloriatus fuerit, Deumque contempserit, (scriptum est enim, Impius, cum in profundum malorum venerit contemnit),[151] tum pronepotem dici: et hanc peccandi quasi familiam a patre in filium, a filio in generationem et generationem, Deus (ut pars est) gravissimis constringit suppliciis.[152]

Non igitur est haec sententia capienda, quasi peccatum unius alterum condemnabit, sed unusquisque pro suo, et non pro alieno peccato luet, iuxta legis sententiam, Deuteronomii 24 *[Deuteron. 24]*. Non morientur patres pro filiis, et filii non morientur pro patribus.[153] Et huic legi testimonium *[Amasia rex Iuda.]* abhibuit facto suo Amasia Rex Iuda, 2. Reg. 14. qui servos suos Ioas Regis patris sui interfectores percussit, filios autem

[23] [171] percussorum non occidit.[154] Sed dicitis, inquit Deus, Ezech. 18., Quare non portabit filius iniquitatem patris? Videlicet, respondit Dominus, Quia filius iudicium et iusticiam operatur, omnia praecepta mea custodit et facit illa, vivet vita: et anima, quae peccaverit, ipsa morietur.[155]

---

[148] *quod concepimus*: viz. the sin.
[149] *eas*: is in agreement with the feminine form of the Greek προπαθείας rather than *stimulos*.
[150] *insoluerit*: This is the (assumed) future perfect from *insolesco*, a verb which in classical Latin has no perfect form.
[151] *Impius . . . contemnit*: Prov. 18.3. V has identical wording, except *malorum* for *peccatorum*.
[152] *ostendit . . . suppliciis*: Jer. Commentariorum in Ezechielem libri, 6.viii : sunt qui ... ita edisserant, ut ad animam humanam sententiam referant, patrem in nobis, levem punctum sensuum, et incentiva vitiorum esse dicentes; filium vero, si cogitatio peccatum conceperit; nepotes si quod cogitaveris atque conceperis, opere perpetraveris; pronepotem autem, hoc est, quartam generationem, si non solum feceris quod malum est et scelestum, sed in tuis sceleribus glorieris secundum illud quod scriptum est impius cum in profundum malorum venerit, contemnit. Deus igitur primos et secundos stimulos cogitationum, quas Graeci προπαθείας vocant, sine quibus nullus hominum esse potest nequaquam punit; sed si cogitata quis facere decreverit, aut ipsa quae fecerit, noluerit corrigere poenitentia (PL 25, cols 168–69). ("There are some who . . . interpret it in such a way that they attribute the pronouncement to a kindly spirit, saying that the light prick of our [moral] sense and incentives to wrong are the "father" in us; but the "son" if deliberation conceives of the sin; "grandsons" if you what you have deliberated and conceived of you put into practice; moreover a great-grandson, that is,

[22] [170] we conceived of the sin, is, as it were, 'the father'. But if we allow what we have conceived of[148] to be brought to fulfilment in deed, and, as it were, to grow, he calls [that] 'the son'. And these first and second spurs for sinning he suggests that the Greeks call 'the early symptoms of a disease'; and just as no human can be without these, so God rarely or never punishes them.[149] But if the sin comes to maturity, [this is] 'a grandson'. Assuredly, if he [then] grows arrogant[150] and exults in his wickedness, and is contemptuous of God, for it is written 'The impious man, when he has reached the depth of evils, is contemptuous',[151] then, he is said to be 'a great-grandson'. And God, as is his business, binds together this 'family of sinning', as it were, from father unto son, from son unto generation and generation, with the most severe punishments.[152]

Accordingly, this pronoucement must not be conceived of as though the sin of one man will condemn another, but [as if] each man, in accordance with the pronouncement of the Law in Deuteronomy 24 *[Deuteronomy 24]*, will pay for his own sin, not for another's. The fathers will not die for the children, nor will the children die for their fathers.[153] And to this law, Amaziah, the King of Judah *[Amaziah, king of Judah]*, added [further] testimony through his own actions in 2 Kings [chapter] 14. He slew his servants, murderers of his own father, King Joash, and yet

[23] [171] he refrained from killing the sons of the assassins.[154] But God says in Ezekiel 18, 'You ask why the son does not bear the sinfulness of his father?' The Lord responds plainly, 'Because the son acts with judgement and righteousness. He keeps all my commands and executes them, and he will live with life; and the soul which has sinned shall itself die'.[155]

---

the fourth generation, if you not only carry out what is evil and wicked, but you [also] exult in your crimes along the lines of that dictum "An impious is contemptuous when he has plumbed the depths of evil". And so, God in no way punishes the first and second spurs of deliberation, which the Greek call "the early symptoms of a disease", without which no mortal can be; but if someone has determined to carry out what has been deliberated or actually carries them out, he is unwilling to restore them through penance'). Asc. adheres closely to the argument of Jer., but his precise wording is quite different.

[153] *Non ... patribus*: Deut. 24.16. V: *non occidentur patres pro filiis nec filii pro patribus*. Asc. follows Pag. (though not the re-numbering of the verse). Such a sentiment is found also in 2 Kings 14.6, which will be cited next, namely: *non morientur patres pro filiis neque filii morientur pro patribus sed unusquisque in peccato suo morietur* ('The fathers will not die for the sons, nor will the sons die for the fathers, but each man will die for his own sin').

[154] *Amasia ... occidit*: The episode is recounted in 2 Kings 14.5–6. I have changed to '2' the reference in the printed copy to '4' before '*Reg*', which is clearly wrong.

[155] *Quare ... morietur*: Ez. 18.19–20. Asc. cleaves closely to V: *et dicitis quare non portavit filius iniquitatem patris videlicet quia filius iudicium et iustitiam operatus est omnia praecepta mea custodivit et fecit illa vita vivet; anima quae peccaverit ipsa morietur*.

Si quis vero instabit, et urgebit, quod nos omnes patris nostri Adami iniquitatem portamus: sic responsum ferat,[156] bifariam dici Adami peccatum: alterum, quo ille peccavit contra DEUM, pro quo ille solus luisset, iuxta Scripturam: Anima quae peccavit ipsa morietur:[157] sed paenitentiam egit, et non mortuus est, iuxta Scripturam: Si impius egerit paenitentiam, et omnia praecepta mea custodierit, vita vivet et non morietur.[158] Alterum originale vocatur, quod per prioris maximeque proprii Adami peccati designationem, in mundum introiit, et in omnes homines propagatum est: quod peccatum, neque Iudaeis qui in Christum venturum crediderunt: neque nobis, qui in Christum mortuum credimus, ad ullam condemnationem propagatum est.

[24] [172] Dicit enim Paulus, Sicut per unius delictum propagatum est malum in omnes homines, ad condemnationem: ita per unius iustificationem, propagatur bonum ad omnes homines ad iustificationem.[159] Et alio in loco: Nulla est condemnatio hiis qui insiti sunt in Christo Iesu, modo non secundum carnem, sed secundum spiritum ambulaverint.[160] Ethnicis vero et infidelibus ad condemnationem, nisi resipuerint:[161] neque id quidem, quia alterius peccatum portant, sed suum, suumque, et proprium iuste vocandum peccatum, quibus iam vel hodie natis adhaerescit mala ad peccatum propensio, tenebrae, ignoratio Dei, quibuscum vitiis nulla omnino Deo est societas. Sed totum hoc negotium, quasi sublimioris intelligentiae, inscrutabili Dei iudicio committamus: et nostram conclusionem, de actuali et voluntario peccato, cum Domino Deo et tota Scriptura ac Doctoribus intelligamus. Sed quid dicemus de iustis, qui propter scelera malorum gravia patiuntur supplicia, quemadmodum inter Sodomitas, pueri et innocentes:[162] et propter peccatum David, multa millia pereuntes?[163]

---

[156] *ferre + responsum*: has a specific meaning, 'to receive / accept a response'.
[157] *Anima... morietur*: Ez. 18.20 again.
[158] *Si... morietur*: Ez. 18.21. Asc. provides a slightly terser version of the verse, but his vocabulary tallies with V.
[159] *Sicut... iustificationem*: Rom. 5.18. Asc. diverges from V: *igitur sicut per unius delictum in omnes homines in condemnationem sic et per unius iustitiam in omnes homines in iustificationem vitae* ('Therefore, just as through the offence of one unto all men to damnation, thus too through the the the righteousness of one, unto all men to justification of life'). He is much closer to *Nov. T*: *itaque sicut per unius delictum propagatum est malum in omnes homines ad condemnationem, ita et per unius iustificationem, propagatur bonum in omnes homines ad iustificationem vitae*. Both V and *Nov. T* are closer to the Greek's εἰς δικαίωσιν ζωῆς at the end of the verse; Asc. does not include *vitae*, but it is possible that he was striving instead for a symmetry in his Latin with his parallel *ad condemnationem... ad iustificationem*. In GNT he has highlighted the Greek words for justification, δικαιώματος and δικαίωσιν.
[160] *Nulla... ambulaverint*: Rom. 8.1. Asc. diverges from V: *nihil ergo nunc damnationis est iis qui sunt in Christo Iesu qui non secundum carnem ambulant*, but is a little closer to *Nov. T*: *nulla*

But if anyone presses [the point] and insists that we all bear the sinfulness of our father Adam, let him accept the following response,[156] that Adam's sin is said to be twofold. On the one hand, he sinned against God for which he alone paid for, as Scripture [says]: 'The soul which sinned will itself die'.[157] But he repented and did not die, as Scripture [says]: 'If the wicked man repents and keeps all my commands, he will live with life and will not die'.[158] The other [form of sin] is called 'original' which, through the perpetration of the first sin, especially Adam's own sin, entered into the world, and was passed down to all men. But this sin has not been passed down for the damnation either of the Jews, who believed in Christ's coming, or to us, who believe in the dead Christ.

[24] [172] Indeed, Paul says 'Just as through the transgression of one man, evil is passed unto all men for their damnation, so through the justification of one man, good is passed unto all men for their justification'.[159] And elsewhere [we read], 'There is no damnation for those who have been grafted in Jesus Christ, provided they have not walked in the flesh but in the spirit'.[160] However, damnation awaits heathens and infidels unless they return to understanding.[161] Indeed, that's not the case because they bear the sin of another, but their own, and it must rightly be called their own native sin; assuredly, for those (i.e. heathens and infidels) already born today, an evil inclination to sin sticks fast, [together with] darkness and an ignorance of God, wrongs which permit no union at all with God. But we should entrust this entire matter to the unfathomable judgement of God, to the wisdom of one on a higher plane, as it were. Moreover, we should comprehend our conclusion about actual and willed sin [along] with the Lord God, the whole of Scripture and the Doctors. Yet what will we say about the righteous who, on account of the crimes of the degenerate, endure severe punishments, as did children and the guiltless in the community of the Sodomites,[162] and [those who] on account of David's sin, perish with many thousands [of punishments]?[163]

---

igitur nunc est condemnatio, his qui insiti sunt Christo Iesu, qui non iuxta carnem versant, sed iuxta spiritum. Both E and Asc. reflect more faithfully the repetition of κατά in the Greek (κατὰ σάρκα ... κατὰ πνεῦμα), but Asc. is quite non-conformist in his use of a proviso rather than a relative clause/s in the Latin. In GNT, Asc. repeats οὐδὲν ἄρα νῦν κατάκριμα τοῖς ἐν χριστῷ ('Now there is no condemnation for those in Christ') in the margin next to this verse.

[161] *resipuerint*: A core meaning of *resipio* is 'have a good flavour', but I have translated the verb as 'return to understanding', a valid meaning of the verb *sapio* of which it is a compound form.

[162] *inter ... innocentes*: For a description of the guiltless dwelling in Sodom and Gomorrah and its subsequent destruction by God, see Gen. 18.20–33 and 19.

[163] *propter ... pereuntes*: The deaths brought about by David's sin are treated in several books of the OT, but Asc. may have in mind here 1 Chronicles 21.14, which refers to the deaths of seventy thousand Israelites through plague as a result of David's sin. *pereo* is an intransitive verb, and *multa millia* [sic], which picks up the earlier *supplicia*, is acting as an accusative of respect.

[25] [173] Huius rei facilis admodum et expedita est explicatio: nam si boni cum impiis puniuntur temporaliter, non malorum peccata luunt, sed acerba ferendo, vitam consequuntur aeternaliter. Supplicia enim, ut sunt malis propter peccatum ad damnationem obiecta: ita supplicia sunt bonis propter patientiam, ad coronam et iusificationem proposita. Ergo, anima quae peccaverit, ipsa morietur: et filius non portabit iniquitatem patris, neque pater filii: sed iusticia iusti semper super eum erit, et impietas impii semper super eum erit:[164] quemadmodum ait Dominus Deus, cui laus et gloria in omne aevum. Amen.

---

[164] *Ergo . . . erit*: Ez. 18.20 again.

[25] [173] An explanation of this matter is quite straightforward and easily supplied. If the good are for a time punished together with the wicked, it's not that they pay for the sins of the degenerate, but [rather], by bearing what is bitter, they attain life eternally. For punishments, just as they are cast in the way of the degenerate for their damnation because of their sin, so [those same] torments are laid before for good men for their crown and justification because of their endurance [of them]. And so, the soul which has sinned will itself die, and the son will not bear the sinfulness of the father, and the father will not bear that of the son. Instead, the righteousness of the righteous man will always be upon him, and the wickedness of the wicked man always upon him,[164] as the Lord God says, for whom (there is) praise and glory unto every age. Amen.

Theme 4
(26–42)

This is by far the longest theme, just over 16 pages in length. Its contents indicate that Ascham composed this piece pursuant to a disputation. The actual wording of the original *quaestio* is not altogether clear. An Augustinian proposition forms the heading of the theme ('Fault lies not in the action, but in the way [it is done]'), though this reference to Augustine seems to relate rather more to the line of argument Ascham himself marshals. Ascham follows closely Augustine's argumentation as set out in book 3 of his *De doctrina Christiana*. It is possible that the original provocation is in fact to be found in the main body of the text (29), namely 'Whether an action [when it is] something simple and without specification of attendant circumstances is a sin or not?' as this would seem to comprise a more standard disputational stimulus. On the other hand, this might also have constituted an attempt by Ascham simply to reformulate the terms of the debate, not least because his opponents (judging by what he writes on 28–29) had been more inclusive in what they deemed to be 'circumscribed' actions.

More obvious are the terms on which Ascham wants the disputation to operate: he is clear about the distinction between (a) a general, unrestricted action which is neither good or bad and (b) a specific, restricted action which is necessarily good or bad. Ascham is also adamant that the concept of the *modus*, the 'way' in which an action is performed, is critical, and that it is only this that determines whether it is good or bad. He makes it clear that 'concerning the nature of sin, we are not now discussing whether it exists, what it is, or what quality it has, because we are not at at all at variance between ourselves on that score, but only *why* a particular action constitutes a sin or is not a sin' (29). In turn, he stresses that what determines the nature of the 'way' is faith: an action is good if it is in conformity with faith; and bad if it contravenes faith. However, Ascham is also open to viewing certain actions as 'indifferent' (*adiaphora*) rather than straightforwardly good or bad.

The ostensible emphasis on sin in the disputation is noteworthy, and may reflect the degree to which Lutheran ideas were by this time driving the theological agenda in Cambridge. In some ways, the piece slots more easily than others into a Reformation framework, and the anti-papal vitriol, plus the common evangelical charge of 'blind custom' (40) used against Catholics, are flagrantly on display. Complicating this, however, is the way that Ascham broadens the focus of the debate to consider virtuous action or 'good deeds' as well as bad, and Ascham presents himself as a reformer who continues to be preoccupied with moral conduct. That said, even as Ascham posits that deeds may be good, he in no way suggests that good deeds actively play a role in an individual's salvation or that they are effected by humans through their own agency, and his overarching message is entirely compatible with a Protestant view of God's ultimate control and man's helplessness.

The weight placed on Scripture again aligns closely with a Lutheran position. Ascham is adamant that biblical examples will render any case watertight (or, in Ascham's words, 'conclusive and incontrovertible', 31). At the same time, Ascham may again be following Augustine who in book 3 of his *De doctrina Christiana* argues that the primary way to resolve ambiguity in Scripture is to consult the 'rule of faith' (*regula fidei*).[165] In addition to citing Augustine (and in some places deploying his vocabulary), Ascham also adhered to the general contours of his argumentation in book 3: like Augustine, Ascham underscored the importance of examining an action in terms of its precise circumstances; he also provides examples of actions from the Old Testament which confound our expectations, and have to be understood as peculiar to the times. Although Ascham is clearly guided in many points by Augustine's *De doctrina Christiana*, he nonetheless underpins and elaborates his suit using various pagan writers, whose status next to Scripture he also addresses: '[Those who had] no concrete and manifest image of the true Law and genuine justification, but relied on semblance and approximations, were to arrive more closely at a comprehension of the truth than we ...' (36).

Classical concepts in fact underpin Ascham's argument at key points. For example, the Greek distinction (one also discussed by Cicero and Quintilian) used in rhetorical practice between 'thesis' and 'hypothesis' that he alludes to on 27 seems to direct his analysis of an 'action' as 'unlimited' or 'limited'. The classical authors (Horace, Xenophon and Cicero) are also harnessed as a means to illustrate a positive code of ethics. Ancients further attest to the all-important 'middle' way, which for Ascham constitutes a life in Christ and an adherence to God's Word. This theme demonstrates well the constructive symbiosis that might exist between the classical canon and Christianity, and even the degree to which the ideas of the pagans might positively kindle religious devotion.

---

[165] Augus. *De doct. Chr.* 3.2.2–3 (*PL* 34, cols 65–66). For Augus. this means the faith as transmitted through Church doctrine, notably via the creed, not personal faith.

[26] [173] Non factum sed modus[166] in culpa est. Augustinus, de doctrina Christiana. 3.12.[167]

Quid factum, quid modus sit, inprimis a nobis diligenter est perscrutandum. Nam verborum, si ambigua sunt, distinctio:[168] sin obscura, explanatio omnem orationem tenebris involutam, qualis haec esse videatur, in lucem evocare solet. Et cum Christiana [174] religio, ipsa lux et veritas sit, nec ullas ex sua natura discrepantes opiniones, nisi primo aliquo aspectu aut hominum culpa admittat, (plus enim una sententia vera in scripturis esse non potest) propterea meas proprias rationes fluctuare non permittam, sed sic oratio nostra solum verbo Dei provehetur,[169] ut eius authoritate,[170] quasi velis quibusdam, gubernata esse videatur.[171] At vero si aliquid a me sive perperam arcessitum, sive non recte intellectum fuerit, non opinioni pravae, quod sic sentiam: sed mediocri meae eruditioni, quod non melius intelligam, hoc a vobis tribui cupio.[172] Non enim ad aliquid statuendum, quod est authoritatis: sed ad aliquid discendum, quod est meae institutionis,[173] ad hanc disputationem accedo. Nam si in errorem aliquem, quod homines solent, incidam, non eum certe acriter, quod pravi consuescunt, defendam: et quantumcunque fuerit ullus error mihi praeceps atque lubricus[174] ad prolapsionem et casum, tantum sane erit voluntas et animus meus paratus ad veritatem, certumque amplectendum sensum: et ad hunc modum caussam meam communitam

---

[166] *modus*: I have translated *modus* as 'way'. However, it is a far from straightforward term to render, as it is a word of several valences, many of which Asc. also applies through the rest of the tract.
[167] *Non ... Christiana*: The wording quoted in the heading of this theme is inspired by, but does not quite match, Augus. *De doct. Chr.* 3.12.18: *In omnibus enim talibus non usus rerum, sed libido utentis in culpa est* (PL 34, col. 73) ('In all such matters what is reprehensible is not the use made of things but the user's desire'); and 3.12.19, *Nam in omnibus huiuscemodi rebus non ex earum rerum natura quibus utimur sed ex causa utendi et modo appetendi vel probandum est vel improbandum quod facimus* (PL 34, col. 73) ('In all matters of this kind actions are made acceptable or unacceptable not by the particular things we make use of, but by our motives for using them and our methods of seeking them'). Translations here and elsewhere of this work are from Green 1996.
[168] *Nam ... distinctio*: The Latin is rather laconic at this point, but Asc. seems to be taking his cue from Augus. Resolution of verbal ambiguities is very much a focus of Augus. *De Doct. Chr.* 3.12.19, where the interpretation of ambiguous signs, particularly those in Scripture, is discussed. Augus. also establishes some rules for differentiating particular words and deeds, stating, *Quid igitur locis et temporibus personisque conveniat, diligenter attendendum est, ne temere flagitia rephrehendamus* (PL 34, col. 73), ('We must pay

[26] [173] 'Fault lies not in the action, but in the way[166] [it is done]'. Augustine in *On Christian Doctrine* 3.12.[167]

We must, from the outset, carefully examine what the action is and what the way [in which it is done] is. If [the meaning] of words is ambiguous, [clarity is found] by distinguishing [between the various meanings],[168] but if obscure, an explanation can shed light on every discourse that is mired in darkness, such as this seems to be. But since the Christian [174] religion is the light and truth itself, and through its own nature admits no divergent opinions, except at first sight or through man's fault – for Scripture does not admit more than one true meaning – for that reason, I will not allow my own arguments to waver, but my speech will proceed[169] only through the Word of God, and in such a way that it seems to have been steered by its authority,[170] on particular sails, as it were.[171] And of course, if I have adduced anything wrongly or have understood anything incorrectly, I insist that you attribute this not to [any] ungodly belief that I hereby habour, but [rather] to an inadequacy of learning on my part and my own lack of understanding.[172] For I come to this disputation not in order to establish anything by virtue of my own status, but in order to learn something pursuant to my own academic cursus.[173] For if I commit some error, as men are accustomed to do, I will definitely not [attempt to] fiercely defend it, as faithless men habitually do. And to the extent that any error on my part seems rash and and reckless[174] [and headed] for a misstep and a fall, I shall be all the more inclined [both] in will and mind to embrace the truth and the proven meaning. Indeed, in this way I want my case to be

---

careful attention to the conduct appropriate to different places, times, and persons, in case we make rash imputations of wickedness').

[169] *provehetur*: the verb *proveho* is being used in the middle sense.

[170] *authoritate*: an alternative form for *auctoritate*.

[171] *plus . . . videatur*: A nod to a subscription to a *sola scriptura* position, but one that is also in conformity with Augus. *De Doct. Chr.* 3.28.39: *per Scripturas enim divinas multo tutius ambulatur; quas verbis translatis opacatas cum scrutari volumus, aut hoc inde exeat quod non habeat controversiam; aut, si habet, ex eadem Scriptura ubicumque inventis atque adhibitis testibus terminetur* (PL 34, col. 80). ('. . .it is much safer to operate within the divine Scriptures. When we wish to examine passages obscured by metaphorical expressions, the result should be something which is beyond dispute or which, if not beyond dispute, can be settled by finding and deploying corroboratory evidence from within Scripture itself)'.

[172] *sed . . . cupio*: a topos of modesty, commonly found in the rhetorical pieces of the time.

[173] *institutionis*: In classical Latin the meaning of *institutio* is more commonly 'education', but later Latin also uses the word to refer to an 'institution', and Asc. probably means here something along the lines of 'by virtue of his progress at the University'.

[174] *praeceps atque lubricus*: Asc. used these exact adjectives in the first theme (1) to describe Adam and the fall and see also n. 12.

[27] [175] esse volo, propter[175] eos, qui nimium in alienas res inquirere solent. Sed iam ad id quod instituebamus. Factum voco quicquid facimus *[Factum quid]*: factum bipartito distribuitur,[176] alterum est generale, simplex et infinitum *[Factum duplex]*, nulla personarum, temporum, locorum designatione notatum, quod Graeci vocant θέσιν[177] ut sacrificare, comedere, loqui, videre, pugnare, et quae sunt eius generis. Alterum factum coniunctum et modificatum, hoc est, certis vel personis vel temporibus, vel locis descriptum atque terminatum, quod Graeci vocant ὑπόθεσιν:[178] ut Cain vel Abel sacrificat, Esau vel Iacob comedit: hic pugnat, ut patriam defendat: alter pugnat, ut seipsum ulciscatur. Iam factum primo loco a nobis explicatum, quod simplex et infinitum dicimus, sine ullo modo, hoc est, sine ullis rebus circumstantibus a nobis praeceptum, neque bonum neque malum est, sed indifferens quiddam atque ἀδιάφορον,[179] alterum factum certis in personis vel temporibus positum, quod modificatum nominamus, aut bonum aut malum est, pro rerum, quae illud circumstant, ratione et modo.[180] Et hoc loco etiam malum peccatum, bonum virtutuem nominamus.

---

[175] *propter*: is difficult to render, and 'bearing in mind' seems like the best option.
[176] Again, Ascham applies taxonomic divisions when mounting his argument.
[177] θέσιν (and ὑπόθεσιν): 'thesis' and 'hypothesis' (mentioned just below) are terms of rhetoric used by Arist. and Hermagoras (a Greek rhetorician of the first century BCE), and by Quint. (*Inst.* 3.5.5–8, where he cross-refers to both Greeks and Cicero). Cic. discusses thesis and hypothesis in a range of rhetorical works, rendering *thesis* as *quaestio* and *hypothesis* as *causa* (*De inv.* 1.6.8, *De or.* 1.138) and as *propositum* and *causa* respectively (*Top.* 21.79–80), though Asc. appears to have *Top.* 21.79–80 in mind here (and see also n. 178 below). The ancient consensus was that the thesis was something unlimited and the hypothesis something limited.
[178] *Factum ... ὑπόθεσιν*: Ascham's language here (and below) is very similar to Cic., who postulates the following in *Top.* 21.79–80: *Quaestionum duo genera sunt: alterum infinitum, definitum alterum. Definitum est quod ὑπόθεσιν Graeci, nos causam; infinitum quod θέσιν illi appellant, nos propositum possumus nominare. Causa certis personis, locis, temporibus, actionibus, negotiis cernitur aut in omnibus aut in plerisque eorum, propositum autem aut in aliquo eorum aut in pluribus nec tamen in maximis. Itaque propositum pars est causae. Sed omnis quaestio earum aliqua de re est quibus causae continentur, aut una aut pluribus aut nonnunquam omnibus.* ('There are two kinds of inquiry, one general and the other particular. The particular is what the Greeks call "ὑπόθεσις" ('hypothesis'), and we call "cause" or "case"; the general inquiry is what they call "θέσις" ('thesis'), and we can call "proposition". The hallmark of a case is that it involves definite persons, places, times,

[27] [175] be rendered secure, bearing in mind[175] those who tend to be overzealous when investigating unfamiliar territory. But now to that [with] which we started. I term anything we do an 'action' *[Action – what it is]*. 'Action' is divided into two.[176] One [type] is general, simple and unlimited *[Action – twofold]* [and] particularised by no demarcation of persons, times and places; the Greeks call this 'a thesis',[177] for example, to sacrifice, to eat, to speak, to see, to fight, and actions of that type. The other [sort of] action is contingent on and limited, that is, to certain persons or times, or defined by and restricted to certain places; this the Greeks call a 'hypothesis',[178] for example, Cain or Abel sacrifices, Esau or Jacob eats, this man fights to defend his fatherland, and another fights to avenge himself. Now the action that I introduced in the first place, the one we speak of as simple and unlimited without any 'way', that is, without any attendant circumstances prescribed by us, is neither good nor bad, but something indifferent and an 'adiaphoron'.[179] The other [sort of] action [that is] peculiar to certain people or times, one we refer to as restricted, is either good or bad, depending on the motive and mode of the circumstances which attend it.[180] And it's at this stage [that] we also refer to sin as bad and virtue as good.

---

actions, or affairs, either all or most of these; a proposition involves one or several of these, but not the most important. Therefore, a proposition is a part of a case. But every inquiry concerns some one of the subjects of which cases consist, that is, it concerns one or more or sometimes all of them'), *LCL*, trans. H. M. Hubbell, 1949.

[179] ἀδιάφορον: Another Greek term, one with a long classical history from Arist. on (and on *adiaphora* generally, see the entry in Hillebrand 1996). However, the usage here is evidently again inspired by Cic. *Fin.* 3.53: *Quoniam autem omne quod est bonum primum locum tenere dicimus, necesse est nec bonum esse nec malum hoc quod praepositum vel praecipuum nominamus; idque ita definimus, quod sit indifferens cum aestimatione mediocri; quod enim illi ἀδιάφορον dicunt, id mihi ita occurrit ut indifferens dicerem.* ('But since we declare that everything that is good occupies the first rank, it follows that this which we entitle "preferred" or "superior" is neither good nor evil; and accordingly, we define it as being indifferent but possessed of a moderate value – since it has occurred to me that I may use the word "indifferent" to represent their term adiaphoron'), *LCL*, trans. H. Rackham, 1914. The Latin translation is *indifferentia*, as per Cic., a term Asc. himself uses at 29.

[180] *alterum ... modo*: Cic. *De inv.* suggests that a key consideration as regards 'action' is the performance, part of which comprises the *modus*, 'the way' in which something is done. At 1.27.41 Cic. treats *modus* as a state of mind in which there is judgement and lack of judgement (*eius partes sunt prudentia et imprudentia*). Ascham harnesses this analysis, though applies it to a distinctly Christian and a more moral context, referring not to any concomitant judgement (or lack of it) but rather to faith and its absence.

[28] [176] Ergo cum duplex factum a nobis sit expositum, iam sequitur, ut explicemus utrum factum infinitum, an factum modificatum illud sit, de quo nos sumus disputaturi. Et cum in disceptationibus omnibus de absoluta et perfecta re quaeri solet,[181] nos in praesenti de facto generali, nullis rebus circumstantibus modificato, sermonem faciemus: quod factum nos extra omnem culpam ponimus et asserimus. Alterum factum, quod designatum est de modo aliquo, utrum bonum an malum sit, nos non multum laboramus, quin illud totum a me disputationis sermone amotum atque segregatum est.[182] Positum ergo hoc sit, et clausum inter nos quatenus dissentimus, et quatenus consentimus: nam sic veritatem ipsam, quam investigamus, disputatione nostra quasi limabimus,[183] et in lucem conspectumque hominum proferemus. Tu dicis peccata omnia, ut adulterium, ut homicidium, fraudem, et furtum,[184] esse semper mala, nec ullo modo posse esse bona: idem et ego dico, et quod tu vocas detestabile peccatum, ego, si vis, vocabo detestabilissimum. Dicis itidem tu factum esse malum, hoc do tibi: sed

[29] [177] [M.] si dicis factum simplex et infinitum, hoc non do tibi, sed solum factum terminatum atque modificatum. Itaque, de natura peccati, an sit, quod sit, quale sit, nunc non disputamus, quia de ea re nos inter nos minime controversamur: sed solum quare aliquod factum sit peccatum aut non peccatum. Et in hac parte etiam consentimus, quod factum est peccatum, si intelligas modificatum. Nostrum igitur κρινόμενον,[185] sive totius nostrae disceptationis certamen, de quo sermonem habebimus, in hac sola quaestione versatur, An factum aliquod simplex, sine rerum circumstantium designatione, peccatum sit, necne? quod ego plane nego,

---

[181] *de . . . solet*: see Cic. *De or.* 3.22.84 which Ascham uses word for word here: . . . [*quacumque de arte aut facultate quaeritur,*] *de absoluta et perfecta quaeri solet* ('. . . [as whatever science or accomplishment is under examination,] it is customary to examine a finished and perfect specimen of it'), LCL, trans. H. Rackham, 1942. These words are spoken by Crassus to Catulus and concern the ideal form of orator. The concept is originally an Aristotelian one: Arist. *EN.* 1.7.8, . . . τέλειον δή τι φαίνεται καὶ αὔταρκες ἡ εὐδαιμονία . . . ('. . . happiness, therefore, being found to be something final and self-sufficient . . .'), LCL, trans. H. Rackham, 1926.

[182] *Alterum . . . est*: Asc. is keen to keep the parameters of the debate as focused as possible. He is not interested in defining actions as good or bad *per se*, but only in the difference between (i) a general action, which he claims is without fault (because it happens without a *modus*), and (ii) an action circumscribed by a *modus*.

[183] *veritatem . . . limabimus*: *veritas ipsa limatur in disputatione* ('when abstract truth is critically investigated in philosophic discussion') is a phrase used in Cic. *Off.* 2.10.35, LCL, trans. W. Miller, 1913.

[28] [176] Thus, since we have set out the twofold [nature of] action, it now follows that we should explain whether that action, about which we are going to debate, is unlimited action or restricted action. And since in all debates there tends to be an enquiry into something that is finished and perfect,[181] we will for the moment direct the discussion to a general [type of] action restricted by no attendant circumstances. This action we take and declare to be beyond all fault. The other [sort of] action, which has been defined in a certain way, [namely] whether it is good or bad, doesn't much concern us, and, in fact, that entire [issue] has been shelved and set aside by me as a talking point in [this] disputation.[182] And so, however much we disagree and however much we agree between ourselves, let [us] deem this matter settled and parked. For in this way, we will, as it were, get down to the truth itself,[183] which we are [primarily] considering in our disputation, and [in this way] we will bring it into the light and sight of men. You claim that all sins such as adultery, such as murder, forgery and theft are always bad,[184] and can be good in no way. I also claim the same, and that which you term 'abominable sin', I will, if you like, term 'most abominable'. Similarly, you claim that the action is bad and this I grant you. But

[29] [177] [M.] if you say that the action is simple and unlimited, this I don't grant you, but only that the action is limited and restricted. Accordingly, concerning the nature of sin, we are not now discussing whether it exists, what it is, or what quality it has, because we are not at all at variance between ourselves on that score, but only why a particular action is a sin or is not a sin. In this respect also, we agree that the action is a sin if you understand it as restricted. And so our enquiry,[185] or [rather] the crux of of our entire disputation pursuant to which we make this speech, turns on this question alone, [namely] whether an action [when it is] something simple and without specification of attendant circumstances is a sin or not? And I simply deny

---

[184] *adulterium...furtum*: This list is taken from from Hosea 4.2, [*maledictum*] *et mendacium et homicidium et furtum et adulterium* [*inundaverunt*] ('cursing and lying and killing and theft and adultery have overflowed').

[185] κρινόμενον: Another Greek term of art, literally, 'the thing being decided'. Cic. also refers to τὸ κρινόμενον in terms similar to Asc. in *Top.* 25.95: *sed quae ex statu contentio efficitur, eam Graeci κρινόμενον vocant, mihi placet id, quoniam quidem ad te scribo, qua de re agitur vocari.* ('The debate which arises from the issue (*status*) is called by the Greeks κρινόμενον, but I prefer to call it *qua de re agitur* ("the question at stake") especially in writing to you'); and in *Orat.* 36.126: *Quicquid est enim illud in quo quasi certamen est controversiae, quod Graece κρινόμενον dicitur, id ita dici placet ut traducatur ad perpetuam quaestionem atque uti de universo genere dicatur ....* ('For whatever that part may be called that deals with the central point of the controversy, which the Greeks call κρινόμενον or the issue, ought to be treated in such a way as to transfer the subject to the realm of universals and bring about a discussion of a general principle'), *LCL*, trans. H. M. Hubbell, 1939.

quodcunque assignaveris factum, videlicet, loqui, videre, comedere, non comedere, carnes edere, pisces edere, pugnare, interficere, re venerea uti, spoliare, et cetera facta omnia, quantum in infinita illorum vi atque natura intelligantur, neque bona neque mala esse, sed solum indifferentia. Verum si haec facta modificabimus, hoc est, ad certam aliquam personam traducemus, tum fient aut peccata aut virtutes: id quod evidentibus exemplis

[30] [178] e sacra Scriptura repetitis planum faciemus, postquam quid modus similter sit, *[Modus]* explicaverimus. Modus nihil aliud, hoc in loco, quam res circumstantes. 1.[186] personam, locum, tempus, et quae sunt huiusmodi, significat:[187] qui modus factum infinitum et late patens, certis quibusdam finibus continet et definit. *[Modus duplex.]* Modus duplex est, bonus et malus. Bonus dicitur modus, quia bonum factum: malus, quia malum factum creat semper et producit. Omnis modus coniunctus cum fide, est bonus: et omnis modus separatus a fide, est malus: nam quicquid non est ex fide, peccatum est: et quicquid est in fide, virtus est. Praeterea, non omnis modus, qui nobis videtur esse bonus, est bonus: neque omnis, qui videtur esse malus, est malus: sed nonnumquam contrario, quodam modo usu venire[188] solet. Neque haec modi indagatio frustra a nobis suscepta est. Neque Divus Augustinus perperam monet, ut quid locis, temporibus, et personis conveniat, diligenter attendamus, ne temere flagitia reprehendamus, aut malum pro bono, vel bonum pro malo usurpemus: nam sic provocemus in nos

---

[186] *1.*: It is not entirely clear why Ascham, or more likely the printer, uses the figure '1' here and elsewhere. It may be to indicate that more than one item is being discussed and be standing for *primum*, which may, in word form, have generated an ambiguity in the text.
[187] *locum ... significat*: Cic. also uses the heads of *locus, tempus, modus* (in addition to *occasio* and *facultas*) in *De inv.* 1.26.38 when considering the category of *gestio* ('action').

that what you have interpreted as 'action', to wit [activities such as] to speak, to see, to eat, not to eat, to consume meat, to feed on fish, to fight, to kill, to indulge in sex, to plunder, and all other actions, insofar as their essence and nature are perceived to be incalculable, are either good or bad; rather they are only indifferent. In truth, if we restrict these actions, that is, [if] we attribute them to some specific person, then they will become either sins or virtues. That [point] which you attack

[30] [178] we will make evident with examples from sacred Scripture, after we have explained how 'the way' *[the Way]* works similarly. The 'way' in this context denotes nothing other than the attendant circumstances:[186] the person, the place, the time and details of this kind.[187] This 'way' contains and defines within certain clear bounds an unlimited action and [one that] lies open in all respects. *[The twofold way.]* The twofold way is good and bad. A way is said [to be] 'good' because it always occasions and produces a good action, and 'bad' because it always occasions and produces a bad one. Every way [which is] conjoined with faith is good, and every way detached from faith is bad. For whatever is not [born] of faith is a sin, and whatever is [done] in faith is a virtue. Furthermore, not every way that seems to be good to us is [in fact] good, and nor is every way that seems to be bad [in fact] bad. But sometimes this tends to happen[188] quite differently. And nor have we embarked on this investigation into the 'way' without good reason. Saint Augustine correctly advises that we carefully attend to how it (i.e. the way) is adapted to places, times and persons, and that we don't rashly censure shameful acts, or label bad for good or good for bad. For [acting] thus, we might rouse up against us

---

[188] *usu venire*: an idiom meaning 'to happen...' or 'turn out' (literally, 'to come by occasion'). Augus. also dwells on the possibility of a counter-intuitive meanings in *De doct. Chr.* 3.25.35–37, *PL* 34, cols 78–79.

[31] [179] [M.ii.] gravem illam Dei comminationem, Vae vobis qui dicitis bonum malum, et malum bonum.[189] Nunc, explicata utriusque et facti et modi natura, ad exempla illa veniamus, quae totam hanc rem, quasi illustrem atque testatam, in omnium vestrum conspectu ponant. Sacrificare, est factum neque bonum neque malum *[Sacrificare, quid.]*, adde modum statim erit alterutrum: nempe sacrificat Cain, malum est factum: sacrificat Abel, bonum factum est.[190] At quare alterum bonum est, alterum malum est? Propter modum: nam modus sacrificandi Cain erat malus, nempe sine fide: modus sacrificandi Abel bonus, videlicet in fide. Interficere hominem, est factum neque bonum neque malum, modifica illud, et statim vel hoc vel illud erit. Es magistratus et interficis hominem? *[Interficere hominem, quid.]* Licet, propter modum coniunctum cum fide: dicit enim scriptura, Non frustra gladium gerit.[191] Interficis hominem hostem? Licet, propter modum copulatum fide:[192] nam Lex divina[193] permittit hostem interficere, quemadmodum David interfecit Golian.[194] Sine ulla caussa, per scripturam comprobata, hominem interficis? Peccatum est.

[32] [180] Quare? Propter modum interficiendi contra fidem: nam dicit scriptura, Non occides.[195] Ergo, interficere hominem est indifferens, sed hoc vel illo modo interficere, licitum aut non licitum est. Concumbere cum muliere, neque bonum neque malum est, adde modum, alterutrum erit. Concumbere cum muliere alterius viri, est peccatum, et adulterium: et hoc propter modum concumbendi contra fidem, quia scriptura dicit, Non moechaberis.[196] Similiter, cum innupta, quia est contra fidem, quae dicit, Fugite fornicationem.[197] Verum, concumbere cum muliere, quae propria uxor est, licitum est, propter modum rei ex fide proficiscentem: nam ait scriptura, Unusquisque possideat vas suum ad sanctificationem:[198] Et iterum,

---

[189] *Vae ... bonum*: Is. 5.20. V (with a slightly different order): *vae qui dicitis malum bonum et bonum malum*. ... Interestingly, Asc. prefers a chiastic arrangement with *bonum* framing the phrase at each end.

[190] *sacrificat ... est*: According to Gen. 4.1–7, the brothers Cain and Abel made sacrifices to God, but God favoured Abel's sacrifice over Cain's.

[191] *Non frustra gladium gerit*: Rom. 13.4. V: *non enim sine causa gladium portat*; Nov. T: *non enim frustra gladium gestat*. L (and indeed Calvin), however, would use the same wording as Asc. Asc. jotted the word for a sword, μάχαιρα in the margin of GNT next to this verse.

[192] *Licet ... Licet ... fide*: This clause is almost identical to the one above, viz. *Licet, propter modum coniunctum cum fide*, but instead of *coniunctum* we have *copulatum* and no *cum* (though *cum* was probably intended, as it so often appears after the verb *copulo*). These terms, *coniunctum* and *copulatum*, belonged to the art of dialectic (Gell. *NA*. 16.8).

[193] *Lex divina*: Judging by what follows, Ascham evidently means the Decalogue (or Ten Commandments) of the OT, and in parallel the guidance established by examples in the NT.

[31] [179] [M.ii.] that serious wrath of God. Damn you who claim that good is bad and bad is good![189] Now that we have explained the nature of each, both the action and the way, let us come to those examples, that they might show in the presence of you all this entire issue [to be] practically conclusive and incontrovertible. To sacrifice is an action that is neither good nor bad *[To sacrifice – what it is]*, but add the way, and it will immediately be one of two [things]. To be sure [when] Cain sacrifices, it is an action [that is] bad, but [when] Abel sacrifices it is an action [that is] good.[190] Yet why is one good and the other bad? On account of the way. For Cain's way of sacrificing was bad, [because it was] obviously without faith, whereas Abel's way of sacrificing was good, [because] of course, [done] in faith. To kill a man is an action neither good nor bad, but restrict that, and it will immediately be this or that. You hold civil office and you kill a man? *[To kill a man – what it is]*. It is lawful because the way is conjoined with faith; indeed, Scripture says 'He does not carry the sword in vain'.[191] You kill a man [who is] an enemy? It is lawful because the way is coupled with faith.[192] That's because divine Law[193] permits the killing of an enemy, just as David killed Goliath.[194] [But if] you kill a man without any reason that has been approved of through Scripture? It's a sin.

[32] [180] Why? Because the way of killing [runs] contrary to faith. For Scripture says 'Thou shalt not kill'.[195] Thus, to kill a man is indifferent, but to kill in this or that way is lawful or not lawful. To sleep with a woman is neither good nor bad, but add the way, and it will be one or the other. To sleep with the wife of another man is a sin and adulterous; this is because the way of copulation [runs] contrary to faith since Scripture says 'Thou shalt not commit adultery';[196] similarly, with a virgin, because that runs contrary to faith, which stipulates 'Flee fornication'.[197] However, to sleep with a woman who is one's own wife is lawful because 'the way' of the matter springs from faith, for Scripture says 'Let each man possess his vessel for sanctification'.[198] And again, 'Let each

---

[194] *David interfecit Golian*: The story of David, namely the young shepherd's killing of the champion of the Philistines, Goliath, is recounted in 1 Sam. 17.
[195] *Non occides*: Ex. 20.13 / Deut. 5.17. Asc. draws on the Decalogue, and will refer to the prohibition on adultery below. Cf. *Apol*, which was structured around the Ten Commandments, and see also Nicholas 2015: 87–100. The Decalogue became increasingly important during the Reformation, displacing the Seven Deadly Sins; it also came to assume a defining role in Protestant doctrine (Willis 2015: 1–2 and *passim*).
[196] *Non moechaberis*: Ex. 20.14 / Deut. 5.18.
[197] *Fugite fornicationem*: 1 Corinth. 6.18. The wording matches V; cf. *Nov. T: fugite scortationem*.
[198] *Unusquisque ... sanctificationem*: 1 Thess. 4.4. V and *Nov. T: [ut sciat] unusquisque vestrum vas suum possidere in sanctificatione et honore*. One wonders whether Asc. opted to conclude the clause with *sanctificationem* rather than *honore* because of the possible sound-effects with *fornicationem*.

Unusquisque habeat uxorem suam ad vitandam fornicationem.[199] His exemplis potissimum usi sumus, quia maxime παράδοξα,[200] et contra hominum opinionem esse videantur. Praeterea, quomodo videre ad[201] concupiscentiam est[202] malum, ad laudandum Deum bonum: comedere ad necessitatem licitum, ad gulam illicitum: pugnare pro patria

[33] [181] [M.iii.] iustum, pro libidine ulciscendi iniustum: et infinita his finitima, facile ostenderemus, nisi quod tempus in nimis longum sermonem producere omnino noluerimus. Cum[203] igitur modus sic terminat factum, ut ex sua ipsius vi et natura, factum nihil sit nisi per propositionem modi: tamen imprimis cavendum est, ne fingamus nobis ipsis modos, sed hoc totum DEI voluntati tribuamus: nam sunt modi quidam, qui non sunt omnium hominum communes, sed quorundam hominum atque temporum proprii et singulares, et qui praecipua quadam DEI voluntatis praerogativa faciunt quaedam facta patrum in veteri testamento licita, quae hoc temporis[204] (quoniam Deus non applicat nunc huiusmodi modos nobis), essent detestabilia.[205]

Et ex his modis alter permissivus,[206] alter imperativus[207] recte potest appellari. *[Modus permissivus.]* Permissivus, ut quando Abraham, propter sterilitatem Sarae, concubuit cum ancilla sua:[208] et quando Iacob decepit patrem, et fraudavit fratrem suum et benedictione et haereditate:[209] et quae sunt his similia prope infinita. *[Modus imperativus.]* Imperativus, ut quando Deus iussit

---

[199] *Unusquisque ... fornicationem*: 1 Corinth. 7.2. V: *propter fornicationem autem unusquisque suam uxorem habeat*; Nov. T: *attamen propter stupra vitanda, suam quisque uxorem habeat*. Both E and Asc. augment the original Greek, which literally translates as 'through fornication, let each man have his own wife'.

[200] παράδοξα: παράδοξος -ον is an adjective commonly used in Greek philosophy. Ascham's use of Greek is a nod to the utility of a Greek concept here, as well as its inability to be easily translated into alternative Latin (the Latinised equivalent is *paradoxus, -a, -um*). It is very likely too that Asc. had in mind Cic. *Parad. St.* 4, where Cic. attempted to explain famous Stoic sayings that appeared to go against common understanding, writing, *inter alia*, in the preface: *quae quia sunt admirabilia contraque opinionem omnium* (*ab ipsis etiam* παράδοξα *appellantur*). ('These doctrines are surprising, and they run counter to universal opinion – the Stoics themselves actually term them "paradoxa"'), LCL, trans. H. Rackham, 1942.

[201] *videre ad*: has the meaning of *spectare*.

[202] *quomodo ... est*: The retention of the indicative, as opposed to the subjunctive, in indirect questions is relatively common in early modern Latin, and there are other instances of this in this text.

[203] *Cum ... tamen ... detestabilia*: I have broken up this long sentence in the translation and have thus not rendered *cum*, which means 'although' (here) and is picked up by the *tamen* that follows.

[204] *hoc temporis*: in Latin it is possible to see certain phrases composed of the accusative neuter of a pronoun followed by a genitive and used adverbially.

[205] *nam ... detestabilia*: See also Augus. *De doct. Chr.* 3.18.26, *Item cavendum est ne forte quod in Scripturis veteribus pro illorum temporum conditione, etiamsi non figurate, sed*

man have his own wife to avoid fornication'.[199] We have adduced these examples in particular because they seem to be especially paradoxical[200] and contrary to people's assumptions. Moreover, how a regard[201] for carnality is[202] bad, but for the purpose of praising God is good; [how] consumption according to [one's] need is lawful, but to satisfy gluttony is unlawful; [how] combat for one's country is

[33] [181] [M.iii.] righteous, but for the love of vengeance is unjust, we could easily demonstrate, and [with] innumerable examples like these, except we are very reluctant to draw out too long a speech in the time [available]. And so,[203] the way limits an action in such a fashion that, through its very own force and nature, an action is nothing except the essence of its way. That said, especial care must be taken not to determine the ways for ourselves, but [rather] to defer this entire business to the will of God. Assuredly, there are certain ways which are not common to all men but peculiar and unique to certain men and times, and which, through a certain superior privilege of God's will, make certain actions of our forefathers in the Old Testament lawful. Such actions, since God does not now permit ways of this kind for us, would at this moment in time[204] be abominable.[205]

And from these ways, it's altogether possible for one to be termed 'permitted'[206] and the other 'compulsory'.[207] *[A way that is permitted]* It is 'permitted' as [for instance] when Abraham, because of Sarah's barrenness, slept with his maidservant,[208] when Jacob deceived his father, and defrauded his brother of his blessing and inheritance,[209] and [in] situations almost innumerable in number which are similar to these. *[A way that proceeds from a command]* It is 'compulsory' as when God ordered

---

proprie intelligatur, non est flagitium neque facinus, ad ista etiam tempora quis putet in usum vitae posse transferri. (PL 34, col. 75). ('Likewise, we must take care not to regard something in the Old Testament that is not wickedness or wrongdoing by the standards of its own time – even when understood literally and not figuratively – as capable of being transferred to the present time and applied to our own lives').

[206] *permissivus*: is a post fifteenth-century word (attested to in *DMLBS*), used especially by grammarians who coupled it with the term *modus*, in this sense a verbal 'mood'. William Lily's *A Short Introduction of Grammar* (first published in 1497) defined it as a sort of exceptional licence, albeit one not quite in accordance with divine law.

[207] *imperativus*: when coupled with *modus*, this term was also used commonly by grammarians, ancient and early modern. Again, Ascham expands the meaning to denote an unequivocal command or injunction from God.

[208] *Abraham ... sua*: The account of Abraham sleeping with his maidservant is set out in Gen. 16. God had promised Abraham that he would be the father of many nations, but his wife, Sarah, was barren. She therefore sought to fulfil the promise by urging Abraham to conceive a child with their maidservant, Hagar. Although God does ultimately acquiesce in this arrangement, the action occurs without his direct sanction.

[209] *Iacob ... haereditate*: The deceit practised by Jacob on his bother Esau, and by extension his father, Isaac, is set out in Gen. 25.29–34. When Esau returned, almost dying of hunger from hunting, Jacob, who was at home and had cooked a stew, compelled Esau to hand over to him his legal birthright as first born, and thus the paternal blessing, in return for some food.

[34] [182] filios Israel spoliare Aegyptum:[210] aut quando Deus iussit Oseam Prophetam concumbere cum meretrice, et ex ea suscipere filios fornicationis:[211] et quando Deus iussit Abraham occidere proprium filium suum Isaac.[212] Haec exempla non sunt nobis proposita ad imitationem, sed sunt nobis relicta ad omnipotentis Dei gloriae significationem. Factum illorum, quatenus factum, erat malum, nec nos possumus probare: sed factum, quatenus per Deum praeceptum, non erat malum, nec nos debemus damnare. Itaque, nec eos, quia sic fecerunt, licitum est, ut imitemur:[213] nec consilia Dei quare sic voluit, fas est ut perscrutemur:[214] sed praeceptum Dei, quia sic iussit, aequum est ut amplexemur.[215] Neque nos illud, quod aliquibus sigillatim[216] et nominatim est permissum, nobis debemus arrogare: sed id quod omnibus generatim et universe vel vetitum sit vel praeceptum, omni cogitatione nostra versare. Ad modum ergo, non ad factum, quicquid ab hominibus vel boni vel mali effectum sit, applicari debet. Sed, quemadmodum prius diximus, diligenter a nobis est cavendum, ne nobismetipsis[217] modos affingamus: nam

[35] [183] [M.iiii.] tum factum nostrum quantumcunque, specie plausibile aut pium esse videatur, Deo tamen displicet et impium est. Est unus modus, et is tantum bonus, nempe praeceptum et voluntas Dei: nam Deus ait in Deuteronom. Hoc tantum facito quod ego praecipio tibi.[218] Si ad praecepta Dei modificemus facta nostra, tum omnia facta nostra sunt bona, quia non nos, sed Deus operatur in nobis, iuxta illud Prophetae, Omnia opera nostra operatus est nobis:[219] et alio in loco, Semita iusti recta est,[220]

---

[210] *Deus ... Aegyptum*: Ex. 3.22. V: *spoliabitis Aegyptum* ('You shall spoil Egypt').
[211] *concumbere ... fornicationis*: Hosea 1.2. Cf. V: *vade, sume tibi uxorem fornicationum et filios fornicationum ...* ('Go, take for yourself a wife of fornications and [have of her] sons of fornications').
[212] *Abraham ... Isaac*: Gen. 22.2. Cf. V: *tolle filium unigenitum ... atque offer eum ibi holocaustum* ('Take your only begotten son ... and there offer him as a sacrifice').
[213] *licitus, -a, -um*: is here followed by *ut* and the subjunctive, as one can also find after the impersonal verb *licet* from which it comes.
[214] *fas est ut perscrutemur*: It is unusual in classical Latin to find *fas* followed by *ut* and the subjunctive, but the formula is mirroring *licitum est ut imitemur* used earlier in the sentence in order to produce a form of symmetry.

[34] [182] the sons of Israel to plunder Egypt,[210] or when God ordered Hosea the Prophet to sleep with a prostitute, and to beget with her sons of fornication;[211] and when God ordered Abraham to kill his own son Isaac.[212] We have not adduced these examples as ones to copy, but they have been left to us as a reminder of the glory of an all-powerful God. What those men did, to the extent that it was 'an action', was bad and we cannot approve of it, but the action, to the extent it was at God's bidding, was not bad and we ought not to condemn it. Nor, accordingly, is it lawful for us to copy them[213] [just] because they acted in this way. Likewise, it is not right for us to scrutinise[214] the plans of God and why he willed it thus. On the other hand, it is appropriate for us to embrace[215] the bidding of God since he ordered it thus. We ought not to appropriate for ourselves that which was permitted to certain individuals,[216] and on a case by case basis, but [rather] to turn in our minds entirely to that which is either forbidden or commanded of everyone generally and universally. And so, whatever has been carried out by men, be it good or bad, ought to be related to the way not to the action. But, just as we said before, we must be scrupulously careful not to determine the ways for ourselves,[217] because

[35] [183] [M.iiii.] then our action, of whatever scale, might seem to be either pleasing or pious in appearance, while [in fact] it displeases God and is wicked. There is one way, and this is the good one only, [and that is], of course, the commandment and will of God. Indeed, so God spoke in Deuteronomy, 'Do only this which I command of you.'[218] If we confine our actions to God's commandments, then all our actions are good, not because of our own [efforts], but [because] God carries them into effect through us, according to that Prophet's [observation], 'He has wrought all our deeds in us'.[219] And elsewhere [we read], 'The path of the righteous [man] is [what is] right[220]

---

[215] *aequum est ut amplexemur*: *aequum est* is commonly followed by *ut* and the subjunctive (as here).
[216] *sigillatim*: an alternative form for *singulatim*.
[217] *nobismetipsis*: This is a very emphatic form, with the suffix *-met* attached to the dative of *nos* and a form of *ipse, -a, -um* added to create a single word; this happens elsewhere in the text too.
[218] *Hoc . . . tibi*: Deut. 12.32. Asc. differs from V: *quod praecipio tibi hoc tantum facito Domino* ('What I command you, do that only to the Lord'). The word order here seems to be very much Asc.'s own.
[219] *Omnia . . . nobis*: Is. 26.12. In V, the Lord is addressed in the second person singular.
[220] *semita iusti recta est*: Is. 26.7. The phrase *semita iusti recta est* is used in V. I have translated *recta* as 'right', but *rectus, -a, -um* can also mean 'straight'.

quia Dominus dirigit gressus eius. Facta igitur nostra, non quia per nos facta, sed quia per praeceptum Dei modificata, bona existimanda sunt, ne nos in nostris gloriemur, sed semper opus haberemus dicere, Non nobis Domine, non nobis, sed nomini tuo da gloriam.[221] Hunc solum et unicum modum bene agendi viderunt, licet non expresse, adumbrate[222] tamen veteres Philosophi, qui ponebant τὸ μέσον[223] inter nimium et parum virtutem, iuxta illud Poetae,[224] Est modus in rebus:[225] et quae sequuntur. Aliquanto propius ad veritatem accessit Xenophon *[Xenophon]*, apud quem Cambyses ait, Modus homini bono aequitas[226] est, non

[36] [184] sua voluntas:[227] qua sententia, quid potest dici divinius, cum Deus sit ipsa aequitas?[228] Sed planissimum est quod Socrates in 4. ἀπομνημονευμάτων[229] respondet Euthydemo interroganti, Quo modo possit esse bonus? Si Deum honorabis, inquit: Sed qua via? inquit alter:[230] *[Socrates apud Xeno.]* Respondet Socrates, πῶς οὖν ἄν τις κάλλιον καὶ εὐσεβέστερον τιμῴη θεοὺς ἤ, ὡς αὐτὸς κελεύει, οὕτω ποιῶν?[231] Hoc est, Quomodo[232] quis maiore cum sanctitate ac religione Deum colet, quam si ad iussum et praeceptum eius omnes factorum suorum rationes applicaverit? Sunt haec exempla a me ab Ethnicorum scholis repetita, non ut probem caussam meam, sed ut nos nostri pudeat,[233] si illi caeci, qui (ut elegantissime ait Cicero)

---

[221] *Non ... gloriam*: Ps. 113.9 (V/S) / 115.1 (H/P). The wording exactly matches V.

[222] *adumbrate*: Literally, 'by way of shadow'. The depiction of the ancients as operating without the light of Christ and the Bible was a common one; see also 36 below.

[223] τὸ μέσον: Asc. probably also has in mind the famous definition of virtue as the 'happy medium' (τὸ μέσον / ἡ μεσότης) as set out in Arist. *EN*. 2.6, where Arist. equates the mean with a quality that lies 'between excess and deficiency', whereby 'hitting the mean' is a form of 'moral virtue'. Asc. would also refer to the mean in *Tox.*, Giles, vol. II, 143–44.

[224] *Poetae*: For Asc., an ancient poet fell into the same category as a 'philosopher', a point he would explicitly make in *Tox.*, Giles, vol. II, 32–33. The poet here is Horace, and see n. 225 below.

[225] *Est modus in rebus*: Hor. *Serm*. 1.1.106. In the first satire of the collection, Horace explores the phenomenon of why so few men are content with their lot. In the part of the poem Asc. quotes from, Hor. is discussing the topic of wealth and suggests that there is a mean between being a miser and being a prodigal, adding ... *sunt certi denique fines, / quos ultra citraque nequit consistere rectum* ('... there are, in short, fixed bounds beyond and short of which right can find no place' (106–7). It is noteworthy that Asc. cited the scriptural use of the adjective *rectus* just above on this page, as though perhaps he discerned some verbal overlap between the ancients and the Bible.

[226] *aequitas*: Again, Asc. has used the related adjective *aequus, -a, -um* just above on 35, and it seems that he is establishing in this tract not just an overlap in thought between the pagans and the Christians, but also one in vocabulary.

[227] *Xenophon ... voluntas*: Xen. *Cyr*. 1.3.18. Ascham has mis-remembered slightly: in the original, it is Cyrus' mother, Mandane, who describes Cambyses I, the father of Cyrus,

because the Lord directs his steps'. And so, our actions, not because they are done by us, but because they are confined within God's commandment, are to be considered good. [This is] to keep us from exulting in our own [deeds], and [to ensure] that there is always need of the statement, 'Not unto us, Lord, not unto us, but unto your name give the glory'.²²¹ The ancient philosophers understood this sole and unique way of behaving well, granted not explicitly but in semblance only.²²² They situated their 'middle way'²²³ between too much and too little virtue following the Poet's²²⁴ dictum, 'There is a mean in things'²²⁵ (and what follows). Xenophon *[Xenophon]* came rather closer to the truth, in whose writings Cambyses says 'The way for the good man is fairness,²²⁶ not

[36] [184] his own will'.²²⁷ What can be uttered more piously than this statement, since God personifies fairness itself?²²⁸ But the most clear-cut [example] is what Socrates in *Memorabilia*²²⁹ 4 replies to Euthydemus, who is asking him 'How can one be good?' 'If you honour God', he (i.e. Socrates) answers. 'But in what way?' the other asks.²³⁰ *[Socrates in Xenophon]* Socrates replies 'How could someone honour God with greater reverence and faith than by doing just as God himself orders?'²³¹ That is, how²³² will someone worship God with more purity and piety than if he directs every basis of his actions according to his (i.e. God's) command and bidding? I have taken these examples from the writing of the pagans, not with a view to proving my case, but that they may stand as a source of shame for us,²³³ if those [who were] blind, [and] who, as Cicero

---

along these lines. While discoursing on the subject of justice and contrasting Cyrus' just father with his rather more unjust grandfather, Mandane states καὶ ὁ σὸς πατὴρ πρῶτος τὰ τεταγμένα μὲν ποιεῖ τῇ πόλει, τὰ τεταγμένα δὲ λαμβάνει, μέτρον δὲ αὐτῷ οὐχ ἡ ψυχὴ ἀλλ' ὁ νόμος ἐστίν ('And your father is the first one to do what is ordered by the State and to accept what is decreed, and his standard is not his will but the law'), *LCL*, trans. W. Miller, 1914. The relevant words here are ψυχὴ and νόμος, which map onto *voluntas* and *aequitas* respectively. On the immense cultural prestige across Europe that the *Cyropaedia* enjoyed in the early modern period, see Grogan 2020: 1–13.

²²⁸ *quid ... aequitas*: In the printed version, there is no question mark at the end of this clause, but one was clearly intended.

²²⁹ ἀπομνημονευμάτων: The genitive plural of ἀπομνημόνευμα, -ατος, the Greek word for a 'memorial', namely, Xen. *Mem.*

²³⁰ *quod ... alter*: Xen. *Mem.* 4.6.2 and ff. It is, however, Socrates who both asks and answers the questions rather than Euthydemus (as the text above seems to indicate). This part of the *Mem.* is also set out in full in on the opening page of GNT.

²³¹ πῶς ... ποιῶν: Xen. *Mem.* 4.3.16. Modern versions of the text read: πῶς οὖν ἄν τις κάλλιον καὶ εὐσεβέστερον τιμῴη θεοὺς ἤ, ὡς αὐτοὶ κελεύουσιν, οὕτω ποιῶν; Fascinatingly, with a Christian sleight of hand, Asc. amends plural 'gods' to one God with his use of αὐτὸς for αὐτοί.

²³² *Quomodo*: I have reproduced the word as it appears in the printed version, i.e. as a single word, unlike *Quo modo*, which appears as two words on this same page just above.

²³³ *nos nostri pudeat*: literally, 'it may shame us of ourselves'.

nullam veri iuris, germanaeque iusticiae solidam et expressam effigiem tenebant, sed umbra et imaginibus utebantur,[234] ad veritatis cognitionem propius accedant quam nos, qui non fictam sequimur imaginem, sed expressissimam DEI patris effigiem, non umbram, sed lucem, qui est Christus Iesus, vera lux et germanissima iusticia nostra.

[37] [185] [M.v.] Sit ergo Christus nobis in omnibus modus, 1.[235] exemplum, (ut ait Scriptura) et norma vitae nostrae, non nosmetipsi: sit ille nobis τὸ μέσον,[236] simus nos conformes illi, non nobis: ut illud, quod Cicero de Philosophia loquitur,[237] nos de Christo verissime usurpemus: Hic est illa de coelo delapsa regula,[238] ad quam omnes vitae nostrae rationes dirigere et formare debemus. Modus ergo hic est. Praescriptio et voluntas Dei, non facta nostra, nos bonos facit: a qua praescriptione sive modo, si unum pedem aberraverimus, Deo placere, aut bonum aliquid facere profecto non possumus, quantumvis bonum et pium illud nostro iudicio et conscientiae esse videatur. Possum adducere in medium Ozam regem, *[Oza rex.]* qui putabat se bene facere, cum admovebat manum ad Arcam Dei ne caderet:[239] sed quia illud factum erat contra modum praescriptionis Dei, bona eius voluntas eum a morte, qua illum propterea percussit Deus, non liberavit. Possum et Saulem memorare, qui bono animo et modo, (ut ille putabat, sed contra praescriptionem Dei), aurum et lapides preciosos[240] ad exornandum

---

[234] *qui ... utebantur*: Cic. *Off.* 3.17.69 almost *verbatim*: *sed nos veri iuris germanaeque iustitiae solidam et expressam effigiem nullam tenemus, umbra et imaginibus utimur* ('But we possess no substantial, life-like image of true Law and genuine Justice; a mere outline sketch is all that we enjoy'). In this part of the work Cic. discusses different types of laws, universal and civil, and various ways to encourage good behaviour, be it through the law, or via philosophers. He also comments that when broaching the important question of who or what *boni* ('good men') are, Romans only have access to a semblance or approximation (*umbra et imaginibus*) of true justice. What is extraordinary here is that the formulation and insight of a classical author are being used by Asc. to delineate the pagans' own place relative to the divine revelation of Christendom, and the principles espoused by Cic. are treated as a direct precursor and bridge to those of Christianity.

[235] *1.*: On the use of the numerical '1', see n. 186.

[236] *sit ... τὸ μέσον*: Asc. explicitly applies the classically defined 'mean' to Christian virtue as directed by Christ (also see 35).

most fluently puts it, had no concrete and manifest image of the true Law and genuine righteousness, but relied on semblance and approximations,[234] were to arrive more closely at a comprehension of the truth than we who don't follow a fictitious approximation but the most manifest image of God the Father, no semblance but the light who is Jesus Christ, the true light and our most genuine righteousness.

[37] [185] [M.v.] Consequently, let Christ be the way in all of us,[235] as [both] the example (as Scripture stipulates) and the governance of our life, *not* we ourselves. Let him be the middle way for us;[236] and let us be like him, not [him] to us, [and in such a way] that we may most truly enjoy in Christ what Cicero speaks of in his philosophy.[237] He (i.e. Christ) is that 'rule'[238] come down from heaven, to which we ought all direct the entire conduct of our life and on which we ought to base it. Consequently, he is the way. The ordinance and the will of God, not our own deeds, make us good. If we depart from this ordinance or way, even if only by a single footstep, we cannot please God or do any [form of] good at all, however good and pious that [action] seems to be in our judgement and conscience. I can introduce into the mix King Oza *[Oza, the King.]*, who thought that he was acting properly when he moved his hand to God's Ark of the Covenant to prevent it from falling.[239] But because that deed was contrary to the way of God's ordinance, his good inclination did not save him from death, [and] for that reason God struck him down. I can also mention Saul, who with good intention and [a good] way (as he thought it, though [it was] contrary to God's ordinance), saved up gold and precious[240] stones [with which] to adorn

---

[237] *quod ... loquitur*: Asc. must mean by this a full comprehension of the truth, as alluded to in 36.

[238] *regula*: This word, meaning some kind of standard, yardstick or rule for life (and derived from the verb *regere* ('to keep straight' and cognate with *rectus*, used above in this theme), is seen regularly in Cic. It was also term often used in the morally charged poems of Walter Haddon, a direct contemporary and friend of Asc. in Cambridge (see Nicholas, forthcoming).

[239] *Ozam ... caderet*: 2 Sam. 6.6-7. V: *extendit Oza manum ad arcam Dei, et tenuit eam quoniam calcitrabant boves, et declinaverunt eam* ('And Oza stretched his hand to the ark of God, and held it, since the oxen were kicking at it and making it lean [to one side]'). This is the first of several episodes in this theme, which are also recounted in Asc. *Apol.*, where there is made a similar point about the importance of adhering to Scripture, notwithstanding someone's 'good intentions' otherwise (Nicholas 2017: 40-43).

[240] *preciosos*: an alternative form for *pretiosos*.

[38] [186] Dei templum ab ignis vastatione reservavit.²⁴¹ Quid illi apud Matthaeum, qui prophetant, qui eiiciunt daemonia, et hoc etiam in nomine Iesu Christi?²⁴² Quia modum et praescriptionem DEI non observant, pro facto optimo, si ullum factum est bonum, contra audiunt dictum gravissimum, Nescio vos.²⁴³ Possum infinita huiusmodi exempla proferre eorum, qui ex bona intentione, (ut ita loquar), male egerunt: sed quia sunt hominum perditorum, facilior ad ea est responsio. Nunc accedamus ad sanctissimos post Christum homines, ad viros Christianae religionis principes, ipsos DEI Apostolos, Petrum, Paulum, Iohannem, quorum facta ex bono animo (ut sibi visum est) profecta, quia praescriptione Dei non erant modificata, Deo displicebant. *[Petrus.]* Sic Petrus valde amanter, sed parum amice monebat Christum ut non²⁴⁴ moreretur: a quo audit, Abi post me Satana.²⁴⁵ Sic Petrus, bono animo, ad defendendum Christum, praecidit auriculam Malco:²⁴⁶ sed ei dictum est, Qui gladio percutit, gladio peribit.²⁴⁷ *[Paulus.]* Sic Paulus rogabat ut stimulus carnis

[39] [187] auferretur ab eo,²⁴⁸ bono animo scilicet, ut liberius Evangelio vacaret:²⁴⁹ sed percussus est, et audivit, Non sufficit tibi gratia mea.²⁵⁰ Sic Ioannes, qui Christo erat intimus, cum Angelum Dei, bono animo, et propter Deum, qui eum misit, opinor, summo quo potuit honore prosequutus fuit, reprehensus est et audivit, Vide ne sic feceris.²⁵¹ Ergo cum facta aposotolorum,

---

²⁴¹ *Saulem ... reservavit*: It is unclear which part of the OT this relates to; Saul certainly displeased God and his kingship was rejected, as is also referenced in *Apol*. (Nicholas 2017: 38–41), but although there are a number of references in the OT to storing up gold and precious stones to decorate the temple, these do not seem to pertain to Saul, and Asc. has evidently conflated episodes here.

²⁴² *qui ... Christi*: Matt. 7.22. V: *multi dicent mihi in illa die, 'Domine, Domine, nonne in nomine tuo prophetavimus et in tuo nomine daemonia eiecimus ...'?* ('Many will say to me on that day, "Lord, Lord, have we not prophesied in your name and cast out devils in your name ...?"').

²⁴³ *Nescio vos*: Luke 13.27. Asc. scribbled οὐκ οἶδα ὑμᾶς next to the verse in GNT.

²⁴⁴ *ut non*: *ne* rather than *ut non* is the correct formulation in classical Latin in a negative indirect command.

²⁴⁵ *Abi post me Satana*: Matt. 16.23 / Mark 8.33. V: *vade post me, Satana* and *Vade retro me, Satana* respectively; *Nov. T* (like Asc.) has *Abi post me Satana* in each verse.

²⁴⁶ *Petrus ... Malco*: Matt. 26.51; Mark 14.47; Luke 22.50; and John 18.10. The latter is the only place which refers to Peter being the one to cut the ear off and names Malcus as one

[38] [186] the temple of God after the devastation of fire.[241] What of those who, according to Matthew, prophesy, [or] who drive out evil spirits, and likewise [do] this in the name of Jesus Christ?[242] Since they fail to observe the way and the ordinance of God instead of [discharging] an action [that is] most worthwhile (if any action is good), they hear against them the most severe pronouncement, 'I know you not'.[243] I am able to produce innumerable examples of this sort concerning those who, with good intention, as I will accordingly suggest, have acted badly. But because they constitute [examples of] men who are utterly ruined a response to these is easier. [For] now, let us come to the most holy individuals after Christ, to the most eminent men of the Christian faith, God's Apostles themselves, Peter, Paul, and John, whose actions were motivated by good intention, as it seemed to them, [yet] because they were not confined by his ordinance, displeased God. *[Peter]* It was in such a way [that] Peter, very lovingly but not in a way that was welcome, enjoined Christ not[244] to die; [accordingly,] Peter heard from him (i.e. Christ) 'Get thee behind me, Satan'.[245] It was in such a way [that] Peter, with good intention and in defence of Christ, cut off Malcus' ear,[246] but the following was said to him, 'He who strikes with the sword, will die by the sword'.[247] *[Paul]* It was in this way [that] Paul asked that the torment of flesh

[39] [187] be removed from him,[248] of course [again] with good intention, so that he might devote himself more freely to the Gospel,[249] but he was struck down and he heard 'My grace is not enough for you'.[250] It was in this way [that] John, a close friend of Christ, who, when, with good intention and, as I think, on account of God who sent him, heaped on the Angel of God as much honour as he could muster, was rebuked and heard 'See that you do it not'.[251] And so, when deeds of the Apostles,

---

of the servants. For John 18.10, V and *Nov. T* have: *abscidit eius auriculam dextram, erat autem nomen servo Malchus* ('He (i.e. Peter) cut off his right ear. Morever, the name of the servant was Malchus').

[247] *Qui ... peribit*: The quoted words of Christ are from Matt. 26.52. V and *Nov. T*: *omnes enim, qui acceperint gladium, gladio peribunt*. Asc.'s wording can be found in Augs. *Serm. ad Populum, sermo* 4.31.34 (*PL* 38, col. 50).

[248] *Paulus ... eo*: 2 Corinth. 12.7-8. V and E refer to *stimulus carnis* in verse 7 but in verse 8 both have: *rogavi ut discederet a me*.

[249] *ut liberius Evangelio vacaret*: This 'evangelical' flourish is Ascham's own; cf. in 2 Corinth. 12.9 Paul proceeds to suggest that he will instead take glory in his infirmities so that the 'power of Christ may rest upon him'.

[250] *Non sufficit tibi gratia mea*: 2 Corinth. 12.9. Unlike V and *Nov. T*, Asc. has – and uniquely as far as searches indicate – added *non* before *sufficit*, perhaps to render God's statement all the more disapproving. He does this again on the next page.

[251] *Vide ne sic feceris*: Rev. 22.9. The wording follows V and *Nov. T*, though Asc. adds *sic*.

quantumvis pia et speciosa, non eo tamen modo, quo Christus vult, effecta, reiecta et refutata sunt, quid de aliorum hominum levioris notae factis dicemus, qui indies novos modos, non a Christo praescriptos, sed a seipsis invectos fingunt et refingunt?[252] Et hic profecto, si non me avocaret nostra instituta disputatio, ingrederer in immensum illum campum dicendi,[253] contra pestem illam Babylonicam, Romanum Episcopum[254] *[Romanus Episcopus Antichristi idolum]*, veram effigiem, et expressum Antichristi idolum, sentinam, ex qua effluxit tanta tamquam perdita novorum modorum faex et eluvies,[255] contra praescriptiones Dei, quae sic totam ecclesiam inundavit, et sic vivam aquam[256] permiscuit et conturbavit, ut multi multis in locis iam sordibus eius involvi quam e fonte Christi aliquid haurire maluerint.

[40] [188] Hic modus suos, pro modis Christi, in Ecclesiam invexit: et propterea dicit scriptura, Hic stabit in loco sancto.[257] Quam hoc verum sit, ex rudi et indocto vulgo facile disces: nam si aliquis dicit, Sic facite[258] ad hunc modum, quem Christus suis apertis verbis praescribit, capiunt verbum illud, nec reprobant: sed duritia cordis, quam illis longa superstitio obduxit, ad illum modum vitam suam instituere nolunt. Sin ipsi habent aliquem peculiarem modum vivendi, quem fortasse Diabolus ipse excogitavit, Romana lues approbavit, hypocrisis in lucem indicavit, caeca consuetude reservavit, ab huiusmodi modo, tanquam Polypus,[259]

---

[252] *fingunt et refingunt*: The phrase *fingunt aut refingunt* is found in L's *Missa privata et unctione sacerdotum libellus* (Wittenberg, 1534), sig. Ii[r], a tome with which it is very likely Asc. was familiar; he certainly was with L's *De abroganda missa privata* (Basel, 1522), as is evident in his *Apol*.

[253] *campus dicendi*: is an expression that became popular in the early modern period. It refers to the Campus Martius, a public open place of assembly in Rome where, *inter alia*, orators might make speeches. It was probably inspired (here) by Cic. *De or*. 3.31.124–25: *in hoc igitur tanto tam immensoque campo cum liceat oratori vagari libere atque ubicumque constiterit consistere in suo, facile suppeditat omnis apparatus ornatusque dicendi* ('Consequently as the orator has the liberty to roam freely in so wide and measureless a field and wherever he takes his stand to find himself on his own ground, all the resources and embellishments of oratory are readily available').

[254] *Romanum Episcopum*: viz. the Pope. At the time Asc. was composing his *Themata*, this was Paul III, whose pontificate ran from 1534 to 1549.

[255] *pestem . . . inundavit*: the first of several aggressively anti-papal barbs.

[256] *vivam aquam*: Christ refers to 'living water' twice in the NT, in John 4.10 and John 7.38. It is not completely clear what the 'living water' is, but it seems likely that Christ was

however pious and plausible, but not carried out in a way that Christ desires, are set aside and opposed, what will we say about actions of a more trivial character of other men who from day-to-day fashion and re-fashion[252] new ways not ordained by Christ but ones introduced by themselves? And certainly at this point, if our disputation [now] in full swing were not beckoning me elsewhere, I would be entering into that immense 'field of speaking'[253] against that Babylonian plague, the Roman Bishop[254] *[The Roman Bishop; and image of the Antichrist]*, an accurate likeness and manifest image of the Antichrist, and bilge from which, as if past recovery, so much sewage and the stink of new ways has flowed[255] contrary to God's ordinances. These have deluged the whole Church in such a way, and have defiled and disturbed the living water[256] in such a way that many have preferred to be enclosed in its many now filthy places than to drink anything from the fountain of Christ.

[40] [188] This 'way' has introduced its own ways into the Church in place of the ways of Christ. And for this reason, Scripture says 'This man will stand in his holy place'.[257] How true this is you will easily learn from the common and untutored folk. For if anyone says 'Act thus'[258] in the way that Christ ordains with transparent words, they (i.e. the common folk) accept that counsel and they do not reject it, but with an insensibility of the heart, which long-standing superstition has instilled in them, they are unwilling to conduct their life according to that way. But [then] if they adopt some private way of living, which the Devil himself has very likely devised, which the Roman curse has sanctioned, and which hypocrisy has led into the light and buttressed through blind custom, they can [only] be dragged and torn from such a way as a polypus[259]

---

referring to the Holy Spirit. Asc. writes the Greek for 'living water' (ὕδωρ ζῶν) in the margin of John 4.10 and also underlines John 7.38 and its final words ὕδατος ζῶντος in GNT.

[257] *Hic... sancto*: Ps. 23.3 (V/S) / 24.3 (H/P). This defines the person who stands in 'His holy place', i.e. the Lord's place, as someone who has clean hands, a pure heart, who has not succumbed to vanity or sworn deceitfully, namely someone who is internally, as opposed to outwardly, moral.

[258] *sic facite*: a phrase found in James 2.12 and also Ben Sira (Ecclesiasticus) 3.2, a work often read by Protestants, but in the fullness of time was not considered to belong to the biblical canon. Asc. must be imagining the words of a priest or a preacher here in the manner of James.

[259] *Polypus*: A polypus is a sort of sea anemone. It is both a Latin and a Greek word, and it is possible that Asc. had in mind Hom.'s *Od.* where a storm-tossed Odysseus is described as clinging to rocks in the manner of a polypus clinging to stones (5.424–35). The point is that a polypus sticks fast to a rock in the same way that sinners cleave to the wrong mode of conduct.

a saxo abstrahi et divelli possunt. At vero, cum non Petro, non Paulo, non Ioanni, aliquando (ut videtur) non ipsi Christo, (nam dicit, Pater, si possibile est, transeat a me calix iste, sed non sicut ego volo, sed sicut tu vis):[260] cum, inquam, non liceat istis, imo non ex bono animo, aliquem novum modum sibi excogitare, quin statim audierint, Abi post me Satana,[261] non sufficit tibi gratia mea,[262] cave ne sic feceris:[263] quid dicemus de modis nostris plurimis,

[41] [189] qui aut ex voluntate hominis, aut voluntate carnis proficiscuntur, sine ulla Dei praescriptione? Non pepercit illis, et parcet nobis? Minime. Quare, cum modus omne factum facit aut malum aut bonum, et unus tantum modus sit bonus, nempe voluntas et verbum Dei, iuxta illud Domini Dei, Hoc tantum facito quod ego praecipio tibi,[264] neque declines ad sinistram, neque ad dextram,[265] hic modus in omnibus nostris factis nobis est perquirendus: quod semper faciemus, si nostram voluntatem ad eius voluntatem adiungamus, adiuvante eo qui dicit, Petite et accipietis:[266] et cum petatis, sic petite:[267] Fiat voluntas tua, sicut in coelo et in terra.[268] Ut voluntas nostra, sic Christi voluntas, duplici modo fit, timendo Deum, et diligendo Deum: timendo, iuxta illud Psalmi, Voluntatem timentium se faciet:[269] diligendo, iuxta illud, Qui diligit me sermonem meum servabit:[270] et sermonem servare, est, voluntatem eius facere, quemadmodum Christus ipse dicit, Non omnis qui dicit. etc.[271] Quamobrem, cum facta nostra nihil sunt, nisi hic modus a me praescriptus illa dirigat,

---

[260] *Pater . . . vis*: Matt. 26.39, and the wording aligns squarely with V and E. The words πλὴν οὐχ ὡς ἐγὼ θέλω ἀλλ' ὡς σύ from this verse have been underlined in GNT. Mark 14.36 contains a similar sentiment, but reads quite differently.
[261] *Abi post me Satana*: Matt. 16.23 / Mark 8.33 See n. 245.
[262] *non sufficit tibi gratia mea*: 2 Corinth. 12.9. See n. 250.
[263] *cave ne sic feceris*: Rev. 22.9. See n. 251, though here Asc.'s wording is different; above he has *Vide ne sic feceris*. He is possibly employing the rhetorical device of *variatio*.
[264] *Hoc . . . tibi*: Deut. 12.32. See n. 218.
[265] *neque . . . dextram*: Prov. 4.27. V: *ne declines ad dexteram et ad sinistram*, and once again, Asc. applies a different word order. The same sentiment is captured in 2 Kings 22.2 concerning Josias.
[266] *Petite et accipietis*: John 16.24, where Christ speaks these words, and V and E use the same phrasing. Asc. underlines the Greek words αἰτεῖτε καὶ λήμψεσθε in GNT.
[267] *cum petatis, sic petite*: In Matt. 6.9, it is Christ who urges the multitude to pray in a similar way with the words *sic ergo vos orabitis . . .* ('Thus therefore shall you pray . . .').

from a rock. But assuredly, since it is not permissible for Peter or Paul or John or sometimes, as it seems, for Christ himself (for he says, 'Father, if it is possible, let that cup pass from me, but not as I want but as you want'),[260] and since, I stress, it is not permissible for those men, even with good intention, to devise any new way for themselves without immediately hearing 'Get thee behind me, Satan',[261] 'My grace is not sufficient for you',[262] and 'Beware not to act thus',[263] what shall we say about the majority of our ways

[41] [189] which originate either in the will of man or the will of the flesh, and without any ordinance from God? He did not spare those men, and [so] will he spare us? Not in the least. Accordingly, when the way makes every action either bad or good, and [since] only one way can be good, that is, the will and the Word of God in keeping with that [instruction] of the Lord God, 'Do only this which I bid you',[264] and 'Turn neither to the left or the right',[265] this is the way that we must search out in all our actions. And this we will always do if we conjoin our will to his will, and with the help of the one who says 'Seek and you will receive',[266] 'Whenever you seek, seek in this way',[267] and 'Let your will be done on earth as it is in Heaven'.[268] Our will, just as the will of Christ, operates in a two-fold way: through fearing God and through loving God. The fear is [encapsulated] in that [part of the] Psalm, 'He will do the will of those who fear him';[269] the love is [encapsulated] in that [pronouncement], 'Whoever loves me will preserve my Word'.[270] And to preserve his Word is to do his will in exactly the way Christ himself enjoins, 'Not everyone who says, etc'.[271] For this reason, since our actions count for nothing unless this way [that is] ordained by me directs them,

---

[268] *Fiat . . . terra*: Matt. 6.10, part of the Lord's Prayer. The wording matches V; cf. *Nov. T: fiat voluntas tua, quemadmodum in coelo, sic etiam in terra*. This part of Matt. is underlined in GNT.

[269] *Voluntatem . . . faciet*: Ps. 144.19 (V/S) / 145.19 (H/P). Asc. follows V.

[270] *Qui . . . servabit*: John 14.23. V and *Nov. T* express this as a conditional: *Si quis diligit me, sermonem meum servabit*, though Ascham may also be conflating this verse and John 14.21 (which is marked up and glossed in GNT): *Qui habet mandata mea et servat ea, ille est qui diligit me* ('He who keeps my commandments and preserves them, he is the one who loves me').

[271] *Non omnis qui dicit. etc.*: Matt. 7.21. The entire verse and sentiment is (as per V) as follows: *non omnis qui dicit mihi 'Domine, Domine', intrabit in regnum caelorum sed qui facit voluntatem Patris mei qui in caelis est ipse intrabit in regnum caelorum* ('Not everyone that says to me "Lord, Lord" shall enter into the kingdom of heaven, but he that does the will of my Father who is in heaven, he shall be the one to enter the kingdom of heaven'). The verse is noted in GNT with the jotting κυε κυε, clearly an abbreviation of Κύριε κύριε.

[42] [190] oremus Deum, ut ipse modificet facta nostra, et tum vera bona opera et salutem nostram operabimur, tum rectis gressibus curremus, et bravium[272] capiemus: tum audacter cum Paulo dicemus, Bonum certamen certavimus, reposita est nobis corona iusticiae, quam reddet, nobis iustus Deus, per eum et propter eum solum, quem misit, Iesum Christum, cui laus in omnem aeternitatem.[273] Amen.

---

[272] *bravium*: a late medieval Latin word, often spelt *brabeum*, and attested to in *DMLBS*.
[273] *Bonum ... aeternitatem*: 2 Tim. 4.7–8, though Asc. has changed the first person singular of Scripture to the first person plural, and more significantly altered quite radically the thrust of the end of 2 Tim. 4.8 so as to place the focus entirely on Christ. Cf. V: *bonum certamen certavi, cursum consummavi, fidem servavi. In reliquo reposita est mihi corona iustitiae, quam reddet mihi Dominus in illa die, iustus iudex* ('I have fought the good fight;

[42] [190] let us pray to God that he restricts our actions, and [then] not only will we bring about truly good works and our salvation, but we will also run on the correct courses and take our reward.[272] Then we shall boldly say with Paul, 'We have fought the good fight; the crown of righteousness is restored to us which he, God [who is] righteous, will render to us through him and on account of him alone whom he sent, Jesus Christ, for whom [there is] praise for all time.[273] Amen'.

I have completed the course; and I have preserved the faith. In what remains, there is laid up for me a crown of righteousness which the Lord, the righteous judge, will return to me in the final day'); *Nov. T*: *certamen bonus decertavi, cursum consummavi fidem servavi. Quod superest, resposita est mihi iusticiae corona, quam reddet mihi dominus in illo die, qui est iustus iudex.*

Theme 5
(43–51)

There is considerable overlap in message and tenor between this theme and theme 4, not least its recurring anti-Roman, anti-Catholic stance. However, unlike the theme above, this one does not appear to have been composed pursuant to a disputation, but rather reads more like a sermon. Its focal point is the image of the 'path' that humans must follow, and Ascham is uncompromising in his assertion that the only correct path is the one that leads directly to God via Christ. Ascham also warns against the creation by men of alternative paths, fashioned through their own volition. The biblical verse from the Old Testament Numbers 22.20 that heads the theme, 'Do only this which I command you', captures the nub of Ascham's argument about the nature of that pathway: it must be one that cleaves always to the Word of God.

Predicatably, given this is a disquisition about Scriptural compliance, both Old and New Testaments are quoted regularly throughout, and lend further ballast to his contention that man must stay within the boundaries of God's Word. The theme also engages in a more obvious way with the Law-Gospel distinction, one that troubled Luther and indeed later Reformed writers.[274] That much is evident in statements such as 'Accordingly, the Father alone must be heard, either under Law, so that we, absolutely terrified, turn from evil, or through Jesus Christ, so that, stout-hearted, we accomplish [what is] good' (44). While Ascham offers no systematic explanation of the function/s or nature of 'moral law', he shows himself cognizant of various suggestions that were then being mooted in contemporary theological debates, including that it served as a form of restraint through fear or as an instrument of guidance, which might help regulate human lives even after Christ's forgiveness of sins. Following an approach similar to one used in theme 4, Ascham additionally provides examples (from both Old and New Testaments) which illustrate how, even in Scripture, good intentions might not be compliant with divine ordinance.

It is at the mid-point of this theme, which comprises a long series of questions and consolatory answers (a similar device was used in theme 1), where it becomes most markedly pastoral in tone. Ascham writes, for instance, and in the manner of a comforting minister:

---

[274] See, for example, Linebaugh 2018.

Surely you are not worried about the entry point onto the path? He himself is the door and the entrance. Are you afraid that you are being led into particular transgressions? He himself is the truth; he will allow you to slip neither to the right nor to the left. Do you dread darkness and night? He himself is the light, illuminating every man coming into this world. (45)

Ascham's next step is to deliberate on the guidance Scripture can offer in three fundamental aspects of life: (i) the civic decrees of leaders; (ii) the rites of the Church; and (iii) our own personal welfare. While seeming at first to concede that Scripture's superintendence in these areas is minimal, Ascham then proceeds to argue that this does not mean that these areas are in any way insignificant, but that all are in fact ordained by God. Ascham then strikingly fuses (i) and (ii), i.e. temporal and sacred power, in what amounts to a confident declaration of the royal supremacy, an issue which would prove so critical during Henry's reign. As for (iii), Ascham suggests that provided care of an individual's person is directed towards the spirit, this also falls within God's purview. Noticeably, Ascham relies on Cicero for a fuller development of this third strand.

[43] [190] Tantum facite quod ego praecipio vobis. Numer. 22.[275]

Vita omnis nostra haec in cursu quodam et perfectione ponitur: civitatem enim manentem hic non habemus, sed ad coelestem illam Hierusalem nos peregrini, qui insiti sumus in Christo Iesu, omni contentione enitimur, ad quam tamen pervenire non poterimus, nisi totum hoc iter nostrum, ex eius sententia solius et consilio (quasi velis quibusdam) gubernatur, qui dicit: *[Propositio]* Tantum facite quod ego praecipio vobis.[276] Nam, qui suas vias unquam ire perrexerunt, quantumvis

[44] [191] directae et pervagatae esse videbantur, non illuc recta contendentes pervenerunt, sed in devia ac transversa loca deflectentes aberrarunt. In hoc ergo humanae vitae curriculo ire pergunt omnes, sed hii recta tantum, quorum gressus dirigit Dominus, et qui in ea persistunt via, quam solam Deus, pater Domini nostri Iesu Christi, tenendam esse praescribit. Unus Deus est, qui est, et in quo est una et omnis bonitas, ad quam una via, licet multifariam patefacta, ut olim apud patres per legem et prophetas, nunc inter nos per Evangelium, sed semper propter Christum,[277] qui ipsa via est, pervenitur. Quaecunque nobis peragenda sunt, in hac demigratione nostra, voce sua praescribit Deus pater: Multifariam enim loquitur Deus, ut olim in Prophetis, ut ait Paulus, nunc in filio qui sermo patris est,[278] dicente ipso patre in Evangelio, *[Confirmatio]*[279] Hic est filius meus dilectus, in quo mihi complacitum est, ipsum audite:[280] solus ergo pater est audiendus, vel in lege, ut perterrefacti declinemus a malo: vel in CHRISTO IESU, ut animati perficiamus bonum.

---

[275] *Tantum ... Numer. 22*: The heading of this theme captures the spirit of Numb. 22.20 but not the actual wording (V: *dumtaxat utquod tibi praecepero facias*). The phrasing is much closer to that of Deut. 12.32, which Asc. cited in the previous theme 4 at 35 and 41. Nevertheless, Asc.'s wording here not only differs from his earlier reference to Deut. (*hoc tantum facito quod ego praecipio tibi*), but also V (*quod praecipio tibi hoc tantum facito Domino*).

[276] *Tantum ... vobis*: A restatement of the heading of the theme, and see n. 275 above. A primary message of the *Themata* is strict obedience to God's mandates.

[277] *olim ... Christum*: Asc. attempts to establish Christ as common to both OT and NT.

[278] *Multifariam ... est*: Asc. relies on Paul's words in Hebr. 1.1-2, but diverges from V: *multifariam et multis modis olim Deus loquens patribus in prophetis novissime diebus istis locutus est nobis in Filio ...* ('God, who, in various ways and multiple ways, formerly

[43] [190] Do only this which I command you. Numbers 22.²⁷⁵

This whole life of ours is placed on a certain course and finite footing. For we don't have a permanent state here, but we travellers, who have been grafted in Jesus Christ, clamber with every effort towards that heavenly Jerusalem, where we, nevertheless, will simply be unable to reach, unless this entire journey of ours is steered as though on particular sails by the judgement and counsel of that one who states, *[The Decree]* 'Do only this which I command you'.²⁷⁶ It is certain that those who have ever continued to follow their own paths, however

[44] [191] direct and well-trodden they seemed to be, [they (i.e. 'those men')] hurrying on, have not [in fact] reached there directly but, by taking a different route, have wandered off into out-of-the-way and outlandish places. Yes, everyone continues to move along this course of human life, but only these [move along it] directly, whose steps the Lord directs, and who adhere to that path which God, the Father of our Lord Jesus Christ, ordains must be the *only* one held to. There is one God who is, and in whom there is one and every goodness to which a single path lies open albeit in various ways, with the result that it was formerly reached by our forefathers, through the Law and prophets and now by us through the Gospel, but *always* by reason of Christ²⁷⁷ who is the path itself. Whatever we must accomplish in this 'migration' of ours God the Father ordains in his own words. Indeed, God speaks in various ways; formerly in the Prophets, as Paul says, and now in the son who is the Word of the Father,²⁷⁸ as the Father himself enunciates in the Gospel *[The adducement of proof]*,²⁷⁹ 'This is my beloved son, in whom I am well pleased: hear him'.²⁸⁰ Accordingly, the Father alone must be heard, either under Law, so that we, absolutely terrified, turn from evil, or through Jesus Christ, so that, stout-hearted, we accomplish [what is] good.

---

speaking unto the fathers by the prophets; and most recently in these days has spoken to us by his son ...'); and from *Nov. T: Deus olim multiphariam, multisque modis locutus patribus per prophetas, extremis diebus hisce locutus est nobis per filium....* Asc. introduces an interesting flourish when he refers to Christ as *sermo patris*.

²⁷⁹ [Confirmatio]: This hanging note is a technical term in rhetoric and can be found, for example, in Cic. *De inv.* 1.24.34 and Quint. *Inst.* 4.3.1 and 4.4.1.

²⁸⁰ *Hic ... audite*: Asc. seems to invoke Matt. 17.5; V: *hic est Filius meus dilectus in quo mihi bene conplacuit ipsum audite*; *Nov. T: hic est meus filius dilectus, in quo bene mihi bene complacitum est, ipsum audite*. Asc., however, has omitted *bene*, and thus may also have in mind any of Matt. 3.17, Luke 9.35 and 2 Peter 1.17. Asc. may also have taken into account the Greek, which also just has a compound verb (εὐδόκησα) and no additional adverb equivalent to *bene*.

[45] [192] Qui extra hanc viam unum pedem ponunt, ad patrem pervenire non possunt: nam sola ea sunt bona et spiritualia, quae praescripta sunt a Deo: et omnia ea sunt mala et carnalia, quae orta sunt ab homine, iuxta illud Evangelii, Quod natum est ex carne, caro est.[281] Viam quam praescribit Deus, et viam quam sibi fingit caro, vel homo, si inter se conferamus, quam haec sola sit proxima et maxime compendiaria ad Deum, illa multis implicata erroribus, rectissima tamen ad interitum, planum admodum et manifestum erit.

Ad patrem via solus Christus Iesus est,[282] quo nihil vel ad sequendum tutius, vel ad ducendum rectius, quo pervenire cupimus: etenim, non solum eo nos recta perducit quo volumus, sed omnem omnium impedimentorum curam summovet quae timere possumus. Num de introitu in viam sollicitus es? Ipse ostium et ianua est.[283] Ne[284] in errores aliquos perducaris extimescis? Ipse veritas est,[285] qui te neque ad dextram, neque ad sinistram delabi patietur.[286] Tenebras et noctes exhorrescis? Ipse lux est illuminans omnem hominem venientem in hunc mundum.[287] Ne de longinquitate viae fessus

[46] [193] [N.] defatigeris, anxius es? Venite ad me omnes qui laboratis et onerati estis, et ego reficiam vos.[288] Digressu Christi a nobis et antecessione eius ad patrem perturbaris? Ob hoc laetare potius,[289] nam vadit paraturus nobis locum.[290] Solus te in hanc viam das? Confide, non derelinquet nos orphanos.[291] Impedimenta, quae mundus obiecerit, formidas? Bono animo sis, ille vicit mundum.[292]

---

[281] *Quod . . . est*: John 3.6. The wording matches V and *Nov. T.* Asc. inscribes the Greek terms ἐκ σαρ[ ], γεγεννημέν[ ] and ἐκ πνε[ ] adjacent to this verse in the margin of GNT (the page is damaged in places).

[282] *via . . . est*: This is the first limb of a prolonged reference to John 14.6 (*ego sum via et veritas et vita*), the three elements of which Asc. will track over this page and the next. John's Gospel dominates this part of the theme. Asc. notes these three elements in GNT, writing, ὁδός, ἀλήθεια, ζωή.

[283] *Ipse ostium et ianua est*: In John 10.7 and 9, Christ (as per V and *Nov. T*) says *ego sum ostium ovium* and *ego sum ostium*. Asc. scribbled ἡ θύρα χος in the margin of GNT next to John 10.7 (χος standing for Christ). This marks the start of another question and answer scheme that Asc. uses in several themes (1 and 8). Each of the answers follows a biblical verse, several of which are re-used from theme to theme.

[284] *ne*: is not an enclitic interrogative, but is rather to be taken after the verb of fearing, *extimescis*.

[285] *Ipse veritas est*: John 14.6 (again); see n. 282.

[45] [192] Those who place one foot from this path are unable to reach the Father. For only those things which have been ordained by God are good and of the spirit; everything which has sprung from man is evil and of the flesh, as that Gospel phrase [indicates], 'Whatever is born of flesh is flesh'.[281] As for the path which God ordains and the path which the flesh – or rather man – fashions for himself, if we were to compare them, it'll be completely plain and clear how only the first path is closest and easily the shortest [route] to God, whereas the latter is entangled in many transgressions and is the most direct [route] to ruin.

Jesus Christ alone is the path to the Father;[282] nothing is safer than him to be followed or more direct to be led along, and [he is] the destination we crave to reach. What's more, not only does he lead us directly to the place we want, but he clears away every concern about every obstacle that we can [possibly] fear. Surely you are not worried about the entry point onto the path? He himself is the door and the entrance.[283] Are you afraid that[284] you are being led into particular transgressions? He himself is the truth;[285] he will allow you to slip neither to the right nor to the left.[286] Do you dread darkness and night? He himself is the light, illuminating every man coming into this world.[287] Are you worried that, exhausted,

[46] [193] [N.] you may be fatigued by the length of the path? Come to me all who toil and are burdened, and I will refresh you.[288] Are you troubled by the departure of Christ from us and the journey [he made] in advance to the Father? Rejoice rather because of this,[289] for he goes in order to prepare a place for us.[290] Do you devote yourself to this path on your own? Be confident; he will not abandon us as orphans.[291] Do you fear the obstacles which the world has cast in the way? Be of good courage; he has conquered the world.[292]

---

[286] *neque ... patietur*: Prov. 4.27 / 2 Kings 22; see also n. 265.
[287] *Ipse ... mundum*: John 1.9; see n. 69.
[288] *Venite ... vos*: Matt. 11.28. The wording matches V and *Nov. T*. This verse is again marked up in GNT.
[289] *Ob hoc laetare potius*: seems to capture the spirit of Luke 10.20, namely ... *gaudete autem, quod nomina vestra scripta sunt in caelis* ('... but rejoice [in this] that your names are written in heaven').
[290] *nam ... locum*: John 14.2. V: ... *quia vado parare vobis locum*. Asc.'s wording is closer to *Nov. T*: *vado paraturus vobis locum*. The switch to the future participle is to avoid the unclassical infinitive of purpose, although it also means for 'improving' the Greek, which also has an infinitive – πορεύομαι ἑτοιμάσαι τόπον ὑμῖν.
[291] *non derelinquet nos orphanos*: John 14.18. V and *Nov. T*: *non relinquam vos orphanos*. This verse has been underlined and highlighted with a manicule in GNT.
[292] *Bono ... mundum*: John 16.33; see n. 75 above.

Peccatorum onera metuis? Ecce agnus Dei qui sustulit peccata mundi.[293] Legis implendae impossibilitatem times? Ipse perfectio legis est ad iusticiam omni credenti.[294] Diaboli vim et tyrannidem, ne te de via deturbet, vereris? Venit Princeps huius mundi, et in illum non potest quicquam.[295] Mortis terrore turbaris? Mors morti fuit, nec post haec mors dominabitur unquam.[296] Perpetuo vivendi desiderio accenderis? Ipse vita est,[297] et semper vivit, ut nos in eo in aeternum vivamus.[298] Solus ergo Christus Iesus via est, quae nos recta sine omni circuitionis errore,[299] periculive metu, fert et perducit ad patrem. Itaque cum quaecunque praecipit pater, praecipit per filium, filius aut non sua, sed quae sunt patris loquatur, (Sermonem

[47] [194] enim quem audistis, etc.)[300] et solus filius a nobis est sequendus: ergo tantummodo nobis sunt facienda quae praecipit pater. Contra, de via hominis plurima sunt loca in Scripturis, sed paucissima attingemus.[301] *[Proverb. 14.]* Via hominis (Prover. 14.) recta est in conspectu eius, sed extremum eius via mortis.[302] *[Deut. 12.]* Et Deut. 12. Non facietis singuli quod sibi rectum videtur.[303] Et Samuel ad Saul: *[1. Sam. 15.]* Numquid voluntas Domini est in holocaustis et victimis, sicut in obtemperando voci eius? Solum enim parere melius est quam sacrificium: et auscultare quam adeps arietum.[304] Zeloticus enim Deus est tuus, nec cum altero quicquam communicat.[305] *[Eccle. 3.]*

---

[293] *Ecce ... mundi*: John 1.29. When Asc. cited this at 10 he used the present tense of the verb, *tollit* (as per V and *Nov. T* – see n. 72 – though here he uses *sustulit*, which appears to have been an independent decision. The Greek has a present participle, αἴρων.

[294] *Ipse ... credenti*: Rom. 10.4; see also n. 74.

[295] *Venit ... quicquam*: John 14.30, except Asc. has *in illum* rather than *in me* (as per V). When Asc. uses the phrase at 10 he has *in illo*, which is more compatible with the Greek, which has ἐν ἐμοί.

[296] *Nec ... umquam*: Rom. 6.9. V: *mors illi ultra non dominabitur*; *Nov. T*: *mors illi non amplius dominatur*.

[297] *Ipse vita est*: John 14.6 (again).

[298] *semper ... vivamus*: Probably a paraphrase of John 11.25: *ego sum resurrectio et vita. Qui credit in me, etsi mortuus fuerit, vivet* ('I am the resurrection and the life. He who believes in me, even though he is dead, will live'); or John 12.25: *qui amat animam suam perdet eam et qui odit animam suam in hoc mundo in vitam aeternam custodit* ('He that loves his life shall lose it, and he that hates his life in this world keeps it unto life eternal').

[299] *error*: denotes both a mistake and a wandering.

[300] *Sermonem ... audistis, etc.*: John 14.24. The full verse is: *et sermonem quem audistis non est meus sed eius qui misit me Patris* ('And the word which you have heard is not mine, but the Father's who sent me'). The start of this part in *Nov. T* is: *sermo quem auditis* ....

Do you fear the burdens of sins? Behold, the lamb of God who has removed the sins of the world.[293] Do you fear the impossibility of fulfilling the Law? He himself is the fulfilment of the Law for the righteousness of everyone who believes.[294] Are you afraid of the power and tyranny of the Devil, that they may force you from the path? The prince of this world is coming, but has no claim over him.[295] Are you troubled by a fear of death? He (i.e. Christ) was death was to death, and death will never have dominion after this.[296] Are you inflamed by a desire to live eternally? He himself is life,[297] and lives always, with the result that we live in him forever.[298] Jesus Christ alone, then, constitutes the path that brings and leads us directly to the Father without every fool's errand[299] or fear of danger. And so, when all that the Father commands, he commands through his son, his son should speak, not indeed with his own words, but those of his Father,

[47] [194] 'For the Word which you have heard ...' etc.,[300] and we must only follow the son; accordingly, we must only do what the father commands. Conversely, there are a multitude of examples in Scripture concerning the path of man, but we will touch on just a few [of them].[301] *[Proverbs 14]* Proverbs 14 [tells us], 'The way of man seems right in his view, but the end of it is the way of death,[302] and Deuteronomy 12 *[Deuteronomy 12]*, 'You shall not do what seems right, each for himself'.[303] Additionally, Samuel [says] to Saul *[I Samuel 15]*, 'Does the will of the Lord lie in burnt offerings and sacrifices, as though [this constituted] compliance with his voice? Indeed, the simple act of obedience is superior to a sacrifice, and attentiveness [is superior] to the fat of rams'.[304] For your God is jealous, and does not communicate anything with another.[305] And [there's also]

---

[301] *Contra ... attingemus*: Although Asc.'s examples point to the potential for man to contravene God's ordinance, each reinforces the need to obey God's Word.
[302] *Via ... mortis*: Prov. 14.12. Asc. diverges from V: *est via quae videtur homini iusta novissima autem eius deducunt ad mortem* ('There is a way that seems righteous to man, but its ends lead to death').
[303] *Non ... videtur*: Deut. 12.8. Asc. produces a rather terser version than V: *non facietis ibi quae nos hic facimus hodie singuli quod sibi rectum videtur*.
[304] *Et ... arietum*: I Sam. 15.22, though the wording differs slightly from V: *Et ait Samuel, Numquid vult Dominus holocausta et victimas, et non potius ut obediatur voci Domini? Melior est enim obedientia quam victimae: et auscultare magis quam offerre adipem arietum*. Asc.'s version is much closer to Pag. This and several of the examples that follow are also alluded to in Asc. *Apol*. (Nicholas 2017: 40–43) and also contribute to his argument in theme 4.
[305] *Zeloticus ... communicat*: The same point appears, almost word for word, in Asc. *Apol*. (Nicholas 2017: 38–39). The phrase 'jealous God' is used in Ex. 20.5 and 34.14. *Zeloticus* is not a classical word (this would normally be *zelotypus*), nor attested to in *DMLBS*, but has evidently been Latinised by Asc. from the Greek ζηλωτικός, found in Arist. *Rhet*. 2.11.1 (here ζηλωτικοὺς).

Et Eccle. 3. Vias novas ne scrutatus fueris, sed quae praecipit tibi Deus, illa cogita semper.[306] Praeterea, quod voluntas hominis etiam bona displicet Deo, si extra praescriptum eius ponatur, et non finibus verbi Dei coerceatur, ex Scripturis manifesto liquet. *[Exod. 32.]* Bono enim animo populus Israeliticus, etiam cum consensu Aaronis, aureos vitulos erexerant, sed absque Mose fuisset, universum illum coetum dominus delevisset.[307] *[Iudic. 8.]* Bono animo etiam Gedeon ephod Domino

[48] [195] [N.ii.] consecravit, qua tamen re magnam Domini offensionem sibi comparavit.[308] *[1. Sam. 15.]* Bono animo et Saul victis Amalichitis armentum in victimam Domini reservavit, sed contra audivit a Samuele, Pro eo quod[309] contempsisti verbum Domini, abiecit te ne sis ultra rex supra Israel.[310] Bono animo Petrus aurem Malco praecidit *[Matth. 26; Marc. 14; Luc. 22; Ioan. 18.]*:[311] bono animo Paulus stimulum carnis auferri sibi rogavit:[312] quae facta quamvis a sanctissimis primariisque viris profecta, Deo tamen displicebant, qui iubet nos facere tantum ea, quae ipse praescribit nobis. *[Confutatio.]* Huic sententiae tres potissimum res sunt, quae primo aspectu nonnihil controversari videntur, Principum civiliaque decreta, Religionis et ecclesiasticae ceremoniae,[313] Vitaeque nostrae ac corporis huius tuendi rationes: quae res, ut magnam authoritatem, summa cum necessitate coniunctam habent: ita nullam aliquam illustrem et insignem earum praescriptam a Deo mentionem, in scriptura sibi vendicare[314] posse videntur. Sed si hoc pro certo tenendum sit, Nihil nobis esse faciendum, nisi quod Deus ipse praecipiat, quem locum istis tribus rebus tribuamus, obscura quaedam res,

---

[306] *Vias ... semper*: Ecclesiasticus 3.22. Asc. has diverged from V: *altiora te ne scrutaveris et fortiora te ne exquisieris sed quae praecepit tibi Deus illa cogita semper*. Ascham may have approved of *scrutatus fueris* used in Pag, but in all other respects Pag matches V. The idiosyncratic phrasing appears in Asc. *Apol.* (Nicholas 2017: 38–39).

[307] *populus ... delevisset*: This episode is recounted in Ex. 32.4–10. The Lord threatened to unleash his wrath because of this false form of worship.

[308] *Gedeon ... comparavit*: Judges 8.27. The verse indicates that Gideon made an ephod (a sleeveless garment worn by Jewish priests), and that it became a ruin to Gideon and his house; there is no *explicit* reference to God's disapproval, though this can of course be inferred. The example is replicated in Asc. *Apol.* (Nicholas 2017: 40–41).

Ecclesiasticus 3 *[Eccles. 3]*, 'Don't be looking out for new ways, but what[ever] God commands for you think on that always'.³⁰⁶ Moreover, that the will of man, even when it is good, displeases God if it falls beyond his ordinance and is not contained within the boundaries of God's Word, is manifestly evident from Scripture. *[Exodus, 32]* For instance, the people of Israel with good intention and even with the consent of Aaron had erected golden calves, but it would have been contrary to [the Law of] Moses, and the Lord would have destroyed that entire company.³⁰⁷ Similarly, with good intention *[Judges 8]*, Gideon consecrated an ephod to the Lord,

[48] [195] [N.ii.] but in so doing earned for himself the great disapproval of the Lord.³⁰⁸ *[Samuel, I, 15]* Also with good intention, Saul, following his conquest of the Amalekites, kept back cattle as a sacrifice to the Lord, but he heard something to the contrary from Samuel, 'Forasmuch³⁰⁹ as you have scorned the Word of the Lord, he has rejected you from being King of Israel any longer'.³¹⁰ With good intention, Peter cut off Malcus' ear *[Matthew, 26; Mark, 14; Luke 22; John 18]*.³¹¹ With good intention, Paul asked for the torment of flesh to be removed from himself.³¹² These actions which, although they were carried out by the most sacred and most important men, were nonetheless displeasing to God, who orders us to do only those things which he himself ordains for us. *[Refutation]* There are three principal strands to this issue [before us], which at first sight seem not to be in dispute at all: (i) the civic decrees of leaders; (ii) the rites³¹³ of religion and the Church; and (iii) the business of our own life and the maintenance of this body [of ours]. These considerations, [even] as they carry great authority together with the utmost importance, seem unable to find³¹⁴ for themselves any clear and distinct basis in what God has ordained in Scripture. But if this [principle] that we must do nothing unless it is what God himself commands must be adhered to as fact, [the question of] what status we grant to these three points ought rightly to seem like a matter of some uncertainty,

---

³⁰⁹ *Pro eo quod*: literally, 'for that which', but more naturally, 'inasmuch as ...' (*OLD* 16c).
³¹⁰ *Saul ... Israel*: a paraphrase of I Sam. 15.21–26 generally, and especially verse 26 – V: *proiecisti sermonem Domini et proiecit te Dominus ne sis rex super Israel* ('You have rejected the word of the Lord, and the Lord has rejected you from being king over Israel').
³¹¹ *Petrus aurem Malco praecidit*: Matt. 26.51; Mark 14.47; Luke 22.50; and John 18.10; and see n. 246. Asc's wording varies from that he used in theme 4.
³¹² *Paulus ... rogavit*: 2 Corinthians 12.7–8. See also n. 248. Asc's wording varies from that he used in theme 4.
³¹³ *ceremoniae*: an alternative form for *caerimoniae*.
³¹⁴ *vendicare*: an alternative form for *vindicare*.

[49] [196] et plena quaestionis, iure videri debet. Ad quam dubitationem hanc facilem responsionem adhibere possumus: Non per hunc locum Scripturae, vel principum decreta tolli, vel Ecclesiasticas ceremonias diminui, vel corporis carnisque nostrae curam negligi[315] debere: sed omnes has res hinc maximam ad se constituenda[316] authoritatem adipisci. Nam Ecclesiae omnes, quarum capita reges sunt post Christum, non sua, sed Christi ferunt decreta: non enim est potestas nisi in Deo, quae autem sunt, a Deo ordinatae sunt:[317] itaque qui resistit potestatibus, Dei ordinationi resistit. Etenim qui Ecclesiam audit, Christum audit, ut est praeclare positum apud Evangelistam, Qui vos audit, me audit: qui vos spernit, me spernit.[318] Et qui Christum audit, Deum patrem audit: nam patris sermo Christus est, quod confirmat et ipse Pater, cum dicit: Hic est filius meus dilectus, ipsum audite:[319] ergo, decreta principum et Ecclesiae inter praescriptiones Dei continentur. Ad haec, religionis nostrae ceremoniae omnes, quae ad pietatem necessariae sunt, ex Dei Patris scriptione (veluti ex fonte quodam)[320] ductae sunt et accersitae:[321]

[50] [197] [N.iii.] dicit enim Paulus, Fiant omnia decenter in Ecclesia.[322] Nam censet sanctus ille Dei vir turpe admodum et vitiosum esse, nos in reliquis omnibus vitae nostrae rationibus summam elegantiam et munditiem solere ostentare, in rerum sacrarum sacrosancta tractatione venustatis omnis dignitatisque plena, rudis cuiusmodi et inhumanae negligentiae velle condemnari.[323] Ceremoniae ergo decentes decenter in Ecclesia sunt retinendae, et tamdiu sunt decentes, quamdiu sunt loquentes, et negotii sui bene gerentes:[324] sin vero fuerint vel mutae et otiosae, vel nimis loquaces et

---

[315] *negligi*: an alternative form for *neglegi*.
[316] *constituenda*: The neuter plural of the gerundive is difficult here, and *constituendas* in agreement with *has res* would have been better.
[317] *quae . . . ordinatae*: must be referring to *ecclesiae* rather than *decreta*.
[318] *Qui . . . spernit*: Luke 10.16. The wording replicates V and *Nov. T*. This verse is underlined in GNT.
[319] *Hic . . . audite*: Luke 9.35. The wording matches V and *Nov. T*, but see also n. 280.
[320] *veluti ex fonte quodam*: The allusion speaks directly to the notion of *ad fontes*, a fundamental axiom for adherents of *sola scriptura*.
[321] *accerso*: from which *accersitae* comes is an alternative form for the verb *arcesso*.
[322] *Fiant . . . Ecclesia*: 1 Corinth. 14.40. Asc. veers from V: *omnia autem honeste et secundum ordinem fiant* and his wording is closer to *Nov. T*: *omnia decenter et secundum ordinem fiant*. Significantly, however, unlike V or E, Ascham has related this injunction expressly to the Church.

[49] [196] and [one] full of doubt. In [the face of] this lack of certainty, we can offer this straightforward response, that this status of Scripture does not mean that the edicts of leaders ought to be annulled, the rites of the Church be minimised, or care of our body and flesh be neglected;[315] rather, all these matters possess enormous standing in the hierarchy of life[316] for this reason: because all churches, the heads of which are kings after Christ, advance not their own edicts but those of Christ, for there is no power unless from God, and those churches that exist have been decreed[317] by God. Accordingly, the man who resists [these] powers resists the decree of God. Conversely, the man who hears the Church hears Christ, as is clearly set out in [the writings of] the Evangelist, 'He who hears you, hears me; he who rejects you, rejects me.'[318] [It] also [follows that] he who hears Christ hears God the Father, for Christ is the Word of the Father, a point the Father himself also confirms when he says, 'This is my beloved son; hear him.'[319] And so, the edicts of leaders and of the Church are included within God's ordinances. In the same way, all the rites of our religion which are necessary for worship have been drawn and derived,[321] just as from some fountainhead,[320] from the writings of God the Father.

[50] [197] [N.iii.] For instance, Paul says 'May everything happen appropriately in the Church.'[322] Indeed, that holy man of God (i.e. Paul) considers it altogether shameful and reprehensible that we in every other aspect of our life habitually apply the utmost fastidiousness and cleanliness, but in the sacrosanct management of sacred business [that's] brimming with every charm and excellence, we are willing to be charged with every type of rough and uncivil neglect.[323] Accordingly, appropriate rites must be appropriately maintained in Church, and while they are appropriate, they are thereby conveying and conducting his business effectively.[324] But if indeed they (i.e. the rites) lie either

---

[323] *inhumanae ... condemnari*: *condemno* is followed by the genitive of the crime. *negligentiae*: an alternative form for *neglegentiae*. The argumentation employed here is very similar to Cic. *Tusc.*, where Cic. says to Brutus: 'Seeing, Brutus, that we are made up of soul and body, what am I to think is the reason why for the care and maintenance of the body there has been devised an art which from its usefulness has had its discovery attributed to immortal gods, and is regarded as sacred, whilst on the other hand the need of an art of healing for the soul has not been felt so deeply before its discovery, nor has it been studied so closely after becoming known, nor welcomed with the approval of so many, and has even been regarded by a greater number with suspicion and hatred?' (3.1.1) *LCL*, trans. J. E. King, 1927. Indeed, in what follows (50–51), Asc. appears to rely regularly on this Ciceronian text, and he refers directly to Cic. at 51.

[324] *negotii sui bene gerentes*: When *gerentes*, the present participle, acts as a pure adjective, it is followed by the genitive, as here (*negotii sui*). See also Cic. *Quinct. sui negotii bene gerens* (19.62).

curiosae, ut iniuste audeant in verae sanctimoniae possessiones irruere, ut bona pars illarum solebat, quae ex eluvie et faecibus Romanae sentinae exhauriebantur, tum profecto sunt vel corrigendae, vel omnino tollendae: potestati enim Principis et Ecclesiae subiiciuntur. Itaque, ceremoniae decentes per potestatem sunt traditae, potestas omnis est ex Deo, ergo ceremoniae sunt ex Deo.[325] Sed cura carnis nostrae tuendae[326] sive per cibum, sive per vestitum, sive per somnum, a Deo nobis non est praescripta, certo est, cum scriptura

[51] [198] dicit, Nemo carnem suam odio habere debet, quia templum spiritus sancti est.[327] Hoc tantum monemur, ne curam carnis agamus ad libidinem: nam tum spiritui Dei resistit, cui semper inservire debet. Praeterea, gratia Dei nos nascimur, atque vivimus, ex qua gratia a primo ortu nostro didicimus, et quasi cum lacte nutricis suximus,[328] nosipsos, vitam, corpusque tueri, et ea omnia declinare, quae nocitura esse videantur, ut praeclare docet Cicero, qui cum de gratia Dei nihil unquam accepit,[329] non sine gratia Dei tamen hoc beneficium Naturae bonitati, quae nomine magis quam re discrepat a gratia, tribuit.[330] *[Conclusio.]* Quamobrem cum ita sunt, clare sequitur, quod decreta Principum, Ecclesiasticae ceremoniae, et corporis nostri tuendi cura, a Deo nobis praescribuntur: et cum hae tres res fines prope sunt et termini, quibus tota haec vita nostra circundata contineatur, quisquis is certe fuerit qui aliam vitam extra hos fines positam sequi vult, ubi ipsi[331] blandiri potest, ego tamen illius vitam probare non audeo, quia Dominus dicit, Tantum facite quae ego praecipio vobis.[332]

---

[325] *Itaque ... Deo*: These propositions are set out in syllogistic form, a technique still viewed as acceptable in the mid-sixteenth century.
[326] *cura carnis nostrae tuendae*: Cic. refers to *corporis curandi tuendique* ('care and maintenance of the body') in *Tusc.* 3.1.1.
[327] *Nemo ... est*: 1 Corinth. 6.19. Cf. V: *An nescitis quoniam membra vestra, templum sunt Spiritus Sancti*. Asc. evidently also has in mind 1 Corinth. 6.15–20 generally.
[328] *cum lacte nutricis suximus*: A striking phrase, also used in Cic. *Tusc.* 3.1.2: ... *ut paene cum lacte nutricis errorem suxisse videamur* (' ... so that it seems as if we drank in deception with our nurse's milk'). Cic. suggests that all human dispositions are endowed with an inbuilt virtue, but as soon as we are born and progress through life, we are led astray. In *Tox.*, Asc. uses the allusion of a babe suckling on mother's pap (Giles, vol. II, 29)

mute and idle, or too verbose and meddlesome, with the result that they have the audacity, without good reason, to seize a claim to true morality, as a good portion of those which were drained from the discharge and dregs of Roman sewage were accustomed [to do], then certainly these must be corrected or altogether annulled. Indeed, they (i.e. the rites) are subordinate to the power of a leader and the Church. It follows that appropriate rites are bequeathed via [some] power; all power derives from God; therefore, rites derive from God.[325] Yet we have not been instructed by God to maintain with [any] care our bodies,[326] be it with food or with clothing or with sleep, and that is for certain. Nay, Scripture [simply]

[51] [198] stipulates 'No one ought to despise his own body; that's because it is the temple of the Holy Spirit'.[327] We are advised only this, not to direct care for the body towards wantonness, because one then resists the spirit of God to which one ought always defer. Besides, we are born and we live by the grace of God, and from this grace we have learnt from the day we were born, just as though suckled by the milk of a wet-nurse,[328] to conserve ourselves, [our] life and body, and to avoid all those things that seem bound to harm us. This is something Cicero teaches very clearly, [a man] who, although he benefitted in no way from the grace of God,[329] nevertheless, not without the grace of God, attributed this benefit to the goodness of Nature, which differs more in name than in substance from grace.[330] *[Conclusion]* Since things are as they are, it clearly follows that edicts of leaders, Church rites, and a care for the maintenance of our body are ordained for us by God. And since these three points in effect constitute the boundaries and parameters by which this whole life of ours should be contained and circumscribed, whoever he is who yet aspires to pursue another [type of] life that goes beyond these boundaries – where [indeed] it is possible for him to delude himself[331] – I don't dare approve of his life because the Lord says, 'Do only what I command you'.[332]

---

[329] *cum ... accepit*: In classical Latin a subjunctive as opposed to an indicative would be expected in a *cum* concessive clause, though Asc., here and elsewhere in the text, is more relaxed about this.

[330] *Praeterea ... tribuit*: I have broken up the sentence in the translation. Again, Asc. seems to have in mind Cic. *Tusc.* 3.1.1–3, where Cic. suggests that Nature can provide all the insight we need for the care of the soul and *ad beatam vitam* ('for the blessed life').

[331] *ipsi*: This should correctly be *sibi* if it is reflexive, but there was a certain flexibility regarding the use of pronouns in early modern Latin.

[332] *Tantum ... vobis*: Asc. ends with the biblical dictum with which he began this theme (from Deut. 12.32), but his wording is here slightly different even to the heading.

Thema 6
(52–54)

One of the shortest themes in the collection, theme 6, hinges on a verse from a Pauline letter, Ephesians 4.26 (and also Psalm 4). Although the piece employs the term *quaestio* (right at the end), it in fact reads more like a philosophical meditation than a disputation, and was possibly intended to serve as a sermon; the term '*oratio*' that Ascham uses in the theme could denote a 'sermon'. The exhortation 'Be angry and sin not' is a theologically complex one, and captures a delicate distinction between just and sinful anger. However, the question of exactly where just anger ends and excessive rage begins requires considerable judgement and interpretation. The nature of anger had been debated extensively in the ancient world (most influentially in the writing of Aristotle (*Nicomachean Ethics*), Cicero (*Tusculan Disputations*, books 3 and 4, in particular), Seneca (*On Anger*) and Plutarch (*On Controlling Anger*)). It was also a well-tilled topic in the writings of the Church Fathers and Doctors of the Church. The early modern period too attached great importance to the mastering, moderating and management of anger, and much space was given over to the topic in philosophical and theological debates.[333] Ascham's theme then falls within a much larger historical preoccupation about the phenomenon.

As is evident in other parts of this collection, a favourite approach is a taxonomic one, as Ascham catalogues different species of anger.[334] Some types contravene God's will, but others are more constructive, and Ascham suggests that anger can be turned to productive use in certain circumstances. One of these is the *ira peccati* ('the anger of sin'), which Ascham, citing Augustine, avers can facilitate a meaningful examination of one's conscience through repentance. The final form in this catalogue Ascham terms *fervor mentis* ('an ardour of the mind'), which he suggests can very effectively work to the 'glory of God'. He elucidates this form with some highly descriptive language, and its main attribute seems to be a form of self-control, a *via media* of the sort he adumbrates elsewhere in the collection. While this may sound rather Senecan / Stoic, it does not appear that Ascham was using *De ira* ('On Anger') or indeed

---

[333] Enenkel / Trainiger 2015: 7–8.
[334] Asc. evinces an interest in anger generally, writing in the margin of GNT next to Matt. 5.22 the Greek word for anger, ὀργή.

had access to it. It is noteworthy, however, that the term *fervor mentis* is a Ciceronian phrase used in *De oratore*.[335] Ascham was by no means alone in synthesising classical and Christian ideas in the matter of *ira*, but this final limb was a very distinctive avenue of argumentation.

---

[335] See n. 345 below.

[52] [199] [N.iiii.] Irascimini et nolite peccare. Ephesi. 4.[336]

Variam ex sacra Scriptura iram docti viri collegerunt,[337] unam a fide non separant, alteram in carne nostra collocant. *[Ira carnis]* Ira carnis,[338] gravissimum delictum est, quam[339] Deo odiosam, hominibus molestam, cum belluis communem habemus. Haec ira hominem immensum in modum foedat et exagitat: nam intus, viscera nostra torquet et enervat: foris, proximum quenque affligit atque cruciat: de cuius universa vi et natura, longam orationem instituerim, nisi quod minime et mihi necessarium, et huius loci proprium illud esset intelligerem.[340] Et propterea, de huiusmodi ira, quam carnis voco, hoc satis hoc tempore dictum sit, non eam esse illam iram, de qua Propheta et Apostolus loquuntur, Irascimini et nolite peccare:[341] quoniam a peccato nullo modo abesse aut separari potest. Ira, qua irasci potest quis, et non peccare, fidei ira dicitur *[Ira fidei]*: quia cum fide rectissime coniungitur: et ad similitudinem huius irae Deum irasci legimus:[342]

[53] [200] quam cum in Deo collocamus, ab omni peccati societate eam segregamus. In hominibus haec ira fidei ex diversis hominum officiis diversa nomina invenit: nam Magistratus omnes, sive hii qui praesunt religioni, sive illi qui dominantur reliquae Reipublicae, iustu nonnunquam irasci dicimus: et eam Correctionis iram nominamus. *[Ira correctionis.]* Ad haec, parentes sive genitores fuerint, quorum beneficio vivimus: sive praeceptores fuerint, quorum praesidio bene vivimus, irasci nobis sine peccato fatemur: *[Ira monitionis.]* et hanc Monitionis iram appellamus. Est et altera ira, quae Peccati ira dicitur *[Ira peccati.]*, cum homo gravissime vitiis et delictis suis irascitur, quae paenitentiam veram quasi socia atque

---

[336] *Irascimini et nolite peccare*: Ephes. 4.26. The wording matches V, but not *Nov. T*: *irascimini et non peccetis*. The sentiment is also found in Ps. 4.5 (V/S) / 4.4 (H/P).

[337] *Variam... collegerunt*: For a fuller overview of the influential (albeit often contradictory) positions on anger that were developed through the ages from Arist. to the Church Fathers, and that Asc. must have in mind here, see Enenkel / Trainiger 2015: 2–4. *collegerunt* could also mean that learned men have 'gathered together' forms of anger from Scripture.

[338] *Ira carnis*: Elsewhere in theological writing sometimes also referred to as '*ira per vitium*' and '*ira per zelum*'.

[52] [199] [N.iiii.] Be angry and sin not. Ephesians 4.[336]

Learned men have reflected on various [forms of] anger in sacred Scripture:[337] one [form] they do not treat separately from faith; the other they confine to our flesh. The anger of the flesh[338] *[Anger of the flesh]* is a very serious offence that[339] we hold to be hateful to God, grievous to men, and an attribute we share with beasts. This anger corrupts and torments a man to a high degree, for within us it twists and weakens our innards, and outside [ourselves] it impairs one's closest neighbour and causes him grief. I could have spoken at length about the universal force and nature of anger were I not of the view that, in this instance, this was not at all necessary or fitting.[340] Henceforth, concerning this type of anger, which I term 'of the flesh', let this which has been said suffice for the moment, [namely that] it does not comprise that anger about which the Prophet and the Apostle say, 'Be angry and sin not'.[341] This is because this [type of anger] cannot be absent from sin or separated from it in any way at all. The anger by which someone can become angry and not sin is called the 'anger of faith' *[Anger of faith]* since it is very correctly conjoined with faith. For an example of this sort of anger, we read that God 'becomes angry'.[342]

[53] [200] Although we situate this anger in God, we distinguish it from all association with sin. Among men, this anger of faith meets with a range of names from the range of men's offices. All public functionaries, whether those who preside over religion or those who govern the rest of the state, we suggest sometimes and justifiably become angry, and we term this 'the anger of correction' *[Anger of correction.]* Additionally, in the case of parents or begetters with whose support we have life or teachers with whose help we live conscienciously, we admit that they are angry with us, but without any sin, and we label this the 'anger of advice' *[Anger of Advice]*. There is also another [form of] anger which is called 'the anger of sin' *[Anger of Sin]* when a man becomes intensely angry because of his own deficiencies and offences, and this is always consequent upon true repentance, as though an ally and a

---

[339] *Ira ... quam*: The antecedent of *quam* is of course *ira* not *delictum*.
[340] *De ... intelligerem*: A rather unclassical formulation here, with a perfect subjunctive (*instituerim*) in the apodosis of the conditional clause (that here comes first), which would normally be an imperfect or pluperfect subjunctive, and a *quod* + subjunctive (*esset*) clause following *intelligerem* in place of an object clause.
[341] *Irascimini et nolite peccare*: A restatement of the theme's heading.
[342] *Deum irasci legimus*: The wrath of God is a constant theme in the OT, for example, Numb. 22.22: *Et iratus est Deus*.

comes[343] semper consequitur: id quod ipse Augustinus docet, ubi ait, Quid est homo paenitens, nisi homo sibi irascens?[344] et hoc modo quivis optime irasci, et minime peccare potest. Demum, et alia ira est, et illa huius loci magis propria est, quae fervor mentis[345] esse dicitur *[Ira quae fervor mentis dicitur.]*: ad hanc iram si inclinamur tantum, (quod boni solent) non nimis concitati in eam[346] efferramur,[347] (quod mali faciunt)

[54] [201] [N.v.] adeo non est culpa et Dei offensio, ut piis mentibus sit summi meriti interdum occasio: nam haec ira, cum afflictio carnis sit, patientiam nostram exercet et probat, e qua re omnis spes nostra certa efflorescit. Et sic Paulus stimulo carnis, ad probationem eius exagitabatur.[348] Ad quas tentationes nobis perquam utiles perferendas, ne illis tamen obruamur, satis nos munit ipsa gratia Dei. Irascimini ergo, hoc est, Sit ira vestra, licet paulum natura sua proclivis, non nimium tamen natura sua praeceps: sit tarda et cunctans, non subita et irruens: motu suo sedata incedat, non ullo impetu rapta excurrat: tacita, verecunda, et prudens conticescat, non immanis, ferina, et insolens intumescat:[349] sic excitata calescat, ut non inflammata exardescat: non pugnax, sed placabilis: non pertinax, sed exorabilis ubique conspiciatur. Irascimini ergo et nolite peccare, hoc est, Iram vestram herbescentem, priusquam maturescat, proterite: incensam, antequam inflammescat, restinguite: solutam, antequam nimis insolescat, comprimite. Ad hunc modum iram, non cum peccato implicatam, [202] sed ad nostrae tollerantiae[350] probationem immissam, ad nostri utilitatem, ad Dei gloriam convertemus, iuxta illud Pauli, Bonis omnia cooperantur in bonum.[351] Et sic quam brevissime potuerimus, hanc quaestionem[352] conclusimus.

---

[343] *socia atque comes*: Cic. uses *comes* and *socia* as a dyad in *Brut.* 12.45 and *Font.* 17.39 and 21.49; for example, in the former, *Pacis est comes otique socia et iam bene constitutae civitatis quasi alumna quaedam eloquentia* ('Upon peace and tranquillity eloquence attends as their ally, it is, one may say, the offspring of well-established civic order'), *LCL*, trans. G. L. Hendrickson, 1939.

[344] *Augustinus . . . irascens*: Augus. *Serm.* 296.9.10: *Etenim omnis homo, quem paenitet, sibi irascitur: paenitens iram exercet in se* (*PL* 38, col. 1358). ('Everyone, after all, who repents, is angry with himself; being repentent, he works off his anger on himself'). Augus. also makes reference to a form of repentence in his *Enarratio in Psalmum IV*.6: *Ergo irascimini, inquit, et nolite peccare; quod duobus modis intelligi potest: aut Etiam si irascimini, nolite peccare . . . aut Agite poenitentiam, id est, irascimini vobis ipsis de praeteritis peccatis, et ulterius peccare desinite* (*PL* 36, col. 80). ('Therefore, Be angry, says he, and sin not. Which may be taken two ways: either, even if you be angry, do not sin; . . . or, repent ye, that is, be ye angry with yourselves for your past sins, and henceforth cease to sin'), trans. https://www.newadvent.org/fathers/1801004.htm).

companion.³⁴³ That is what Augustine himself teaches when he says 'What is a repentant man unless a man angry with himself'?³⁴⁴ And in this way, anyone can become angry most advantageously and not sin in the least. Finally, there is another [form of] anger and one that is more suited to the subject in hand; this is said to be 'the ardour of the mind'³⁴⁵ *[Anger which is called 'the ardour of the mind']*. If we only incline to this [form of] anger as good men are accustomed to do, and, may not, overmuch roused unto it,³⁴⁶ become carried away³⁴⁷ as bad men do,

[54] [201] [N.v.] it is not so much a fault and an affront to God as a possible opportunity for the greatest reward for those who are piously minded. For this [form of] anger, since there is a pain of the flesh [present], exercises and tests our endurance, and from this every sure hope of ours blossoms. It was for this reason that Paul was provoked by the torment of the flesh – as a means to test him.³⁴⁸ The grace of God itself defends us sufficiently that we can bear these trials as profitably as possible, and that we are not, on the other hand, overwhelmed by them. And so, 'Be angry' essentially means may your anger, even if a little prone to excitement by nature, be not however too headstrong by nature. May it be slow and hesitant, not sudden and impetuous; may it emerge, calmed by its own impulse, and not rush forth, captive to passion; may it come to rest, silent, moderate and cautious, and not swell up in a monstrous way, wild and excessive;³⁴⁹ and roused in this way, may it glow, but not so that, [even] though kindled, it can catch fire; may it be appear everywhere, not as bullish but placable, not as unyielding but tractable. And so 'Be angry and do not sin' essentially means banish your anger as it grows and before it ripens. Snuff it out when it's hot, but before it becomes inflamed. Restrain it when it is unfettered, but before it becomes too uncontrolled. In this way, we will turn an anger that is not entangled in sin [202] [but rather one] that has been sent to test our resolve,³⁵⁰ to our own advantage, [namely] to the glory of God. Paul says as much [with the words], 'All things work together for the good of those that are good'.³⁵¹ Thus we have concluded this investigation³⁵² as succinctly as we were able.

---

³⁴⁵ *fervor mentis*: A phrase used in Cic. *De or.* 1.51.220.
³⁴⁶ *concitati in eam*: *concito* can be followed by *in* plus accusative, and is commonly followed by *in iram* (as per Cic. *Verr.* 2.3.3.6).
³⁴⁷ *efferramur*: an interesting form of the verb *effero, -re*, which appears with double 'r' (and also at the start of theme 7), possibly to differentiate it from *effero, -are*, which would have a single 'r'.
³⁴⁸ *Paulus . . . exagitabatur*: 2 Corinth. 12.7, an episode referred to regularly in the *Themata*.
³⁴⁹ *Sit . . . intumescat*: Cic. discusses anger in *Tusc.* 3, where he classifies it as a 'disease of the soul'. Cic., as Asc. also does here, refers to the 'swelling' of anger (*turgescit / tumor / tumidum / turgidum / tumens*) (3.9.18–19).
³⁵⁰ *tollerantiae*: an alternative form for *tolerantiae*.
³⁵¹ *Bonis . . . bonum*: Rom. 8.28. Cf. V: *diligentibus Deum omnia cooperantur in bonum*; Nov. T: *qui diligunt Deum, omnia simul adiumento sunt in bonum*. Ascham evidently favoured the polyptoton effect of *bonis . . . bonum*.
³⁵² *quaestionem*: *quaestio* can denote a simple investigation as well as a debating motion in a disputation.

Theme 7
(55–57)

In this next (again) short theme, Ascham produces another philosophical piece, this time one that engages with the issue of human knowledge and its limitations concerning God. He begins with a verse from 1 Corinthians 8.2 ('If anyone thinks that he knows something, he has not yet got to know as he ought to know'). He then immediately sets out some of the original Greek for this verse, providing not only a reminder of Ascham's Greek language skills but also his biblical independence, for he produces a Latin translation of the Greek without example elsewhere.[353]

Following the Pauline citation, Ascham quickly reverts to the classical world with an extensive reference to the ancient Greek philosopher, Socrates, who was celebrated for his aperçu that the wisest person is the one who knows that they know nothing. Pursuant to this, and still with a close eye on Paul, Ascham then proceeds to insist that in our worthless, bodily condition (or 'prison') we are are unable to perceive God. He clarifies that God is not seen and is not understood as he really is, but only believed. Then, asking 'How can God, since he is infinite, be perceived by a finite mind?' (56), Ascham adumbrates a fairly standard medieval philosophical view of the infinity of God, 'He is the greatest without quantity, the best without quality, the parent of everything without any contribution from another...' and so on (57), his argument being that man simply does not have the capacity in his fallen state to comprehend the Lord. At the end, Ascham circles back to Socrates.

While the emphasis in this theme on man's helpless and ignorant state certainly has a Lutheran flavour, the language Ascham uses, and more importantly, the image of Socrates, seem to have been inspired to a large extent by Cicero and a Ciceronian view of this Greek philosopher. Yet again we have an example of a Christian message – here, the prescription of a godly attitude towards God – parcelled up as an amalgam of biblical and pagan words and concepts.

---

[353] See p. 13 of the main introduction.

[55] [202] Si quis putat se aliquid scire, hic nondum[354] cognovit quemadmodum oportet scire. 1. Cor. 8.[355]

Si quis putat se aliquid εἰδέναι nondum quicquam ἔγνωκεν, quemadmodum oportet γνῶναι.[356] Haec sententia Pauli tantum redigit in memoriam nobis, quales nam sumus, quam viles, quam humi repentes, ut nosmet ipsi non efferramus, sed humiliter et demisse sentiamus.[357] Hic scientissimus est, qui scit quam nihil ipse sciat, hoc est, qui ignorantiam suam et inscitiam scit[358] ob quam rem Socrates, licet ab Apolline, divinitus tamen iudicatus est sapientissimus, quod hoc solum sciret, quam esset omnium rerum inscius.[359] Socrates etiam, in Apologia sua, putat multos viros, qui habebantur valde sapientes, hoc nomine

[56] [203] fuisse ab Apolline iudicatos stultiores, quia sibi ipsi videbantur esse sapientissimi.[360] Scientiam habemus, fateor, sed eo sane maiorem, quo nos illam minorem esse sentimus: nec est ut ulla de eximia virtute gloriemur,[361] quamdiu hiis corporum vinculis retenti fuerimus. Sapienter enim Sapiens in sapientia sua,[362] Terrena inhabitatio deprimit sensum

---

[354] *nondum*: appears as two separate words in the printed version.
[355] *Si ... scire*: 1 Corinth. 8.2. Asc.'s wording diverges slightly from V: *si quis se existimat scire aliquid, nondum cognovit quemadmodum oporteat eum scire*; cf. *Nov. T*: *si quis sibi videtur aliquid scire nondum quicquam novit quemadmodum oporteque scire*. A possible reason for Asc.'s choice of *putat* (rather than V's *existimat* or E's *sibi videtur*) was the fact that Cic. in the quote below used the verb – see n. 359.
[356] εἰδέναι ... ἔγνωκεν ... γνῶναι: Asc. highlights verbs that are used in the the Greek Bible and are the equivalent of *putat ... scire* and *cognosco* and *scire* respectively. The Greek of *Nov. T* (and of GNT) is εἴ τις δοκεῖ εἰδέναι τι, οὐδέπω οὐδὲν ἔγνωκεν καθὼς δεῖ γνῶναι.
[357] *humiliter et demisse sentiamus*: Asc. harnesses Ciceronian wording; see *Tusc.* 5.9.24 [... *non ausus est elate et ample loqui,*] *cum humiliter demisseque sentiret* ('... [he did not venture to speak in an exalted and dignified strain], as his thoughts were mean and low').
[358] *Hic ... scit*: This is sometimes referred to as the 'Socratic paradox', albeit it sprang from a particular episode (recounted by both Plat. and Xen.) whereby in reponse to a statement issued by the oracle of Apollo at Delphi that 'Socrates is the wisest person in Athens', Soc., convinced that he knew nothing, was said to have concluded that *nobody* knew anything, and that he was only wiser than others because he was the only person who recognised his own ignorance. However, it was in fact Cicero who was the first to claim that Socrates knew he knew *nothing* (Altman 2015: 8) – see also the note below.

[55] [202] If anyone thinks that he knows something, he has not yet[354] got to know as he ought to know. 1 Corinthians 8.[355]

If anyone thinks that he knows something, he has not yet got to know anything in the way he ought to know.[356] This sentiment of Paul merely recalls to our memory what we certainly are, how worthless we are, how we crawl on the ground so that we don't exalt ourselves, but instead become conscious of our humble and lowly station.[357] The wisest man is the one who knows that he knows nothing,[358] that is, who knows his own ignorance and lack of knowledge. Wherefore, Socrates, albeit by Apollo, was judged by the gods to be the wisest because he knew only this, namely how ignorant about everything he was.[359] Socrates in his *Apology* also thinks that many men who were regarded as very wise

[56] [203] were, despite this name, judged by Apollo to have been rather stupid for the reason that they seemed to themselves to be the wisest.[360] We are in possession of knowledge, I admit, but it's a fact that the greater it is, the less we feel it is. Nor should we boast[361] of any exceptional virtue while we are held fast by these chains of our bodies. Indeed, wisely the wise man in his wisdom[362] [knows that] '[our] earthly dwelling diminishes a capacity

---

[359] Cic. *Acad.* 1.6.16 alludes to Soc. in very similar terms to Asc.: ... *nihil se scire dicat nisi id ipsum, eoque praestare ceteris quod illi quae nesciant scire se putent, ipse se nihil scire, id unum sciat, ob eamque rem se arbitrari ab Apolline omnium sapientissimum esse dictum quod haec esset una omnis sapientia, non arbitrari se scire quod nesciat.* ('...to assert that he knows nothing except the fact of his own ignorance, and that he surpassed all other people in that they think they know things that they do not know, but he himself thinks he knows nothing, and that he believed this to have been the reason why Apollo declared him to be the wisest of all men, because all wisdom consists solely in not thinking that you know what you do not know'), *LCL*, trans. H. Rackham , 1933. See also *Acad.* 2.23.74: (re. Soc.) *scire se nihil se scire* ('[He said that] he knew that he knew nothing').

[360] *Socrates ... sapientissimi*: This is almost a certainly a reference to Plat. *Ap.* 21a–e, where Soc. describes his visits following the oracular response to supposedly wise citizens, only to find they are less wise than him. It is less likely that Asc. means Xen. *Apol.* 14–17, since in this account the oracle states that there was no man 'more free, more just, or more sound of mind' rather than 'wiser'.

[361] *nec* (or *non*) *est ut*: Used with the subjunctive, this constitutes a set Latin formula, and is the equivalent of the Greek οὐκ ἔσθ' ὅπως ....

[362] *Sapienter ... Sapiens ... sapientia*: Asc. underscores the point, using a cognate adverb, adjective and noun in close succession.

ut multa cogitet.³⁶³ Et noster intellectus, quo scimus, sic undique circumfusus est tenebris, ut homo coniectus in carcerem,³⁶⁴ aut de nocte in caligine vigilans, nihilo certius (quae oportet) percipiens, quam homo hospes et advena in aliena religione: quod sane verum est, nam ait Paulus, Quamdiu sumus in carne hac, peregrinamur a Domino:³⁶⁵ peregrini autem omnes rudes et rerum imperiti semper esse solent. Scire, quemadmodum oportet scire, est scire Deum *[Scire quid]*. Sed hoc facere non possumus, nisi aliqua ex parte, ut ait Paulus, quamdiu compingimur in hoc gurgustium corporis nostri.³⁶⁶ Deus, sicuti est, non videtur, non comprehenditur, sed solummodo creditur. Quomodo Deus, cum sit infinitus, a mente finita percipi potest, cum vel iuxta

[57] [204] Philosophiam,³⁶⁷ Finiti ad infinitum nulla sit proportio? Quomodo Deus, qui³⁶⁸ solus ENS³⁶⁹ est, non tamen ex numero eorum quae sunt, neque ex numero eorum quae non sunt, qui maximus est sine quantitate, optimus sine qualitate, parens omnium sine ulla collatione cum altero, omnia agens et semper quiescens, omnia continens et tamen impatibilis,³⁷⁰ ubilibet extra locum, aeternus sine tempore, formosissimus sine omni habitu aut forma corporis: Quomodo, inquam, tanta natura, sicut est, perfecte cognosci potest? Cum evolaverimus ex carcere corporis nostri, cognoscemus eum sicut sumus cogniti ab eo,³⁷¹ adquam cognitionem adipiscendam vix est ulla alia via proprior, ex nostra parte, quam est ea, quam Socrates Alcibiadi ostendit, nempe, si putemus nos fere nihil scire.³⁷² Nam omnis nostra nunc cognitio, si cum ea conferatur, qua oportet nos aliquando Dominum cognoscere, non solum incohata est, et prope nulla, sed mera quaedam ignoratio atque inscitia. Ergo, Si quis putat se aliquid scire, hic nondum cognovit, quemadmodum oportet scire.

---

³⁶³ *Terrena ... cogitet*: Book of Wisdom 9.15. Cf. V: *deprimit terrena inhabitatio sensum multa cogitantem*. The Book of Wisdom (or 'Sapientia' or 'Wisdom of Solomon') is included in the deuterocanonical books by the Catholic Church, but most Protestants now consider it part of the Apocrypha. It was, however, considered to be part of the OT by Augus.
³⁶⁴ *coniectus in carcerem*: A phrase used in Cic. *Tusc.* 1.40.96.
³⁶⁵ *Quamdiu ... Domino*: 2 Corinth. 5.6. Cf. V: *quoniam dum sumus in corpore peregrinamur a Domino*; Nov. T: *quod cum domi sumus in corpore peregrinamur a deo*. Asc. uses different vocabulary to both V and E.
³⁶⁶ *quamdiu ... nostri*: Asc. seems to have in mind 2 Corinth. 5.5–7 again, where Paul speaks about the importance of the spirit over the body, though his own language is rather more striking.
³⁶⁷ *iuxta Philosophiam*: Asc. proceeds to outline a medieval philosophical view of the infinity of God.

to think in depth'.³⁶³ And our intellect through which we know [things] is as hemmed in by darkness in every direction as a man who has been thrown into prison,³⁶⁴ or as one wakeful during the night in the pitch black and perceiving the things he ought to with no more certainty than a man who is an alien and a foreigner in an unknown faith. This is evidently true, for Paul says 'For as long as we are of this flesh, we are a stranger to God'.³⁶⁵ Moreover, all strangers always tend to be clumsy and inexperienced in their ways. To know as one ought to know *is* to know God *[To know – what it is]*. But we are not able to do this except to the least degree, just as Paul says, 'for as long as we confined to this ghetto of our body'.³⁶⁶ God is not seen [and] is not understood as he really is, but only believed. How can God, since he is infinite, be perceived by a finite mind, or since, according to

[57] [204] philosophy at any rate,³⁶⁷ there is no equivalence between what is finite and what is infinite? God³⁶⁸ alone is 'What is',³⁶⁹ but not from the number of those entities that exist, nor from the number of those entities which do not. He is the greatest without quantity, the best without quality, the parent of everything without any contribution from another, doing everything and always quiet, holding all in check, however insupportable,³⁷⁰ in every place beyond extent, eternal without time, and the most beautiful without any semblance or bodily form. In what way, I ask, can such a nature be fully comprehended as it really is? When we take flight from the prison of our body, we shall comprehend him just as we are comprehended by him.³⁷¹ From our perspective, in order to obtain this understanding, there is really no way more apposite than that which Socrates showed to Alcibiades, namely [that] if we are to think that we know almost nothing.³⁷² For our entire intelligence [as it is] now, [even] if it were conjoined to that [power] with which we ought at last to comprehend the Lord, is not only incomplete and almost nothing but [also] a form of pure ignorance and lack of knowledge. And so, if anyone thinks that he knows something, he has not yet got to know as he ought to know.

---

³⁶⁸ *quomodo ... qui*: I have not translated these words that come at the start of a long sentence in Latin, which I have broken up in English.

³⁶⁹ *ENS*: There is no present participle of the verb 'to be' (*esse*) in classical Latin, but this hypothetical form started to be used in the philosophical and theological writers of the medieval age.

³⁷⁰ *impatibilis*: an alternative form *impetibilis*.

³⁷¹ *cognoscemus ... eo*: A play on 1 Corinth. 13.12: *nunc cognosco ex parte tunc autem cognoscam sicut et cognitus sum* ('Now I know in part, but then I shall know even as I am known').

³⁷² *Socrates ... scire*: Ascham probably has in mind *Alcibiades I* or *II*, two dialogues featuring Soc. and Alcibiades, the principal motif of which are self-knowledge; these were considered, until the nineteenth century, to be a works by Plat.

Theme 8
(58–69)

Like many theologians of the Reformation, Ascham would pore over the detail of Paul's epistles in the New Testament; here we have a commentary on Galatians 6.14, 'May I be kept from boasting, except in the cross of our Lord Jesus Christ'. The piece bears a marked Lutheran influence, not only through its use of phrasing found in Luther's commentary on the Galatians, but also in terms of its Lutheran emphases. An important and recurring motif throughout Ascham's exposition is the cross of Christ, and again the thrust of the argument has much in common with Luther's *theologia crucis* ('theology of the cross').[373] For Ascham, just as for Luther, the cross was more than the wood to which Christ was affixed; it was rather the key to understanding Christian ethics and experience, as well as the process of righteousness (one without any obvious exchange between God/ Christ and man).[374] Ascham places great emphasis on the suffering Christ undergoes on behalf of mankind. The kinship possible with God and Christ through the cross is underscored by Ascham through the repeated verbal scheme 'his x is our x', for example, 'His glory is our glory; his righteousness is our righteousness, his works are our works ... His sanctification is our sanctification; his inheritance is our inheritance' (62).

Luther contrasted the *theologia crucis* with *theologia gloriae* ('the theology of glory'),[375] and in this theme Ascham also draws a sharp distinction between *gloria vera* and *gloria vana*. Only the former, Ascham stresses, comprises a life in Christ. Ascham also identifies several aspects of the latter, including misplaced or wordly glory, including (as described elsewhere in Paul's Epistle to the Galatians) circumscision, the Law, superstition, the search for fame and wealth, and the fashioning of one's own path to righteousness. This type of glory, according to Ascham, who once again reminds us of his knowledge of Greek, may be more precisely understood via the Greek term δοξα ('reputation'). Ascham's repeated and overt criticism of the *maledictum legis* ('the curse of the Law') is not only a reference to Galatians 3.13, but also a clear nod to Luther, whose theology drew a clear line between the Law and the Gospel.

A Lutheran consolatory approach is also in evidence. As Ascham suggests, the image and concept of the cross can bring much comfort, and he writes

---

[373] For more on this, see pp. 28–29 of the main introduction.
[374] Westhelle 2014: 161–62.
[375] ibid: 156.

Audi crucis consolationem ('Heed the comfort of the cross') (69) before embarking on another series of questions and answers, where Ascham first anticipates a worshipper's fear, only to respond in quick succession with a New Testament verse. Once again, however, we can also glimpse a variance between Ascham and Luther when it comes to 'works' (*opera*). In one of Luther's most developed pronouncements on the *theologia crucis*, the theses in the Heidelberg Disputation of 1518, a key point of emphasis was the sinful nature of human works. By contrast, Ascham explicitly acknowledges the value of works (albeit ones that he ultimately credits to God), writing, for example, 'his works are our works, as in Isaiah 26, "You have wrought all our works in us"' (61).

Features already outlined in other themes are in play again here, such as Ascham's rhetorically-wrought Latin and his pronounced biblical allegiance. And once more, he presents himself as a religious reformer: after inveighing against 'superstition, ignorance and blindness', he demands that 'all rotten and unfruitful branches of misuse must be cut down' (65).

[58] [205] Absit mihi gloriari[376] nisi in cruce Domini nostri Iesu Christi. Gal. 6.[377]

Cum[378] antiqui patris nostri Adami culpa et incuria, Evae levitate et inconstantia, Serpentis fraude et calumnia,[379] tota humani generis universitas, imperio Carnis, Legis, Peccati, Mortis, Diaboli, Inferni,[380] subiecta fuerat, unigenitus Dei filius, Patri aeternitate coaevus, substantia et potestate par et aequalis, e patris sinu exiliens, semetipsum exinanivit, Deus pro perditis et mortalibus, altissimus pro infimis et humi serpentibus, omnium Deus pro mortis et peccati servis, innocens pro reis et irae filiis, formam servi accipiens, in similitudinem hominum homo factus est, et lignum crucis, lignum supplicii et ignominiae pertulit, ut non solum lignum praevaricationis hoc ligno, quasi clavum clavo pelleret,[381] et hominum genus e legis maledicto,[382] et mortis carcere, in veterem libertatis dignitatem assereret: sed ut aeternum peccati, mortis, diaboli victoriae monumentum, crucis signum, et trophaeum in coelis ad

[59] [206] dextram patris, ad perpetuam Christi et cum Christo omnium Christianorum gloriam poneret et collocaret. Et haec est benevolentia illa, qua prius nos ante iacta mundi fundamenta dilexit, quam[383] mundus non cognovit, quam caro abhorruit, ad quam ratio obstupuit, magnis et prudentibus ignota, parvis et idiotis revelata, Iudaeis ignominia, gentibus stulticia,[384] Christianis vere nomen eius invocantibus, decus et sempiterna gloria. Absit ergo mihi gloriari, nisi in cruce Domini nostri Iesu Christi.

---

[376] *gloriari*: I translate this verb as both 'boast' and 'exult in' in this theme.
[377] *Absit ... Christi*: Gal. 6.14. The wording follows V, but differs from *Nov. T*: *ego vero, absit, ut glorier, nisi in cruce nostri Iesu Christi*. Grammatically, Asc. (and V) are in fact more in line with the Greek, which reads ἐμοὶ δὲ μὴ γένοιτο καυχᾶσθαι εἰ μὴ ἐν τῷ σταυρῷ τοῦ κυρίου ἡμῶν Ἰησοῦ Χριστοῦ.
[378] *cum*: This clause ushers in a very long sentence that runs to the start of the following page, and the sentence is accordingly broken up in the English.
[379] *Adami ... calumnia*: Note the striking symmetry of the three phrases.

[58] [205] 'May I be kept from boasting[376] except in the cross of our Lord Jesus Christ', Galatians 6.[377]

When,[378] through the fault and negligence of our ancient father Adam, through the shallowness and inconstancy of Eve, and through the deception and cunning of the serpent,[379] the entire body of the human race had become subjugated to the sovereignty of Flesh, the Law, Sin, Death, the Devil, and Hell,[380] the only born son of God, coeval with the eternity of the Father, equal and the same in substance and power, springing from the bosom of his Father, made himself powerless. And God, on behalf of those lost and subject to death, the highest [being] on behalf of the lowest and those crawling on the ground, God of everything on behalf of the slaves of death and sin, an innocent on behalf of the accused and the sons of anger, taking on the form of a slave, became a man in the likeness of men, and bore the wood of the cross, the wood of torment and dishonour, with the result that he not only expelled the wood of wickedness with this wood, as if a nail with a[nother] nail,[381] and liberated the human race from the curse of the Law[382] and the prison of death, [restoring it] unto the ancient dignity of freedom, but [also] established and erected as an eternal monument to sin, death and victory over the Devil, a sign of the cross and a trophy in heaven at

[59] [206] the right hand of the Father for the perpetual glory of Christ and of all Christians with Christ. And this is that goodwill with which he loved us in former times before the foundations of the world were set in place, which[383] the world did not understand, which the flesh shrank from, at which reason amazed; it was unknown to the great and the experienced, but disclosed to the lowly and inexperienced, a [source of] scandal for the Jews, folly[384] for the Gentiles, but for the Christians who rightly call on his name [a source of] honour and eternal glory. Accordingly, may I be kept from boasting except in the cross of our Lord Jesus Christ.

---

[380] *Legis ... Inferni*: This list (except for the first item *carnis*) was also used by L in his commentary on the Gal., *In Epistolam S. Pauli ad Galatas commentarius ex praelectione D. Martini Luth. collectus* (Wittenberg, 1535), 286.

[381] *clavo clavum eicere*: an ancient Greek proverb, used in Cic. in *Tusc.* 4.35.75.

[382] *legis maledicto*: a clear nod to Gal. 3.13, *Christus nos redemit de maledicto legis* ('Christ has redeemed us from the curse of the Law'), but also to L, who, used Paul's teaching in Gal. to stress Christ's self-substituting submission to the Law in his own penal suffering.

[383] *quam*: the antecedent is of course *benevolentia*, and so too for each *quam* that follows.

[384] *stulticia*: an alternative form of *stultitia*.

Gloria planius a Graecis δοξα dicitur,[385] cum praestantes, eminentes, eximii videri cupimus. Ea duplex est: altera legis et mundi, altera Christi et crucis: et altera vana, altera vera et est et esse dicitur. Vana fuit gloria pseudapostolorum eorum, qui apud Galatas Pauli doctrinam calumniantes, et ad circumcisionem et legis observationem eos adhortantes, applausum vulgi, et insignium Doctorum nomina sibi ipsi[386] acquirere studuerunt, contra quos homines, quia suam in aliorum carne, non Christi in animarum salute gloriam quaerebant, dixit Paulus, Absit mihi gloriari etc. Vana est et nunc eorum gloria, qui

[60] [207] vel novis dogmatibus inferendis, vel hypocrisi et superstitionibus retinendis, tranquillitatem Ecclesiae perturbant. Vana fuit gloria eorum, quos Christus Matth. 6.[387] redarguit, qui cum fistulis et tubis eleemosynas dividebant, et in plateis stantes orabant, et faciem suam occultantes ieiunabant, et omnem suam iusticiam coram hominibus faciebant, ut ab eisdem conspicerentur,[388] hoc est, ut inanem rumorem et aliquam vel falsae gloriae umbram aucuparentur: at non gloriam a Deo sed mercedem suam a mundo acceperunt, ait Christus.[389] Vana est et eorum gloria (ut summatim omnia complectar), qui potentias consectando, opes accumulando, honores aucupando, iusticiam propriam venando, vel pacem mundi, vel plausum populi, vel quietem carnis, sibi ipsi[390] comparare velint: quas res omnes, quamvis plausibilis ad tempus, et popularis quaedam iactatio comitatur, ad extremum tamen (quia nihil nisi umbra et fumus[391] Aegypti sint) summa profecto confusio necessum ut consequatur. Et haec de vana gloria: quam vitium maxime detestabile et pestiferum, si D.[392] Hier. credimus, censeri debet: *[Hieronymus.]* scribit enim sanctus ille vir, se novisse multos

---

[385] *a Graecis δοξα dicitur*: another Greek form, and further attempt on the part of Asc. to establish an equivalence between certain Greek and Latin terms.
[386] *ipsi*: I have left this nominative plural form 'themselves' untranslated.
[387] *vana...velint*: Asc. bases his argument on Matt. 6, which warns against showy displays of righteousness and hypocrisy, pretences of piety, for example, when giving alms and fasting, and also against hoarding of wealth.
[388] *omnem ... conspicerentur*: Asc. relies on Matt. 6.1. V: *adtendite ne iustitiam vestram faciatis coram hominibus ut videamini ab eis* ('Take care not to perform your righteousness before men so as to be seen by them'). *faciem ... occultantes* is perhaps influenced by *fronte occultare*, wording used in Cic. in *De am.* 65 and scribbled on the final page of GNT.

Glory is more precisely termed by the Greeks as 'reputation',[385] since we desire to appear pre-eminent, esteemed and elevated. That glory is two-fold: one [form] [resides] in the Law and the world, the other in Christ and the cross. One both is and is said to be empty, and the other both is and is said to be true. Empty was the glory of those false apostles who misrepresented Paul's teaching among the Galatians, coaxed them in the direction of circumcision and an observance of the Law, and strove to win for themselves[386] the approbation of the ordinary folk and the reputation of high-ranking scholars; against such men, insofar as they sought their own glory in the flesh of others, not that of Christ in the health of souls, Paul proclaimed 'May I be kept from boasting etc.' Empty too is the glory of those nowadays who

[60] [207] disturb the peace of the Church, either with the introduction of new dogmas or through the retention of ersatz sanctity and superstition. Empty was the glory of those whom Christ refuted in Matthew [chapter] 6,[387] who, with pipes and trumpets, were dividing the alms and, standing in streets, were begging and were fasting while concealing their own face; [these] were fashioning entirely their own [form of] righteousness in the presence of men by whom they contrived to be seen,[388] that is, so that they might go in quest of worthless fame or else some semblance of false glory. But, says Christ, they have [in fact] taken receipt of not [so much] glory from God but their own 'fee' from the world.[389] Empty too is the glory of those who, to sum up the whole matter briefly, by pursuing power, by amassing wealth, by questing after honours, by hunting for their own righteousness, hope to obtain for themselves[390] either peace on earth, the approbation of the people, or rest for the body. [While] a certain ostentation, praise-winning at the time and gratifying, accompanies all these things, nevertheless, in the final analysis ([not least] because Egyptians are nothing but shadow and smoke),[391] the greatest disorder surely and necessarily follows. And so much for empty glory. If we set store by St[392] Jerome *[Jerome]*, what an altogether loathsome and pernicious [form of] wickedness it should be regarded. Indeed, that holy man writes that he knew many

---

[389] *mercedem... acceperunt*: Matt. 6.2 and 4 employ the refrain *receperunt mercedem suam*.
[390] *ipsi*: Again, I have not translated this rather redundant (in English) pronoun, which, as above, must be nominative plural.
[391] *umbra et fumus*: two words that often appear together in Latin and denote death, just as σκιὰ καὶ καπνός ('shadow and smoke') do in Greek.
[392] D.: stands for *divus*.

[61] [208] viros, qui foedas libidines coercere, qui sitim et inediam multos dies sustinere, qui omnes rerum asperitates subire, qui mortem ipsam sponte et voluntate sua oppetere potuerunt: verum, qui proprias laudes et honores contemneret, non vidisse, sed ne legisse quidem confitetur.[393] Et eam ob rem, Paulus ipse dicit, in hoc sibi datum fuisse Angelum Satanae, qui eum colaphis cederet, ne efferretur gloria et magnitudine revelationis.[394] *[Vera gloria qua in re consistit.]* Vera gloria omnis in Christo cruceque eius posita et defixa est. Crux Christi non solum passio eius est in ligno, sed totum illud vitae eius in carne curriculum, nuditati, inopiae, frigori, siti, ludibriis, calumniis, verberibus, cruci, morti, expositum et obiectum. Praeterea, crux nostra et totius Ecclesiae, crux Christi est: nam, tam affluenter effusa est bonitas Dei erga nos, ut quae bona Christi, nostra bona: quae vero mala nostra, Christi mala dici et haberi voluit: gloria eius gloria nostra, iusticia eius iusticia nostra, opera eius opera nostra,[395] ut Isaiae 26: Omnia opera nostra operatus es in nobis:[396] sanctificatio eius sanctificatio nostra, haereditas eius haereditas nostra: ait

[62] [209] [O.] enim Paulus, Quem Pater pro omnibus nobis tradidit, cum eo nobis omnia donavit.[397] Contra incommoda nostra incommoda eius, ut, Qui vos laedit me laedit:[398] peccata nostra peccata eius, ut in Psalmo, Longe a salute verba derelictorum meorum:[399] contemptio nostri contemptio eius, ut in Evangelio, Qui vos spernit me spernit:[400] blasphemia nostri blasphemia eius, ut in Propheta, Non filios Israel, sed me blasphemasti:[401] ad haec,

---

[393] It is not entirely clear which part of Jer.'s corpus Ascham has in mind here, but it may be his most famous Letter 22.27, in which Jer. discusses with Eustochium (Julia) the hazards of vainglory (*inanis gloria*), citing Gal. and writing: *plures enim paupertatis, misericordiae, atque, ieiunii arbitros declinantes, hoc ipso cupiunt placere, quo placere contemnunt, et mirum in modum laus, dum vitatur, appetitur* (PL 22, col. 413) ('For many, who screen from all men's sight their poverty, charity, and fasting, desire to excite admiration by their very disdain of it, and strangely seek for praise while they profess to keep out of its way'), trans. https://www.newadvent.org/fathers/3001022.htm. If this is the passage Asc. has in mind, he has embellished it.

[394] *Paulus ... revelationis*: The sentiment is from 2 Corinth. 12.7. Asc.'s formulation diverges from V: *Et ne magnitudo revelationum extollat me, datus est mihi stimulus carnis meae angelus Satanae, qui me colaphizet,* and also from *Nov. T*: *datus fuit mihi stimulus per carnem, nuncius satanae, ut me colaphis caederet, ne supra modum efferrer*. It is noteworthy that Asc. incorporates the term *gloria* which fits with his argument, a term neither the other two versions, nor the Greek, contain.

[61] [208] men who were able to restrain shameful lusts, who were able to withstand thirst and hunger for many days, who were able to undergo all depredations, and who were able to meet death itself voluntarily and of their accord. On the other hand, he (i.e. Jerome) admits that he has never seen and not even read [of anyone] who places no value on his own praise and honour.[393] And on that account, Paul himself says that for this reason the Angel of Satan was brought to him to yield him up to buffetings to prevent him from being puffed up by glory and the size of the revelation.[394] *[True glory stops in this business]* All true glory has been placed and set in Christ and his cross. The cross of Christ consists of not just his passion on the wood but that whole course of his life in the flesh, exposed and forsaken to: nakedness, poverty, cold, thirst, derision, malicious charges, lashings, the cross and death. For that reason, our cross and that of the whole Church is the cross of Christ. What's more, the goodness of God has been so liberally offered to us that what are Christ's boons [become] our boons; and truly [in turn], he willed it that these afflictions of ours be said and considered to be the afflictions of Christ. His glory is our glory; his righteousness is our righteousness; and his works are our works,[395] as in Isaiah 26, 'You have wrought all our works in us'.[396] His sanctification is our sanctification; his inheritance is our inheritance.

[62] [209] [O.] Paul likewise says 'Together with the one whom the Father handed over for all our sakes, he [also] gave us everything'.[397] Conversely, our misfortunes are his misfortunes, as in 'He who harms you, harms me'.[398] Our sins are his sins, as in the Psalm, 'Far from my salvation are the words of my abandonment'.[399] Our disregard is his disregard, as in the Gospel, 'He who despises you, despises me'.[400] Our sacrilege is his sacrilege, as in the Prophet, 'You have slandered not the sons of Israel but me'.[401] Additonally, our

---

[395] *eius ... nostra*: Asc. repeats this eye- and ear-catching pattern 'his *x* is our *x*' in what follows.
[396] *Omnia ... nobis*: Is. 26.12. The wording is practically identical to V.
[397] *Quem ... donavit*: Rom. 8.32. The wording is very similar to V, though V expresses the words as a question, as does E, who also uses *donet* rather than *donavit*. Next to this verse in GNT, Asc. has inscribed ΑΓΑΠΗ, the Greek word for love.
[398] *Qui ... laedit*: Asc. is probably quoting L here, who uses this form of wording in his commentary on Gal., 441.
[399] *Longe ... meorum*: Ps. 21.2 (V/S) / 22.2 (H/P), and Asc. follows V.
[400] *Qui ... spernit*: Luke 10.16. A citation used above in theme 5; see n. 318.
[401] *Non ... blasphemasti*: Possibly a reference to Ez. 20.27: *adhuc et in hoc blasphemaverunt me patres vestri cum sprevissent me contemnentes* ('Moreover in this also your fathers blasphemed me, when they had despised and contemned me'), but Asc.'s wording matches exactly that used by L in his commentary on the Gal., 441.

commoditas nostra commoditas eius, ut Isaiae 28: Haec est requies mea: reficite lassum, hoc est refrigerium meum.⁴⁰² Et Matth. 25. Quatenus fecistis uni de his fratribus meis minimis, mihi fecistis.⁴⁰³ Ad extremum, passio et crux nostra crux eius est: ut primo ad Col: Adimpleo ea quae desunt passionum Christi in carne mea, pro corpore eius, quod est Ecclesia.⁴⁰⁴ Et Actorum 9, Saule, Saule, quid me persequeris?⁴⁰⁵ cum Saulus nullam vim Christo, sed Ecclesiae nobis inferebat.⁴⁰⁶ Praeterea, cum nos sumus corpus Christi, ut ait Paulus,⁴⁰⁷ et ille caput nostri, certe quicquid membra aut corpus mali patiatur, ad perturbationem capitis necessum est ut perveniat: nam scinde

[63] [210] manum, et totum caput doloribus statim erit peregravatum, vultus turbabitur, genae moerebunt,⁴⁰⁸ oculi rigescent, os contrahetur, pendebunt labra: sensus enim omnis in capite, quam in membris, semper est patibilior. Et haec cogitatio, quod Christus particeps sit nostrae afflictionis, facit ut non desperemus, non nimis contristemur, id quod faceremus, si tot passiones quasi tantum nostras, nostrisque humeris⁴⁰⁹ tantum tollerandas⁴¹⁰ consideremus: nam essent et nimium molestae atque intollerabiles⁴¹¹ nobis, et nos illis multum impares et inferiores. Verum, si una cum Psalmista dixerimus, Propter te Domine occidimur tota die,⁴¹² non solum omnia melius sustinebimus, et cum Christo gloriabimur, quod onus nostrum leve sit et iugum suave: sed magnum etiam gaudium et consolationem in illis perferendis capiemus. Dicit enim Paulus, quod sicut abundant passiones Christi in nobis, ita et per Christum abundat consolatio nostra.⁴¹³ Porro, sicut

---

⁴⁰² *Haec . . . meum*: Is. 28.12. Asc.'s wording is practically identical to V.
⁴⁰³ *Quatenus . . . fecistis*: Matt. 25.40. Asc. is identical to V and *Nov. T*, though V has *quamdiu* in place of *quatenus*. The verse is flagged up in GNT.
⁴⁰⁴ *Adimpleo . . . Ecclesia*: Coloss. 1.24. Asc. has identical wording to V, but *Nov. T* is rather different: *suppleo quod deerat afflictionibus Christi in carne mea pro corpore ipsius, quod est ecclesia*. Asc. glossed the verse in GNT, jotting in the margin ὑστερήμα[ ] θλίψ[ ], the equivalent of *ea quae desunt passionum*.
⁴⁰⁵ *Saule . . . persequeris?*: Acts 9.4. The wording is identical to V and *Nov. T*.
⁴⁰⁶ *cum . . . inferebat*: a reference to Paul's role as persecutor just prior to his famous conversion on the road to Damascus. Paul had been threatening disciples of Christ with execution, but then Christ, speaking as the Lord, intervened. L in his commentary on Gal. has the same quote from Acts (n. 405) and also the words *Saulus nullam vim inferebat Christo, sed ipsius Ecclesiae* (440). In the printed version of *Themata* there is a 'I' after *Ecclesiae*, but it is unclear what this indicates, and has been omitted.
⁴⁰⁷ *nos . . . Paulus*: There are a number of biblical passages that suggest that Christians / the Church are the body of Christ, and that Christ is the head of the body, but the relevant

advantage is his advantage, as in Isaiah 28, 'This is my respite; restore the weary, [for] this is my consolation'.⁴⁰² [We] also [read] in Matthew 25, 'Inasmuch as you have done it unto one of the least of my brethren, you have done it unto me'.⁴⁰³ Ultimately, our suffering and cross is his cross, as in the first [chapter of the Epistle to] the Colossians, 'I fill up in my flesh that which is wanting as regards the sufferings of Christ, for his body's sake, which is the Church'.⁴⁰⁴ [We] also [read] in Acts 9, 'Saul, Saul, why do you persecute me?'⁴⁰⁵ [at a time] when Saul was employing no force towards Christ [himself], but [rather] [the force] of the Church towards us.⁴⁰⁶ Moreover, since we are the body of Christ, as Paul states,⁴⁰⁷ and he (i.e. Christ) is our head, it follows that whatever affliction he (i.e. Christ) might suffer in limbs or body, this necessarily also means for a disturbance of the head. For wound

[63] [210] the hand, and the whole head will immediately be burdened by pains, the face will be disturbed, the cheeks will grieve,⁴⁰⁸ the eyes will grow stiff, the mouth will grow sad, and the lips will hang low. For every sensation in the head is always more sensitive than in the limbs. And this notion that Christ shares our pain, means that we do not despair, and don't become too downhearted, something we would [certainly] do if we were to contemplate that so many sufferings must be borne⁴¹⁰ as though ours alone, and on our shoulders⁴⁰⁹ alone. For [sure] these would be both too difficult and intolerable⁴¹¹ for us, and we are most unequal and inferior to them. However, if we say together with the Psalmist, 'Through you, Lord, we are undone in a whole day',⁴¹² not only will we endure everything better and exult with Christ because our burden is light and the yoke sweet, but we will also derive great joy and comfort in bearing those things. Indeed, Paul says that just as the sufferings of Christ abound in us, so also our comfort abounds through Christ.⁴¹³ Furthermore, just

---

verses seem to be: (a) 1 Corinth. 12.12–27; in these lines Paul outlines how Christian believers should be thought of as one body of Christ, culminating in 12.27: *vos autem estis corpus Christi* ('...and you are the body of Christ'); and (b) Coloss. 1.18, where Paul states *et ipse est caput corporis* ('And he himself is the head of the body'). This verse of Coloss. was marked up in GNT.
⁴⁰⁸ *moerebunt*: an alternative form for *maerebunt*.
⁴⁰⁹ *humeris*: an alternative form for *umeris*.
⁴¹⁰ *tollerandas*: an alternative form for *tolerandas*. *esse* has been omitted.
⁴¹¹ *intollerabiles*: an alternative form for *intolerabiles*.
⁴¹² *Propter ... die*: Ps. 43.22 (V/S) / 44.22 (H/P). Asc. uses different vocabulary to the V, which has: *propter te mortificamur omni die*. Asc.'s wording was, however, used by Augus. in *Enarratio in Psalmum IX*.13 (*PL* 36, col. 123), and the verb *occidimur* was also utilised in Ps. 43 in Pag.
⁴¹³ *sicut ... nostra*: 2 Corinth. 1.5. Asc. quotes V *verbatim*; *Nov. T* has the same, except *afflictiones* in place of *passiones*.

crux nostra crux Christi est, ita gloria nostra gloria Christi: et sic intelligendus est locus ille Pauli, cum dicit, Unusquisque probet opus suum, et sic in semetipso, et non in alio gloriam habebit:[414] nam gloriam nostram

[64] [211] [O.ii.] et gloriam habere in semetipso, vocat Paulus Testimonium conscientiae nostrae,[415] cum sumus, aut esse debemus, conformes imaginis filii eius,[416] cum recta incedimus, sicut ille per gloriam et ignominiam, per infamiam et laudem, per crucem et scandalum: et hoc modo si illum honorificaverimus, et ille nos (ut ait Ioan.) glorificabit.[417] Gloriari in cruce dicitur superbire, gaudere, et placere sibi ipsi in cruce Christi: ut 2 Cor. 12. Placeo mihi in persequutionibus[418] et angustiis pro Christo.[419] Et Matth. 5. Gaudete et exultate cum persequuti vos fuerint homines propter me, quoniam merces et gloria vestra copiosa est in coelis.[420] Et Act. 5. Ibant gaudentes a conspectu consilii, quia digni habiti sunt pro nomine Iesu Christi contumeliam pati.[421] De gloriando in cruce, Paul. 2 Cor. 11:[422] Si gloriari oportet, quae infirmitatis meae sunt gloriabor.[423] Et ad Rom. 5. Gloriamur in afflictionibus.[424] Neque hic volo omnes afflictiones humanas crucem Christi dici, sed eas tantum, quas pro Christo et eius iusticia patimur: nam passus est Cain, Pharao, et Saul: passus est Pilatus, et Nero: patiuntur etiam nunc Iudaei, infideles, et falsi Christiani: sed hae afflictiones

---

[414] *Unusquisque ... habebit*: Gal. 6.4. V follows a different order: *opus autem suum probet unusquisque et sic in semet ipso tantum gloriam habebit et non in altero*. Likewise, Asc. does not follow E (whose wording is very similar to the V) except in his use of *in alio*.

[415] *Testimonium conscientiae nostrae*: 2 Corinth. 1.12. The fuller wording of V is: *nam gloria nostra haec est testimonium conscientiae nostrae* ('For our glory is this: the testimony of our conscience'). The same verse proceeds to define this testimony of conscience as follows, '[namely] that in simplicity of heart and sincerity of God, and not in carnal wisdom, but in the grace of God, we have conversed in this world, and more abundantly towards you'; Asc. also develops the term, but in a way that keeps Christ and the cross more central.

[416] *conformes imaginis filii eius*: Asc. may have in mind Rom. 8.29, which contains similar wording, *conformes fieri imaginis filii eius*. The Greek equivalent of these words are underlined in GNT.

[417] *si ... glorificabit*: Asc. is not quoting directly here, but summarising in his own words the content of John 8.49–54.

[418] *persequutionibis*: an alternative form for *persecutionibus*.

as our cross is the cross of Christ, so the glory of Christ is our glory. And it's in this way that that passage in Paul must be understood, when he says 'Let every man prove his own work, and thus he will have glory in himself, and not in another'.[414] What's more, to enjoy

[64] [211] [O.ii.] our glory and glory in himself, Paul calls the 'Testimony of our conscience',[415] when we are, or ought to be, like the image of his son;[416] when we advance directly, just as he (i.e. Christ) [did], through glory and humiliation, through shame and praise, through the cross and ignominy. And if we honour him in this way, he will, as John says, also glorify us.[417] To exult in the cross is said to be proud, to rejoice, and to take pleasure for oneself in the cross of Christ, as [described] in 2 Corinthians 12, 'I take pleasure for myself in persecutions[418] and difficulties for Christ's sake',[419] and in Matthew 5, 'Rejoice and be exceedingly glad when men have persecuted you for my sake, since your reward and glory in heaven is plentiful',[420] and [again] in Acts 5, 'They were going from the presence of the council, rejoicing because they were accounted worthy to suffer reproach in the name of Jesus Christ'.[421] Concerning exultation in the cross, Paul [writes] in 2 Corinthians 11[422] 'If it is necessary to exult, I will exult in the causes of my deficiency'.[423] And in the Epistle to the Romans 5, 'We exult in tribulations'.[424] Nor am I here willing that all human tribulations be taken as the cross of Christ but only those which we suffer on behalf of Christ and his righteousness. For example, Cain, Pharaoh and Saul suffered; Pilate and Nero suffered; even now the Jews, infidels and false Christians suffer, but these tribulations

---

[419] *Placeo ... Christo*: An abridged version of 2 Corinth. 12.10. V refers to: *infirmitatibus, contumeliis* and *necessitatibus* ('infirmities, reproaches, and necessities') in addition to *persecutionibus* and *angustii*; *Nov. T* has: *anxietatibus* in place of *angustiis*.

[420] *Gaudete ... coelis*: Matt. 5.12. V and *Nov. T* follow a different word order, and both versions refer to the prophets of earlier times being persecuted. Asc., in a more immediate way, renders the reader the one who is persecuted and inserts the key term *gloria* into this verse even though it is not there in the original.

[421] *Ibant ... pati*: Acts 5.41. The wording follows V exactly, except Asc. uses *quia* where V uses *quoniam*. He does not follow *Nov. T*, which has in the latter part of this verse: *quod digni habiti essent, ut pro nomine eius contumelia afficerentur*. Ascham jots in the margin of GNT the word χάρμα ('joy') next to this verse.

[422] *Paul. 2 Cor. 11*: In the printed version '1' is used rather than '11'; this is evidently a mistake, and has been corrected here.

[423] *Si ... gloriabor*: 2 Corinth. 11.30. The wording closely tracks both V and *Nov. T*.

[424] *Gloriamur in afflictionibus*: Rom. 5.3. Asc. veers in his vocabulary from V: *gloriamur in tribulationibus*, but is closer to *Nov. T*: *gloriamur super afflictionibus*, but follows exactly the wording of L's commentary on Gal., 439 and also Pag.

[65] [212] omnes sunt improbis et quasi poenarum ingressiones ad condemnationem. Sic crux Christi, et piorum res adversae, sunt bonis verae et expressae probationes ad perfectionem. Et hactenus quid sit gloria et vana et vera, quid crux et Christi et nostra, et quid sit gloriari, et quomodo in cruce, apertis Scripturarum verbis aperuimus.[425] Iam, quare sit gloriandum, et qui veri fructus ex arbore crucis Christi nobis sunt decerpendi, paucis explicabimus. Decidui[426] quidam sunt crucis et vieti fructus, qui non sunt in cruce, sed de cruce exciderunt: qui in terra iacentes putrescunt, non Christo nec hiis qui in Christo vivunt placentes: sed immundis tantum et suibus sapientes,[427] ut superstitio, ignoratio, caecitas. Neque hic probatos Ecclesiae ritus despicio,[428] sed omnes putidos et infrugiferos abusionis ramos decidendos esse sentio. Ascendamus nos in verticem crucis Christi, et veros fructus colligamus. Haec arbor in duos praecipuos ramos se spargit:[429] alter generalem illam omnium, qui sub legis maledicto fuerant subiecti, redemptionem: alter cunctorum, qui insiti sunt in Christo Iesu, nec amplius in

[66] [213] [O.iii.] carne, sed in spiritu et sanctificatione ambulant, glorificationem continet. Agnosce ergo, o homo, quid fecit prius pro omnibus, et nunc vide atque gloriare quid facit pro Christianis: nam cum humanum genus, malicia[430] Diaboli, in maledictum legis fuerat conclusum, et in omnem ignominiam et obscuritatem demisissimum, nostrae tamen imbecillitatis assumptione et crucis suae portatione, in libertatem illam priorem et dignitatem restituit, hoc est, omnia quae erant nostra mala accepit, et omnia quae erant sua bona nobis tribuit.[431] Primum e sinu patris in terras se demisit, ut hominem ex inferorum voragine, ad coelum usque duceret:[432] et Deus

---

[425] *apertis ... aperuimus*: Asc. amplifies through his language the revelation that Scripture offers using two cognate forms.
[426] *Decidui*: This term may also connote man's fall.
[427] *sapientes*: Asc. evidently intends that the present participle of the multivalent verb *sapio, sapere* to convey two ideas: (a) that for the reprobate these bad fruits are flavoursome and attractive; and (b) that they make sense to the reprobate.
[428] *probatos Ecclesiae ritus*: surely denoting state-sanctioned religious observances.

[65] [212] are [reserved] entirely for the depraved, and constitute, as it were, the entry points of punishments for their damnation. On the other hand, for good men, the cross of Christ and the setbacks of the pious constitute true and clear tests for their fulfillment. So far, we have demonstrated with the express words of Scripture[425] what glory is, both empty and true, what the cross is, both that of Christ and ours, and what it is to exult, and how [to exult] in the cross. Now we will explain in a few [words] on what account we must exult, and what is the genuine fruit that we must pluck from the tree of Christ's cross. Some fruits of the cross are easily shed[426] and are shrivelled. These are not [actually] on the cross, but have fallen from the cross, and, lying on the ground, they rot, and are pleasing in no way to Christ or those who live in Christ; they are of appeal[427] only to the unclean and to swine, just like superstition, ignorance and blindness. I am not here looking down on approved liturgy of the Church,[428] but I do feel that all rotten and unfruitful branches of misuse must be cut down. Let us climb to the summit of Christ's cross and pluck the genuine fruits. This tree spreads its branches in two particular directions:[429] one [of these] comprises that universal redemption of all those who have been subjects under the curse of the Law; the other comprises the glorification of all those who have been grafted in Jesus Christ,

[66] [213] [O.iii.] and who no longer walk in flesh but in the spirit and sanctification. And so, acknowledge, o mankind, what he did previously for the sake of everyone, and behold and exult in what he does now for the sake of Christians. Indeed, when the human race, through the wickedness[430] of the Devil, had been confined to the curse of the Law and all humiliation and the most debased oblivion, nevertheless, by taking responsibility for our helplessness and by carrying his cross, he restored [us] to that former freedom and dignity; that is, he took on all that was evil in us, and [instead] bestowed on us all that was good in him.[431] First, he cast himself down from the bosom of his Father to the earth in order that he might lead man from the abyss of Hell all the way up to heaven.[432] Thus God

---

[429] *in . . . spargit*: literally, 'spreads itself into two particular branches'.

[430] *malicia*: an alternative form for *malitia*. In all other cases where this word has been used in the tract, it has been spelled *malitia*.

[431] *Diaboli . . . tribuit*: The stark contrast between man's degeneracy and Christ's goodness is accentuated through the symmetrical clauses that Asc. again deploys.

[432] *ut . . . duceret*: This is the first of a long sequence of purpose clauses which I have translated in such a way as to draw attention to the benefits Christ bestowed on man. Cumulatively, these have an almost prayer-like quality.

factus est homo, ut homo factus esset Deus:⁴³³ et filius voluit esse hominis, ut homo haeres esset Dei: ex muliere natus est, ut Evae praevaricationem deleret: vehementer esurivit, ut hominem sua carne saturaret: saepius⁴³⁴ sitivit, ut homo in aeternum, ut ait Ioan. non sitiret:⁴³⁵ super asinum sedebat, ut hominem super angelos et potestates collocaret: seipsum vendi permittebat, ut hominem e captivitate redimeret: Pilato adstitit, ut hominem ad

[67] [214] dextram patris consedere faceret: cruci et ignominiae se obtulit, ut hominem gloriae ac vitae restitueret: et fecit se peccatum,⁴³⁶ et omnium pessimum, ut hominem redderet iustificatum et optimum. Nam pro Noë fuit ebrius,⁴³⁷ pro Loth incestus,⁴³⁸ pro Mose homicida,⁴³⁹ pro Davide adulter,⁴⁴⁰ pro Petro periurus,⁴⁴¹ pro Paulo persequutor,⁴⁴² et denique pro lege lex, pro peccato peccatum, pro morte mors, ut legem abrogando libertas, peccatum damnando iusticia, mortem destruendo⁴⁴³ vita universo humano generi restauraretur. Atque in hunc modum cum⁴⁴⁴ Christus, Crucem, Legem, Mundum, Peccatum, Mortem, Diabolum,⁴⁴⁵ cruci suae affixisset, et totam humani generis universitatem, e tam abiecta et iacenti conditione, ad tam excaelsum⁴⁴⁶ gloriae fastigium, crucis beneficio evexisset, adhuc etiam tantis beneficiis non contentus, omnibus illis, qui animam suam perdere, et carnem suam ac mundum cruci una cum Christo figere et mactare (ut ait Paulus) voluerint,⁴⁴⁷ hanc gloriam tutam, sartam, tectam, et spiritus sancti praesidio septam atque munitam, ab omni serpentinae fraudis metu et periculo vacuam conservabit.

---

⁴³³ *Deus ... Deus*: This is based on Augus. The phrase *factus est Deus homo, ut homo fieret Deus* appears in several of his sermons, including *Serm.* 128.1 (*PL* 39, col. 1997), although it has been pointed out that this formulation might in fact be Ps. Aug., albeit one that was very popular through the centuries and, in any case, based on a simplified version which is genuinely Augustinian, viz. *deos facturus qui homines erant, homo factus est qui Deus erat* (Oberman / Trinkaus 1974: 430).

⁴³⁴ *saepius*: this comparative, which might have been rendered 'quite often' or even 'very often', here sounds better as 'often'.

⁴³⁵ *Sitivit ... non sitiret*: a paraphrase of John 4.13/14, and referred to in theme 2; see n. 115.

⁴³⁶ *peccatum*: literally 'a sin', though 'a sinner' sounds more appropriate here.

⁴³⁷ *Noë fuit ebrius*: Noah, having built a vineyard, becomes drunk in Gen. 9.21.

⁴³⁸ *Loth incestus*: Lot's daughters, concerned about preserving humanity in their solitude in the hills, decided to get their father drunk and to have intercourse with him with the goal of getting pregnant, as per Gen. 19.32–38.

⁴³⁹ *Mose homicida*: Moses killed an Egyptian in Ex. 2.12 after seeing (in Ex. 2.11) an Egyptian striking one of his Hebrew kinsmen.

⁴⁴⁰ *Davide adulter*: David committed adultery by sleeping with Bathsheba, the wife of one of his own soldiers, Uriah, in 2 Sam. 11.4

was made man in order that man might be made God.⁴³³ In addition, his son was willing to take on the characteristics of a man in order that man might be the heir of God. He was born from a woman in order that he might destroy the wickedness of Eve. He suffered great hunger in order that he might feed man with his own flesh. He often⁴³⁴ went thirsty in order that man, as John says, would not go thirsty for the rest of time.⁴³⁵ He sat on an ass in order that he might elevate man above the angels and the powerful. He allowed himself to be sold in order that he might rescue man from captivity. He stood before Pilate in order that he might

[67] [214] enable man to sit down at the right hand of the Father. He offered himself over to the cross and humiliation in order that he might restore man to glory and life; and he rendered himself a sinner⁴³⁶ and the most debased of all men in order that he might return man justified and as good as they could be. For instance, he became intoxicated on Noah's behalf,⁴³⁷ incestuous for Lot,⁴³⁸ a murderer for Moses,⁴³⁹ an adulterer for David,⁴⁴⁰ a perjurer for Peter,⁴⁴¹ a persecutor for Paul,⁴⁴² and finally the Law for the Law, sin for sin, death for death, so that, by repealing the Law, freedom might be restored to the entire human race, [so that] by condemning sin, righteousness might [too], [and so that] by dismantling death,⁴⁴³ life might [also be restored]. And in this way,⁴⁴⁴ Christ had affixed the Cross, the Law, the World, Sin, Death and the Devil⁴⁴⁵ to his own cross and had rescued, through his service on the cross, the entire community of the human race from so slavish and supine a condition to such an elevated⁴⁴⁶ summit of glory. Even so, he, still not even satisfied with such great services, will keep this [form of] glory safe, in good repair, protected, guarded and fortified by the garrison of the Holy Spirit, free from all fear and danger of the serpent's deceit for all those who have been willing, as Paul says, to forgo their own soul and to affix and to sacrifice their own flesh and the world to the cross together with Christ.⁴⁴⁷

---

⁴⁴¹ *Petro periurus*: This is a reference to Peter's denial that he knows Jesus. The denial is predicted by Jesus in all four Gospel accounts, and, following Jesus' arrest, Peter does indeed disown him, as set out in Luke 22.57, 58 and 60, Mark 14.68 and 71, Matt. 26.74, and John 18.17, 25 and 27.

⁴⁴² *Paulo persequutor*: Paul persecutes St Stephen in Acts 7.58, and there are further references to Paul's persecutions in Acts 8.2, 9, 22.4 and 19, and 26.9–11. Paul also confesses to persecuting others in 1 Corinth. 15.9, Gal. 1.13 and 1 Tim. 1.13. *Persequutor* is an alternative form from *persecutor*.

⁴⁴³ *legem abrogando ... peccatum damnando ... mortem destruendo*: A rhetorically effective tricolon of gerunds, each of which takes an object.

⁴⁴⁴ *Atque ... conservabit*: I have broken up this long sentence in the English and not translated *cum*.

⁴⁴⁵ *Crucem ... Diabolum*: L has a very similar catalogue of words in his commentary on Matt.: *peccatum, legem, mortem, carnem, mundum, Diabolum*. L's *Werke*, vol. 38, 527.

⁴⁴⁶ *excaelsum*: an alternative form for *excelsum*.

⁴⁴⁷ *qui ... voluerint*: Presumably a reference to Gal. 2.20: *cum Christo confixus sum cruci, et iam non vivo, vivit autem in me Christus* ('I am affixed to the cross with Christ; and now I do not live, but Christ lives in me').

[68] [215] [O.iiii.] Nam si conformis imaginis illius (ut ait Paulus) fueris,[448] si afflictionibus Iesu Christi (ut ait Petrus) communicaveris,[449] hoc est, si carnem et concupiscentias tuas crucifixeris,[450] si mundo et peccato morieris, si morti et Diabolo liber eris, si hae res non florebunt, aut ultro dominabuntur in te, nec sensum ullum, vel illae in te, vel tu in illis habueris, tum non amplius tu vives, sed Christus vivit in te: nec amplius homo in terris, sed e terris, quasi deducta colonia,[451] in coelum DEUS commigrabis: et hic existens quasi non existens,[452] illic conversationem[453] tuam, ut ait Paulus,[454] et totius vitae tuae quasi tabernaculum[455] collocabis. Tum non amplius hospes et advena, sed civis et domesticus DEI, nec id tantum sed cohaeres cum Christo in omnem sempiternitatem fueris. Et haec gloria nostra est, quam non mundus cognovit, nec caro nec sanguis revelavit: hoc summum illud gaudium quod, spondente Christo, nunquam a nobis tolletur. Ad hanc gloriam tutandam et protegendam illi, quicunque crucem suam tollunt, et vestigiis Christi insistunt, in quascunque

[69] [216] afflictiones compingantur, certissima praesidia et adiumenta in cruce, hoc est, in humanitate Christi invenire poterunt. Nam primum, parentibus et amicorum ope orbatus es?[456] Audi crucis consolationem, Non relinquam vos orphanos, veniam ad vos.[457] E patrio solo eiiceris, et in exilio degis? Quamvis Paulus multum te levare poterit, Non habemus hic manentem civitatem:[458] unice tamen te consolabitur crucifixus, qui dixit: Vado paraturus vobis locum.[459] Vim et persequutionem mundi times? Bono animo sis, Ego vici mundum.[460] Maledictum legis extimescis? Perfectio legis Christus est ad iusticiam omni credenti.[461] Faecem peccati abhominaris?[462]

---

[448] *Nam ... fueris*: Rom. 8:29; see n. 416.
[449] *si afflictionibus ... communicaveris*: 1 Peter 4.13. This wording does not match either V: *sed communicantes Christi passionibus* or *Nov. T: consortes estis afflictionum Christi*.
[450] *si ... crucifixeris*: A loose reference to Gal. 5.24: *qui autem sunt Christi carnem suam crucifixerunt cum vitiis et conscupiscentiis* ('Moreover those who are of Christ have crucified the flesh with their vices and lusts').
[451] *coloniam deducere*: a technical phrase in classical Latin meaning 'to relocate a colony'.
[452] *existens*: an alternative form for *exsistens*.
[453] *conversatio*: While this can mean 'abode', a meaning which seems to fit well in this context, it can also mean 'intercourse' and 'conversation'.
[454] *illic conversationem*: Asc. probably has Philipp. 3.20 in mind here, *nostra autem conversatio in caelis est* ('Furthermore, our conversation is in heaven').

[68] [215] [O.iiii.] For if, as Paul says, you are a direct likeness of him;[448] if, as Peter says, you partake in the sufferings of Jesus Christ,[449] that is, if you crucify the flesh and your carnality;[450] if you die with this world and sin; if you are free from death and the Devil; if these elements do not flourish, or if they do not overly control your actions, and you don't have any awareness of them [being present] in you or you in them, then you will no longer live, but Christ lives in you. Then, no longer a man on the earth but from the earth, you will travel as GOD into heaven just as one might relocate one's dwelling.[451] And here, having life though not having life,[452] you will, as Paul says,[454] locate your abode[453] there and, as it were, the tabernacle[455] of your whole life. Then you will no longer be a guest and a foreigner but a citizen and kinsman of GOD; and not only that, but a joint heir with Christ into all eternity. And this is our glory, which the world has not understood, nor flesh or blood disclosed. This is that most supreme joy which, while Christ continues to pledge it, will never be taken from us. As for the protection and preservation of his glory, those who raise up their own cross and follow in the footsteps of Christ

[69] [216] will be able to find, in whatever difficulties they may be placed, the surest garrisons and assistance in the cross, that is, in the humanity of Christ. To begin with, are you deprived[456] of your parents and the help of friends? Heed the comfort of the cross, 'I will not abandon you as orphans; I will come to you.'[457] Are you being cast out from the soil of your fatherland, and do you live in exile? Although Paul will be able to bring you considerable relief [when he says], 'We do not have here a lasting state here,'[458] only the one who has been crucified will comfort you, he who said, 'I go to prepare a place for you.'[459] Do you fear the violence and persecution of this world? 'Be of good courage; I have conquered this world.'[460] Do you dread the curse of the Law? 'The fulfillment of the Law is Christ for the righteousness of everyone who believes.'[461] Do you abhor[462] the filth of sin?

---

[455] *tabernaculum*: Paul refers to heaven as a 'tabernacle' in Hebr. 8.2.
[456] *orbatus es*: I have rendered *orbatus* as an adjective rather than as a perfect passive form with *es*, so that the tense matches the present verbs of the questions that follow on this page. As Asc. also did in themes 1 and 5, he here asks a series of questions to which he supplies the answers using quotations from the NT. Much of his phrasing is repeated.
[457] *Non ... vos*: John 14.18. The wording is identical to V and *Nov. T.*
[458] *Non ... civitatem*: Hebr. 13.14. The wording matches V and *Nov. T.*
[459] *Vado ... locum*: John 14.2. Used above in theme 5; see n. 290.
[460] *Bono ... mundum*: John 16.33. Used above in themes 1 and 5; and see n. 75.
[461] *Perfectio ... credenti*: Rom. 10.4. Used above in themes 1 and 5; and see n. 74.
[462] *abhominaris*: An alternative form for *abominaris*.

Ecce agnus Dei, qui tollit peccata mundi.[463] Diaboli tyrannidem vereris? Venit princeps huius mundi, et in me non habet quicquam.[464] Mortis aculeum exhorrescis? Mors ero mors tua,[465] et vivo ego, ut vos in aeternum in me vivatis.[466] Ergo, cum a lege ad libertatem, a peccato ad iusticiam, a morte ad vitam, a Diabolo ad Christum, crucis beneficio, adducimur, Absit mihi gloriari, nisi in cruce Domini nostri Iesu Christi.[467]

---

[463] *Ecce ... mundi*: John 1.29. Used above in themes 1 and 5, and Asc. uses the present tense *tollit* as he does in theme 1 but not theme 5.
[464] *Venit ... quicquam*: John 14.30. Used above in themes 1 and 5.
[465] *Mors ero mors tua*: Hosea 13.14. The wording matches V.

'Behold, the lamb of God who removes the sins of the world'.[463] Are you afraid of the tyranny of the Devil? 'The prince of this world comes, and he has nothing in me'.[464] Do you shrink from the sting of death? 'Death, I will be your death',[465] and 'I live so that you may live forever in me'.[466] And so, since we are led by the service of the cross from the Law to liberty, from sin to righteousness, from death to life, from the Devil to Christ, may I wholly refrain from boasting except in the cross of our Lord Jesus Christ.[467]

---

[466] *vivo . . . vivatis*: Probably a paraphrase of John 14.19, *quia ego vivo et vos vivetis* ('because I live, you shall also') and 14.16, *ut maneat vobiscum in aeternum* ('so that he may remain in you forever'), the latter of which is also marked up in GNT.

[467] *Absit . . . Christi*: a restatement of the verse which heads this theme, Gal. 6.14.

Theme 9
(70–72)

This is the shortest of all the themes. It comprises another New Testament commentary, this time on a verse from John 5, a chapter in which Jesus *inter alia* discusses the question of witnesses to his own true identity and nature. Jesus suggests that, although the question of his relationship to God needs no corroboration by another human, he will adduce it in any case: this is via evidence of John the Baptist, whom Jesus also describes as a lamp. Following this, Jesus additionally refers to his own works or miracles as proof of his identity as the son of God, the Father's testimony, and also that of the written Scriptures. These proofs Ascham also alludes to in the second part of the theme.

The theme, though brief, points to an exegetical confidence on the part of Ascham, and he deftly draws on relevant Scriptural passages beyond John 5. As he also makes clear at the end, he had plans to develop elsewhere the motifs broached here. The pronounced christological and scriptural motifs are consistent with other themes.

[70] [217] [O.v.] Ego testimonium ab homine non accipio, sed ut vos salvi sitis. Ioan. 5.[468]

Summum illum Dei Patris erga hominem amorem potius admirari, quam vel mediocri aliqua laude eum celebrare possumus, qui non solum omnia, quae essent scribenda, in nostram doctrinam scribi voluerat,[469] et fragmenta illa panum et piscium in cophinos in spem multorum colligi iusserat:[470] sed omnem etiam suam Deitatem, ad utilitatem humani generis amplificandam converterat, et fere (ut ita dicam) in nostram naturam, nostro amore, penitus se transfuderat. Nostri enim caussa, et irasci et subsannare, aures manus et pedes habere, et pro nobis in alios irridere legimus,[471] quas res in illo esse suspicari, non impietatis tantum, sed crassae cuiusdam dementiae esset. Eodem modo Christus, cum sit summa bonitas et summa scientia Patris, sciri tamen per aliorum testimonia, ut homines salvi essent, non dedignabatur: quae

[71] [218] sane testimonia omnia ipsi Christo, nec lucem nec authoritatem ullam adiicere potuerant: et hoc est quod dicit, Ego testimonium ab homine non accipio.[472] Nam, cum Christus, Et vos eritis mihi testes, non solum Hierosolymis etc.[473] Et in Actis Petrus, Nos testes sumus, omnium quae fecit Iesus in regione Iudaeorum:[474] et Ioan. 1. Non erat ille lux, sed ut testaretur de luce.[475] Hae scripturae omnes in hanc sententiam sunt accipiendae, quod Christus, non sui caussa opus habuit testimonio, sed homines hoc eguerunt, ut facilius crederent Christo. Clarissimum de Christo testimonium perhibuit Pater, cum diceret, Hic est filius meus dilectus, in quo bene mihi complacitum est.[476] Et Iesum esse Christum testantur opera Christi: nam cum[477] Ioan. duos

---

[468] *Ego ... sitis*: John 5.34. The wording is practically identical to V and *Nov. T*, though each of these have *sed haec dico* before *ut* (and the Greek has the equivalent).

[469] *Summum ... voluerat*: The ultimate agency of God the Father and the importance of the scriptural testimony are important themes in John 5.

[470] *et ... iusserat*: A reference to the miracle of feeding the 5,000 as outlined in John 6.10–14, where John reports that Jesus used five loaves and two fish to feed a multitude. The miracle is also outlined in Matt. 14.13–21, Mark 6.31–44, and Luke 9.12–17. In GNT, Asc. copies out the Greek text of one of the Sibylline Oracles (8.275–78) which is meant as an analogue to John 6:13.

[471] *et ... legimus*: *eum*, referring to Christ, must be understood in this indirect statement, but, as Asc. did not use the pronoun, I have tried to mirror his syntax in the English. The rough treatment endured by Jesus is a constant theme in the Gospels.

[472] *Ego ... accipio*: John 5.34 again, following the main premise.

[70] [217] [O.v.] 'I do not accept testimony from man, but [I mention it] that you may be saved', John 5.[468]

We can wonder at that immense love of God the Father towards man, rather than honour him with some half-baked praise. He is the one who not only willed it that everything which needed to be recorded was inscribed into our doctrine,[469] and ordered those fragments of bread and fishes be gathered into baskets for the hope of many,[470] but he also altered his entire divinity for the immense advantage of the human race, and, almost, as I will go on to say, infused himself deep into our nature through his love for us. Indeed, we read about – and on our account – anger and taunting, the adoption of ears, hands and feet, and the mocking of others instead of us.[471] But to surmise that such qualities were in that man would be not only impious but crassly mad. In the same way, Christ, even though [already] bestowed with the utmost goodness and utmost knowledge of the Father, nevertheless, did not refuse to be known through the testimonies of others so that men might be saved.

[71] [218] Truly all these testimonies could add neither light nor any authority to Christ himself. And this is what he pronounces, 'I do not receive a testimony from man',[472] for example, when Christ [says], 'And you shall be witnesses unto me, not only in Jerusalem' etc.;[473] and [when] in Acts, Peter [says], 'We are witnesses of everything that Jesus did in the land of the Jews';[474] and in John 1, [John says], 'That man was not the light, but [was sent] to bear witness of the light'.[475] All these scriptural passages must be understood in this sense – that Christ did not have need of testimony for his own sake, but men needed one that they might believe more easily in Christ. The Father issued the clearest testimony about Christ when he said 'This is my beloved son in whom I am well pleased'.[476] The actions of Christ also testify that Jesus is Christ. For instance,[477]

---

[473] *Et ... Hierosolymis*: Acts 1.8. The printed version has *aut* in place of *et* (which this edition uses), but it seems much more likely that *et* was meant in line with V, *et eritis mihi testes in Ierusalem* and also *Nov. T* (which, like Asc., has *non solum* before *Hierosolymis* rather than *in*). Asc. jots down the word μάρτυρες ('witnesses') next to this verse in the margin of GNT.
[474] *Nos ... Iudaeorum*: Acts 10.39. The wording is almost identical to V and *Nov. T* (except Asc. has inserted the subject *Iesus*). Again, the word μάρτυρες is inscribed in the margin of this verse in GNT.
[475] *Non ... luce*: John 1.8. Asc. diverges in wording from both V: *non erat ille lux sed ut testimonium perhiberet de lumine*, and from *Nov. T*: *non erat ille lux illa, sed missus erat ut testaretur de luce*, but has identical wording to Pag.
[476] *Hic ... complacitum est*: Matt. 3.17 or 2 Peter 1.17; and see n. 280.
[477] *cum ... cum*: these have been left untranslated, as I have broken this long sentence up in the English.

ex eius discipulis ad Christum, non quod ipse dubitaret, sed ut illos confirmaret, misisset ut interrogarent illum, An esset Christus, vel alium expectarent? Non statim nomen suum indicabat, sed re ipsa illud patefaciebat, cum dixerat, Dicite Ioan. caeci vident, claudi ambulant, etc.,[478] ut cum viderent opera, qualia praeter Christum

[72] [219] nemo operari potuisset, tum firmiter crederent, quod testimonio illorum operum Christus illis significatus fuisset. Porro, cum Christus in scripturis apte et congruenter quidem Sol dicatur, ut in illo Zachariae, Visitavit nos oriens ex alto:[479] et Ioannes Baptista a Davide Lucerna nominetur, ut illic, Paravi lucernam Christo meo:[480] profecto, non magis Christus testimonio Ioannis egebat, quam opem lucernae in medio die sol desiderat. Praeterea, si testimonio Ioannis Christo nihil sit adiectio, non est ut aliorum testimonia requiramus, cum Inter natos mulierum maior Ioanne Baptista nullus unquam surrexerat.[481] Et haec de priore, quod ideo brevius perstrinximus, quoniam in posteriorem longe diligentiores fuerimus.

---

[478] *Dicite ... ambulant*: Matt. 11.4–5. Cf. V: *renuntiate Iohanni quae auditis et videtis: caeci vident et claudi ambulant*; *Nov. T* follows V but has *visum recipiunt* (instead of *vident*) after *caeci*. In GNT, Ascham has commented on the verse in the margin with a reference to 'the works of Christ'.

[479] *Visitavit ... alto*: verse 78 from the Benedictus or Song of Zechariah, a song of thanksgiving given by Zechariah on the occasion of the circumcision of his son, John the

John sent two of his followers to Christ, not because he himself was in doubt, but so that he might instill courage in them, and to ask [him] whether he *was* Christ, or whether they should await another. He (i.e. Christ) did not immediately indicate his name, but let the matter speak clearly for itself when he said 'Tell John, the blind see and the lame walk', etc.,[478] so that when they perceived deeds of the sort which

[72] [219] no one had been able to perform except Christ, they would then have a sure faith because Christ had been made known to them through the testimony of those deeds. Hereafter, although Christ is openly and indeed fitly called 'the Sun' in Scripture, as in that [book] of Zechariah, 'Rising, he visited us from on high';[479] and John the Baptist is named 'a Lamp' by David, as in that statement, 'I have prepared a lamp for my Christ',[480] to be sure, Christ did not need the testimony of John [any] more than the sun has need of a lamp in the middle of the day. Moreover, if the added testimony of John was as nothing to Christ, it is not for us to seek the testimonies of others, since 'from those born of women, none has ever come into this world greater than John the Baptist'.[481] And we have touched on these items above rather briefly since we will deal with them much more carefully later on.

Baptist, and set out in Luke 1.68–79. Asc.'s wording follows V and *Nov. T.* Asc. highlights the song in the margin of GNT.

[480] *Paravi lucernam Christo meo*: Ps. 131.17 (V/S) / 132.17 (H/P). The link between the Psalm wording and John was identified by Augus. (Martinez / Luttikhizen 2003: 18), by whom Ascham may well have been influenced here.

[481] *Inter . . . surrexerat*: based on wording in Matt. 11.11 and Luke 7.28.

Theme 10
(73–89)

This is the longest theme in the collection, running to some sixteen pages, and, even so, it is incomplete, as indicated by the Latin words *pauca desunt* at the end. It functions as another disputational speech (indeed, Ascham makes an explicit reference to a disputation in it). Another Pauline verse serves as the stimulus for this debate, this time from the second Epistle to Timothy (often believed to be Paul's last letter before execution), 'Everyone who is willing to live piously in Jesus Christ will endure persecutions'. This theme is one of the most partisan and obstreperous items in the collection, with its explicit assaults on important Catholic shibboleths, and it is very much implicated in the dynamics of the Henrician Reformation. It is also a rhetorically assured production, that again repeatedly boasts of its own scriptural integrity.

The theme begins almost devotionally with an invocation of Christ and the guidance God provides through the preaching of the Gospel. In many ways, this captures the core theological message of the theme, one that suffuses the majority of the themes, namely a rigid adherence to the Word of God. The early reference to Augustine is interesting in confessional terms. Ascham writes that Augustine 'declared that just as the life of all be credited to the providence of divine will, so the death of all must be attributed to [God's] refusal to heed the human will' (73), and within a Reformation context it points to a Lutheran stress on man's powerlessness before God. As elsewhere, Ascham carefully examines each element of the biblical verse in order to pin down the meaning of each phrase. Ascham also demonstrates a keen awareness of seminal doctrinal controversies, and, unsurprisingly, the term 'willing' in the verse from the Epistle to Timothy prompts an engagement (of sorts) with the issue of the 'will'. While he overtly circumvents the larger Free Will debate, the positions of which had been become well-set in the earlier disagreement between Luther and Erasmus,[482] he does offer his own definition of the will, one that is formed from his independent reading of Scripture. Yet Ascham's aversion to abstruse doctrinal distractions is evident when he dismisses those who advocate 'predestination', and this prompts him to comment that such people 'have entangled themselves in a totally inexplicable matter' (74). As discussed above, Ascham was also not prepared to accept a theological model that neglected personal human conduct, and he added 'they reject all wisdom and all concern and regard for conducting a

---

[482] For more, see Rupp / Watson 1969.

better life' (74). The theme constitutes a clear manifestation of Ascham's twin priorities – moral conduct and strict observance of God's Word.

In addition to explaining piety *in Christo*, Ascham then branches out to consider piety *extra Christum*. Interestingly, he includes all Christians, both those who live in and outside of Christ, as members of a collective 'church militant' and he redeploys an argument, along with certain *exempla* he has used elsewhere, which illustrates how, even in the most devout, a Christian zeal can contravene God's will. He then, however, proceeds to assail certain quarters of that church militant, including monastic personnel, partisans of the Pope and Cardinal Reginald Pole. Ascham also issues a warning against another type of Christian who live *extra Christum*, those he terms 'gospellers' who, despite their reading of the Gospel, nevertheless behave immorally. Within this survey, he invokes what was effectively the Tudor cliché of the 'middle way', referring to the Charybdis of the gospellers and the Scylla of the religious radicals. Of course, at a time when Protestants were being accused of innovation by their religious opponents, their own charge of 'radical' was a form of deflection.

In the final part of the theme, Ascham addresses the matter of persecution. He presents suffering as an important aspect of Christian life, suggesting that it is a condition of especially pious men. In support of this, Ascham produces a number of scriptural dicta which suggest the same, as well as examples of biblical and historical figures who suffered persecution. Ascham also includes a two-line poem about the spiritual benefit of suffering by John Redman, one of Ascham's close contemporaries at Cambridge. Then, in an attempt to explain why the righteous are more oppressed than the bad (possibly in response to a disputational opponent), Ascham cites a hemistich of Ovid that, for Ascham, effectively articulated the ultimate reward of such persecution. Despite Ascham's clear commitment to the principle of *sola scriptura*, he once again demonstrates a ready willingness to supplement the Bible with material that he deemed compatible with it. The two poetical citations also point to the value Ascham placed on formal structures of language and their elevated form, and the degree to which he believed in words' power to redirect the soul.

[73] [219] Omnes qui volunt pie vivere in Christo Iesu persequutiones patientur. 2. Tim. 3.[483]

Dominus noster Iesus Christus, qui fuit, est, erit lumen et splendor Dei Patris, per viscera misericordiae suae visitare nos, veluti oriens ex alto, dignabatur: ut omnes homines in hunc mundum venientes, qui lucem illam non reiecerunt, vultus [220] sui splendore illuminaret: et omnium hominum pedes, qui in tenebris, et in umbra mortis sederent, in viam pacis dirigeret atque confirmaret.[484] Hic est qui (attestante Psalmista) salvos nos fecit, quoniam voluit nos:[485] voluit enim omnes, omniumque generum et conditionum homines salvari,[486] et ad agnitionem veritatis per Evangelii sui praedicationem pervenire, ut nulla omnino existeret condemnatio hiis, qui insiti in eo essent, modo non in viam carnis ambularent, sed omnem vitae suae cursum, clavum regente spiritu, gubernarent. Itaque, Divus Augustinus, ut vitam omnium divinae voluntatis providentiae assignandam, ita mortem omnium humanae voluntatis neglegentiae[487] imputandam esse iudicabat.[488] Ergo, cum omnes, qui volunt pie vivere in Christo Iesu, persequutionem patientur, hoc est, vel (ut ait Paulus) per patientiam, probationem, spem ad vitam aeternam pervenient:[489] vel (ut ait Christus) regni Dei possessionem quasi haereditario quodam iure occupabunt:[490] nam qui compatiuntur, una cohaeredes erunt et conregnabunt.[491] Et cum[492] haec sit promissio

---

[483] *Omnes ... patientur*: 2 Tim. 3.12. Asc. has altered slightly the wording of V and *Nov. T*, both of which have *persecutionem* rather than *persequutiones*. In this letter, Paul, awaiting execution, reflects movingly on the example of Tim., who embraced, *inter alia*, an acceptance of persecution.
[484] *per ... confirmaret*: inspired by the Song of Zechariah in Luke 1.78–79, a passage Asc. also cites in theme 9 (see n. 479). Asc.'s wording of this particular verse departs quite noticeably from V: *per viscera misericordiae Dei nostri, in quibus visitavit nos oriens ex alto, inluminare his qui in tenebris et in umbra mortis sedent, ad dirigendos pedes nostros in viam pacis*. ('Through the inmost workings of the mercy of our God, whereby he, rising, visited us from on high to bring light to these who sit in darkness and the shadow of death, [and] to direct our feet in the way of peace'); cf. *Nov. T*: *per viscera misericordiae Dei nostri, quibus visitavit nos oriens ex alto: ut illucesceret his qui in tenebris et umbra mortis sedebant ad dirigendos pedes nostros in viam pacis*. The song's main themes of hardship and hope complement the argument Asc. adumbrates in this theme.
[485] *salvos ... nos*: Ps. 17.20 (V/S) / 18.19 (H/P), albeit V has *salvum me faciet*. Like Asc., the Coverdale Bible (which had relied on Tyndale's New Testament translation and, *inter alia*, Luther's German version) also uses the past tense rather than the future ('delyuered me'). Asc. has conflated the salvific powers of God (as referred to in the Ps.) with Christ's.
[486] *salvos ... salvari*: Asc. is clearly focused on the process of salvation.
[487] *neglegentiae*: This is working in parallel with *providentiae*, and must refer to God's divine 'disregard' of the human will.
[488] *Divus ... iudicabat*: Asc. cites Augus. as an authority for the position that there was no liberty of human will and that God directs both live and death, albeit I have been unable to match Asc.'s wording to a particular Augustinian work. In fact, Augus.'s views on the

[73] [219] 'Everyone who is willing to live piously in Jesus Christ will endure persecutions'. 2 Timothy 3.[483]

Our Lord Jesus Christ who was, is, and will be the light and lustre of God the Father, deemed it worthy, through the inmost workings of his mercy, to visit us, just as if rising from on high, in order that he might illuminate with the lustre of his countenance all men coming into this world who did not reject that light; [220] also [in order that] he might direct and secure the feet of all men who tend to sit in darkness and the shadow of death unto the way of peace.[484] This is the one who, as the Psalmist testifies, has saved us, since he willed us [to be so];[485] for he willed [it] that all men of every sort and type be saved,[486] and arrive at an understanding of the truth through the preaching of his Gospel in order that there might be absolutely no damnation for these who were grafted in him, provided they did not walk in the way of the flesh, but steered the whole course of their lives with the spirit governing the rudder. Accordingly, St Augustine declared that just as the life of all be credited to the providence of divine will, so the death of all must be attributed to [God's] refusal to heed[487] the human will.[488] Therefore, when all who are willing to live piously in Jesus Christ endure persecution, that is: either, as Paul says, through patience, experience and hope, they will reach an eternal life;[489] or, as Christ says, they will occupy possession of the kingdom of God, as if by a certain inherited right.[490] For those who suffer together will be joint heirs as one and will reign jointly.[491] This[492] is the promise of one

---

human will and predestination were rather more complicated than Asc.'s allusion suggests, and it was only in the latter part of his life, following his conflict with Pelagius, when Augus. came to resist in a more robust way the notion of human will. God's total control of humans was certainly a standpoint promoted by L, and the sentiment certainly speaks to a Protestant view of the degeneracy of mankind and the paramount importance of faith in the Lord, but, as will become clear below (and see also n. 495), Asc. qualifies an extreme subscription to the doctrine of predestination, which in some ways his reference to Augus. here might seem to point to.

[489] *per ... pervenient*: a paraphrase of Paul in Rom. 5.3–4, *scientes quod tribulatio patientiam operatur; patientia autem probationem, probatio vero spem* ('knowing that hardship brings about patience; moreover, patience experience; and truly experience hope'). Asc. has inscribed the Greek terms for these qualities in the margin of GNT, namely θλίψεις, ὑπομονή, δοκιμή and ἐλπίς.

[490] *regni ... occupabunt*: Asc. is paraphrasing, but this is presumably another reference to Rom. (here, 8.17): *si autem filii, et haeredes: haeredes, quidem Dei, cohaeredes autem Christi si tamen compatimur ut et conglorificemur* ('Moreover, if sons, also heirs; heirs indeed of God, and joint heirs with Christ [only] if however, we suffer with him to as to be glorified with him'). Asc. would inscribe in the margin adjacent to this verse in GNT the Greek words for 'children' and 'heirs'.

[491] *compatiuntur ... conregnabunt*: The two compound verbs (using the preposition *cum* in combination with *coharedes* and *una* arguably convey an even more powerful sense of togetherness than the scriptural verse that inspired it.

[492] *Et ... censendi*: I have broken up this long Latin period with a series of English sentences, and thus not fully captured the *cum* clause and the one that follows.

[74] [221] eius, qui semper iustus et numquam mendax (ut ait Paulus) extiterit,[493] cum haec sit spes illa nostra, afflictionis comes atque socia,[494] quae numquam confusa, sed semper certissima fuerit: hii ergo, qui nescio quid de praedestinatione[495] somniantes, nullam aut honestae aut flagitiosae vitae rationem habent, praeterquam quod certissimam salutis suae viam, cum desperatione quadam insigni, ignave negligentes, re longe inexplicabili, nec umquam ulli vel angelo coeli cognita sese irretiverint,[496] stulti merito sunt habendi: praeterea etiam, quod tam immortale certumque beneficium, quale nunquam nec in terris, nec in coelis audiebatur, contempserunt, ingrati impiique[497] sunt censendi.[498] Nam, qui[499] vitam suam in tam angustos praedestinationis terminos, et veluti cancellos quosdam includunt, et in ea re sola perpetuas cogitationes suas ad stuporem usque defigunt, praeterquam quod omnem providentiam, omnemque vitae melioris gerendae curam atque rationem abiiciunt, totos se pronos, expansissimo illo gratiae velo contempto, Christoque clavo tutissimo deserto, et Ecclesia nave fundatissima

[75] [222] relicta, in immensum illud flagitiorum pelagus, stupida et insensili quadam salutis suae desperatione misere praecipitant ac devolvunt. Est haec ergo sententia certe cuiusdam consolationis plena, Omnes qui volunt pie vivere in Christo Iesu persequutionem patientur.[500] Qui volunt pie vivere in Christo Iesu. Neque hic retexendum, neque leviter quidem attingendum perplexum illud et implicatum de Libero Arbitrio[501] caput esse iudico, sed quasi huius loci et instituti minime proprium praetereundum potius censeo: hoc satis et tantum de hac re a me dictum sit, Humanam voluntatem Adami lapsu multum esse depravatam, et veluti in domum quandam pessime

---

[493] *qui ... mendax*: This is not Pauline wording, but it is likely that Asc. has in mind Rom. again, probably 7.12: *itaque lex quidem sancta et mandatum sanctum et iustum et bonum* ('And so the law indeed is holy, and the commandment holy, and just and good'), and Asc. would mark up this verse in GNT with the Greek words for 'holy law'. It is probably not a coincidence that Asc. employs language here which has something in common with L's famous paraphrase, *semper peccator, semper iustus*.

[494] *comes atque socia*: see n. 343, though here the phrasing is reversed.

[495] *praedestinatione*: The issue of predestination became a major fault-line in the Reformation debates. At the radical end, which Asc. here criticises, adherents of a religious determinism considered predestination to be the sole source of salvation and consequently the role of good works was accordingly marginalised. But see also n. 159 of the main introduction.

[496] *irretiverint*: A pejorative application of this verb is seen in Cic. *Tusc.* 5.21.62, *iis enim se adolescens improvida aetate irretierat erratis eaque commiserat* ('for with the inconsiderateness of youth he had entangled himself in such errors and been guilty of

[74] [221] who was always righteous and never false, as Paul says;[493] this is that hope of ours, the companion and partner[494] of suffering, which was never in doubt but always most certain. Thus, these men, who, as they dream up all sort of things about predestination,[495] have no regard either for a pure or profligate life, except only the surest way to their own salvation. Since, with a certain remarkable foolhardiness and in their lazy indifference, they have entangled[496] themselves in a totally inexplicable matter – one that has never been known even to any angel of heaven – they must correctly be considered idiots. What is more, because they have scorned so everlasting and sure a gift, the kind that was never heard of either on earth or in heaven, they must be regarded as ungrateful and wicked[497] [aswell].[498] For they[499] confine their own lives within such narrow bounds of predestination, as though [within] certain railings and, in that matter alone, incline their thoughts constantly and exclusively in the direction of 'fascination', except that they reject all wisdom and all concern and regard for conducting a better life. In their wretchedness, they hurl and roll themselves in an altogether downward trajectory into that immense sea of shame,

[75] [222] scorning that wonderfully unfurled sail of grace, deserting Christ, the most safe rudder, and abandoning the Church, the most steady ship, in some senseless and insensible foolhardiness regarding their own salvation. For this reason, there is this maxim that is so full of comfort, 'All who are willing to live piously in Jesus Christ will endure persecution'.[500] 'Those who are *willing* to live piously in Jesus Christ': and I do not consider that the bewildering and involved principle of Free Will[501] must be unravelled here, nor indeed superficially broached, but rather I propose rather that it be passed over on the grounds that it is not at all pertinent to this topic and the debate that has been instituted. Regarding this matter, let it be sufficient that I say only this: [that] the human will was greatly corrupted by the fall of Adam, and, as it were, led back into a certain house which was very badly

---

such acts ...'). In his Latin works generally, Asc. often harnessed classical references against his religious opponents.

[497] *ingrati impiique*: The adjectives 'ungrateful' (*ingrati*) and wicked (*scelesti*) are used in 2 Tim. 3.2 of the reprobate.

[498] *praeterquam ... censendi*: Note the symmetrical formation of these two clauses which draws out the stark contrast between the upholders of predestination, on the one hand, and the true faith, on the other.

[499] *Nam ... devolvunt*: I have broken up this long Latin sentence in the English and thus omitted the relative clause.

[500] *Omnes ... patientur*: a restatement of the verse that forms the heading of the theme, 2 Tim. 3.12, although Asc. uses the singular *persequutionem* rather than the plural *persequutiones* as above (see also n. 483).

[501] *Libero Arbitrio*: Following the high-profile debate in print in the 1520s between L and E, the issue of Free Will became a hotly contested topic in the Reformation. Asc. stresses that he does not wish to become too embroiled in the intricacies of it here.

materiatam⁵⁰² redactam, eandem vero mortis Christi beneficio insigni quodam modo esse reparatam, et quasi novo aliquo lumine et nitore mirifice esse illustratam. Quid hic voluntas sit, liquide ex aliis Scripturae locis omnibus innotescit: aliquando enim amor nominatur, ut in eo Psalmo, Quis est homo qui vult vitam, et diligit videre dies bonos?⁵⁰³ Novumque studium, ut ad Hebraeos sexto:

[76] [223] Cupimus autem ut unusquisque vestrum idem praestet studium, ad plenam spei certitudinem, et c.⁵⁰⁴ Et alibi Iesus, Ut zelum habent, sed non secundum scientiam.⁵⁰⁵ *[Velle quid]* Velle ergo, hoc in loco, est promptam quandam et paratam animi inductionem ad quidvis praestandum habere, quod conatus fueris.⁵⁰⁶ Vivere pie in Christo Iesu. Vivere *[Vivere quid.]*, est omnium hominum Iudaeorum, Turcarum, Christianorum, Regum, Subditorum, Publicorum, Privatorum, Sexuum, et Aetatum, vitae conditio, id quod proprio quodam nomine a Paulo, inter Christianos, vocatio dicitur.⁵⁰⁷ Sunt ergo qui vivunt, et id tantum: nam neque pium aliquid in Christo, neque extra Christum moliuntur, ut Iudaei, et Saraceni.⁵⁰⁸ Est aliud genus hominum, quorum partim in Christo, partim extra Christum, ut ita dicam, pie vivunt, qui omnes communi quodam nomine, postquam baptismate regenerentur, Christiani appellantur: quod nomen primum illis in Antiochia inditum est, ut refert in. 11. Actuum Lucas.⁵⁰⁹ Et hic coetus cum contineat in se bonos et malos, triticum et zizaniam,⁵¹⁰ Haereticos et

---

[502] *domum quandam pessime materiatam*: cf. Cic. *Off.* 3.13.54: *aedes . . . male materiatae* ('a house . . . built of unsound timber').

[503] *Quis . . . bonos?*: Ps. 33.13 (V/S) / 34.12 (H/P). V: *quis est homo qui vult vitam cupit videre dies bonos*, but Asc. seems to have followed Augus. *Ennaratio in Psalmum XXXIII*.17 (*PL* 36, col. 317), where *diligit* is used. Pag. also has *diligit*, but otherwise follows different wording to Asc.

[504] *Cupimus . . . certitudinem, et c.*: Hebr. 6.11. Asc. diverges from V: *cupimus autem ununquemque vestrum eandem ostentare sollicitudinem ad expletionem spei usque in finem*, but he follows *Nov. T.* verbatim. *c.* stands for *cetera*.

[505] *Ut . . . scientiam*: Rom. 10.2. Asc. diverges from V, which, as the first part of this, has: . . . *quod aemulationem Dei habent* and from *Nov. T*: . . . *quod studium dei habent*. Jer. in letter 54.6 (to Furia) (*PL* 22, col. 552) used *zelum*, but Asc. almost certainly had the ζῆλος of the Greek in mind; indeed, he inscribes this word in the margin in GNT next to this verse.

[506] *Velle . . . fueris*: Asc. offers a meaning of *volunt* of the verse from 2 Tim. that he began with, but the definition he offers does not easily flow from the two verses he has just cited.

built;⁵⁰² but somehow the same house was renovated by the extraordinary service of Christ's death and marvellously adorned as if with some new light and sheen. What the will comprises here becomes patently obvious to everyone from other passages of Scripture. Indeed, sometimes love is mentioned, as in that Psalm, 'Who is the man who desires life and loves to see good days?'⁵⁰³ It is a 'new diligence', as in the sixth [chapter of the Epistle] to the Hebrews,

[76] [223] 'Moreover, we desire that each one of you shows the same diligence to the full assurance of hope etc.'⁵⁰⁴ Elsewhere Jesus [says], 'Though they have zeal, it is not in accordance with knowledge'.⁵⁰⁵ Thus, in this passage 'to be willing' *['To be willing' – what it is]* is to have a certain quick and ready inclination of the mind to discharging anything which you have attempted.⁵⁰⁶ 'To live piously in Jesus Christ': 'to live' *['To Live' – what it is]* is a condition of life peculiar to all men – Jews, Turks, Christians, kings, subjects, public figures, private figures, [of all] sexes and ages; it is that which is referred to with its own particular name of 'a calling' by Paul among the Christians.⁵⁰⁷ Indeed, there are those who live and only that; for they venture [to do] nothing pious in Christ nor outside of Christ, like the Jews and the Saracens.⁵⁰⁸ There is another type of men, some of whom live piously in Christ and, so to speak, some outside of Christ; these are all called by the universal name of 'Christians' after they are reborn through baptism. This name was first given to them in Antioch, as Luke reports in Acts 11.⁵⁰⁹ And this company, since it contains in itself both good and bad, wheat and tares,⁵¹⁰ heretics and

---

⁵⁰⁷ *a ... dicitur*: Paul refers to a 'calling' in, for example, 1 Corinth. 1.26, *videte enim vocationem vestram, frates* ('For see your vocation, brethren').

⁵⁰⁸ *Saraceni*: i.e. Arab Muslims.

⁵⁰⁹ *quod ... est*: Acts 11.26. V: *ut cognominarentur primum Antiochiae discipuli Christiani* ('so that at Antioch the disciples were first named "Christians"'); the same wording used in *Nov. T*, albeit it empoys a different word order. Acts is generally credited to Luke, hence Asc.'s *refert ... Lucas*.

⁵¹⁰ *contineat ... zizaniam*: wording inspired by the parable in Matt. 13.24–25: ... *qui seminavit bonum semen in agro suo ... venit inimicus eius et superseminavit zizania in medio tritici* ('... [a man] who sowed good seed in his field, ... an enemy came and sowed tares among wheat ...'). *zizania* in Latin (and Greek) is neuter plural, and the accusative *zizaniam* is incorrect on the part of Asc. (or the printer). The verse is underlined in GNT.

[77] [224] Papistas, Ecclesia militans⁵¹¹ vocatur. *[Ecclesia militans]* Et primum quidem, quid sit pie vivere in Christo Iesu, ex fonte Scripturarum,⁵¹² et sanctorum Patrum rivulis exhauriendum esse iudico: volo enim omnem orationis meae sermonem et cursum, vel verbi Dei authoritate, vel Patrum testimoniis, tanquam velis quibusdam et clavis, regi atque gubernari. *[Pietas in Christo]* Est pietas ergo in Christo, quam Graeci apte et plane εὐσέβειαν vocant, ut definit D. I.⁵¹³ Chysost. *[Chrysostomus]* ἡ μετὰ πίστεως ὀρθῆς, ἐπιμέλεια τοῦ βίου.⁵¹⁴ 1. coniuncta cum recta et sana fide diligens vivendi ratio. *[sana fides]*. Est autem recta et sana fides, ut Graeca scholia tradunt,⁵¹⁵ quae nihil in se externum continet, nec Iudaïcum, nec Graecum, nec Haereticum,⁵¹⁶ nec Papisticum,⁵¹⁷ sed quae se in praefixos verbi Dei terminos abdiderit et incluserit. Nam quemadmodum nulla caro,⁵¹⁸ ab illa immensa illuvione fuerit erepta,⁵¹⁹ quae in Arcam Noe⁵²⁰ sese non receperat: ita, nullam in Christo Iesu pietatem esse existimem, quae non omnem, quem instituerit cursum, in sola Arca testamenti eius (ut ait in Apocalypsi Ioannes)⁵²¹ ad exoptatissimum portum Christum

[78] [225] [P.] confecerit. Praeterea, volo pietatem sic Christo inesse *[Pietas quomodo in Christo]* (quamvis leviore exemplo utar) quemadmodum accidens aliquod inseparabile, quod nullo modo a subiecto,⁵²² nec actu nec potentia, separari potest. Hanc pietatem et cultum divinum habuit Paulus, qui dixit: Quis nos separabit a dilectione Dei?⁵²³ Et c. Si quis explicatiorem rectae et sanae fidei institutionem requirit, sanctissimum sanctissimi viri Athanasii⁵²⁴ symbolum perlegat.

---

⁵¹¹ *Ecclesia militans*: The expression is traditionally ascribed to Pope Clement V who used it in his letter to King Philip IV in 1311, and it indicates all living Christians.
⁵¹² *ex fonte Scripturarum*: see n. 320.
⁵¹³ D. I.: standing for *divus*
⁵¹⁴ Oec.: ΕΙΣ ΤΗΝ ΠΡΟΣ ΤΙΜΟΘΕΟΝ Α. ΕΠΙΣΤΟΛΗΝ: [τοῦτο γὰρ εὐσέβεια,] ἡ μετὰ πίστεως ὀρθῆς ἐπιμέλεια τοῦ καθαροῦ βίου (*Oecumenius' Exegesis on Acts and the Letters of Paul*, 1844, 435 / PG 119, col. 169). Cf. Chrysos.: [Ἅγιοι δέ εἰσι πάντες, ὅσοι] βίον καλὸν μετὰ πίστεως ὀρθῆς [ἔχουσιν ἄν] in his *Homily XIV on 1 Tim.* (according to the Laurentianus codex of the eleventh century), although βίου δὲ ἐπιμέλεια is also used in Chrysos. *Homily on Matthew*, 46.485A. It seems very likely Asc. here accessed Chrysos. via Oec., not least because Asc. would undertake a larger translation of Oec. around this time.
⁵¹⁵ *Graeca scholia*: Presumably Asc. means Oec. here and Oec.'s reference to 'the concern of life with upright faith'.
⁵¹⁶ *nec Iudaïcum . . . Haereticum*: cf. Gal. 3.28, *non est Iudaeus neque Graecus non est servus neque liber . . .* ('There is neither Jew nor Greek; there is neither slave of free man. . .'), which then also suggests that all these people have the same opportunity to be Christians.
⁵¹⁷ *Papisticum*: Asc. made his own anti-papal addition to the list found in Gal. (as n. 516 above).
⁵¹⁸ *caro*: literally, 'flesh'.

[77] [224] papists, is called 'the church militant'[511] *[Church militant]*. And first indeed, I adjudge that what it is to live piously in Jesus Christ must be drawn from the fountainhead of the Scriptures[512] and the streams of the holy Fathers. For it is my will that the entire discourse and progress of my speech be governed and steered either by the authority of the Word of God or the testimonies of the Fathers, as if by certain sails and rudders. *[Piety in Christ]* And accordingly, there is a piety in Christ, which the Greeks appropriately and clearly call 'eusebeia', that St[513] Chrysostom defines *[Chrysostom]* [as] (in Greek) 'the concern of life with upright faith'[514] and (in Latin) 'the attentive concern of living coupled with an upright and wholesome faith' *[wholesome faith]*. There is, moreover, an upright and wholesome faith, as the Greek scholia transmit it,[515] which contains in itself nothing extraneous, neither Jewish, nor Greek, nor heretical,[516] nor papistical,[517] but which has confined and kept itself within the pre-determined boundaries God's Word. For just as there was no [species of] animal[518] that was carried away[519] by that boundless overflow, which had not taken itself into the ark of Noah,[520] so I should think that there has been no piety in Jesus Christ which has not brought every journey that he instituted in the unique 'ark of his testament', as John puts it in Revelation,[521] to the most longed for harbour, Christ.

[78] [225] [P.] Beyond this, I mean that piety resides in Christ *[Piety – how [it works] in Christ]* just as, although I use a rather frivolous example, some inseparable quality which can be separated in no way from its subject[522] nor through [any] impulse or power. Paul had in mind this piety and divine worship when he uttered 'Who will separate us from the love of God? etc.'[523] If anyone seeks a clearer exposition of upright and wholesome faith, he should examine thoroughly the most holy Creed of that most holy Athanasius.[524]

---

[519] *fuerit erepta*: these words do not belong together, and *fuerit* must be taken with *nulla caro*.
[520] *Noe*: is in the genitive, and is either the indeclinable form, *Noe*, or *Noae*, with contracted diphthong.
[521] *Arca testamenti eius*: a reference to Rev. 11.19, *et visa est arca testamenti eius*.
[522] *accidens . . . subiecto*: The vocabulary used here is taken from the realm of logic.
[523] *Quis . . . Dei?*: Rom. 8.35. V: *Quis nos separabit a caritate Christi?* Asc.'s *dilectione* matches E, who has *dilectio*, which was considered a better rendering of the Greek ἀγάπη; indeed, Asc. notes this very term next to this verse in GNT.
[524] *viri Athanasii*: St Athanasius, Bishop of Alexandria and early Greek Church Father of the fourth century CE. He is, however, no longer considered to be the author of Latin statement of belief named after him. The so-called Athanasian Creed (or *Symbolum Athanasianum*) is a statement of Catholic faith that was popular in many early Protestant churches, appearing in, for example, the Augsburg Confession and the Thirty-Nine Articles. The first half of the Creed emphasises a belief in the Trinity, and the second half is concerned with christology. Its opening words, namely *Quicumque vult salvus esse* ('Whoever is willing to be saved') complemented the verse from 2 Tim. that Asc. was elucidating, and in his reference to *rectae et sanae fidei*, Asc. may be thinking in particular about verse 30 of the Creed, *Est ergo fides recta ut credamus et confiteamur . . .* ('For the right Faith is that we believe and confess . . .').

Altera pars huius definitionis[525] in ratione vivendi vertitur, quae duobus locis, uno Davidis, altero Pauli, veluti penicillo quodam depingitur.[526] Davidis hic est *[Psal. 34]*: Quis est homo qui vult vitam, diligit dies videre bonos? Prohibe linguam tuam a malo, et labia tua ne loquantur dolum: diverte a malo et fac bonum, inquire pacem et persequere eam.[527] *[Tit. 2.]* Pauli ad Titum. 2. est, Abnegemus impietatem et mundanas concupiscentias, ac sobrie, ac iuste, et pie vivamus in hoc seculo, et c.[528] Sic ergo pietas illa in Christo Iesu, et ex fidei sanitate, et ex vitae integritate conflata est atque perfecta. *[Pietas extra Christum quid]* Pietas vero extra Christum est zelus quidem, sed non secundum

[79] [226] scientiam, quae[529] stulta quadam officii erga DEUM opinione inniti videatur. Itaque, non omne quod a bono proposito proficisci dicitur, statim DEO placet, sed quod praecepto DEI eiusque voluntate comprobari solet: Est enim via (Proverbiorum. 14) quae videtur homini iusta, novissima autem eius deducunt ad mortem.[530] *[Pietas Sauli]* Sic pius erat Saul, qui iussus a Domino, ut[531] omnes hostes eius[532] usque ad mingentem ad lapidem trucidaret, ut aurum et argentum eorum et opes universas igni perurenda[533] traderet, cum tamen zelo et pietate quadam templum DEI decorandi, aurea quaedam monumenta reservarat, pariter et e regno, et e perpetuo DEI favore eiectus et deturbatus fuerat.[534] *[Pietas Petri.]* Sic pius erat Petrus, qui cum Christus crucem et mortem suam Apostolis praedicabat, assumens illum pia quadam mente dixit, Propitius tibi sis Domine, nequaquam erit tibi hoc:[535]

---

[525] *Altera pars huius definitionis*: viz. the definition of piety in Christ.
[526] *veluti penicillo quodam depingitur*: This presumably means that there is considerable correspondence between the Ps. account and Paul.
[527] *Quis... eam*: Ps. 33.13–15 (V/S) / 34.12–14 (H/P). Asc. has referred to verse 12 (H/P) and 13 (V/S) above (75), though he quotes more here. The wording of the additional verses matches V, although the hanging note again makes reference to the H/P numbering.
[528] *Abnegemus... seculo*: A summary of the exhortations in Titus 2.
[529] *quae*: its antecedent is *pietas*.
[530] *Est... mortem*: Prov. 14.12. Asc. follows V.
[531] *sic... ut*: *ut* is almost certainly operating in a result clause construction following *sic* rather than an indirect command after *iussus*, as *iubeo* is generally followed by an infinitive rather than an *ut* construction, although there it is just possible that an indirect command is intended, as *ut* (+ subjunctive) is used below following a part of *iubeo* (albeit together with other verbs) – see also n. 616.

The other part of this definition[525] turns on a way of living, and [is found] in two places: one in David, and the other in Paul, as if being depicted by some painter's brush.[526] This is David's [version] *[Psalm 34]*: 'Who is the man who desires life, [and] loves to see good days? Keep your tongue from evil and don't let your lips tell a lie; turn from evil and do good; search after peace and pursue it'.[527] [The account] of Paul is in his Second [Epistle] to Titus *[Titus 2.]*, 'Let us abstain from wickedness and worldly carnality, and let us live soberly, righteously and piously in this lifetime etc'.[528] Thus, therefore, that piety in Jesus Christ has been produced and achieved from both a soundness of faith and a purity of life. *[Piety beyond Christ – what it is]* In truth, piety beyond Christ is indeed enthusiasm, but not in accordance with

[79] [226] knowledge, insofar[529] as it seems to rest upon some misplaced belief of duty towards God. In like manner, not everything which is said to derive from a sound proposition is immediately pleasing to God, but [only] that which is routinely sanctioned by God's commandment and his will. 'For there is a way,' as per Proverbs 14, 'which seems righteous to man, yet its ends lead to death'.[530] *[Piety of Saul]* Saul was 'pious' in such a way that,[531] following God's orders, he killed all his[532] enemies as far as pissing against a stone, and handed over their (i.e. his enemies') gold and silver and every treasure for burning[533] on a fire; however, when, [moved] by enthusiasm and a certain piety to decorate God's temple, he had kept aside some gold monuments, he was simultaneously cast out from and deprived of his kingdom and the eternal favour of God.[534] *[Piety of Peter]* Peter was 'pious' as follows: when Christ was foretelling the cross and his own death to the Apostles, he (i.e. Peter), upon hearing him with a certain pious mind, said 'You should be kind to yourself, Lord; in no way shall this happen to you'.[535]

---

[532] *eius*: the reflexive *suos* (in agreement with *hostes*) would have been preferable in classical Latin, unless it refers to God's enemies.

[533] *perurenda*: a gerundive in the neuter plural referring to *aurum, argentum* and *opes* collectively.

[534] *Sic ... fuerat*: What follows is a very loose paraphrasing of the disobedience of Saul as set out in 1 Sam. 15. The example is also used in theme 4 (37–38), although there Asc. uses rather different vocabulary. However, the striking language *mingentem ad lapidem* has possibly been taken from another OT account of transgression, that by Jereboam in 1 Kings 14.10, where *mingentem ad parietem* ('pissing against the wall') is used.

[535] *Propitius ... hoc*: Matt. 16.22. V: *Absit a te, Domine; non erit tibi hoc*. However, Asc.'s wording exactly tracks *Nov. T*, which produced a more direct translation of the Greek: Ἵλεώς σοι, Κύριε· οὐ μὴ ἔσται σοι τοῦτο.

sed audiebat contra a Domino, Vade post me Satana, scandalum es mihi.[536] Ut praeteream quod idem Petrus pia erga

[80] [227] [P.ii.] Christum voluntate Malco aurem praeciderat,[537] sed hanc gratiam a CHRISTO reportabat, Qui gladio percutit, gladio peribit.[538]

Quid vas illud DEI Paulum referam? *[Pietas Pauli]* qui cum satis pia mente stimulum carnis auferri sibi oraret, responsum accepit, Sufficiat tibi gratia mea.[539] Atque ut a sanctis illis viris deflectat oratio nostra, quid turba illa Fratrum et Monachorum nostrorum[540] *[Fratrum et Monachorum pietas superstitiosa]*, ut sibi visi sunt, admodum pia, qui in multis et non loquacibus ceremoniis, nec e prisca patrum memoria profectis, spem magnam figebant: qui principum imperia excutientes, et ab omni honesta politeia[541] se abducentes, in domicilia quaedam propria se abdiderunt, et[542] non e mundo, quemadmodum illi falso mentiebantur, se deduxerunt, sed in mundo principatum quendam tenebant, et in omnia carnis opera, immunditias, ebrietates, commessationes, simulachrorum cultus, contentiones, aemulationes demersi sunt[543] atque devoluti: artis Magicae quam Scripturae peritiores, mundi quam DEI

[81] [228] studiosiores, Papismo quam Christo multo addictiores. Et hic memorari possunt quidam nostrates, qui olim, et vera pietate, et praestantissimis ingeniis instructi postea tamen contra omnem pietatem, Papae, quam in Christo Iesu, Regi, parere maluerunt. Sed Deus optimus est orandus, ut nec hiis nec consimilibus peccata sua[544] imputare velit.[545] *[Reginaldus Polus optima nominis allusione perstringitur]* An-non nominatim

---

[536] *Vade ... mihi*: Matt. 16.23 as per V, but not *Nov. T*, which has: *Abi post me satana, obstaculo es mihi*. However, in theme 4, Asc. used wording for the first part of this citation that was utilised by E (*Abi post me Satana*). While Ascham's *scandalum es mihi* (not quoted in theme 4) cleaves to V, it may be that Asc. preferred *scandalum* as it relates more closely to the Greek σκάνδαλον, a word he glosses in GNT several times, including next to Matt. 16.23.

[537] *Petrus ... praeciderat*: An episode referred to in Matt. 26.51, Mark.14.47, Luke 22.51 and John 18.10–11, and also in themes 4 and 5.

[538] *Qui ... peribit*: Matt. 26.52. Asc. also used the example in theme 4.

[539] *qui ... mea*: 2 Corinth. 12.7–9. Asc. is again redeploying points used in themes 4 and 5, although here, he uses the less eccentric *Sufficiat tibi gratia mea*, which he had earlier negatived.

But from the Lord he heard the opposite in reply, 'Get you behind me, Satan; you are a cause of offence to me'.[536] And [this is] to pass over the fact that the same Peter, [albeit] with a pious will

[80] [227] [P.ii.] towards Christ, had cut off the ear of Malcus,[537] but got in return this thanks from Christ, 'He who strikes with the sword will die by the sword'.[538]

Why need I mention that vessel of God, Paul? *[Piety of Paul]* When this man, with a pious enough disposition, was praying that the torment of the flesh be removed from him, he received the response, 'Let my grace be sufficient for you'.[539] And to shift my speech away from those holy men, what a crowd of our brothers and monks[540] [*The superstitious piety of Brothers and Monks*], altogether 'pious', as they seemed to themselves, who used to place great hope in many a ceremony not based on words, and that did not originate in the ancient memory of the Fathers. These men, repudiating the might of monarchs and removing themselves from all respectable state business,[541] have taken themselves off into certain habitations of their own. Yet[542] they did not withdraw themselves from the world, as they kept fraudulently claiming, but maintained a certain dominion in the world, and have submerged and sunk themselves in every form of profligacy, in smut, drunkenness, carousing, the worship of idols, strife and jealousy;[543] more skilled in the art of magic than in Scripture, more occupied with this world than with God,

[81] [228] and much more devoted to Papism than Christ. And at this point, some of our own can be mentioned, men who once upon a time were versed in true piety and in the most excellent qualities, but thereafter and, contrary to all piety, preferred to obey the Pope than the King in Jesus Christ. But we must pray to God pre-eminent to will it that his (i.e. the Pope's) sins[544] are not imputed to these men nor to similar men.[545] [*Reginald Pole is referred to with an excellent pun on his name*] Or should I not mention

---

[540] *turba ... nostrorum*: a very contemporary reference to Henry VIII and Thomas Cromwell's dissolution of religious houses of monks, friars and nuns.
[541] *politeia*: a transliteration of the Greek word; the equivalent Latin term is *politia*.
[542] *et*: I have made this adversative in the translation.
[543] *carnis ... sunt*: The sibilance on display is noticeable, and underscores Asc.'s contempt.
[544] *peccata sua*: These must refer to the sins of the Pope, even though the reflexive adjective *sua* should technically refer to God.
[545] *ut ... velit*: a positive indirect command introduced by *ut ... velit* with *nec ... nec* being attached to *hiis* and *consimilibus* respectively.

perstringam Reginaldum illum Polum,[546] quo, inter utrumque polum, sceleratior et abhominabilior[547] numquam extitit, qui pietate, si diis placet,[548] extra Christum? non, sed impietate inaudita in Diabolo, non solum a Patria ingrate, a Rege[549] perfidiose, a Christo impie veluti ignavissimus quidam Demas[550] ad Papam et Diabolum deficit: sed ingentem quandam perditorum hominum[551] faecem et coluviem[552] in easdem sordes involvit. Atque ut hinc ad aliud hominum genus, ut ab hiis longe diversissimum, ita omni[553] scelerum labe aspersissimum perveniam, sunt quidam, qui ut illi κατ' ἀντίφρασιν[554] religiosi, qui longissime abessent a religione: sic Evangelici ab Evangelio,[555] et dici et haberi contendunt. Hii pietatis speciem legendo

[82] [229] [P.iii.] Evangelium habentes, virtutem tamen eius improbitate vitae negantes, testamentum Dei prophanant:[556] nam omnem carnis libertatem sibi vendicantes, cunctos bonos ritus, qui (ut omnia in ecclesia decenter fiant), salutariter, et cum scripturis traditi sunt, convellentes, et rectae pietatis perturbatores, et verbi Dei male audiendi authores[557] existunt. Itaque, vita nostra, quasi navis quaedam, sic cursum suum in medio horum scopulorum tenere debet, ut neque ad Chraribdin Evangelicorum illisa, nec ad Syllam[558] Religiosorum attrita et absorpta sit.[559] Et hactenus a nobis de hiis qui pie volunt vivere, sed non in Iesu Christo, explicatum est. Quae sequuntur breviter perstringam: Persequutiones patientur.[560]

---

[546] *Reginaldum illum Polum*: Reginald Pole (1500–1558), an Oxford-educated cleric, who broke with Henry VIII over the King's proposed annulment of his marriage to Catherine of Aragon. Pole spent much of his life on the continent, and was appointed a Cardinal and papal legate of the Catholic Church in 1536/7.

[547] *abhominabilior*: an alternative form for *abominabilior*.

[548] *si diis placet*: a phrase commonly found in the pagan corpus.

[549] *Rege*: This must be Henry VIII.

[550] *Demas*: This figure, mentioned in the NT, was involved in the ministry of preaching Christ as a companion of Paul, but later turned his back on the faith. In 2 Tim., Paul declares 'Demas has forsaken me, having loved this present world...' (4.10).

[551] *perditorum hominum*: a phrase used regularly in Cic. *Cat.* 1–4.

[552] *coluviem*: an alternative form for *colluviem* or *colluvionem*.

[553] *omni scelerum labe*: I have made *omni* agree with *scelerum* though technically it belongs with *labe*.

[554] κατ' ἀντίφρασιν: this is a Greek phrase that also appears in the Latin of Gell. *NA*. 11.1.5–6. It is a concept borrowed from the field of grammar and rhetoric.

that fellow Reginald Pole by name?[546] Than *Pole* there has never lived [anyone] between each *pole* more wicked and more execrable,[547] who, if it pleases the gods,[548] [lives] with 'piety' beyond Christ. And not [just that], but with an impiety unheard of in the Devil, not only has he gone over ungratefully from his fatherland, treacherously from his King,[549] and impiously from Christ, to the Pope and the Devil, just like some very cowardly Demas,[550] but he has [also] swept up into the same state of uncleanliness a certain immense detritus and swill[552] of the most degenerate men.[551]

And to move from here to another type of men, as so very different to these men as it (i.e. this new type) is utterly spattered with the taint of every disgrace,[553] there are some, as those who, according to the principle of opposites,[554] were 'religious' even though very far [removed] from religion. Accordingly, they scramble both to be called and to be considered 'gospellers' from the [term] 'Gospel'.[555] Yet these men, with the appearance of piety

[82] [229] [P.iii.] because of their reading of the Gospel, nevertheless, by negating its goodness through the immorality of their lives, desecrate[556] the testament of God. For they lay claim to every licence of the flesh and they tear away all good observances which, along with Scripture, have been handed down for our salvation with the result that everything is performed properly in the Church. They are disturbers of correct piety and instigators[557] of a misguided mode of hearing the Word of God. Therefore, our life, as if a ship, ought thus to hold its course between these crags, so that it is neither forced towards the Charybdis of the gospellers, nor enfeebled and devoured by the Scylla[558] of the religious radicals.[559] Thus far, I have described these men who wish to live piously but not in Jesus Christ. What follows I will mention briefly, 'They will endure persecutions'.[560]

---

[555] *Evangelici ab Evangelio*: 'gospeller' was a multivalent label at this point in the Reformation. At one level it was used to denote a full commitment to the Gospel, but it also carried pejorative connotations, and was often bound up with an accusation of insurgence. This is illustrated well in Cranmer's *A Sermon concerning the time of Rebellion* (1549) as set out in *The Remains of Cranmer*, ed. H. Jenkyns, vol. 2 (1833), 248–73, at 260.

[556] *prophanant*: an alternative form for *profanant*.

[557] *authores*: an alternative form for *auctores*.

[558] *Syllam*: This should be *Scyllam*.

[559] *neque . . . Syllam*: Scylla and Charybdis were two mythical monsters that featured *inter alia* in Hom. *Od*. Here they are being used to articulate a *via media*, or an Aristotelian golden mean, a position which was considered a virtue in the early modern period, even as it could also be deployed in some very one-sided and belligerent argumentation.

[560] *Persequutiones patientur*: A return to the wording of 2 Tim. 3.12 with which Asc. began this section.

Est hic locus huius disputationis maxime meo iudicio proprius, de quo ita nobis est dicendum, ut primum, Quid sit persequutio: tum, Cur patimur: ad extremum, Quod omnes, praecipue viri pii et Christi imitatores, persequutiones patientur. Est autem persequutio tentatio quaedam, qua fides nostra quasi aurum igne indies probatur et exercetur.[561] Persequutionis

[83] [230] princeps et dux est (Vita enim nostra militia super terram, ait Ioannes),[562] Diabolus: Tribuni militum, et quasi primipili[563] quidam Mundus et caro, Milites sunt gladii, timor, scandala, sectae, haereses, scommata, insidiae, vincula, carceres, verbera, naufragia, praecipitia, conciliabula, frigora, calores, fames, inopia, nuditas:[564] et in hiis Veterani quidam milites, ut lingua dolosa, labia iniqua et falsi fratres,[565] et id genus alia, quae in sacris literis recensentur. In hiis infestissimi milites semper fuerunt, sunt, erunt falsi fratres, qui delatores perfidi et quadruplatores[566] pessimi, corpus, animam, nomen una perdere omni contentione moliuntur. Atque haec non mea sententia est, sed D. Augustini, qui supra[567] hunc locum ait, Caetera pericula quiescere possunt, pericula a falsis fratribus usque in finem seculi cessare non possunt.[568] Huius militiae (si placet) Dictatorem constituemus ipsum Deum, qui dictavit Diabolo quousque in affligendo Iob progrederetur, et qui nos ultra vires tentari nunquam sinit. De persequutione ergo et eius militia, et qualis sit, ita a nobis statuatur.

---

[561] *aurum . . . exercetur*: Asc. probably has I Peter 1.6–7 in mind that he will proceed to cite more fully below (see n. 577), but he may also be thinking about Prov. 17.3: *sicut igne probatur argentum et aurum camino ita corda probat Dominus* ('Just as silver is tested by fire and gold by the furnace, so the Lord tests our hearts').
[562] *ait Ioannes*: The reference to John is incorrect; these words appear in Job 7.1, *militia est vita hominis super terram*.
[563] *primipili*: These were the leaders of the *triarii*, a division of the Roman army.
[564] *milites . . . nuditas*: Many of items in this list comprise the ordeals faced by Paul in his service to Christ (2 Corinth. 11.25–27).

This is the part of the disputation where I can make my own thoughts especially known. Concerning this, I will start by stating what persecution is, then why we suffer, and finally, [about] the fact that everyone, especially pious men and imitators of Christ, will endure persecutions. There is, moreover, a certain [form] of persecution [that stands] as a trial by which our faith is proved and disciplined on a daily basis, just like gold by fire.[561]

[83] [230] The head and leader of persecution is the Devil (for our life on earth is warfare, as John says).[562] This world and the flesh are his military tribunes and, as it were, his 'leading spears'.[563] His soldiers are swords, fear, temptations, factions, heresies, taunting, traps, fetters, prisons, beatings, shipwrecks, lapses, brothels, coldness, heat, hunger, poverty, and nakedness.[564] In these [are to be found] certain veteran soldiers, such as lying language, vindictive chatter, false brethren,[565] and other things of that ilk which are surveyed in holy Scripture. Of these, the most dangerous warriors have been, are and will always be, false brethren who, as treacherous informers and the worst tricksters,[566] strive with every effort to ruin body, soul and reputation at all once. And in fact, this is not my formulation, but St Augustine's who about this passage[567] writes, 'Other dangers can remain muted, but dangers from false brethren cannot cease till the end of the world'.[568] We will (if it seems appropriate) appoint as the commander of this warfare God himself, who determined for the Devil how far Job should be submitted to ruin, and who never allows us to be assailed beyond what we can withstand. And so, as regards persecution and its warfare and what its nature is, let it be judged by us as such.

---

[565] *falsi fatres*: 'false brethren' are also referred to in 2 Corinth. 11.26 (see n. 564 above), and denote people who masquerade as Christians but in reality only serve themselves.

[566] *quadruplatores*: These were public informers in ancient Rome who received a fourth part of the thing informed against.

[567] *supra*: literally 'above'.

[568] *Augustini . . . possunt*: cf. Augus. *Serm*. 111.4 (*PL* 39, col. 1966) (commenting on 2 Corinth. 11.26): *caetera pericula possunt quiescere: pericula a falsis fratribus quiescere usque ad finem saeculi non noverunt* ('Other dangers can fall quiet, but dangers from false brethren do not admit quiet till the end of the world').

[84] [231] [P.iiii.] Quare patimur, ex ipso scripturarum *[Quare patimur]* fonte[569] omnis nostra oratio quasi rivulus quidam accersenda et deducenda est. Primum affligimur ut probemur, ut Exodus. 16. dixit Dominus ad Mosen, *[Exod. 16.]* Ecce ego pluam vobis panem e coelo, et egredietur populus, et colliget de die in diem, ut tentem eum utrum ambulet in lege mea an non.[570] Et Deuteronomii. 8. *[Deut. 8.]* Memento omnis viae tuae per quam ambulare te fecit Dominus DEUS tuus, iam quadraginta annis in deserto, ut affligeret te, ut tentaret te, ut sciret quae sunt in corde tuo, utrum custodires praecepta eius an non.[571]

In similibus exemplis citandis, et temporis recensendi inopia, et inveniendi copia plurimum laborarem, cum venio ad novum testamentum, video longe sublimiorem persequutionis eventum tradi. Sic Christus, Afficiemini moerore,[572] sed moeror vester vertetur in gaudium, et in tale gaudium, quod nemo tollet a vobis.[573] Sic Paulus, Gloriamur super afflictiones, scientes quod afflictio patientiam pariat, patientia probationem, probatio spem, quae spes nunquam

[85] [232] confunditur.[574] Et alibi Paulus, sed longe memorabilissime, Simul cum eo patimur, ut una cum eo glorificemur.[575] Sic Iacobus, Beatus vir qui suffert tentationes, quoniam cum probatus fuerit, accipiet coronam vitae, quam promisit dominus hiis qui diligunt eum.[576] Sic Petrus, Nunc ad

---

[569] *ex ipso scripturarum fonte*: We see again an allusion to the *ad fontes* nature of Scripture; see also n. 320.

[570] *Ecce ... an non*: Ex. 16.4. Asc. diverges from V in minor ways; Ascham uses *panem* in place of V's *panes*, the future indicative in place of the V's subjunctives *egrediatur* and *colligat*, and *de die in diem* in place of *per singulos dies*. The wording, however, matches Pag. exactly (with the exception of *pluo* for Asc.'s *pluam*).

[571] *Memento ... an non*: Deut. 8.2, but Asc.'s vocabulary is quite different to V: *et recordaberis cuncti itineris per quod adduxit te Dominus Deus tuus quadriginta annis per desertum ut adfligeret te atque temptaret et nota fierent quae in tuo animo versabantur utrum custodires mandata illius an non*. Asc.'s wording matches Pag. exactly.

[572] *moerore*: an alternative form for *maerore*.

[573] *Afficiemini ... vobis*: Asc. has melded two verses from John 16.20 and 16.22. His vocabulary deviates noticeably from V for verse 20, which reads *vos autem contristabimini, sed tristitia vestra vertetur in gaudium*, but matches Nov. T more or less exactly, albeit Asc. applies the future tense *tollet* where both V and E have the present *tollit* (in line with the Greek).

[84] [231] [P.iiii.] *[Why we suffer]* [On the question of] why we suffer, our entire speech, as if some rivulet, must be derived and drawn from the very fountainhead of Scripture.[569] First, we are cast down in order to be tested, just as the Lord said to Moses in Exodus 16 *[Exodus 16]*, 'Behold, I will rain down bread for you from heaven, and the people shall go out and assemble from day to day so that I may test whether they walk in my law or not'.[570] And in Deuteronomy 8 *[Deuteronomy 8]* [we read], 'Be mindful of your every path along which the Lord your God has made you walk, now for forty years in the desert, so that he might cast you down, that he might test you, and that he might know what was in your heart, whether you were keeping his commandments or not'.[571]

If I were to cite similar examples, I would be in real difficulty owing both to the limited time for reviewing them and the [limited] opportunity for locating them, but when I come to the New Testament, I see a by far more elevated form of persecution being offered. Christ [speaks] thus, 'You will be vexed with sorrow,[572] but your sorrow will be converted into joy, and into a special joy such that no man will take from you'.[573] Likewise, Paul [says], 'We rejoice in tribulations, knowing that tribulation breeds endurance, endurance experience, experience hope, and hope is never

[85] [232] expunged'.[574] And elsewhere Paul says, and really very memorably, 'We suffer along with him so that we may be glorified together with him'.[575] James [speaks] as follows, 'Blessed is the man that endures temptations, for when he is tried, he shall receive the crown of life, which the Lord has promised to those that love him'.[576] Peter [speaks] as follows,

---

[574] *Gloriamur ... confunditur*: Rom. 5.3–5. The vocabulary diverges from V: *gloriamur in tribulationibus scientes quod tribulatio patientiam operatur patientia autem probationem probatio vero spem. spes autem non confundit*, and Asc. is in some, though by no means all, respects closer to *Nov. T*: *gloriamur super afflictionibus, scientes quod afflictio patientiam pariat, patientia vero probationem, probatio autem spem. Porro spes non pudefacit.* See also n. 424 and 489 on Rom. 5.3–4.

[575] *Simul ... glorificemur*: Rom. 8.17. V: *conpatimur ut et conglorificemur*, but Asc.'s wording matches *Nov. T*.

[576] *Beatus ... eum*: James 1.12: The wording is similar to but does not quite tally with either V: *Beatus vir qui suffert tentationem, quoniam cum probatus fuerit, accipiet coronam vitae, quam repromisit Deus diligentibus se*, or *Nov. T*: *beatus vir qui suffert tentationem, quoniam cum probatus erit, accipiet coronam vitae quam promisit dominus iis, a quibus fuerit dilectus*. Ascham has glossed in Greek the words for 'blessed', 'tried' and 'crown' in the margin next to this verse in GNT.

tempus afflicti variis tentationibus, si opus sit, ut probatio fidei vestri multo pretiosior auro quod perit, et tamen per ignem probatur, reperiatur in laudem et gloriam, et honorem, tum cum revelabitur Iesus Christus.[577] Ex hoc loco Petri definitio illa persequutionis, quae a me tradita est, veluti ramus quidam ex arbore, decisa est.[578] His sacris scripturae locis Distichon[579] quoddam doctissimi simul et integerrimi viri Ioannis Redmanni[580] quasi coronidem[581] quandam adiiciam.

[Ioannis Redmanni Distichon] Exercet pravam non prava molestia carnem,

Ut queat in tuto spiritus esse vado.[582]

Praeterea, cur iusti plus quam mali premuntur, facilis est responsio. Ideo hic

[86] [233] [P.v.] premuntur iusti, quia quasi peregrini et advenae sunt, atque aliena in patria detinentur, manentem hic civitatem non habentes, sed aliam longe expectantes: mali hic minus premuntur, sed securius laetantur, ut alio in loco gravius puniantur. Iusti aliquando non premuntur, ne virtus et probitas nimis odiosa videatur: mali aliquando hic cruciantur, ne vitia nimium bona et plausibilia esse iudicentur. Postremo, iusti hic premuntur, ut in apparatione Christi, (testante Petro) laudem, gloriam, et honorem accipiant:[583] non omnes mali hic vexantur, ne dies illa irae et resurrectionis expectatio penitus e memoria hominum excidat. Ut omnes persequutiones aequo animo ferantur, infinita sunt quae nos impellunt et adhortantur: nam primum (ut Hemistichio[584] Nasonis in re sacra, ut non inepte, ita minus impie utar).

Dulcis erit mercede labor[585]

---

[577] *Nunc ... Christus*: I Peter 1.6–7. The vocabulary diverges markedly from V: *modicum nunc si oportet contristari in variis tentationibus ut probatio vestrae fidei multo pretiosior auro (quod per ignem probatur) inveniatur in laudem, et gloriam, et honorem in revelatione Iesu Christi*. Asc. is closer in some, but not all, respects to *Nov. T*: *nunc ad breve tempus afflicti in variis experimentis, si opus est, quo exploratio fidei vestrae, multo preciosior auro, quod perit, et tamen per ignem probatur, reperiatur in laudem et gloriam et honorem, tum cum revelabitur Iesus Christus*.

[578] *quae ... est*: Asc. seems to acknowledge the potentially distorting effect of extracting citations from their context.

[579] *Distichon*: A unit of verse consisting of two lines; an elegiac couplet with hexameter in the first line and pentameter in the second.

[580] *Ioannis Redmanni*: John Redman (1499–1551) was fellow of St John's College Cambridge, Public Orator of the University and also the first Master of Trinity College. He was a leading theologian and greatly respected by members of both sides of the confessional divide. This is, to my knowledge, the only source for Redman's poem. The way Asc. refers

'Now, if necessary, afflicted for a season by diverse temptations so that the trial of your faith, [being] much more precious than gold that perishes, and though it be tried with fire, might be found unto praise and glory and honour whenever Jesus Christ is revealed'.[577] From this passage of Peter, that definition of persecution which I have adduced has been cut off, as if a branch from a tree.[578] I will [therefore] supplement these holy passages of Scripture, as if by way of a *coronis*,[581] with a certain distich[579] [written] by a man supremely learned and honourable in equal measure, John Redman:[580]

[*Distich of John Redman*] 'A vexation that is not indecent disturbs the flesh that is indecent so that the spirit can be kept in safe water'.[582]

Moreover, [as for] why the righteous are more oppressed than the bad, there is an easy response.

[86] [233] [P.v.] The righteous are oppressed here because they are as though travellers and foreigners, and are being detained in an alien land without any permanent state here, but long awaiting another. [Conversely,] the bad are oppressed less [grievously] here and rejoice more carelessly so that they might be punished more severely in another place. Sometimes the righteous are not oppressed so that virtue and goodness do not seem too hateful; and sometimes the bad are afflicted here so that their transgressions are not viewed as too positive and acceptable. Finally, the righteous are oppressed here so that – and a point Peter attests to when Christ appears – they might receive praise, glory and honour.[583] Not all those who are bad are troubled here so that that day of wrath and anticipation of the resurrection does not fall completely out of men's memory. So that all persecutions might be borne with a calm mind, there exist infinite resorces that impel and encourage us. To begin with, and to apply a hemistich[584] of Ovid to a religious matter, which for being so apposite, it is less profane: 'The labour will be sweetened by its reward'.[585]

---

to it as a supplement to Scripture both reflects the respect that Redman was held in and also points to a Protestant humanist tendency to establish a canon of works that would sit alongside the Bible.

[581] *coronis*: a Greek term which denotes the curved line or flourish made with a pen that writers or transcribers were accustomed to make at the end of a book or chapter.

[582] *in vado*: by itself (and notwithstanding *tutus*) can mean 'in safety', as well as '(shallow) water'.

[583] *in . . . accipiant*: 1 Peter 1.7 again. Asc. has just referred to this epistle on the previous page (85), although he adjusts his vocabulary here.

[584] *Hemistichio*: a half-verse.

[585] *Dulcis erit mercede labor*: The first half of a hexameter line from Ov. *Fast.* 6.661, although standard versions of the text have the imperfect *erat* in place of Asc.'s future tense *erit*. The use of a future is more effective in the context here, and it seems that, just as with biblical quotations, Asc. was also prepared to adapt classical authors to suit his purpose.

In praesenti enim vita, labores et studium: in futura, praemia, et coronae. Praeterea, cum[586] in hoc vitae nostrae curriculo

[87] [234] comparatum est, ut antea[587] perferatur labor, maria traiiciantur, quam videatur merces: sudores exantlentur,[588] glacies hyemesque[589] tristes sollicita quadam spe superentur, quam fructus percipiantur: adeantur discrimina, quam postulentur cornonae. Cumque nos ad eam fructus spem enitimur et contendimus, quem non venti et tempestates, duae res incertissimae moderantur, quem non absorbet naufragium, non proterit calamitas, non ensis rapit, sed in aeterno quodam tenore atque perpetuitate vigeat et efflorescat, certe et labores hii, quibus ad illius fructus usuram et occupationem perveniendum sit, non solum leves et perfaciles, sed iucundi et suaves sunt habendi: et nos, si torpore ullo aut mollitia labores illos devitemus, aridi, sine oleo, sine veste, adeoque servi nequam et inutiles, merito quidem nostro meritissimo, sumus censendi.

Quamobrem persequutiones patimur, satis a nobis fuse et copiose explicatur. Quod nostrae orationis est residium,[590] brevem

[88] [235] quandam (id quod pollicebamur) Christi imitatorum recensionem complectatur. Et primum, quemadmodum ad omnia membra unius corporis, vel exiguae partis dolor diffunditur: ita universa DEI ECCLESIA vexatur, *[Sympatheia*[591] *Ecclesiae DEI]* si vel unum membrum eius afflictione aliqua teneatur. Dicit enim Augustinus, nullam esse graviorem boni viri persequutionem, quam cum aliquem in peccatum incidisse sentiat.[592] Patiuntur et patientur ergo omnes.

Sic Abraham e patrio solo eiectus *[Abraham]*, uxoris sterilitate confectus, inopia victus, longinqua difficilique peregrinatione lassus, uxoris pulchritudine in discrimine vitae positus,[593] ne filii parricida existeret, moerore agitatus persequutionem patiebatur.[594]

---

[586] *cum*: I have not translated this as it starts a subordinate clause which Asc. in fact does not complete.
[587] *antea*: more commonly *ante* (and here *ante . . . quam*).
[588] *exantlentur*: an alternative form for *exanclentur*.
[589] *hyemes*: an alternative form for *hiemes*.
[590] *residium*: clearly *residuum* is meant.
[591] *Sympatheia*: The hanging note uses the transliterated word from the Greek rather than the Latin *sympathia*.

In our present life there is toil and effort, but in the future, rewards and crowns. Furthermore,[586] in this course of our life,

[87] [234] it has been ordained that toil be endured and seas be traversed before[587] it can seem like a reward; [that] severe heat be suffered[588] and ice and miserable winters[589] be survived with a certain anxious hope before profits can be felt; [that] dangers be submitted to before crowns can be demanded. When we strive and hurry towards that hope of profit, which neither winds nor storms – two very unpredictable phenomena – impede, which a shipwreck does not swallow, mishap does not crush, the sword does not seize, but on some eternal and endless journey it may grow and flourish, certainly even these trials, which are the surest route to the enjoyment and possession of that profit, must be perceived as not only trivial and very easy [to bear] but [even] pleasant and sweet. If we are to avoid those trials with any inactivity or weakness, we must be regarded as dry and without oil, without clothing, extremely worthless and useless like slaves, our desert being a very deserved one indeed.

As to [the question of] why we suffer persecutions, this lengthy and full explanation is [surely] sufficient. As for the rest[590] of our speech,

[88] [235] let it comprise, as we promised, a brief review of the imitators of Christ. To start with, just as pain even in small measure spreads to all limbs of a single body, so the universal Church of God is troubled even if one limb is beset by some injury [*The mutual interdependence*[591] *of the Church of God*]. Indeed, Augustine says that there is no more serious a persecution of a good man than when he (i.e. God) senses someone has fallen into sin.[592] They suffer and thus everyone will suffer.

Accordingly, Abraham *[Abraham]*, after being cast out from his homeland, worn down by the sterility of his wife, overcome by privation, exhausted from protracted and difficult wanderings, and compelled by the beauty of his wife into risking his life[593] for fear that the murder of his son may ensue, was shaken by grief and suffered persecution.[594]

---

[592] *Augustinus ... sentiat*: It is not clear which Augustinian work Asc. has in mind here.

[593] *Sic ... positus*: Abraham's departure from his homeland (at God's behest), his journey and suffering though famine, and the problems he faced in Egypt because of the beauty of his wife, Sarah, are recounted in Gen. 12.

[594] *ne ... patiebatur*: God's trial of Abraham's faith reaches a climax in Gen. 22, where God orders to him to sacrifice his own son Isaac, albeit an Angel of God prevents this happening once Abraham has shown willing.

Isaac eodem fere modo cum patre *[Isaac]*, victus inopia, longinqua peregrinatione, uxoris pulchritudine afflictus premebatur.[595] Sic Iacob *[Iacob]*, fratris odio, Laban soceri sui iniuria, Liae lippitudine[596] et fastidio, Rachael forma et desiderio misere vexabatur.[597]

[89] [236] *[Iob]* Si in vitam Iob et graves eius persequutiones[598] sermonis nostri cursum inflecterem, introitus latissimus, iter viarum varietate perplexum, exitus sane nullus pateret. *[David]* Quid David? quantis primum Saul, dein Absalon (ut interiectas afflictiones praeteream) eum persequutionibus invadebant?[599] *[Prophetae]* Omittam etiam Prophetas illos universos, qui non solum persequutiones, sed ipsam mortem oppetierunt.[600] *[Christus]* Quid Christum ipsum referam, qui nullam aliam a patre hominem reparandi viam habebat, quam afflictionem per crucem, per mortem? Quid caeteros Apostolos? *[Paulus]* Quid Paulum illum? qui dum omnia sua tempora Christianorum temporibus transmittenda esse iudicabat,[601] in insidias, verbera, carceres, naufragia, conciliabula, et id genus alia discrimina praecipitabat.[602] *[Primitiva Ecclesia]* Quid universam illam Primitivam Ecclesiam, ubi vix centesimus quisque[603] pius vir, unum aut alterum annum superare poterat? *[Triginta martyres ecclesiae Romanae]* Iure praeterire non debeo triginta illos[604] ecclesiae Romanae et syncerae[605] religionis antistites, qui singuli, (modo annalibus fides habenda sit), non tam vivendi [237] integritate sese ornabant, quam praesenti et intrepida quadam pro Christo moriendi constantia, cum Deo tum posteritati omni sese commendabant.[606]

---

[595] *Isaac... premebatur*: Gen. 26 charts the challenging fortunes of Isaac, who, like Abraham, leaves his homeland, which is beset with famine, and risks his life for the beauty of his wife Rebekah.

[596] *lippitudo*: is used with *diuturna* in Cic. *Tusc*. 4.37.8; V uses the adjective rather than the noun: *sed Lia lippis erat oculis* (Gen. 29.17).

[597] *Sic... vexabatur*: Jacob incurred the hatred of his brother Esau when the former took the latter's birthright (Gen. 25.29–34, 27 *passim*, especially 27.41). Jacob was then tricked by his uncle and father-in-law, Laban, into marrying Laban's eldest daughter, Leah, rather than the youngest, Rachel, with whom Jacob had fallen in love (Gen. 29.16–26, especially 29.25). Leah is described as bleary-eyed and not as beautiful as Rachel (Gen. 29.17); consequently, Jacob loathes Leah (Gen. 29.31) and loves Rachel (Gen. 29.18).

[598] *Iob... persequutiones*: a reference to the suffering of Job in the OT Book of Job.

[599] *Quid David... invadebant?*: The account of the attempts by Saul, the King of Israel, to kill David are set out in 1 Sam. 19; the rebellion of Absalom, David's third son, against his father are set out in 2 Sam. 15.1–12 and 18.1–19.15. David's responses to persecution are also recorded in many of the Psalms.

Isaac *[Isaac]* in almost the same way as his father, overcome by privation and protracted wanderings and struck down by the beauty of his wife, was oppressed.[595] So too Jacob *[Jacob]* was wretchedly tormented by a hatred of his brother, by the violence of his own father-in-law, Laban, by the bleary-eyedness[596] and loathing of Leah, and by the beauty of and his desire for Rachel.[597]

[89] [236] If I were to steer the course of our discussion towards the life of Job *[Job]* and his severe afflictions,[598] my introduction [would be] very extensive, and the way complex through the range of its avenues, and certainly there would be no obvious conclusion. What of David? *[David]* By what great abuses were first Saul, then Absalon (to skip over the intervening tribulations) assailing him?[599] I will also leave out all those many Prophets *[Prophets]* who not only met with persecution but death itself.[600] What should I say of Christ *[Christ]* himself who was granted by his Father no other way to restore man than to suffer on the cross and death? What of the other Apostles? *[Paul]* What [of] that man Paul? He, while he was pronouncing that the entirety of his own times should be entrusted to those of Christians,[601] repeatedly fell foul of traps, beatings, prisons, shipwrecks, brothels, and other predicaments of that sort.[602] *[The earliest Church]* And what of that universal and earliest Church where scarcely each hundredth[603] pious man was able to survive one year or the next? Rightly, I ought not to pass over those thirty[604] *[Thirty Martyrs of the Roman Church]* of the Church of Rome and the overseers of a true[605] religion, each of whom, provided we can place faith in the chronicles, [237] distinguished themselves, not so much through their purity of lifestyle, as through a resolute and undaunted steadfastness in dying for Christ when they commended themselves both to God and to the whole of posterity.[606] *[The city*

---

[600] *Prophetas ... mortem oppetierunt*: Prophets persecuted in the OT include Jeremiah, and in the NT, John the Baptist.

[601] *dum ... iudicabat*: A rather odd phrase, but it must refer to Paul's Christianising mission generally.

[602] *in insidias ... praecipitabat*: Asc. has already referred to a (longer) catalogue of similar ordeals, as outlined by Paul in 2 Corinth. 11.24–27, earlier in this theme.

[603] *vix centesimus quisque*: meaning 'scarcely each hundredth man' is an eye-catching phrase, though used quite commonly in the early modern era.

[604] *triginta illos*: A group of thirty martyrs killed by Emperor Diocletian because they refused to surrender the Scriptures to the Roman authorities.

[605] *syncerae*: an alternative form for *sincerae*.

[606] *non tam ... commendabant*: I have altered the balance of the sentence in the English for reasons of felicity: strictly, the imperfect verbs belong to the *tam* and *quam* respectively: *non tam ... sese ornabant ... quam ... sese commendabant.*

[Urbs Roma deficiens a Christo, non patitur cum Christo]. At postquam abhominatio desolationis sanctum illum locum irrepsisset, una ab omni vera in Christo Iesu pietate urbs Roma excidebat, et ab omni gravi persequutione satis caute sese communiebat.

Pauca desunt.[607]

---

[607] *Pauca desunt*: an editor's note to indicate that Asc's prose in this theme breaks off here. This may in part explain the used of *inchoata* in the main title of the volume, a term literally meaning 'begun, but not completed'.

of Rome deserting Christ does not suffer with Christ] But after a distate for wretchedness had insinuated itself into that sacred place, the city of Rome began to fall altogether from all true devotion for Jesus Christ and, sufficiently wary, began to fortify itself against all serious persecution.

A small part is missing.[607]

Theme 11
(90–99)

This final theme is the most overtly didactic of the collection. Ascham situates the piece in the final days of Jesus' life on earth, and depicts Jesus offering both consolation and teaching to his disciples before his betrayal and execution. The verse of John's Gospel (15.16 / 16.23) which heads the piece signals the form of instruction that Ascham then proceeds to offer, and serves as a springboard for some extensive and detailed guidance in the correct form of prayer. The theme is an audacious one, not least because Ascham makes Christ himself the 'tutor' through a remarkable form of religious ventriloquism. The recommendations essentially comprise a confetti of biblical precepts that have been stitched together into a new *sola scriptura* roadmap for prayer. What is additionally exciting about this theme is the way we can almost plot its composition in the moment, as it were, via annotations in Ascham's Greek New Testament. While Ascham's Greek Bible was a key resource for all his themes, his numerous margin notes that relate to the practice of prayer enable us almost to visualise the scholar during the very process of creation of this theme. He inscribes, for instance, the Greek term for prayer (προσευχή) in multiple places, and in Matthew 26 he notes (in Latin) *Christi modus orandi* ('Christ's way of praying').

While the theme is evidently intended at some level to bring comfort to the reader, it also contains a starkness of message that sounds distinctly Lutheran; Ascham is quite blunt about about the inherent sinfulness of the person at prayer. The production may be viewed as part of a reformist programme to overhaul the content and tenor of forms of worship more generally, and the theme thus offers another interesting window on the areas of religion in which Ascham felt reform was most urgent.[608]

---

[608] For more on this, see pp. 44–45 of the main introduction.

While Scripture forms the obvious inspiration for much of the language throughout this theme, Ascham is often more expansive than the Bible, and he regularly reworks the original wording of the Holy Writ before him. His prose has panache, constructed as it is around various rhetorical devices, and the theme as a whole serves as a reminder of the vital role Ascham (and others) believed *eloquentia* could play in the business of faith.

[90] [237] Quicquid petieritis patrem in nomine meo dabit vobis. Ioan. 15.[609]

Dominus noster Iesus Christus mortem iam iam, ut vitam omnibus restitueret, subiturus: et ad patrem, ut locum nobis pararet, ascensurus: Apostolos suos et discipulos, nec eos tantum sed cunctos, qui per sermonem illorum credituri essent in Christo, in summum moerorem et sollicitudinem post eius discessum iniicere videbatur. Quapropter, ut eorum animos in

[91] [238] quandam quasi desperationem abiectos et demissos levet et recrearet, semota turba,[610] apud illos orationem non solum parabolis et mysteriorum circuitu vacuam, sed spei certae, gaudii, pollicitationis, consolationis plenam, ut est apud Ioan. 10. 4. 5. et 6.[611] habebat. Nam primum spiritum suum omnis consolationis datorem promittit, qui moerorem illorum in gaudium verteret perfectum, qui patrem, qui omnem illis ostensurus esset veritatem: deinde, pollicetur se iterum reventurum ad illos, et illos ad se assumpturum, ut ubi ipse esset, illi essent: postremo, ne mundi interea saevitia, qui[612] Christum et qui[613] sunt Christi semper odit, oppressi, ne rerum inopia nimis coarctati,[614] in nimias angustias compellerentur, opem suam praesentem semper illis pollicetur,[615] hortans, impellens, iubens ut peterent,[616] dicens, Hactenus non petistis quicquam, petite et accipietis, nec ullam repulsam patiemini:[617] imo, quicquid illudcunque[618] fuerit, quod petieritis patrem in nomine meo, dabit vobis.[619] Iactate curam vestram in me, in me respicite, in omni tempore, nam semper pauperes eritis: sine ulla intermissione, nam

---

[609] *Quicquid ... vobis*: John 15.16. V: *quodcumque petieritis Patrem in nomine meo det vobis*, and has the subjunctive 'may he give it to you' as opposed to the future *dabis*; *Nov. T* also has *det*, but uses *quicquid*. Asc. may also be thinking of John 16.23, *si quid petieritis Patrem in nomine meo, dabit vobis*; indeed, this verse has been marked up with the Greek word for 'prayer' in GNT.

[610] *turba*: John 12 describes Jesus amid the multitude, but chapter 13 has him speak with his disciples about the necessity of his departure from the world.

[611] *apud Ioan. 10.4.5. et 6.*: These verses from John clearly belongs to the earlier clause (*parabolis et mysteriorum circuitu vacuam*), and this is the order I have adopted in the translation. John 10.4–6 comprises part of the parable of the Good Shepherd, the message of which is that Jesus is the true shepherd for those who put their faith in him. However, John 10.6 indicates that his disciples did not understand his words.

[612] *qui*: The antecedent of *qui* is *mundus*.

[613] *qui*: the assumed antecedent of *qui* is *eos*.

[90] [237] 'Whatsoever you ask of the Father in my name he will give it to you'. John 15.[609]

Our Lord Jesus Christ was at any moment about to submit to death in order to restore life to all. He was about to ascend to his Father in order to prepare a place for us. He appeared to be causing his apostles and disciples the greatest sorrow and concern after his departure, and not only them, but all those who, because of their preaching, were destined to believe in Christ. For this reason, so as to

[91] [238] console and revive their spirits, [then so] downcast and sunken in a sort of hopelessness, once the crowd[610] had dispersed, he made a speech in their presence that was not only devoid of parables and a circling around the mysteries, as one finds in John, chapter 10, verses 4, 5 and 6,[611] but full of sure hope, joy, promise and comfort. For initially he promises his own spirit as granter of all comfort to turn their sorrow towards complete joy, [and one] that might reveal the Father and the whole truth to them. Then he promises that he will return again to them and lead them to himself, so that wherever he was, they [too] would be. Finally, so that they are in the meantime not forced into straits too narrow, overwhelmed by the savagery of this world, which[612] always hates Christ and those who[613] are of Christ, and overmuch constricted[614] by privations, he promises that his own aid will always be available to them.[615] He encourages, spurs them on, and orders them to seek,[616] saying 'Hitherto you have not asked for anything; but seek and you will receive, and nor will you experience any rejection.[617] Indeed, whatsoever[618] it may be that you shall ask the Father in my name he will give it to you.[619] Cast your care on me, and look to me at all times, for you will always be poor; for you will always, without any cessation,

---

[614] *coarctati*: an alternative form for *coartati*.

[615] *nam . . . pollicetur*: Asc. paraphrases and condenses the counsel contained in John 16.

[616] *ut peterent*: *ut* + subjunctive is appropriate following *hortans* and *impellens* (albeit, according to the sequence of tenses, a present rather than an imperfect subjunctive would be technically more appropriate) but after *iubens* an infinitive would be more correct. It is likely that Ascham was here more interested in the rhetorical immediacy of a tricolon of present participles.

[617] *Hactenus . . . patiemini*: John 16.24. The wording diverges considerably from V: *usque modo non petistis quicquam in nomine meo; petite et accipietis ut gaudium vestrum sit plenum*; Nov. T has *hactenus* like Asc., but otherwise quite different wording, especially at the end: *gaudium vestrum sit perfectum*. As far as searches indicate, Asc.'s unconventional version is peculiar to him; see also n. 266.

[618] *illudcunque*: In the printed version *illud* and *cunque* are shown as separate words.

[619] *quicquid . . . vobis*: a restatement of the heading of this theme.

[92] [239] semper egebitis: in spiritu et veritate, non carnis viribus et mendaciis fisi:[620] quem modum orandi servus meus Paulus spiritu meo ductus, latius postea explicabit.[621]

Non laudem et iactationem[622] mundi in plateis orantes quaerite, ne pars vestra ponatur cum hypocritis, et sic non a me, sed a mundo mercedem capietis:[623] neque βαττολογίαν[624] in precibus accumulate *[Battologia, sive multiloquium]*,[625] sed auferte (ut dixit Amos Propheta meus), tumultum et turbam carminum vestrorum:[626] nec faciatis ut Ethnici, qui putant se ob multiloquium suum exaudiri.[627] Prudenter ergo dixit Solomon, In multiloquio non deerit peccatum.[628] Quapropter, vos ad utilitatem vestram, non ad laudem aliorum: mente, non labris: fiducia, non haesitatione: veritate, non hypocrisi preces vestras in sinum Patris fundite. Et hoc totum est, quod dixi Petite. Quid vero sit petendum, et quid primum petendum *[Quid petendum]*, alio tempore vos abunde satis docui: nempe, Primum quaerendum esse[629] regnum DEI,[630] et tum caetera omnia facile adiicerentur vobis.[631]

---

[620] *Iactate ... fisi*: These paraphrased injunctions are based on the content of various books of John's Gospel.

[621] *quem modum ... explicabit*: Paul recorded many spirit-inspired prayers throughout the books of the NT he authored.

[622] *iactatio*: meaning 'popular approval' is a term used frequently by Cic.

[623] *Non ... capietis*: A clear (albeit loose) reference to Matt. 6.5: *Et cum oratis, non eritis sicut hypocritae, qui amant in synagogis et in angulis platearum stantes orare, ut videantur ab hominibus. Amen dico vobis: Receperunt mercedem suam* ('And when you pray, don't be as the hypocrites who love to pray while standing in the synagogues and on the corners of streets so that they might be seen by [other] men: Amen I say to you; they have received their reward'). Asc. has marked up the margin next to this verse with the Greek word for 'prayer' in GNT.

[624] βαττολογίαν: a reference to the Greek term used in Matt. 6.7, which reads προσευχόμενοι δὲ μὴ βαττολογήσητε ('But when you pray, use not vain repetitions'). The term has been noted (in Greek) by Asc. next to this verse in GNT.

[92] [239] be in need, if you have placed your trust in the spirit and the truth, not in the force and falsehoods of the flesh.[620] My servant Paul, guided by my spirit, will afterwards explain at more length the mode of prayer.[621]

As you pray, seek not praise and popular approval[622] in the wide ways of this world lest your lot is set alongside that of hypocrites, and, as such, you will take profit not from me but from this world.[623] And don't amass idle talk[624] in your prayers,[625] *[Battologia or talkativeness]* but "Remove", as my Prophet Amos said, "the noise and disorder of your songs".[626] Nor should you act as the pagans, who think that they are heard because of their talkativeness.[627] Solomon thus spoke prudently, "In talkativeness there's no lack of sin".[628] Accordingly, for your own benefit and not for the praise of others, utter your prayers unto the bosom of the Father with your mind not your lips, with trust not irresolution, and with truth not hypocrisy. And all this of which I have spoken seek. To be sure, what must be sought *[what must be sought]* and what must be sought first, I informed you in more than ample detail at a different point. It is certainly the case that the kingdom of God must be sought[629] first,[630] and thereafter everything else may be readily added for you.[631]

---

[625] *Non ... accumulate*: a general allusion to Matt. 6.5–7, verses which outline good practice in prayer just prior to the Lord's Prayer.
[626] *auferte ... vestrorum*: Amos 5.23. V: *aufer a me tumultum carminum tuorum*. Asc. has added the word *turba* for rhetorical effect.
[627] *nec ... exaudiri*: Matt. 6.7, though a different configuration to V: *orantes autem nolite multum loqui sicut ethnici putant enim quia in multiloquio suo exaudiantur*; and also from *Nov. T*: *verum orantes, ne sitis multiloqui, sicut ethnici. Putant enim fore, ut ob multiloquium suum exaudiantur*.
[628] *In ... peccatum*: Prov. 10.19. The wording follows V.
[629] *docui ... esse*: There is an implied indirect statement following *docui*, and hence the infinitive *quarendum esse*.
[630] *Primum ... DEI*: a reference to one of the injunctions from the Sermon on the Mount, Matt. 6.33: *quaerite ergo primum regnum Dei*. The verse is underlined in GNT.
[631] *vobis*: Given what follows, it is possible that *vobis* is a dative agent ('by you') after the passive (imperfect subjunctive) *adiicerentur*, but 'for you' also works.

[93] [240] Nam si quaeratis quae sunt spiritualia, propter honorem meum, et haec una cum omnibus temporalibus capietis, ad magnam gloriam vestram. Si enim me honorificabitis, et vos ego glorificabo. Primum ergo exoptate, ut nomen Patris mei in omnes gentes sit sanctificatum, hoc est, ut omnes cognoscant illum verum et solum esse Deum, et quem[632] misit Iesum Christum, ut praedicatio Evangelii et nominis Christi liberum cursum ad generalem, per omnem terrarum orbem, Ecclesiam meam fundandam habeat:[633] ut vos et ego quasi unum corpus simus, purum, immaculatum, et sanctum, neque ut[634] ulla pollutione a corpore et nomine meo separemini, sed mecum quasi coniuncti et adhaerentes, omnis haereditatis et regni mei participes sitis. Ad quod regnum consequendum, non debetis anniti vestris viribus aut cerebro, sed totos vos semper ad Patris mei voluntatem deferatis, hoc est, sive fueritis reges, pastores, et magistratus, sive plebei et subditi, iuxta voluntatis meae testamentum, et quaecunque in eo conscripta fuerint, vitam vestram instituatis.

[94] [241] [Q.] Sic primum quaerenda est gloria patris, tum vestra salus spiritualis, quas res si primum vere quaeratis, audacter ad caetera, quae sunt vitae usus et necessitatis vestrae, ut panem, ut victum quotidianum, ut sanitatem, ut pacem et tranquillitatem animi, et alia vitae commoda, quibus patri meo liberius inservire potestis, aspicite et expectate.[635] Praeterea, cum quamdiu in mundo fueritis, ut non peccetis, nullo modo effugere valetis: nam si dicetis quod peccatum non habetis, mendaces estis, nec veritas in vobis est:[636] indesinenter orate, ut illa vobis remittantur, vos ipsos inter vos, quasi sacramento quodam astringentes, vos mutua vestra delicta remissuros,[637] quo nihil Patri meo ad vestra vobis peccata condonanda potest esse impetrabilius.[638] Ad extremum, cum Diabolus omnia loca et tempora circuit, quaerens quem devoret, hoc diligenter precibus vestris praecavete, ne in fauces eius incidatis: de quo Diabolo propterea ultimo loco vobis dixi, quod sic erit mea virtute et cruce depulsus atque debilitatus, et[639] quamvis non multum erit vobis formidabilis, tamen

---

[632] *quem*: standing for *eum qui* ....
[633] *ut ... habeat*: I have understood the *ut* clauses in this part as following *exoptate* (a verb often followed by *ut*) rather than as purpose clauses.
[634] *neque ut*: used for *ne* here. Again, I have taken the *ut* clauses as following *exoptate*.
[635] *aspicite* and *expectate*: are imperatives, which I have rendered 'you may ...'.
[636] *si ... est*: A paraphrase of 1 John 1.8 and 10; V: *si dixerimus quoniam peccatum non habemus ipsi nos seducimus et veritas in nobis non est* ('If we say that we have no sin, we deceive ourselves and the truth is not in us') / *si dixerimus quoniam non peccavimus mendacem facimus eum et verbum eius non est in nobis* ('If we say that we have not sinned, we make him a liar: and his word is not in us').

[93] [240] Now, if you seek by means of [your] worship of me whatever is spiritual, you will also take possession of this along with all that is temporal to your great glory. For if you worship me, I will also glorify you. Accordingly, to begin with, desire it that the name of my Father be sanctified among all people, that is, that everyone recognises that he is the true and only God and the one who[632] sent Jesus Christ. [Desire it] that preaching of the Gospel and Christ's name has an unimpeded course for the universal establishment of my Church through the whole world.[633] [Desire it] that you and I may be as though one body, pure, immaculate and sacred, and that you may not[634] be separated by any defilement from that body and my name, but, as though joined and fixed to me, you may be participants in the whole of the inheritance and my kingdom. In order to attain this kingdom, you ought not to rely on your own power or understanding, but you should always commit your whole selves to the will of my Father, that is, whether you are kings, ministers or magistrates, whether commoners and subjects, and you should organise your life around the testament of my will and whatever has been written in it.

[94] [241] [Q.] So, first of all, the glory of the Father must be sought, then your spiritual health. If you truly seek these things first, you may confidently look towards and anticipate[635] [all] the rest that is vital for life and and your basic subsistence, such as bread, daily sustenance, health, quietude, and peace of mind, and other benefits in life, by which you are able to serve my Father more freely. Furthermore, for as long as you are in this world, you in no way have the power to escape the act of sinning. Indeed, if you say that you have no sin, you are liars and there is no truth in you.[636] Pray incessantly that among yourselves you can forgive your mutual transgressions, as if becoming bound together through some sacrament, so that those things may be forgiven for you;[637] than this, nothing can be more likely to make my Father amenable to pardoning you of your sins.[638] Ultimately, since the Devil surrounds all places and times, seeking someone to swallow up, vigilantly guard against this with your prayers so as to avoid falling into his jaws. Moreover, concerning this Devil I mentioned to you a moment ago, as for the fact that he will be deterred and weakened by my truth and cross and[639] although he will not fill you with much fear, nonetheless

---

[637] *orate ... remissuros*: I have taken *remissuros* as a future infinitive (with *esse* understood) after *orate* and *ut ... remittantur* as a purpose clause.

[638] *ut ... impetrabilius*: A paraphrase of Matt. 6.14; V: *Si enim dimiseritis hominibus peccata eorum, dimittet et vobis Pater vester caelestis*. ('For if you forgive men their sins, your heavenly Father will also forgive you your offences').

[639] *et*: in the printed version this word reads *ut*, but this would be very awkward syntactically, and *et* offers a much happier reading.

[95] [242] declinatio eius tam vobis erit necessaria,[640] ut illud in precibus vestris omittere non debeatis. Iam quid sit petere, et quid sit petendum accepistis: quae omnia, si in nomine meo faciatis, Pater omnes petitiones vestras adimplebit. Nam, quemadmodum solus ego[641] ero pontifex,[642] ut omnia mundi peccata cruci affigam, ut illic[643] sacrificem et mactem: sic ego solus sum precum et indigentiarum vestrarum ad Patrem deportator: nam ego semper et solus intercessor et advocatus vester, ego thronus gratiae,[644] propitiatorium et mediator vester, ego patri solus dilectus, nemo ascendit ad coelum, nemo ad patrem nisi solus ego.[645] Ergo si aliquid impetrare velitis, hoc in meo nomine facietis:[646] ne alio deflectatis,[647] nam ego sum via: ne latebras et fenestras quaeratis, nam ego sum ostium et ianua:[648] ne diffidatis, nam ego sum iustus et ipsa veritas:[649] ne in tenebris palpetis, nam ego sum lumen de lumine,[650] et splendor Patris. Praeterea, cum in nomine meo Daemonia eiecistis, cum morbos et infirmitates depulistis, de caeteris rebus ne desperate:[651] nam nominis mei confessione coeli

[96] [243] [Q.ii.] aperiuntur, tyrannis mundi devincitur, Diabolus conculcatur, et nova quasi facies et regeneratio hominis instituitur. Et quamobrem? Nam nemo potest dicere IESUM CHRISTUM nisi in spiritu sancto. In nomine meo. Hoc est, in voluntate patris: sum enim ego filius ille dilectus, in quo sibi complacuit.[652] Sit haec ergo fiducia vestra apud DEUM, quod, si quid petieritis, secundum voluntatem eius, audiet vos. Vel, in nomine meo.

---

[640] *declinatio... erit necessaria*: literally, 'there will be for you so necessary an avoidance'; *erit* is sometimes used gerundivally in the early modern period.
[641] *solus ego*: The continued emphasis on *solus* ('I alone') in this theme reinforces the christological voice.
[642] *quemadmodum... pontifex*: a possible nod to Hebr. 4.14: *Habentes ergo pontificem magnum qui penetravit caelos, Iesum Filium Dei* ('Having therefore a great high priest who has passed into heaven, Jesus, the son of God') or 9.11: *Christus autem adsistens pontifex futurorum bonorum* ('But Christ being present, a high priest of good things to come'). This part of verse 9.11 is underlined in GNT and the term ἀρχιερεύς has also been inscribed in the margin.
[643] *illuc*: 'unto the other world' is a valid meaning of *illuc*, as used, for example, in Cic. *Tusc*.1.31.75.
[644] *thronus gratiae*: The throne of grace is mentioned in Hebr. 4.16.
[645] *nemo... ego*: Asc. perhaps has in mind John 14.6: *nemo venit ad Patrem, nisi per me* ('no man comes unto the Father, but by me').

[95] [242] you must avoid him to such a degree[640] that you should not omit that in your prayers. You have [now] been told what it is to seek and what must be sought. If you do all this in my name, the Father will answer all your requests. What's more, just as I alone[641] will be the high priest,[642] to affix all the sins of this world to the cross and to sacrifice, [and] magnify unto the other world,[643] thus I alone am the means of carrying your prayers and wishes to the Father. Indeed, I am your only intercessor and advocate forever; I the throne of grace,[644] your means of atonement, and your mediator; I alone beloved of my Father. No one ascends to heaven and no one [ascends] to the Father except I alone.[645] And so, if you wish to accomplish anything, do[646] this in my name. You should not turn[647] in another direction, for I am the way; you should not seek hiding places and recesses, for I am the entrance and the door;[648] you should not despair, for I am righteous and truth itself;[649] you should not grope in the shadows, for I am the light from light[650] and the radiance of the Father. Moreover, when you have expelled the demons in my name, when you have driven back illness and infirmity, do not despair[651] about everything else, for the heavens are opened by the acknowledgement of my name,

[96] [243] [Q.ii.] the tyrant of this world is conquered, the Devil is trodden under foot, and it is as if a new form and beginning of man is inaugurated. Why [should this be] so? Certainly, no one can say 'Jesus Christ' unless through the Holy Spirit. 'In my name'. That is, through the will of the Father, for I am his beloved son in whom he is well pleased.[652] And so, may this trust of yours be with GOD, because if you seek something in accordance with his will, he will hear you. Assuredly, 'in my name'.

---

[646] *facietis*: I have translated this future simple as an imperative.
[647] *ne ... deflectatis*: This prohibition, as well as the ones that follow (*ne quaeratis, ne diffidatis* and *ne palpetis*) are all formed using *ne* and the present subjunctive, a less standard construction than *nolite* + infinitive), but perfectly acceptable (especially in verse). The cumulative effect is very striking.
[648] *ostium et ianua*: a coupling used in theme 5.
[649] *via ... veritas*: Asc. is gesturing to John 4.16 again, as he also does in themes 1 and 4.
[650] *lumen de lumine*: a form of words used at the start of theme 2 and taken from the Nicene Creed. Asc. also uses *erit lumen et splendor Dei Patris* at the beginning of theme 10.
[651] *ne desperate*: This prohibition is different again to those above (see n. 647), comprising as it does *ne* + the imperative, an unusual construction in classical Latin, but Asc. may also have the Greek μή + present imperative in mind.
[652] *sum ... complacuit*: Matt. 3.17 or 2 Peter 1.17 cited twice above, and see n. 280.

Hoc est in spiritu, veritate, et fide: nam pater meus odit hypocrisin et mendaces, qui diligunt ore et lingua, cum cor eorum procul sit ab eo: aspernatur haesitantes, nam nihil hii accepturi sunt ab eo: Oculi enim Patris mei (ut ait Ieremias Propheta) in fidem respiciunt,[653] et fidei oratio penetrat coelos.[654] Quamobrem, dico vobis, Quaecunque orantes petitis, credite quod accipietis, et erunt vobis:[655] nam si petitis, et non accipitis, eo fit, quod male et non in fide petitis: ad concupiscentias enim vestras explendas, non ad voluntatem Patris petitis. Nescitis vos quid expedit vobis, at Pater priusquam oratis novit qua re opus habeatis.

[97] [244] Etenim, si mala petieritis, non impetrabitis. Quare? Nam non in nomine meo, hoc est, neque ad vestram salutem, neque ad patris voluntatem petitis. Prosperas enim res petetis? Videte ne corrumpant vos, et nimium feroces reddant. Longitudinem dierum postulabitis? Sed ecce quam dies malae sint, et quam praestat dissolvi et mecum esse. Cavete ergo petatis quae cum malo vestro accipiatis: nam servus meus Paulus, quamvis ter rogabit patrem ut angelum Satanae tollat ab eo, non impetrabit: etenim, quod Paulo videbitur sibi esse impedimentum, hoc a patre meo iudicabitur ei necessarium.[656] Quamobrem, petite secundum eius voluntatem, et gratia eius satis superque vobis in omnibus sufficiet.[657] Itaque, ego in Psalmo in persona vestra, et totius Ecclesiae meae, quae non semper exaudit vos, Patri quodam modo gratias ago, dicens, Verba derelictorum meorum clamavi ad te per diem, nec exaudies: et nocte, et non ad insipientiam mihi:[658] hoc est, Nocte dieque clamabitis, et Pater non exaudiet, et tamen hoc ipsum, quod non exaudiet, non ad malum vestrum et insipientiam

---

[653] *Oculi ... respiciunt*: Jeremiah 5.3. There is very similar phrasing in V: *Domine oculi tui respiciunt fidem*.

[654] *fidei oratio penetrat coelos*: Probably a reference to Ecclesiasticus 35.21, *oratio humiliantis se nubes penetrabit* ('The prayer of the one humbling himself shall pierce the clouds').

[655] *Quamobrem ... vobis*: Mark 11.24. Ascham diverges subtley from V: *propterea dico vobis omnia quaecumque orantes petitis credite quia accipietis et veniet vobis*, but tallies almost exactly with *Nov. T.* Again, Asc. has inscribed the Greek word for 'prayer' next to this verse in GNT.

That is, in spirit, truth and faith, for my Father hates hypocrisy and liars who delight in the mouth and tongue, since their heart is very much absent from him. He rejects those who equivocate, and these men are destined to receive nothing from him. Indeed, the eyes of my Father, as the Prophet Jeremiah states, look towards faith,[653] and a prayer of faith penetrates the heavens.[654] On which account, I say to you, whatever you seek in prayer, believe that you will receive it and it will be yours.[655] If you seek and do not receive, it is because you seek badly and without faith, insofar as you seek that your desires be satisfied but not the will of the Father. You do not know what is held in store for you, but the Father, [even] before you pray [for it], knows what you have need of.

[97] [244] For sure, if you make unworthy requests, you will not achieve them. Why? It's because it is not [done] in my name; that is, you seek neither in accordance with your salvation, nor in accordance with the will of the Father. For instance, will you seek favourable fortunes? Beware that they don't corrupt you and rebound on you too forcefully. Will you demand a longer life? But behold how days can be injurious, and how much better it is to be released and to be with me. And so, beware seeking what you may receive to your own detriment. Certainly, my servant Paul, although he will ask the Father three times to remove the angel of Satan from him, shall not achieve it, for what seems to Paul to be be a hindrance, will be deemed by my Father to be necessary for him (i.e. Paul).[656] As such, seek in accordance with his (i.e. God's) will, and his grace will be more than sufficient for you in all things.[657] Consequently, in the Psalm, on the part of yourselves and that of my whole Church which does not always heed you, I give thanks in a particular way to the Father, saying "I have shouted the words of my offences to you by day and by night, and you will not hear; and it shall not be [regarded as] folly in me";[658] that is, by day and night you will shout, and the Father will not heed you, and it's not to your detriment or [regarded as] folly

---

[656] *Paulus ... necessarium*: 2 Corinth. 12.7–10. A summary of an episode already referred to above (in themes 4, 5 and 10), whereby Paul asks three times for a *stimulus carnis* to be removed, only to be set on the correct path again by God.

[657] *gratia ... sufficiet*: a nod to 2 Corinth. 12.9, a verse regularly cited in the *Themata*, though see n. 250.

[658] *Patri ... mihi*: loosely based on Ps. 21.2–3 (V/S) / 22.2–3 (H/P).

[98] [245] [Q.iii.] non exaudiet, sed magis ad bonum et sapientiam vestram non exaudiet, ut intelligatis quid a Patre petere debeatis. Sequamini ergo vos non voluntatem hominis, sed voluntatem Dei: nam quatenus ego sum Christus, hoc est, Deus et homo, utrasque has voluntates in me, humanam et divinam, multum inter se diversas et dissentientes habeo. Itaque, quando oro Patrem iuxta humanam voluntatem, non impetro, ut quando dico, Pater, si possible est transeat a me calix iste: sed ex divina voluntate aliud sentio, addens, Non sicut ego volo, sed sicut tu.[659] Igitur, si Paulus, qui videbitur prudenter petere, ut stimulus carnis tollatur, non impetrabit: si ego ipse, et in persona Ecclesiae, et in persona mea, sed iuxta humanam voluntatem orans, voti compos non ero, ne moerore vos ipsos conficiatis, si vel ad tempus repulsi, vel omnino aliquibus votis frustrati fueritis. Nam ut quaedam obtinuisse, ita quibusdam caruisse summum beneficium reputare debetis. Etenim, si aliquod bonum dabit Pater, accipietis beneficium: sin aliquod malum avertet Pater, accipietis beneficium. Sic sive

[99] [246] accipiatis sive non accipiatis, beneficium semper aliquod a patre capietis. Ergo, si primum quae sunt regni DEI, tum quae vestrae necessitatis quaeratis, et ea omnia in nomine meo, hoc est, in spiritu, in fide, in iusticia, in voluntate, et beneplacito Patris a Patre petatis, impetrabitis: nam, Quicquid petieritis patrem in nomine meo dabit vobis.[660]

---

[659] *Pater ... tu*: Matt. 26.39, as also quoted in theme 4.

[98] [245] [Q.iii.] that he will not heed you. Rather, he will not heed you for your [own] good and your [own] edification, that you might understand what you ought to seek from the Father. Accordingly, you should follow not the will of man but the will of God. Indeed, to the extent that I am Christ, that is, God and man, I have each of these wills in me – human and divine – [even though] each is contrary [to the other] and they differ considerably. And so, when I pray to the Father in accordance with human will, I do not achieve [anything], as when I say "Father, if it is possible, may that cup be moved from me". But from divine will I perceive another aspect, by adding "Not just as I want, but just as you want".[659] It follows that if Paul who will seem to ask wisely that the flesh's torment be removed will not achieve it, and if I myself, both on the part of the Church and my own part, yet praying in accordance with human will, shall not obtain my wish, you should not wear yourselves out with grief if you have either been put off for the moment, or have been altogether frustrated in any of your prayers. Indeed, just as you ought to reflect on the benefit of taking hold of certain things, so you ought to reflect upon the fact that the greatest benefit is to lack certain things. What's more, if the Father grants anything good, you will receive the benefit; equally, if the Father averts anything bad, you will [likewise] receive the benefit. Thus, whether

[99] [246] you receive or don't receive, you will always take some benefit from the Father. In conclusion, if initially you seek the things which belong to the kingdom of God, and then what you need, and you ask for all those things in my name, that is, in spirit, in faith, in righteousness, in will and gracious purpose of the Father from the Father, you will obtain them, for 'Whatsoever you ask of the Father in my name he will give it you'.[660]

---

[660] *Quicquid . . . vobis*: a restatement of John 15.16 (and also John 16.23), and the heading of the theme.

Bibliography

Adams, S. (2002), *Leicester and the Court: Essays on Elizabethan Politics*, Manchester.
Altman, W. H. F., ed. (2015), *Brill's Companion to the Reception of Cicero*, Leiden / Boston.
Backus, I. (2012), 'Moses, Plato and Flavius Josephus: Castellio's Conceptions of Sacred and Profane in his Latin Versions of the Bible', in B. Gordon and M. McLean (eds), *Shaping the Bible in the Reformation: Books, Scholars and Their Readers in the Sixteenth Century*, 143–65, Leiden / Boston.
Baker, T. (1869), *History of the College of St John the Evangelist Cambridge*, ed. J. E. B. Mayor, 2 vols, Cambridge.
Bartlett, K. R. and M. McGlynn, eds (2014), *The Renaissance and Reformation in Northern Europe*, Ontario / New York.
Belt, van den, H. (2016), 'Sola scriptura: an inadequate slogan for the authority of Scripture', *Calvin Theological Journal*, 51.2, 204–26.
Ben-Tov, A. (2009), *Lutheran Humanists and Greek Antiquity: Melanchthonian Scholarship between Universal History and Pedagogy*, Leiden / Boston.
Binns, J. W. (1990), *Intellectual Culture in Elizabethan and Jacobean England: The Latin Writings of the Age*, Leeds.
Brammall, S. (2018), 'Laurence Humphrey, Gabriel Harvey, and the Place of Personality in Renaissance Translation Theory', *The Review of English Studies*, 69.288, 56–75.
Cameron E., ed. (2016), *The New Cambridge History of the Bible: From 1450 to 1750*, Cambridge.
Clegg, C. (2021), 'Ascham and Queen Elizabeth's Religion', in L. R. Nicholas and C. Law (eds), *Roger Ascham and his Sixteenth-Century World*, Leiden / Boston.
Cox, V. and J. O. Ward, eds (2006), *The Rhetoric of Cicero in its Medieval and Early Renaissance Commentary Tradition*, Leiden / Boston.
Craig, H. (1950), 'Religious Disputation in Tudor England', *The Rice Institute Pamphlet*, 37.1, 21–47.
Cratty, F. (forthcoming), 'The Christian Humanists and their Prayers to Jupiter', in M. Lazarus and L. R. Nicholas (eds), *Classical Reformations: Beyond Christian Humanism*, Turnhout.
Crawforth, H. and R. Leo, eds (2021), *Scholarship, Sacrifice and Subjectivity: The Renaissance Bible Today*, Oxford / New York.
Cubillos, R. H. (2009), 'Consolation as Theme in Luther's Sermons and Correspondence: Insights into his Theological Ethics', *The Asbury Journal* 64.2, 36–67.
Cummings, B. (2002), *The Literary Culture of the Reformation: Grammar and Grace*, Oxford.

Enenkel, K. A. E. and A. Trainiger, eds (2015), *Discourses of Anger in the Early Modern Period*, Leiden / Boston.
Eskhult, J. (2012), 'Latin Bible Translations in the Protestant Reformation: Historical Contexts, Philological Justification and the Impact of Classical Rhetoric on the Concept of Translation Methods', in B. Gordon and M. McLean (eds), *Shaping the Bible in the Reformation: Books, Scholars and Their Readers in the Sixteenth Century*, 167–85, Leiden / Boston.
Hamel, de, C. (2001), *The Book: a History of the Bible*, London.
Ford, P., J. Bloemendal and C. Fantazzi, eds (2014), *Brill's Encyclopaedia of the Neo-Latin World*, Leiden / Boston.
Friedenthal, M., H. Marti and R. Seidel, eds (2020), *Early Modern Disputations and Dissertations in an Interdisciplinary and European Context*, Leiden / Boston.
Frigo, A. (2020), *Inexcusabiles: Salvation and the Virtues of the Pagans in the Early Modern Period*, New York.
Gibbs, F. W. (2018), *Poison, Medicine and Disease in Late Medieval and Early Modern Europe*, Abingdon.
Giles, J. A., ed. (1865–67), *The Whole Works of Roger Ascham*, 3 vols, London.
Gordon, B. (2010), 'The Authority of Antiquity: England and the Protestant Latin Bible', in P. Ha and P. Collinson (eds), *The Reception of Continental Reformation in Britain*, 1–22, Oxford.
Gordon, B. and E. Cameron (2016), 'Latin Bibles in the early modern period', in E. Cameron (ed.), *The New Cambridge History of The Bible from 1450 to 1750*, Part II, 187–216, Cambridge.
Gordon, B. and M. McLean, eds (2012), *Shaping the Bible in the Reformation: Books, Scholars and Their Readers in the Sixteenth Century*, Leiden / Boston.
Gray, H. (1963), 'Renaissance Humanism: The Pursuit of Eloquence', *Journal of History of Ideas* 24.4, 497–514.
Green, I. (2009), *Humanism and Protestantism in Early Modern English Education*, Farnham.
Green, R. P. H., ed. and trans. (1996), *Augustine, De Doctrina Christiana*, Oxford.
Grendler, P. F. (2004), 'The Universities of the Renaissance and the Reformation', *Renaissance Quarterly*, 57.1, 1–42.
Grogan, J. (2020), *William Barker's Xenophon's 'Cyropaedia'*, MHRA Tudor and Stuart Translations, vol. 13, Cambridge.
Hamilton, A. (1996), 'Humanists and the Bible' in J. Kraye (ed.), *The Cambridge Companion to Renaissance Humanism*, 100–17, Cambridge.
Hannibal, H. (2015), 'Reading the Bible in Tudor England', *Oxford Handbook Topics in Literature*, online edn, Oxford.
Hardy, N. (2017), *Criticism and Confession: The Bible in the Seventeenth Century Republic of Letters*, Oxford.
Hatch, M. A. (1946), 'The Ascham Letters: An Annotated Translation of the Latin Correspondence', PhD Thesis, Cornell University.

Hettler, A. (1915), *Roger Ascham: Sein Stil und seine Bezeihung zur Antike*, Elberfeld.
Hillebrand, Hans. J, ed. (1996), *The Oxford Encyclopedia of the Reformation*, Oxford.
Houghton, H. A. G. (2016), *The Latin New Testament: A Guide to its Early History, Texts, and Manuscripts*, Oxford.
Hudson, W. S. (1980), *The Cambridge Connection and the Elizabethan Settlement of 1559*, Durham NC.
Ijsewijn, J. and D. Sacré, eds (1998), *Companion to Neo-Latin Studies*, 2 vols, Leuven.
Jonge, de, H. J. (1988), 'The Date and Purpose of Erasmus's *Castigatio Novi Testamenti*', in A. C. Dionisotti, A. Grafton and J. Kraye (eds), *The Uses of Greek and Latin: Historical Essays*, 97–110, London.
Kachuck, A. J. and B. C. F. McDougall (2022), 'Why Tudor Cambridge Needs Greek', in G. Manuwald and L. R. Nicholas (eds), *An Anthology of Neo-Latin Literature in British Universities*, 59–87, London / New York / Dublin.
Katterfeld, A. (1879), *Roger Ascham: sein Leben und seine Werke: mit besonderer Berücksichtigung seiner Berichte über Deutschland*, Strasbourg / London.
Kennerley, S. (2020), 'Patristic Scholarship and Ascham's "troubled years"', in L. R. Nicholas and C. Law (eds), *Roger Ascham and his Sixteenth-Century World*, 61–81, Leiden / Boston.
Killeen, K. and H. Smith (2015), 'Introduction. "All other books ... are but Notes upon this": The Early Modern Bible', in K. Killeen, H. Smith and R. Willie (eds), *The Bible in Early Modern England, c. 1530–1700*, 1–18, Oxford.
Killeen, K., H. Smith and R. Willie, eds (2015), *The Bible in Early Modern England, c. 1530-1700*, Oxford
Kirby T. (2013), *Persuasion and Conversion: Essays on Religion, Politics and the Public Sphere in Early Modern England*, Leiden / Boston.
Kolb. R, I. Dingel and L. Batka, eds (2014), *The Oxford Handbook of Martin Luther's Theology*, Oxford.
Kristeller, P. O. (1961), *Renaissance Thought: The Classic, Scholastic, and Humanistic Strains*, New York.
Law, C. (2021), 'Roger Ascham and the Idea of a University in Sixteenth-Century England', in L. R. Nicholas and C. Law (eds), *Roger Ascham and his Sixteenth-Century World*, 23–40, Leiden / Boston.
Lazarus, M. (2021), 'Ascham's Bookshelf', in L. R. Nicholas and C. Law (eds), *Roger Ascham and his Sixteenth-Century World*, 297–320, Leiden / Boston.
Lazarus, M. and L. R. Nicholas, eds (forthcoming), *Classical Reformations: Beyond Christian Humanism*, Turnhout.
Leader, D. R. (1988), *A History of the University of Cambridge: The University to 1546*, vol. 1 of *A History of the University of Cambridge*, ed. C. Brooke, Cambridge.
Leedham-Green, E. S. (1986), *Books in Cambridge Inventories: Book lists from Vice-Chancellor's Court probate inventories in the Tudor and Stuart periods*, Cambridge.

Leeuwen, van T. M., K. D. Stanglin and M. Tolsma, eds (2009), *Arminius, Arminianism and Europe: Jacobus Arminius (1559/60–1609)*, Leiden / Boston.
Linebaugh, J. (2018), *God's Two Words: Law and Gospel in Lutheran and Reformed Traditions*. Grand Rapids, MI.
Logan, D. (1991), 'The First Royal Visitation of the English Universities, 1535', *English Historical Review*, 106, 861–88.
Long, A. A. and D. N. Sedley (1987), *The Hellenistic Philosophers*, vol. 1, Cambridge.
Lugioyo, B. (2010), *Martin Bucer's Doctrine of Justification: Reformation Theology and Early Modern Irenicism*, Oxford.
MacCulloch, D. (1996), *Thomas Cranmer: A Life*, New Haven / London.
MacCulloch, D. (2004), *Reformation: Europe's House Divided, 1490–1700*, London.
Mack, P. (1996), 'Humanist Rhetoric and Dialectic', in J. Kraye (ed.), *The Cambridge Companion to Renaissance Humanism*, 82–99, Cambridge.
Marenbon, J. (2015), *Pagans and Philosophers: the Problem of Paganism from Augustine to Leibniz*, Princeton.
Marshall, P. (2006), *Religious Identities in Henry VIII's England*, Aldershot.
Martinez, F. G. and G. P. Luttikhizen, eds (2003), *Jerusalem, Alexandria and Rome*, Leiden / Boston.
Matheson, P. (2004), *Rhetoric of the Reformation*, London / New York.
Mayor, J. E. B., ed. (1859), *Early Statutes of College of St John the Evangelist in the University of Cambridge*, Cambridge.
McConica, J. K. (1965), *English Humanists and Reformation Politics under Henry VIII and Edward VI*, Oxford.
McConica, J. K. (1991), *Erasmus*, Oxford.
McDiarmid, J. F. (2022), 'Perfecting Eloquence, Perfecting England', in J. F. McDiarmid and S. Wabuda (eds), *The Cambridge Connection in Tudor England: Humanism, Reform, Rhetoric, Politics*, 21–50, Leiden / Boston
McDiarmid, J. F. and S. Wabuda, eds (2022), *The Cambridge Connection in Tudor England: Humanism, Reform, Rhetoric, Politics*, Leiden / Boston.
McGrath, A. E. (1982), 'Humanist Elements in the Early Reformed Doctrine of Justification', *Archiv für Reformationgeschichte*, 73, 5–20.
McGrath, A. E. (1986), *Iustitia Dei: A History of the Christian Doctrine of Justification*, Cambridge.
McKerrow, R. B. (1949), *Printers' and Publishers' Devices in England and Scotland, 1485–1640*, London.
McKerrow, R. B. (1968), *A Dictionary of Printers and Booksellers in England, Scotland and Ireland and of Foreign Printers of English Books 1557–1640*, London.
McLaughlin, M. L. (1995), *Literary Imitation in the Italian Renaissance: The Theory and Practice of Literary Imitation in Italy from Dante to Bembo*, Oxford.
Moss, A. (2003), *Renaissance Truth and the Latin Language Turn*, Oxford.

Muller, R. A. (1996), 'Biblical Interpretation in the Era of the Reformation: The View from the Middle Ages', in R. A. Muller and J. L. Thompson (eds), *Biblical Interpretation in the Era of the Reformation*, 3–22, Grand Rapids, MI.

Nicholas, L. R. (2015a), 'Roger Ascham's Defence of the Lord's Supper', *Reformation*, 20.1, 26–61.

Nicholas, L. R. (2015b), 'Sin and Salvation in Roger Ascham's *Apologia pro Caena Dominica*', in J. Willis (ed.), *Sin and Salvation in Reformation England*, 87–99, Aldershot.

Nicholas, L. R. (2016), 'Exploring Polemical Theology in Humanism Through a Little-Known Tract on the Eucharist by the Great Tudor Humanist, Roger Ascham', in S. Zavarský, L. R. Nicholas and A. Riedl (eds), *Themes of Polemical Theology Across Early Modern Genres*, 67–84, Newcastle.

Nicholas, L. R. (2017), *Roger Ascham's 'A Defence of the Lord's Supper': Latin Text and English Translation*, Leiden / Boston.

Nicholas, L. R. (2020), 'In Search of the Truth: Mid-Sixteenth Century Disputations on the Eucharist in England', in M. Friedenthal, H. Marti and R. Seidel (eds), *Early Modern Disputations and Dissertations in an Interdisciplinary and European Context*, 105–44, Leiden / Boston.

Nicholas, L. R. (2021), 'The Special Relationship: Ascham and Sturm, England and Strasbourg', in L. R. Nicholas and C. Law (eds), *Roger Ascham and his Sixteenth-Century World*, 145–64, Leiden / Boston.

Nicholas, L. R. (2022), 'New Perspectives on Cambridge's Role in the Religious Reformation; Roger Ascham and the Early Edwardian Religious Debates at the University', in J. F. McDiarmid and S. Wabuda (eds), *The Cambridge Connection in Tudor England: Humanism, Reform, Rhetoric, Politics*, 159–79, Leiden / Boston.

Nicholas, L. R. (forthcoming), 'Humanism and Reform in Sixteenth Century England re-examined through the Latin Works of Walter Haddon', *Brill Research Perspectives in Latinity and Classical Reception in the Early Modern Period*, Leiden / Boston.

Nicholas, L. R. and C. Law, eds (2021), *Roger Ascham and his Sixteenth-Century World*, Leiden / Boston.

Novikoff, A. J. (2013), *The Medieval Culture of Disputation: Pedagogy, Practice and Performance*, Philadelphia.

Oberman, H. A. (1981), *Masters of the Reformation: The Emergence of a New Intellectual Climate in Europe*, trans. D. Martin, Cambridge.

Oberman, H. A and C. E. Trinkaus, eds (1974), *The Pursuit of Holiness in Late Medieval and Renaissance Religion*, Leiden.

Olsen, D. L, N. H. Petersen and R. A. Rosengarten (2014), *Encyclopedia of the Bible and its Reception*, vol. 8, Berlin / Boston.

Pabel, H. M. (1997), *Conversing with God: Prayer in Erasmus' Pastoral Writings*, Toronto.

Pereira, J. L. (2013), *Augustine of Hippo and Martin Luther on Original Sin and Justification of the Sinner*, Göttingen.

Poleg, E. (2020), *A Material History of the Bible, England 1200–1553*, Oxford.
Rabil, A. (1993), *Erasmus and the New Testament: The Mind of a Christian Humanist*, London.
Racaut, L. and A. Ryrie (2005), *Moderate Voices in the European Reformation*, Oxford / New York.
Reinhardt, T. (2003), *Cicero's Topica*, Oxford.
Remer, G. (1996), *Humanism and the Rhetoric of Toleration*, Pennsylvania.
Rex, R. (1991), *The Theology of John Fisher*, Cambridge.
Rex, R. (1999), 'The Role of English Humanists in the Reformation up to 1559', in N. S. Amos, A. Pettegree and H. F. K. van Nierop (eds), *The Education of a Christian Society: Humanism and Reformation in Britain and the Netherlands*, 19–40, Aldershot.
Rex, R. (2011), 'The Sixteenth Century', in P. Linehan (ed.), *St. John's College, Cambridge: A History*, 5–93, Woodbridge.
Rex, R. (2019), *The Making of Martin Luther*, Princeton / Oxford.
Rex, R. (2021), 'Ascham & Co: St John's College, Cambridge, in the 1540s', in L. R. Nicholas and C. Law (eds), *Roger Ascham and his Sixteenth-Century World*, 41–60, Leiden / Boston.
Richards, J. (2019), *Voices and Books in the English Renaissance: A New History of Reading*, Oxford.
Rodda, J. (2014), *Public Religious Disputation in England, 1558–1626*, Aldershot.
Rummel, E. (1995), The Humanist-Scholastic Debate in the Renaissance and Reformation, Cambridge Mass. / London.
Rummel, E. (2000), *The Confessionalization of Humanism in Reformation Germany*, Oxford.
Rummel, E. (2008), *Biblical Humanism and Scholasticism in the Age of Erasmus*, Leiden / Boston.
Rupp, E. G. and P. S. Watson (1969), *Luther and Erasmus: Free Will and Salvation*, London.
Ryan, L. (1963), *Roger Ascham*, Stanford / London.
Ryrie, A. (2002), 'The Strange Death of Lutheran England', *The Journal of Ecclesiastical History*, 53.1, 64–92.
Ryrie, A. (2003), *The Gospel and Henry VIII: Evangelicals in the Early English Reformation*, Cambridge.
Ryrie, A. (2009), 'Paths not taken in the British Reformations', *The Historical Journal*, 52.1, 1–22.
Ryrie, A. (2013), *Being Protestant in Reformation Britain*, Oxford.
Scott-Amos, N. (2015), *Bucer, Ephesians and Biblical Humanism: The Exegete as Theologian*, Heidelberg / New York / Dordrecht / London.
Shagan, E. H. (2011), *The Rule of Moderation*, Cambridge.
Shrank, C. (2020), 'The Bow and the Book', in L. R. Nicholas and C. Law (eds), *Roger Ascham and his Sixteenth-Century World*, 208–25, Leiden / Boston.
Shuger, D. K. (1994), *The Renaissance Bible: Scholarship, Sacrifice and Subjectivity*, California.
Shuger, D. K. (2022), *Paratexts of the English Bible, 1525–1611*, Oxford

Spranzi, M. (2011), *The Art of Dialectic between Dialogue and Rhetoric: the Aristotelian Tradition*, Amsterdam / Philadelphia.
Tadmor, N. (2010), *The Social Universe of the English Bible: Scripture, Society and Culture in Early Modern England*, Cambridge.
Trueman, C. R. and C. Euler (2012), 'The Reception of Martin Luther in Sixteenth- and Seventeenth-Century England', in P. Ha and P. Collinson (eds), *The Reception of Continental Reformation in Britain*, 63–81, Oxford.
Venn, J., ed. (1910), *Grace Book Delta*, Cambridge.
Verkamp, B. J. (1977), *The Indifferent Mean: Adiaphorism in the English Reformation to 1554*, Ohio.
Vos, A., ed. (1989), *Letters of Roger Ascham*, trans. M. Hatch and A. Vos, New York.
Ward Holder, R. (2009), *A Companion to Paul in the Reformation*, Leiden / Boston.
Weaver, W. P. (2022), *Homer in Wittenberg: Rhetoric, Scholarship, Prayer*, Oxford.
Westhelle, V. (2014), 'Luther's *Theologia Crucis*' in R. Kolb, I. Dingel and L. Batka (eds), *The Oxford Handbook of Martin Luther's Theology*, 156–67, Oxford.
Willis, J., ed. (2015), *Sin and Salvation in Reformation England*, Farnham.
Wooding, L. E. C. (2015), *Henry VIII*, London.
Yost, J. K. (1975), 'Protestant Reformers and the Humanist *via media* in the Early English Reformation', *Journal of Medieval and Renaissance Studies*, 5, 187–202.

Index of Biblical and Patristic Citations

Acts 180–81
  1   181 n.473
  5   168–69
  7   173 n.442
  8   173 n.442
  9   166–67
  10 181 n.474
  11 190–91
  22 173 n.442
  26 173 n.442
Amos
  5   217 n.626
Augustine
  De civitate Dei
    22   62, 66 n.17, 71 n.40,
         73 n.48/49
  De doctrina Christiana
    3   104–7, 113 n.188, 116 n.205
  Enarratio in Psalmum
    IV   150 n.344
    XXXIII 190 n.503
    XXXVI 80 n.82
  Sermones
    4   125 n.247
    111 201 n.568
    128 172 n.433
    296 150 n.344

Book of Wisdom
  9   156 n.363

1 Chronicles
  21 101 n.163
Chrysostom
  Homily on Matthew
      192 n.514
  Homily on 1 Timothy
      21, 192 n.514
Colossians
  1   166–67

1 Corinthians
  1   191 n.507
  6   115 n.197, 144 n.327
  7   116 n.199
  8   7, 152, 154–55
  13 157 n.371
  14 142 n.322
  15 75 n.62, 77 n.79,
      173 n.442
2 Corinthians
  1   168 n.415
  5   156 n.365/366
  6   90 n.129
  11 168–69, 200 n.564,
      201 n.565/568, 209 n.602
  12 18, 125 n.248/249/250,
      128 n.262, 141 n.312,
      151 n.348, 164 n.394,
      168–69, 196 n.539,
      223 n.657
Daniel
  3   84 n.107
Deuteronomy   11, 118–19
  5   96 n.144, 97 n.145,
      115 n.195/6
  8   202–3
  12 119 n.218, 128 n.264,
      134 n.275, 138–39,
      145 n.332
  24 98–99, 99 n.153

Ecclesiasticus
  3   127 n.258, 140–41
  35 222 n.654
Ephesians   26 n.135
  2   74 n.58
  4   7, 38, 74 n.60, 146,
      148–49
  6   30 n.153, 75 n.66

Exodus 11
2   172 n.439
3   118 n.210
16 202–3
18 41
20 96–97, 115 n.195/196,
    139 n.305
32 140–41
34 139 n.305
Ezekiel 29, 79, 94–99
18 41, 82–83, 94–99,
    100 n.157/158, 102 n.164
20 165 n.401

Galatians 158, 162–63, 164 n.393
1   173 n.442
2   173 n.447
3   88 n.121, 158, 161 n.382,
    192 n.516/517
5   174 n.450
6   7, 18, 28, 76–77, 158, 160–61,
    168 n.414, 177 n.467
Genesis
3   27
4   114 n.190
9   172 n.437
12 207 n.593
16 117 n.208
18 101 n.162
19 101 n.162, 172 n.438
22 118 n.212, 207 n.594
25 117 n.209
25–34 208 n.597
26 208 n.595
27 208 n.597
29 208 n.596/597

Hebrews
1   134 n.278
4   220 n.642/644
6   33, 190–91
8   175 n.455
9   220 n.642
13 175 n.458

Hosea
1   118 n.211
4   111 n.184
13 176 n.465

Isaiah
5   114 n.189
26 119 n.219/220, 159,
    164–65
28 166–67
54 86–87

James
1   203 n.576
2   127 n.258
4   75 n.63
Jeremiah
5   222 n.653
31 96 n.142/143
Jerome
    Commentariorum in Amos libri
    3   80 n.82
    *Commentariorum in Ezechielem
    libri*
    6   97 n.147, 98 n.152
    Letters
    22 164 n.393
    54 190 n.505
Job   208 n.598
7   200 n.562
John
1   76 n.69/72, 136 n.287,
    138 n.293, 176 n.463, 180–81
3   136 n.281
4   86 n.115, 126–27 n.256,
    172 n.435, 221 n.649
5   7, 178, 180–81
6   180 n.470
7   126–27 n.256
8   168 n.417
10 136 n.283, 214–15
11 77 n.80
12 138 n.298, 214 n.610
13 214 n.610

Index of Biblical and Patristic Citations

14	14, 44, 75 n.68, 77 n.77, 129 n.270, 136 n.282/285, 137 n.290/291, 138 n.295/297/300, 175 n.457/459, 176 n.464, 177 n.466, 220 n.645	8	124 n.245, 128 n.261
		11	222 n.655
		14	124 n.246, 128 n.260, 140–41, 173 n.441, 196 n.537
		Matthew	41, 45, 56
15	8, 212, 214–15, 225 n.660	3	135 n.280, 181 n.476, 221 n.652
16	13, 77 n.75, 128 n.266, 137 n.292, 175 n.460, 202 n.573, 212, 214 n.609, 215 n.615/617, 225 n.660	5	18, 146 n.334, 168–69
		6	14, 82 n.100, 128 n.267, 129 n.268, 162–63, 216 n.623/624, 217 n.625/627/630, 219 n.638
17	44		
18	124 n.246, 140–41, 173 n.441, 196 n.537	7	124 n.242, 129 n.271
1 John		11	137 n.288, 182 n.478, 183 n.481
1	218 n.636	13	191 n.510
Jonah		14	180 n.470
1–2	84 n.106	16	77 n.78, 124 n.245, 128 n.261, 195 n.535, 196 n.536
Judges			
8	140–41	17	135 n.280
1 Kings		25	166–67
14	195 n.534	26	124 n.246, 125 n.247, 128 n.260, 140–41, 173 n.441, 196 n.537/538, 212, 224 n.659
17	85 n.108/109/110		
2 Kings			
6	86 n.112	Numbers	
7	86 n.113	22	7, 132, 134–35, 149 n.342
14	98–99		
22	128 n.265, 137 n.286	1 Peter	
Luke		1	200 n.561, 204 n.577, 205 n.583
1	15–16, 183 n.479, 186 n.484		
2	81 n.91	4	174 n.449
7	183 n.481	2 Peter	
9	135 n.280, 142 n.319, 180 n.470	1	135 n.280, 181 n.476, 221 n.652
10	137 n.289, 142 n.318, 165 n.400	Philippians	
		3	174 n.454
13	124 n.243	Proverbs	
22	124 n.246, 140–41, 173 n.441, 196 n.537	4	128 n.265, 137 n.286
		10	217 n.628
Mark		14	138–39, 194–95
6	180 n.470		

17	200 n.561			187 n.490, 193 n.523,
18	98 n.151			203 n.575
Psalms			10	33, 76 n.74, 138 n.294,
17/18	186 n.485			175 n.461, 190 n.505
21/22	165 n.399, 223 n.658		11	138 n.298
23/24	127 n.257		13	114 n.191
33/34	33, 190 n.503, 194–95			
36/37	41, 78–79, 80 n.82,		1 Samuel	
	82 n.96/99, 88 n.119/123,		15	138–41, 195 n.534
	89 n.125, 91 n.136		17	115 n.194
70/71	81 n.92		19	208 n.599
113/115	120 n.221		2 Samuel	
116	30 n.155		6	123 n.239
131/132	183 n.480		11	172 n.440
144/145	129 n.269		15	208 n.599
			18	208 n.599
Revelation	192–93		19	208 n.599
11	193 n.521			
22	125 n.251, 128 n.263		1 Thessalonians	
Romans	11		4	115 n.198
3	30 n.155		1 Timothy	
5	62, 100 n.159, 168–69,		1	173 n.442
	187 n.489, 203 n.574		2 Timothy	184
6	138 n.296		3	18, 33, 41, 186–87,
7	63, 188 n.493			189 n.497/500, 190 n.506,
8	15, 62–63, 71 n.37, 73 n.46,			193 n.524, 199 n.560
	74 n.52/57, 87 n.118,		4	130 n.273, 198 n.550
	100 n.160, 165 n.397,		Titus	
	168 n.416, 174 n.448,		2	194–95

Index of Classical Citations

Aristotle
  Art of Rhetoric   37
    2   139 n.305
  Nicomachean Ethics   146
    1   110 n.181
    2   120 n.223

Cicero
  Academica
    1   155 n.359
    2   155 n.359
  Brutus
    12   150 n.343
  De amicitia
    65   162 n. 388
  De finibus
    1   89 n.127
    3   42, 109 n.179
  De inventione   40–41, 79
    1   108 n.177, 109 n.180,
          112 n.187, 135 n.279
    2   82–83
  De officiis
    2   110 n.183
    3   122 n.234, 190 n.502
  De oratore   37, 147
    1   108 n.177, 151 n.345
    2   65 n.14
    3   110 n.181, 126 n.253
  In Catilinam   37, 198 n.551
  In Verrem
    2   151 n.346
  Orationes Philippicae
    5   65 n.12
  Orator
    36   111 n.185
  Paradoxa Stoicorum
    4   116 n.200
  Pro Fonteio
    17   150 n.343
  Pro Publio Quinctio
    19   143 n.324
  Topica   39
    21   108 n.177/178
    25   111 n.185
  Tusculanae disputationes   146
    1   156 n.364, 220 n.643
    3   143 n.323, 144 n.326/328,
          145 n.330, 146, 151 n.349
    4   146, 161 n.381, 208 n.596
    5   154 n.357, 188 n.496

Columella
  De re rustica   41, 90–91
    2   90 n.134

Gellius, Aulus
  Noctes Atticae
    11   198 n.554
    16   114 n.192

Homer
  Odyssey   199 n.559
    5   127 n.259

Horace
  Sermones
    1   120 n.225

Ovid
  Fasti
    6   205 n.585

Quintilian
  Institutio oratoria
    3   108 n.177
    4   135 n.279

Plato
  [Alcibiades]   157 n.372

Apologia 41
  21 155 n.360

Xenophon
  Apologia Socratis
    14–17 155 n.360

Cyropaedia 221 n.227
  1 120 n.227
Memorabilia 41, 120–21
  4 121 n.230/231

Index of Subjects and Names

Aaron 140–41
Abel 80–81, 108–9, 114–15
Abraham 40, 88–89, 116–19, 206–7
Absalon 208–9
Adam 29, 30, 36, 38, 64–75, 94, 100–1,
　　107 n.174, 160–61, 188–89
adiaphoron/a 42–43, 104, 108–9,
　　112–13
Agricola, Georgius 70 n.28
Alcibiades 156–57
Amaziah 98–99
Ambrose 20, 31 n.158, 62
Amos 216–17
anger 7, 28, 38, 46, 68–69, 74–75,
　　146–51, 160–61, 180–81
Antioch 190–91
anti-papal / -Roman 24, 38–39, 104,
　　126 n.255, 132, 144–45,
　　192 n.517
Apollo 154–55
Aquinas 62
Aristotle 37, 41, 108 n.177, 109 n.179,
　　110 n.181, 146, 148 n.337
Arts faculty 2, 8, 44, 46
Ascham
　　Apologia pro caena Dominica 4, 8,
　　　20, 30, 57, 61, 75 n.66, 78,
　　　115 n.195, 123 n.239,
　　　124 n.241, 126 n.252,
　　　139 n.304/305, 140 n.306/308
　　biblical scholarship 9–22 and
　　　passim
　　classical learning / scholarship
　　　35–43 and *passim*
　　clerical path 8, 44
　　Greek New Testament 13, 17,
　　　26 n.135, 41, 56, 60–61, 212
　　　(and *passim* in the
　　　annotations)
　　lecturing 3, 8
　　library 1
　　Master of St John's 3
　　patristic scholarship 9–22 and
　　　passim
　　philology / language skills *passim*
　　Public Orator 2, 16
　　religious reform/er 22–35 and
　　　passim
　　rhetoric (use of) 35–43 and
　　　passim
　　theologian 43–47 and *passim*
　　tutor / educator 1, 2, 72 n.43
　　Scholemaster, The 2, 37 n.183,
　　　38 n.186, 72 n.43, 88 n.122
　　Themata Theologica passim
　　Toxophilus 2–3, 24, 91 n.134,
　　　120 n.223/224, 144 n.328
Aristotle / Aristotelian 37, 39, 41,
　　108 n.177, 109 n.179,
　　110 n.181, 120 n.223,
　　139 n.305, 146, 148 n.337,
　　199 n.559
Athanasian Creed 20, 192–93
Athanasius 20–21, 192–93
Augsburg Confession 20 n.99,
　　193 n.524
Augustine 17, 20, 26–27, 29, 30–31,
　　39, 62, 66 n.17, 71 n.37/40,
　　80 n.82, 94, 104–7, 112–13,
　　116 n.205, 125 n.247, 146,
　　150–51, 156 n.363, 172 n.433,
　　183 n.480, 184, 186–87,
　　190 n.503, 200–1, 206–7
Ps. Augustine 172 n.433

baptism 79, 190–91
Barbaro, Ermolao 44
Bathsheba 172 n.440

Belgic Confession 20 n.99
Bible / bibles 9–22 and *passim*
 biblical translations 9–16 and
  passim
 Complutensian Polyglot 9
 Coverdale Bible 10, 186 n.485
 Geneva Bible 60
 Great Bible (King's) 10, 23,
  25 n.126
 King James Bible 60
 Luther's German Bible 186 n.485
 Tyndale's New Testament 10,
  186 n.485
 Zurich bibles 10
biblical commentary 5, 7, 10, 17, 78
Bishops' Book 8
Bohemian Confession 20 n.99
Brenz, Johannes 10 n.45
Bruni, Leonardo 44
Brutus 143 n.323
Bucer, Martin 26, 44
Bullinger, Heinrich 5 n.18

Cain 108–9, 114–15, 168–69
Calvin, Jean 59 n.3, 114 n.191
Cambridge, University of 1, 3, 4, 7–8,
  11, 13, 16, 20–23, 26, 29, 44, 46,
  57, 63, 104, 107 n.173, 185,
  204 n.580
 Injunctions 11, 23
 St John's College 3, 5–6, 23, 25, 44,
  57
Cambyses 120–21
care of body 133, 142–45
Castellio, Sebastian 10, 17
Catherine of Aragon 198 n.546
Catholic/ism / conservative 4, 8, 19,
  21, 24–26, 29, 31, 34, 42, 78, 94,
  104, 132, 156 n.363, 184,
  193 n.524, 198 n.546
Catulus 110 n.181
Cecil, William 5 n.16, 72 n.43
Charles V 42
Charybdis 25, 185, 198–99
Cheke, John 5 n.16, 21, 46

Christ/ian *passim*
Chrysostom 4 n.14, 20–21, 192–93
Church 15, 19, 27, 34–35, 46, 80–83,
  105 n.165, 126–27, 140–45,
  162–63, 166–67, 170–71,
  188–89, 206–9, 218–19, 222–23
 of England 23
 rites / litugy 24, 133, 140–45, 170–71
 Rome (of) 27, 156 n.363,
  198 n.546, 208–9
church militant 25, 185, 192–93
Cicero/nian 10, 17, 36–42, 65 n.12/14,
  79, 81 n.95, 82–85, 89 n.127,
  105, 108 n.177/178,
  109 n.179/180, 110 n.181/183,
  111 n.185, 112 n.187,
  116 n.200, 120–23, 126 n.253,
  133, 135 n.279, 143 n.323/324,
  144–47, 150 n.343,
  151 n.354/346/349, 152,
  154 n.355/357/358, 155 n.359,
  156 n.364, 161 n.381, 162
  n.388, 188 n.496, 190 n.502,
  198 n.551, 208 n.596,
  216 n.622, 220 n.643
Clement 20
Coldocke, Francis 5 n.18
Columella 41, 79, 90–91
confessionalism 2, 22, 27, 34, 38–39,
  43, 46, 184, 204 n.580
consolation / comfort 28–29, 132,
  159, 166–67, 174–75, 188–89,
  212, 214–15
Coverdale, Myles 10, 186 n.485
Cranmer, Thomas 20, 25 n.126,
  199 n.555
 Sermon concerning... Rebellion
  199 n.555
Crassus 37, 110 n.181
Croke, Richard 21
Cromwell, Thomas 23–24, 197 n.540
custom/s 27, 104, 126–27
Cyprian 13 n.64, 20, 71 n.37
Cyril 4 n.14
Cyrus 120–21 n.227

Index of Subjects and Names 243

David 78, 80–83, 100–1, 114–15, 172–73, 194–95, 208–9
Decalogue 8, 114 n.193, 115 n.195
Demas 39, 198–99
Devil / Satan 72–75, 77 n.76, 77 n.77, 88–91, 124–29, 138–39, 160–61, 164–65, 172–77, 196–201, 218–23
dialectic 8, 37, 39, 44, 55 n.223, 79, 114 n.192
Diocletian 209 n.604
disputation/s 4–7, 10, 61, 94, 104, 106–7, 110–11, 126–27, 132, 146, 151 n.352, 184, 200–1
Doctors, *see* Fathers
Donato, Bernadino 21 n.103
Dudley, Robert (Earl of Leicester) 4 n.11, 5
Duke of Somerset 5 n.16

Edward VI / Edwardian 4, 8, 25, 46
Egypt/ians 40, 118–19, 162–63, 172 n.439, 207 n.593
Elias 84–85
Elizabeth I 2, 5, 25, 43
Erasmus, Desiderius 8–11, 13, 15–18, 31–32, 35, 44–45, 59–60, 184, 189 n.501 (and *passim* in the annotations)
Esau 108–9, 117 n.209, 208 n.597
Estienne, Robert 9, 60
Eucharist / Lord's Supper 4, 20, 34, 57
Euthydemus 120–21
Eve 36, 64–65, 94, 160–61, 172–73
Exeter Conspiracy 24

Fathers (of the Church) / Doctors 10, 17, 19–20, 26, 74 n.55, 78–81, 88–89, 92–93, 100–1, 146, 148 n.337, 192–93, 196–97
  Greek Fathers 20, 57
felix culpa 5, 26–27, 62
Fisher, John 23, 25
Formula of Concord 20 n.99, 77 n.74
Foxe, Edward 7 n.34

Free Will (and debates about it) 3, 31–33, 184, 186 n.487/488, 188–89

Gellius, Aulus 114 n.192, 198 n.554
Gideon 140–41
Gnesio-Lutherans 42 n.211
God / God the Father / the Lord *passim*
Goliath 114–15
Goodrich, Thomas (Bishop of Ely) 8
(good) works / deeds 30–32, 78–79, 104, 122–23, 130–31, 158–59, 164–65, 184, 188 n.495
Gospel/s *passim*
'gospeller' 185, 198–99
grace of God 27, 30–32, 61–62, 64–65, 70–71, 74–75, 77 n.77, 124–25, 128–29, 144–45, 150–51, 168 n.415, 188–89, 196–97, 220–23
Grant, Edward 4, 5, 57, 61
Greek/s 4, 8–9, 13–16, 18, 21, 23, 39, 42, 45, 58–60, 98–99, 100 n.159, 101 n.160, 105, 108–9, 111 n.185, 116 n.199/200, 121 n.229, 127 n.259, 128 n.266, 135 n.280, 136 n.281, 137 n.290, 138 n.293/295, 146 n.334, 152, 154 n.356, 155 n.361, 158, 160 n.377, 161 n.381, 162–63, 164 n.394, 165 n.397, 168 n.416, 180 n.470, 187 n.489, 188 n.493, 190 n.505, 191 n.510, 192–93, 195 n.535, 196 n.536, 197 n.541, 198 n.554, 202 n.573, 203 n.576, 206 n.591, 212, 214 n.609, 216 n.623/624, 221 n.651, 222 n.655
Gregory of Nazianzus 21
Gregory of Nyssa 21
Gryson, Roger 60

Haddon, Walter 46, 123 n.238
Hatfield House 14, 56
Hebrew 9, 12, 14, 23, 59, 90–91,
    172 n.439
Heidelberg Disputation 28, 159
Henry VIII (King) / Henrician 4, 6, 8,
    22–26, 35, 39, 46, 78, 133, 184,
    196–99
Hermagoras 108 n.177
Holgate, Robert (Bishop of Llandaff)
    8
Holy Spirit 64–65, 80–81, 127 n.256,
    144–45, 172–73, 220–21
Horace 41, 43, 105, 120 n.224/225
Hosea 40, 118–19
Hugo of Saint-Cher (Cardinal) 12,
    90–91
    In Psalterium universum
    92 n.139

inheritance 29, 40–41, 97 n.147,
    116–17, 158, 164–65, 186–87,
    218–19
Irenaeus 20
Isaac 118–19, 207 n.594, 208–9
Israel/ites 16, 40, 80–85, 95–97,
    101 n.163, 140–41, 164–65,
    208 n.599
iustitia/iustus, *see* righteousness /
    righteous

Jacob 40, 108–9, 116–17, 208–9
James 11, 127 n.258, 202–3
Jereboam 195 n.534
Jeremiah 209 n.600, 222–23
Jerome 9, 12–13, 15, 17, 20, 59, 94,
    96–97, 98 n.152, 99 n.152,
    162–65, 190 n.505
Jerusalem 134–35, 181 n.473
Jesus *passim*
    see also Christ
Jew/s/ish 100–1, 160–61, 168–69,
    180–81, 190–93
Joash 98–99
Job 200–1, 208–9

John (Apostle / Gospel) 11, 30, 44–45,
    124–25, 128–29, 136 n.282,
    168–69, 172–73, 180–83,
    192–93, 200–1, 212
John the Baptist 178, 182–83,
    209 n.600, 216 n.620
Jonah 84–85
justification 3, 26–28, 30–31, 43,
    62–63, 70–71, 94, 102–3
    by faith alone 23, 27–29

King's Book 23
knowledge (human) 7, 13, 152,
    154–57

Laban 208–9
Latin (use of / style / sound) 2–4,
    8–10, 13–15, 17–18, 20–21,
    35–36, 39, 42–43, 47, 57–58,
    60–61, 100 n.159, 115 n.198,
    116 n.200/202/204, 118 n.214,
    124 n.244, 127 n.259, 130 n.272,
    139 n.305, 145 n.329/331, 152,
    155 n.361, 163 n.391, 174 n.451,
    184, 191 n.510, 192–93,
    195 n.532, 197 n.541, 206 n.591,
    212, 221 n.651
Law 28, 80–85, 98–99, 105, 114–15,
    117 n.206, 122–23, 132, 134–35,
    138–39, 158, 160–63, 170–77
Law and Gospel 63, 77 n.74, 132,
    158
Leah 208–9
Lee, Edward (Archbishop of York) 8
Leipzig Interim 42
Lily, William 40, 117 n.206
logic (discipline of) 6, 193 n.522
Lot 172–73
Luke 190–91
Luther / Lutheran 1, 7, 9–10, 18–19,
    23, 25–33, 35, 43–45, 63,
    77 n.74, 78–9, 94, 104–5,
    114 n.191, 126 n.252, 132, 152,
    158–59, 161 n.380/382,
    165 n.398/401, 166 n.406,

169 n.424, 173 n.445, 184,
186 n.485, 187 n.488,
188 n.493, 189 n.501, 212
Bondage of the Will 30
Commentary on Galatians 17, 28,
158, 161 n.380, 165 n.398/401,
166 n.406, 169 n.424
Commentary on Matthew 173 n.445
De Abroganda Missa 126 n.252
Missa Privata 126 n.252
Lyra, Nicholas 10

Malcus 124–25, 140–41, 196–97
Mandane 120–21 n.227
Martial 40
Mary I 24
Mass 4, 57
Matthew (Apostle) 21, 41, 45, 56,
124–25, 129 n.268
medieval 4–6, 11, 32, 68 n.23, 78,
130 n.272, 152, 156 n.367,
157 n.369
Melanchthon, Philip 9, 42 n.211, 43, 45
Middleton, Henry 5
Mirandola, Pico della 44
moderation 34
monasteries / monks 23–24, 196–97
More, Thomas 23
Moses 96–97, 140–41, 172–73, 202–3
Münster, Sebastian 10

New Testament *passim*
Nebuchadnezzar 84 n.107
Nero 168–69
New Testament *passim*
Nicene Creed 81 n.90, 221 n.650
Nicodemite 24 n.125
Noah 172–73, 192–93
Novum Testamentum (of Erasmus) 9,
13, 15, 18, 59–60 (and *passim*
in the annotations)

Odysseus 127 n.259
Oecumenius 4, 8, 17, 21, 57,
192 n.514/515

Old Testament *passim*
orator/y, *see* rhetoric
Origen 21
Osiander, Andreas 10 n.45
Ovid/ian 41, 46, 185, 204–5
Oxford, University of 23, 198 n.546
Oza (King) 122–23

Pagninus, Santes 9, 59, 71 n.37,
99 n.153, 139 n.304, 140 n.306,
169 n.424, 181 n.475,
190 n.503, 202 n.570/571
papist/m 24–25, 192–93, 196–97
see also antipapal
Paul (Apostle) / Pauline 4, 17, 30, 41,
57, 70–71, 84–87, 90–91, 94,
100–1, 124–25, 128–31,
134–35, 140–43, 146, 150–52,
154–58, 161 n.282, 162–69,
172–75, 184, 187 n.489,
188–89, 191 n.507, 192–97,
198 n.550, 200 n.564, 202–3,
208–9, 216–17, 222–23
Pelagius 187 n.488
anti-Pelagian 62, 94
persecution 11, 18, 168–69, 172–75,
184–85, 198–99, 200–11
Peter (Apostle) 124–25, 128–29,
140–41, 172–75, 180–81,
194–97, 202–5
Petre, William 72 n.43
Pharoah 168–69
Philemon 4, 17, 57
Philip IV (King) 192 n.511
Philippists 43 n.212
philosophy/ical/ers 5, 7, 16, 32, 37,
42–43, 116 n.200, 120–23, 146,
152, 156 n.367, 157 n.369
Pilate 168–69, 172–73
Plato 41, 154 n.358, 157 n.372
Plutarch 146
Pole, Reginald (Cardinal) 24, 38, 39,
185, 196–99
Pope 23–24, 39, 126 n.254, 185,
196–99

Clement V 192 n.511
Paul III 126 n.254
prayer 6, 8, 37, 44–46, 129 n.268,
  130–31, 171 n.432, 212, 216–25
preaching/er 5, 17, 127 n.258, 184,
  186–87, 218–19
predestination 31, 33, 184, 187 n.488,
  188–89
priest/hood 44, 46, 127 n.258, 220–21
Propertius 40
Protestant/s 4–5, 9, 12, 15, 19–20,
  22–23, 25–28, 30, 31, 34–35, 42,
  45, 61, 78–79, 104–5, 115 n.195,
  127 n.258, 156 n.363, 185,
  187 n.488, 193 n.524
Psalm/s/ist 7, 60–61, 82–83, 128–29,
  164–67, 183 n.480, 186–87,
  190–91, 194 n.526, 208 n.599,
  222–23
  Hebrew / Protestant numbering
    61, 78, 194 n.527
  Vulgate / Septuagint numbering
    61
puritan/ism 22

Quintilian 105, 108 n.177, 135 n.279

Rachel 208–9
radical/s/ism 22 n.107, 25, 34, 43, 185,
  188 n.495, 198–99
Rebekah 208 n.595
Redman, John 21, 26 n.137, 46, 185,
  204–5
Reformed 1, 19, 22, 26, 32, 132
rhetoric 1, 4–6, 14–16, 34–43, 45,
  58–59, 79, 84 n.105, 105,
  110 n.181, 126 n.253,
  135 n.279, 173 n.443,
  198 n.554, 212
righteousness/righteous 7, 12, 29–30,
  41–42, 78–79, 80–94, 96–97,
  102–3, 116–19, 122–23,
  130–31 n.273, 138–39, 158,
  162–65, 168–69, 172–73, 185,

188–89, 194–95, 204–5,
  224–25
Rome 4, 23, 37, 46, 126 n.253,
  201 n.566, 210–11
royal supremacy 23–24, 133
Ryan, Lawrence 3, 22, 33–34, 72 n.43,
  73 n.44

Sampson, Richard (Bishop of
  Chichester) 7
Samuel 138–41
Saracens 190–91
Sarah 40, 116–17, 207 n.593
Satan, see Devil
Saul 122–23, 124 n.241, 138–41,
  166–67, 194–95, 208–9
scholastic/ism 11, 37, 44
Scripture, see Bible / bibles
Scylla 25, 185, 198–99
Second Helvetic Confession 20 n.99
Seneca 146
sermon/s 5, 7–8, 28, 78, 132, 146,
  217 n.630
Seven Deadly Sins 115 n.195
Sibylline Oracles 180 n.470
sin/sinners 3, 28–31, 36, 38–39, 46,
  62, 66–71, 74–75, 77 n.74, 78,
  94–104, 108–15, 127 n.259,
  132, 138–39, 146, 148–49,
  159–61, 172–77, 196–97,
  206–7, 212, 216–21
Six Articles 23
Smith, Thomas 46
Socrates 41, 120–21, 152, 154–57
Sodom/ites (and Gomorrah)
  100–1
sola scriptura 10, 19–27, 33, 94,
  107 n.171, 142 n.320, 185, 212
Solomon 156 n.363, 216–17
State (and edicts of) 24, 46, 73 n.44,
  121 n.227, 142–45, 148–49,
  170 n.428, 196–97
Stephen 173 n.442
Stoic/ism 42, 116 n.200, 146

Strasbourg 26
suffering 11, 32, 62, 66–71, 158,
    161 n.382, 166–69, 174–75,
    185, 188–89, 202–3, 206–11
superstition 24, 66–67, 126–27,
    158–59, 162–63, 170–71,
    196–97
Sutcliffe, Matthew 44 n.223
syllogism 144 n.325

Tertullian 20
Theodoret 4 n.14
Theological faculty 2, 44
theology 2, 5, 7, 11, 12, 26, 30, 34,
    39, 43–46, 146, 157 n.369,
    184
theology of the cross 28, 158–77
thirty martyrs 208–9
Thirty-nine Articles 20 n.99,
    193 n.524
Titus 4, 57
transubstantiation 34
Turks 190–91
Tyndale, William 10, 60,
    186 n.485

Uriah 172 n.440

vernacular 3, 10, 15, 21 n.105, 23
Vetus Latina 9
via media ('middle way') 23, 25,
    43, 105, 120–23, 146, 185,
    199 n.559
Virgil 40
Vulgate 9, 12–13, 15–18, 59
    (and *passim* in the
    annotations)
  Clementine Vulgate 60
  Stuttgart Vulgate 60

Watson, Thomas 6 n.27
Weber, Robert 60
Westminster School 4
widow of Zarephath 84–85
Windsor Castle 72 n.43
Wittenberg 10

Xenophon 41, 56, 105, 120–21,
    154 n.358

Zechariah 15, 182–83, 186 n.484

www.ingramcontent.com/pod-product-compliance
Lightning Source LLC
Chambersburg PA
CBHW071822300426
44116CB00009B/1403